XO

Krissi Ayward

Michael Bexley

100

Voices

of Inspiration Awakening and Empowerment

A SoulSpiration ™ Series

Soulful Pen Publishing

2016-2017

An Anthology filled with dynamic inspiration.

ISBN-13: 978-1537649948
ISBN-10: 1537649949

Special Thanks to our Sponsors

Carol Starr Taylor, Author of Life in Pieces
Candy Kastanis, Author of Sacrificed
Sundi Sturgeon and Holistic Rejuvenation Center, HI
Joshua Adam Mancil, Owner of Bold Impressions Web

www.TheSoulfulPen.com

Table of Contents

Foreword by Dr. Markesha Miller

100 Voices of Inspiration, Awakening & Empowerment is a strong empowering piece that makes room for each voice to be heard. The title, within itself, gives amplification to the magnitude of these voices and the messages that they convey. As a reader, you will be inspired through the trials and tribulations, awakened to your own beauty and presence through the self-discovery of others, and empowered to pursue your own greatness by the journeys that these wonderful authors have taken.

These individuals have assembled together through their writing and allowed their stories to unfold. As a professional support to this group, I could witness the depth that these individuals submerged into to bring their story to life. This story speaks great volume to the power of writing. These authors could complete a healing process that may ignite healing and truth inside of you.

As a psycho-therapist, I know the power of the voice. Throughout my time in college, I was taught that the voice can be used to persuade, captivate, and command attention. However, throughout my career, I have come to realize that the voice has the ability to convey healing, peace, awareness, and love. Often times, lending our voice is not easy. For some, it takes a while to discover your voice. For many, it takes a journey to discover the power of your voice. This book speaks to the definition of all the above. These authors have utilized their voice to persuade you as the reader that you have the ability to make room for your greatness, captivating you to be empowered and commanding you to awaken. In an ever-changing world, we are often trying to discover our inner peace, ourselves, and how we relate to the world around us. As a clinician, I believe that one of the best modalities of accomplishing this is through group support. This book serves as a great avenue to such. The beauty is finding something in each story that you can relate to and apply to some aspect of your own life. It only takes one voice to be heard to signify change...in this book 100 voices are uplifted and unified.

It is my hope as a reader that you find yourself, your inspiration, your empowerment, and that you are awakened to your truth and your destiny!

100 Voices Corporate Sponsor

Carol Starr Taylor, Author of Life in Pieces

I have had the pleasure of watching this book unfold in the Facebook group where all the writers were growing their author wings. As an author, myself, I know how difficult it can be to write a tough story. Carla Wynn Hall asked me if I would be a sponsor of the Soulful Pen Publishing "SoulSpiration" anthology series of books. After truly seeing what her team did for authors, just at the level of empowerment, I knew this was a great opportunity for me.

My book is Life in Pieces, From Chaos to Clarity and released this year 2016. Here is a little more about the book. Please feel free to contact me if you have media opportunities or would like more information on my book.

Life in Pieces: From Chaos to Clarity

Have you ever felt STUCK? Stuck spinning your wheels, searching for happiness, love, money or purpose?

Have you ever felt as though you were moving through life on auto-pilot, seeing with no vision, hearing without listening, tasting without savoring, touching without connection? Carol did; many times, throughout her life only to come through it all on the other side to find her truth and embrace her PERFECT IMPERFECTION.

In 'Life in Pieces', Carol gives you a glimpse into the moments, the experiences that have shaped who she is as she candidly shares the valuable learnings, and the love she has found within herself and the courageous life she leads today.

Website: http://www.carolstarrtaylor.com

100 Voices Angel Sponsor

Candy Kastanis, Author of "Sacrificed"

Contributing my written voice to the newest compilation 100 Voices of Empowerment, Awakening, and Inspiration has been a beautiful experience. Through every moment of writing, authors gain insight similar to the reader. Lending our experiences though the written word is truly the best form of philanthropy. It takes a lot to open up and allow certain vulnerabilities to be highlighted.

As I close this year, 2016, my greatest achievement will be that of my newest book SACRIFICED. It will be my first entry into the fictional genre. Sacrificed tells a story of a deep, but very dysfunctional romance riddled with dark entities that encompass some mysterious spiritual journeys. I am hoping my audience will love this book as much as I do!

http://www.waytoomuchsugar.com Visit my Website

Find Candy on Facebook: Way Too Much Sugar

Gratitude and Honor

From the Soulful Pen Support Team to You

www.TheSoulfulPen.com

We Publishing Heirlooms

This anthology is part of the SoulSpiration Series ™ of anthologies featuring brand new writers who have never been published before, and seasoned authors of Bestselling books. In the summer of 2016 this team of writers came together with one voice and one mission: They worked as a team to achieve the status of Amazon #1 International Bestseller. Early in the program one of the authors, Lyn Kyrc, stepped up with both feet and supported the development of this publication with relentless joy. I am thankful to Lyn for her support of all the writers.

I am delightfully grateful that we had three writers under the age of 13 participate in this project. I am happy and grateful for our sponsors Carol Starr Taylor, author of Life in Pieces: From Chaos to Clarity and Candy Kastanis, author of "Sacrificed" for helping our writers feel empowered. Special thanks to all the team leaders and to all the family and friends who ordered the Kindle version of our book.

In dedication to all great authors now and who have gone, this book was created to build a new legacy and fill bookshelves with new stories.

Carla Wynn Hall

10 Time #1 International Bestselling Author

Recognizing Deliberate Soul Suppression for Societal Acceptance in a Materialistic Era

Welcome to 100 Voices. I want to write you a story today about suppression of the soul and feeling acceptance in a rather hard and materialistic era. The years have taught me many lessons. "The older you get the more lessons you learn", Grannie.

My 95-year-old great-grandmother (in law) gave me some awesome advice this past Thanksgiving. Haven tricked death for a long time, she was stunned that life was still with her. Her soul is doing fine and she is ready to cross over, but there are many people in the world who suppress their soul for fear of what others think of them. In a materialistic era where what we drive, where we live and how we play is how our successes or failures are defined, it is easy to get caught in the trap.

My very short story is meant to make a very broad point: There is only perfection. Imperfection is an illusion. Do your best and write the rest.

Xoxo

Carla

1 0 0

Voices

of Inspiration Awakening
and Empowerment

Disclaimer:

The stories you are about to read and enjoy, were contributed by over 100 women, men and young adults toward the betterment of our world. When we opened the anthology for submissions there were no specific topics given. What resulted was a collaboration of voices speaking on what is most important to them at this moment in time. I hope you enjoy the words within and get a blessing doing so. Please go back to Amazon and leave a review for your favorite stories and authors.

To keep the native speech and language of our international authors, you may read some words that are focused on a culture. Keep an open heart and mind.

Joanna Intara Zim

<u>Transformative Love and our "Little Bear"</u>

"Never forget that your fears whatever they are, are a call for love."

I remember the amazing times when I gave birth to my children. A friend told me that having children feels like your heart is forever outside your own body. **When they hurt, you hurt**. When they are ecstatic, you are ecstatic. And so, the deep bond between parent and child unfolds and does it's' magical work on us all.

While it's true that when they hurt, you hurt, it is also true that when they are happy and healthy, so are you as a parent.

What I discovered this summer, was the truth of that statement was never more potent and powerful to change the course of human life because it runs both ways - your children ignite and initiate you into deep awakenings, and you have the opportunity, when they need you, to role model for them how to do the same. The call came.

My daughter Pema is a huge ray of sunshine not just in my life, but her whole world. She's loved by all her friends, and her teachers light up when they talk about her with a glimmer of amazement at the life and love her little five-year-old body beholds.

When she was born, my husband described his experience of being in her presence, calling it "blazingly mindless". With dark brown eyes, and a wicked rapturous laughter like Krishna, the Indian God of divine love, play, magic and so much more, little spirit sings songs all day long as she dances through the house, delighting all those who come all those who cross her path.

All of that came to a screeching halt late June this year when the flu struck our home. Our son got it first, and any parent who has had a child with flu knows, it's not fun or pretty. Fortunately, he recovered quickly and was back to his monkey self in a flash.

It was a good thing our son recovered quickly because our daughter was next. Maybe because she's smaller, or more sensitive, it hit her much harder. She was in agony. The stomach cramping, the out of control feeling of throwing up, or having to wear a pull up - not able to run to the potty fast enough frustrated her even more.

We did everything we could; plenty of fluids, rest, tummy massage, soup, coconut water, songs and love. Her symptoms seemed to resolve and she went back to school, but something was terribly off and we didn't realize it until a week later when her teacher contacted us to say our little sunshine was not herself. We had thought she might have regressed, or just had low energy. Laying her head on her desk at school and sleeping on the playground was not normal.

Then, a mysterious rash showed up. That, coupled with a deeply unhappy child, sent us to the emergency room where we got the news no parent ever wants to hear, once the blood test results came. "She has acute renal failure, her kidneys are not working and she needs to be transferred by ambulance to tonight to Kaiser Oakland, and have immediate kidney dialysis."

I could feel my throat close. My breathing tightened and my heart pounded as tears flowed down my cheeks. The disbelief, the shock, the Oh My God, we should have got her checked sooner, the why is this happening all ruptured and ached through my whole being.

We planned and packed; we organized our son staying at friends. We hugged each other. We let our nearest beloveds know. We prayed. Watching as they transported my daughter in an ambulance with tubes in her arms was a sight no mother wanted to see. My heart ached.

There wasn't even a moment to ask why. That would have been getting sidetracked.

I started getting messages, phone calls and emails at the hospital, just as the doctors were telling me that they would need to put a catheter in her leg to be ready for dialysis as soon as possible. It was all happening so fast and my little girl had no idea what was coming to her. I feel the tears for her confusion as to what was happening as I share this with you.

And faster than I could kiss her before they started, the doctors ushered us out of the room for the procedure for sanitary reasons, and into the waiting room, complete with hospital grade 'comfy' chairs thick with vinyl. We laid together on the floor, my hubby and I, holding hands, clinging in deep raw nerve vulnerability to each other, for support, solace, and consolation. The next thing I remember, the nurse came and woke us gently to tell us everything went great and we could come back into her room, which was now filled with a team of top experts, intensive care doctors and interns, IC nurses, child kidney specialists, child autoimmune specialists, bacterial specialists. The faces were long and serious but their voices were totally positive.

Exhaustion was hitting me. Dehydration made me feel weak and I suddenly realized I had been out of my body in shock. I wondered what I was missing as the dialysis nurse named Jai Ma, which means Victory to the Mother in Sanskrit, entered the room. My breath released and I started to cry as the reality set in that dialysis was happening and we had no clue how shut down her kidneys were, what the cause was, or when in God's name they would be functioning again.

Giant unknowns, were followed by more texts and calls from family and close friends now wanting to know. My private, let's deal with this and get through it self, and THEN share, was about to be blown apart.

Little Bear, as we have called Pema, struggled to squeak out in her tired voice, "what happened to me mama?" Throat choking up. Then, Jai Ma pulled my teary hubby and I close to her, hugging us.

This *light being nurse* pretty much gave us a Yoda quality teaching of being strong and positive for her. Our Zen master of the moment, the dialysis angel. Of course, she was right, and we would deal with our sadness later, if we still had it.

There was no time to lose. My hubby wrote the most amazing post for all our thousands of Facebook friends and followers with one request; no "sorrys" or worry or fear our way, -- transform all that energy, leverage all the intensity (and believe me, there was lots of it), put all your intention, your heart energy, your imagination, your mind stream into one thing and one thing only; see, feel and know in your whole being, your soul that Pema be completely 100% well, her kidneys functioning and totally healthy.

We asked people to post their intentions and visualizations in the thread. There were hundreds of comments and shares. Everyone's words and prayers were so beautiful. Offers flew in for healings, understandings, and help. The beauty of Facebook algorithms is that when someone is in distress, those posts are priority. Bless Mark Zuckerberg for that. For five days, solid, this is what we were immersed in. And, if you've ever doubted in the power of your own thoughts, feelings and intentions, visualizations and prayers to save a life, and create a miracle, it's time for that to dissolve now. They can, and they will.

We literally felt what we called, a tangible and palpable grace-force field to envelop our family. Within a few days her numbers started to get better. We weren't sure if it was because dialysis, but in the end, after five days in the intensive care unit and four days in the regular ward, her kidneys were eventually functioning on their own. We came home on 4th of July holiday, Independence Day, with our daughter practically singing down the Hall, "I'm so happy to be free."

We cried. A lot. Happy, soft, and warm tears. And she was part of it, most likely orchestrating it, for the spiritual Upleveling of us all. She played her part, like when she asked what happened to her and I explained best I could to a five-year-old, "Well honey, your kidneys basically went on a very long vacation, and it's time for them to come back now, like right NOW. Can you tell them, 'come back from vacation now?" Little Pema Bear piped up nice and sassy, mighty arms strong and waving, "kidneys, you come back right now." Our little fierce Goddess.

Love asked for all of this. Fear asked for all this and love gave it. This love we felt and that was born in her, us and our community healed everyone. For weeks afterwards, people wrote to me and said things like; it seemed like your request for intentions and positivity was for her, but in this healing way, it ended up helping us too."

Although that wasn't what we led with, it's what happened. We were all in this collective healing miracle mandala. This awakening mandala - the love inside of it, the imagery, the intention and positivity, the pure hearted care and compassion, the uncontrived, totally sincere way it came together and healed. Never forget that your fears whatever they are, are a call for love, so they can be dissolved into the place they come from and from there life can birth anew. This is the power of deep love, pure intention, and unwavering devotion to the work at hand.

This is the transformation that becomes possible when the collective inner circle of clear minds, undefended hearts and open bodies come together to honor the wishes of your soul and spirit. If it can happen to my daughter with a shutdown kidney, it can unfold for you in whatever place is closed off or separate from these awakening and transformative qualities.

This is what I offer you and the hundreds of men, women, and couples I work with every year. Fear or pain or challenge is the call. Love had our back. Love brought our daughter "Little Bear" through her sudden illness to teach our family and the world that with love, there is deep and profound healing. I would love to invite you to "The 366 Day Fear Into Love Challenge on Facebook https://www.facebook.com/joannaintarazim/. Take a minute to reach out to me and let's connect.

Learn more about Joanna Intara Zim

Joanna Intara Zim is a modern-day psycho-spiritual guide, teacher and healer, a massive courage awakener who delivers her programs to hundreds of women, men and couples every year on the topics of fierce love and wisdom, healing, deep empowerment and sacred transformation. Lit up and on heart-fire about supporting others to live a life embodied with the courage, compassion and confidence to meet the transformational challenges of life, Joanna provides soul-centered of their life, Joanna provides healing and life-changing programs to further bring home her message of strength, devotion and love, which deeply impacts her clients' lives and gives lasting results of peace freedom and happiness.

Website: www.joannaintarazim.com

Candice Gentry

<u>Unexpected Joy</u>

Human beings. Raw. Fragile. Delicate. Beautiful. Unique. Always tottering close to the point of toppling.

We want to be tough, but in reality, it only takes one to bring us down. One word. One mishap. One tragedy. One disappointment. One heartbreak. It only takes one to leave us clamoring to pull ourselves back up and cling to our dream. The precious dream that we see as the goal of our life. Everything we do is built around it. What is your dream?

If you had told me in high school that one day I would be where I am today, I would not have believed you. In fact, I'm pretty sure I would have given that condescending smile of youth outfitted with all the pomp and cluelessness of a budding adult. Now I want to hug the young folks and warn them to just wait. Wait until the moment they discover they actually don't know anything about anything. But that is something learned and experienced, not told. Life ages us. Somehow our journeys transform us into a very different person than originally anticipated with a completely unexpected life. Each step you take leads you there. Tread carefully. Tread expectantly. Be brave.

My journeys have led me to a minivan, stained shirt, and purse full of crushed cheerios. It is true. But friend, my life is beautiful. I have been married 16 years to man who has provided a life of travel, adventure, laughter, and love. We have more children than I ever thought appropriate, one shy of Brady Bunch status. Our children have more medical needs than I can count on all my fingers and toes. My husband and I managed to go from the fruitful 5 year plan (no kids, graduate degree, savings accounts) to having 5 little humans in 8 years. We wouldn't change a thing.

Our youngest two were adopted from a country I never even dreamed of visiting, far on the other side of the world. A beautiful country and culture which now is part of my life, my heart, my home, my everything. Japan.

I don't speak though of just the Japanese culture, but also the special needs culture. It is a completely different world than I have ever known before. Some days I am on my knees in prayer and tears and others I am rejoicing from the beauty I have discovered in a precious moment. Who are we kidding? I can rollercoaster between emotions within an hour! My youngest two blessings have Trisomy 21, Down Syndrome.

Truth be told I never really gave any thought to special needs. No one in my life had special needs. I lived in a world of abled bodied people. When I was pregnant I prayed for a "healthy" pregnancy, just like every other mom: code for no special needs. My second pregnancy was, surprise, twins! They developed Twin to Twin Transfusion at 19 weeks and survived a very troubled pregnancy. One that landed me 3 months of hospital stay on bedrest and on my knees, figuratively, that they would born alive and "healthy."

And then, somehow, the next set of delightful little humans, crashed into my world. Children full of life, music, and dance. Contagious laughter. Smiles that light up the whole world. Just like my other children, but also different.

I cannot help but be haunted by the truth. Steps were taken so they wouldn't be here. They shouldn't be out and about meeting and greeting the world as if life is a big parade. They survived. They are walking miracles.

The good Lord had other plans for our little guy, Noah, or he would have perished long ago. He was born in Japan at a hospital with a pediatric cardiologist who did not value him because he was born with Trisomy 21. He was sent home with his birth mother, despite severe heart defects. He was not deemed worth saving. The doctor knew he would die. He knew surgery could save him but told his dear birth mother "take him home." He went into heart failure at 6 weeks old and almost died waiting for surgery. I met Noah 2 days after he was given to the ministry that helped saved him. His body was limp. He gasped for breath and could only move his head slightly. I will never forget his arms and legs completely limp to his sides, but his eyes spoke to me. They shined with not just determination, but personality. I knew him and loved him. And I knew from the beginning he was not the one blessed by the relationship. It was me.

His story is long and worth being told but for now I just want you to close your eyes and sit with the reality: my 4-year-old should be dead, but he is alive. Our family comedian, artist, and thespian. Alive. Intervention and miracles. Every person who meets him is impacted in some precious way.

 The Japanese cardiologist is not the enemy though. More recently than I'd like to admit, this same practice was common in America. Just like in Japan, our America has an astounding abortion rate for children diagnosed with Down Syndrome in utero. They are being wiped off the face of this earth because of their extra chromosomes. That is so many smiles and so much laughter that this world will never know. It is a loss for us all.

Now, let me tell you about my baby girl, Hannah Joy. We debated over naming her Hannah and Joy. In the end, we named her both. We had saved the name Hannah for years. But Joy. We wanted to scream out to the world that this baby, our surprise baby, brought us joy! Silly us. Our girl has a smile that melts your heart right down to your soul. No need for the name. She would show the world.

Hannah was not born with any heart problems and came to us as a healthy one month old, with the chubbiest cheeks you ever did see.   After several doctor visits and specialist appointments we thought she was in the clear. And then at 10 months she was diagnosed with infantile glaucoma and rushed to Hawaii for surgery. We were living in Okinawa, Japan at the time. Surgery was successful. They put a high-tech valve in her eye with the highest pressure. It controls optometric pressure so it never goes too high or too low. Her vision was partially saved, but not before permanent damage was done. She has greatly reduced vision in that eye and I am told it can never come back. A few months later she had surgery on the other eye. No irreversible damage was done on that eye but infantile glaucoma is serious. It will be a life long struggle to keep her vision.

You would never guess it. She doesn't let it slow her down one bit. Hannah Joy is bound and determined to keep up with all the big kids. She can climb, run and jump with the best of them. She is pure joy, this little one. You cannot help but smile no matter what turmoil is in your life or clouding your mind. And friends, just think. She was going to be placed in a children's home.   What kind of life would a blind baby with Down syndrome have there? Would she smile and dance, climb and run giggling all day like she does at our house? I wonder. Even my overly optimistic glass half full heart knows the truth.

The truth haunts me.

Let me admit to you, my deep-down secret. I want to adopt them all. All orphans. All orphans with Down syndrome. All orphans with special needs. All. Of. Them.

But praise the Lord, I have a logical, level headed husband who understands that perhaps all the orphans in the world is a wee bit too many for our little family. That leaves one for you!

I am not saying life with a special needs child is easy. Nothing worthwhile is easy. I am letting you in on a colossal secret: you will be changed. You will see the world through new lenses. You will start to celebrate each victory, no matter how small. You will appreciate the simple things you can do so easily. You will start noticing the quirks YOU have and realize that each of us has special needs that must be met in order for us to succeed in this world. We all do. Then your past dreams will shatter around you, and all the trivial things in your life will melt away. New dreams are formed. And you notice that it is not the world that changed. You have been changed. One adoption. One child. One life. One story.

Just as it only takes one to tear you down, it only takes one to lift you up. To change your world. Imagine how different the world would be if every able family was willing to take in one precious child. Just one.

Goosebumps.

Learn More about Candice Gentry

Candice Gentry is a wife, mother, and teacher with a great sense of humor, adventure, and compassion. She has been married since 2000 to Rodney Gentry, a dedicated U.S. Marine and loving husband and father. Though they have endured hardships, they have enjoyed growing up together, traveling the world, and parenting 5 children. They share a love of adoption and hope their family will continue to grow. They believe children are a blessing.

Candice holds a Master of Social Work degree from Virginia Commonwealth University and is an LSW (Licensed Social Worker). Though she has worked as an adoption social worker, her primary job has been teaching as a homeschool mother for the past 7 years. She remains committed to helping her children develop a love of learning, life, and people. After the adoption of her family's two youngest children, her eyes were opened to the world of special needs. She now helps others understand and not fear the uniqueness of children who have special needs. She hopes all children will be valued and more families will open their homes and their hearts to orphans and experience the joy of adoption.

Elizabeth "Liz" Hassaan

Australia

<u>From a Frightened Child to an Empowered Adult: Love Letters to Liz</u>

"Through forgiveness, love and validation I was able to grow from a very wounded child to an empowered woman" - Liz

As a young child, there are plenty of memories I have forgotten. Born and raised in Australia, I knew my childhood was not normal. Today I write this story on behalf of the little girl, me, and the tears still flow but I know there is more love inside me now that there will ever be tears, for I have grown up.

My father, a brick layer and my mother a well-respected legal secretary and Paralegal worked hard for their living. I and my siblings were all given the privilege of going to private schooling, primary and secondary. I now know this probably placed a strong burden on the family. Sadly, my father became an alcoholic and at what time of his life I do not know, all I remember as a very young child is an aggressive drunk towards my mother. I remember one argument that stands strong on my memory of my mother asking my father to please eat his dinner. He became so angry that he said "you know what I think of this dinner, and threw it through the kitchen window". **I distinctly remember standing so still with intense fear as to what was going to happen next.**

My only constant memory is the arguing and yelling, and I would stand beside my mother as if I was programmed to go into PROTECTIVE MODE to ensure that he would not hurt her. I have another strong memory of my childhood and that is sitting up most nights beside my mother on the couch. No TV, no sound and waiting and waiting to hear the fearful sound of my father's car and the horrible fear that would pour over me, not knowing was he going to walk in the door and start screaming and yelling at my mother or siblings.

I have no memory of any parent saying "I Love You" or for that matter as a little girl even seeing it. I grew blaming my mother for not leaving my father and could not understand as a child why she would allow this to happen to her and my siblings. Why was I the protector of the family? How did I manage it? Where did the strength come from? All I had come to know was that I was MUM to my siblings and my mother. I was the protector of our family. I was not given the chance to be a child, I was tormented.

I was unable to bring friends home, why would I, how could I explain my father's drinking and rage? To me, all my other school friends lived in a different world to me and I could only somehow fake it, and at such a young age, I had learned to hide the sadness I felt and the abuse that was within our four walls and just kept on moving through school life as if all was fine. I was envious of these other families.

Mum, why won't you leave him? My mother looked down at me, thus my small scattered memories of my childhood, I gather I was very young, and she said "I will never leave your father".

My heart and soul were now gone from my body. I had only myself. I do not have any recollection of my sister who is only 6 years my junior, being anywhere within the walls of the home and out at school or around the house playing. Where was she? I know now she was there but how cruel is the brain to block that one precious memory of never knowing any fun or growing experiences with her?

I have a few scattered memories of my brother. I remember times of yelling and seeing the look of terror on his face and I would stand beside him or in front of him so that the barrage of abuse would stop or that he would not get hit. I don't not know, nor can I tell you from any memory HOW DID I GET AWAY WITHOUT BEING HURT OR SCREAMED DOWN TO, from my father?

Did I have some protective barrier around me or was I a strong-willed child. Was I just now solely the mother of the household and had to stand tall? Standing tall was scary. I was a fearful child.

I could not have been more than 9 or 10, as these memories I write as primary school years of my life. I never knew from one day to the next, if someone be hurt or if it would be a night of complete screaming and insults to us all. Why was my father's anger so deep and intense towards us as a family?

"What did I do wrong Daddy?"

Adult Liz, has seen a psychologist, for two years to try and unravel my brain as to why I cannot remember the so called normal memories children have. I don't remember my bedroom or anything about the room, the bed, any ornaments etc. Nothing. I don't remember where my siblings slept. I don't remember seeing my siblings coming and going from the home, but I do remember I was in charge and had to prepare meals at night as my parents were working.

I don't remember walking to school. I don't remember a lot of classmates in school photos, worse I don't remember even having them taken year by year. I don't remember Christmas or any year or birthdays till my 16th. I don't remember what I ate at school for lunch. I don't remember any of my teachers. I don't remember the inside of any of my classrooms. I don't remember any of the homes we lived in, only THE ONE, but my siblings can remember the others and they are younger than me.

I don't remember my Grandmother, I look, I study her face in an old picture, she is foreign to me, yet the only memory I have of her is a figure walking down the pathway to a house I don't remember anything inside it, and she would stop walking, put her hands behind her back, as she would always have lollies (lollipop) for me. Why can I not see you or your love Nana in your face of the picture I have of you. How could that memory be erased?

Was my life as a child so unknowingly abusive that the adult Liz has lost all memory? I know through education of seeing a psychologist that my memories are there, but they are so embedded deeply that even he as a professional said "there is no reason for you to remember". In one session with him I closed my eyes and with the psychologist guiding my thoughts, we took "little Lizzie" home, I tucked her into bed, I told her she is safe and no one could hurt her as I was here and I would protect her always. Amazingly this worked wonders for me and it was like for the first time ever I had released a pressure valve inside me.

The protection mode is now like a built-in system to me to always protect my family and friends. I did not know what my purpose in life was, especially as a young child growing up under these extreme conditions but, I have come to learn that there was a purpose in life for me at that time and a lesson in life for me during that time, to get me to where I am today.

It has taken me many years to learn how to forgive. Forgiveness is the only way to heal childhood trauma. It's the hardest thing I have ever done and will be the hardest thing you ever do.

I as an adult, could now go to the grave sites of my parents and talk to them both and to say out loud I FORGIVE YOU, as this was the only way I could move forward. I grew to understand that holding onto what my childhood had been was only making me dark and angry internally.

Understanding Why I Am Mother to So Many I Meet

I often wondered why I was put in the family I was in. Why didn't I have happy childhood memories? Liz as an adult now is understanding why. My faith is in Jesus and I thank him for keeping me safe, for giving me the strength to be MUM TO SO MANY, for the knowledge I learnt as a struggling lost and I felt unloved child, having to act the role of protective mother. I am aware that I can use my love to help others heal, and I thank Jesus for this. But, it all started with forgiveness. Forgiveness is not an easy task.

The Babies: My Life's Truest Blessing

Aged 26 I fell pregnant. Yes, with a mother whom was a strong Catholic I was the shame. I didn't feel any shame, I felt joy. I didn't care that I would have to do this alone, I felt strong and believed in myself. I was blessed, and her name is Bianca. "Little Ray of Sunshine" could a song have been more perfect for her.

Bianca is my ROCK and I could not have done things, gone through life, reeducated myself, if it was not for her. At the drop of a hat, my beautiful daughter comes to my aid. My Little Ray of Sunshine is my strength.

Aged 32 I fell pregnant again. The man of my dreams was born. The most amazingly good looking Son. My heart was full. Simon has been and will always be my son, but more so the man in my life. He is my protector and guardian angel watching in the distance always, over his mother with such love.

Many more times than I can recall, I have been called upon to be a mother (mum) to friends, my children's friends and people I meet on Facebook. Being and feeling so unloved by my mum, created doubt that I would not be a good mum to anyone, but the love letters arrived just in time.

Defining my Purpose: The Love Letters

LOVE NOTE FROM BIANCA: - to help me understand why I am mother to so many and why so many come to me for mothering.

"You're not just my mum, you are everybody's mum."

"Nurturer, provider, carer."

"Without any prejudice, you take anyone in, helps, listens, understands their struggles, open and non-bias."

LOVE NOTE FROM ANNA - a dear friend who is there always even when long times have passed.

"To a Woman, through thick and thin is there if you need her. We all now come to ask the wisdom of a well-rounded accepting mature woman with the biggest unjudging heart. We cry, we laugh, we miss periods of time but pick up again without missing a beat, but most of all her love is true."

LOVE NOTE FROM COCO SOLIMAN - My friend and Soul mate.

"They say in your life your soul mate appears in many forms whether it's your friend, your son, your daughter, a stranger you meet. The only way I can describe my dear friend Lizzie of 36 years is just that my soul mate, despite all her own challenges in life, she has stood beside me and so many other people who have come into her life. She has helped guide them on their journeys in life...BUT.... even the strong can become weakened. Liz once asked me why everyone turns to her with their issues and problems, which seems to be her entire life.

My answer to her is that she has been given the roll of Mothering. The mothering roll is to heal people and help them on the next journey in their lives whether on earth or in spirit. Liz has many times been my tower of strength for me and my family. I have met thousands of people over my life span, but Liz will be there until the end. I love you Liz and you are my blessing in life my dear friend"

LOVE NOTE FROM VICTORIA CRUZ:

From the moment I was born and I met aunty Liz I felt protected and knew I'd never be alone. In 2011 I sadly lost my son in a terrible drowning accident and my life as I knew it had stopped. I found myself in a dark place with no hope and no light... and there she was, with her beaming smile and glimmer of hope, my rescuer. Aunty Liz. She took me in, loved me, cared for me, listened to me when I needed her and got me back on my feet. She helped me stand when I couldn't find the strength, she made me laugh at moments I wanted to cry and made me see that although my precious boy was no longer with me, my life still needed to go on, not only for my little ANGEL but for myself also.

In 2014 I was blessed yet again. I had found my strength, had a loving family and home and I awaited the arrival of a new baby boy. Once again my hero and Savior aunty Liz was there by my side. My son (now 3) and I are so thankful for a woman who is so loving, caring, understanding and warm, that not only gave me HOPE, but saved my life.
Love Victoria

CRUZ
3/12/2009- 30/7/2011 RIP

I am humbled and blessed to receive these love notes and others I have over the years. These are not for my ego, or to impress or feel validity. These "LOVE NOTES" are here to show me that through the darkest moments of my life, not knowing why, not understanding the lessons, not understanding the magnified hurt, I felt, I finally came to believe, I have a guardian angel watching over me every moment.

With my Creator knowing my purpose, as a middle-aged woman, I now don't question "why am I mum to all?". This was my lesson, not a Burdon a BLESSING AND A GIFT FROM GOD.

My Truest Source of Empowerment

Through my growing life people have opened to me and trust me with their inner most secrets, just ask for general help or put a roof over their head. I now know God has put them into my life for the time that is only needed then he removes them and I know that for everyone I have helped, they have also helped me by moving forward with more knowledge and fulfilment which has enabled me to heal myself one step at a time and this brings me closer to who I want to be and who I will be tomorrow.

Only through Forgiveness

Learn More about Elizabeth Hassan

Elizabeth Hassan is a full time Professional AIN (Assistant in Nursing) currently working as a Personal Carer. As an AIN, she has extensive experience with professionals in the mental health, physical health, legal, hospice, mediation, suicide, drug, palliative and family communication areas. In addition, she has previous experience as a legal secretary, personal office assistant to a CEO, and a property manager.

Education and Credentials include: Certificate III AIN in Age Care and Disability Certificate III in Child Care and Disability, Certificate in Anger Management for Youth. Elizabeth has volunteered for the Lions Club Program, Special Education Department Unit, After School Care Benowa Primary and DOCS (Department of Children Services) Elizabeth (Liz) is passionate about caring for people. She acts on her skills, expertise and passion by dedicating her life to the service of others mental, physical and spiritual well-being.

Liz cares so deeply for the life of others, she feels blessed that through her experience with social media she found deep connection, relief from her isolation, and common ground with other like-minded women. This connection allowed her story of hope, strength and love "Caring for Sarah" to be born. Liz has lived her entire life in Melbourne Victoria, and Gold Coast Queensland, Australia. She is a mother, grandmother and loves water and nature. She is currently continuing the story of the journey of "Caring for Sarah" and writing a book about how personal childhood struggles are often the blessings that bring forth our diamonds.

Facebook @Elizabeth Hassan (Liz Doyle)

Susanne Scott Blumer

Becoming a Farm Girl

I didn't choose to become a farm girl. I didn't grow up on a farm, didn't dream about having a farm, and honestly the only animal I liked was a cat. Little did I know how my life was about to change. Seven years ago, I was living in a beautiful home in a fancy neighborhood in a lovely suburb. I owned a bridal salon full of gorgeous dresses. Happy marriage, two kids, lots of friends. Life was good, safe and comfortable even if it was much the same thing every day. I wasn't unhappy but I wasn't fulfilled either. And I certainly wasn't inspired about anything.

Our backyard consisted of a huge pool with a lot of concrete around it. The only grassy area had two huge old trees that provided a lot of shade and little sun. I suggested taking the trees down because I had fallen in love with a picture on the internet of a French potager. A potager is just a fancy French word for a kitchen garden, but oh it was so beautiful! I wanted it. I needed it. I wanted to grow my own vegetables. I needed more sun! My husband just shook his head and told me no. I even contemplated putting in the front yard but knew the Home Owners Association would never go for that. So I put a few tomatoes in pots and did my best. My dreams of a French potager would just have to stay a dream.

Or not. Out of the blue my husband announced over breakfast one morning that he wanted some land. Huh? What do you mean land? Land to own or land to move to and live? He wasn't very specific except telling me that land meant possibilities. I love my husband (and hadn't forgotten about my potager), so I told him that was a fabulous idea. Off we went in search of land.

We found it. The minute we stepped foot on the property, we both knew it had to be ours. Over 110 acres with twelve acres of ponds, rolling hills and gorgeous views, this "land" touched my heart in a way I never expected. We were an hour from our home in a little town that boasted a Walmart and not much else. I didn't care. I knew I was finally in the place I was meant to be.

Our new land didn't have a house on it or a barn or very many trees. What it did have when we arrived after signing our closing papers was an ornery mule, two donkeys and seven goats. We didn't want an ornery mule, two donkeys and seven goats, but they were in one of the pastures when we got here, and so they became ours. Suddenly we were not just land owners. We were farmers.

The previous owner lived in a single-wide trailer on the property and offered to rent it to us while we built our home. Thankfully he had made some improvements to it on the inside, and it felt like a nice, albeit very long and narrow, condo on the inside. I didn't care. Our friends were convinced we had actually lost all of our sense as we packed up our 4,000-square foot house, put most of our belongings in storage and moved into our new place. One of my friends pointed out that our new town didn't even have a Target! We still don't by the way, but I have discovered that Amazon will deliver just about anything I want in two days for free. Thank goodness for the internet!

Our children were nine and five at the time so they thought the whole thing was a big adventure. My husband was self-employed and could live anywhere. We moved to our new farm completely oblivious that we had a very steep, but very satisfying, learning curve ahead of us.

I couldn't wait to get up every morning and just walk around taking in all of the beauty God had created for us. Our farm is mostly pasture land so there is nothing to block the view anywhere. I could actually see the sky now, the whole sky, not just a little peek. I could see storms rolling in from miles away, geese flying overhead, stars peeking out at twilight, and majestic herons visiting the pond.

Two weeks after we moved in, the mule and the male donkey got in a fight over the female donkey and ripped half of her lip off. In the middle of an ice storm. Several frantic calls later, we found a large animal vet to come out to the farm and take care of Brownie's poor lip. If you ever visit, you'll know Brownie because she looks like she has a permanent sneer. She's sweet though. The vet told us to get rid of the mule. She said he was unmannered, had never been handled and was mean. One post to Craigslist and that ornery mule was gone by the next day. It's honestly amazing what you can sell on Craigslist. I had no idea!

I couldn't tell which of the goats were boys and which were girls. I went online and posted my question on Hobby Farm magazine's bulletin board. Farmers are nice people overall and several sent me pictures, gave me advice and tried to help me out. I spent way too much time out in that pasture, pictures in hand, staring at the backside of my goats. I swear it all looked the same to me. I laugh about it now because a female udder and the male anatomy on a goat honestly do not look the same, but I had been selling bridal gowns. I didn't know anything about goats. I was also convinced that my donkeys would sneak up on me and kick me in the head (they don't). They scared me and for weeks I was afraid to go in the pasture if they were anywhere near the gate. A few months later I was reading the latest issue of Hobby Farm magazine and they published my question in there! I'm sure the readers got a good laugh from that one.

We bought a book about farming and it said chickens are hard to kill and a good first animal for new farmers. That was the start of my Chicken Addiction. I figured if I couldn't sell bridal gowns, I could sell chickens. I bought the rarest and best quality chickens I could find, talked my husband into letting me buy fifteen beautiful playhouses that I turned into chicken coops (all painted a different color of course), and began my new career as a chicken breeder. When my husband talked about possibilities, I doubt he meant me having 500 chickens, people traveling from all over the country to buy chicks, and having a bathtub full of them. Poor guy! My mother-in-law always wondered how could I possibly go from the bridal salon to a life filled with chicken poop. My answer was and is always the same. I'm happy. This is the life I was meant to live. I've been mostly cured of my Chicken Addiction but do still have my own little flock that lay beautiful blue eggs and love their human mama.

We now have seven donkeys, a herd of cattle, miniature baby doll sheep, a flock of hair sheep, pygmy goats, chickens, ducks, a pet goose named Gus, guineas, cats and three Great Pyrenees dogs. Most of my animals have escaped at some point and the Sherriff Department knows us well. I believe we are infamous for animals roaming the countryside. Every day is different, unique, blessed. I have a huge wraparound front porch on my farm house and I spend a lot of time there rocking, dreaming and writing.

After years of thinking about becoming an author, I decided to just do it. I've had six number one best-selling children's books on Amazon and have two more coming out in the next few months. My animals provide lots of good writing material! I have an orchard, a little vineyard and finally my kitchen garden! My son and I became certified beekeepers and I became a Master Gardner. And I am so lucky to be able to homeschool my children. Our next big project is the construction of a wedding/event venue here on the farm. Everyone always tells us this farm is magical, and I can't wait to share that with others on their special day.

I had no idea I was meant to be a farm girl until I had a farm. I had a lovely life before but something was missing. Now my heart is content. The farm is where I am meant to be, and I am so thankful that we took a chance, left what was comfortable and leapt into the unknown. God knew what he was doing when I fell in love with the French potager. I just wasn't dreaming big enough, so He did it for me.

Learn more about Susanne Blumer

Susanne Blumer lives on Huckleberry Farm in Upstate South Carolina with her husband and two children. A former model and city girl, Susanne became an accidental farm girl and fell in love with her new life. Her adventures on the farm are the inspiration for many of her books. As Susanne puts it, "Having a farm is like a story. Sometimes it's a comic book. Sometimes it's a horror story. But mostly it's a fairy tale." In short order, Susanne became a chicken breeder, goat wrangler, shepherdess, homeschool mom, donkey whisperer and fence repairer.

She is also a Master Gardener and a Certified Beekeeper. When she is not writing, she is tending to her chickens, sheep, garden and little vineyard.

In addition to chickens, the farm is home to cows, donkeys, guineas, ducks, cats, Barbados sheep, miniature Baby doll sheep, three Great Pyrenees and a pet goose named Walker. Susanne is the author of the best-selling Pip! Zip! Hatch! Love! and Wooly Meets the Chickens: Book 1 of the Huckleberry Farm series. She is also the author of the Piper Periwinkle™ series and the Explorer series. You can contact her at www.susanneblumer.com

Judy Mark

<u>In Search of Unconditional Love</u>

My name is Judy Mark. This is a story about how I felt as a young girl.

Being part of a strict religion made me feel insignificant and small but I kept believing and dreaming. Today I am a happy mother and use my skills as a barefoot, nature-loving abilities to help others. Enjoy my story. You will find diary entries from when I was a young girl, followed by my view on the entry.

Tales from a Mennonite Experience

Growing up in the foothills of the mountains on the backs of hours and hair flying in the wind... You would think it was this young girl's dream and you are right, it was. But it was too rocked with many nightmares. And today I will take you through her experience of finding unconditional love. She was shuffled multiple times through deeply dark and religious churches. During this time, she grew up watching her parents being told that their son had died because they had sinned and watched the use of conditional love and fear used. As she grew up she began to experience this conditional love in her own life.

The very first time she experiencing this feeling was with the tool of abandonment. She was only 11 at the time but remembers that moment clearly as if it were yesterday. Something had transpired during the day and the actions of an active little 4-year-old pushed her mother's patience over the edge. She had never experienced that look of anger before as her mother angrily walked out the door, saying: "When you can maybe OBEY ME again, I'll come back. Or maybe, I'll never come back!" Hours went by and her mom returned, albeit from art class, but the damage had been done. In her little 4-year-old mind she had been abandoned, and was no longer loved for those long hours. For many, many years after that her mother would use the this as a threat for obedience, always saying things like "Do you want me to leave?" and "Can you raise your brothers and sisters, and I'll go live on the streets?

It always worked. But was it right?

Another episode that cut deep like a knife was found in an entry in her diary.

Age 12

Dear Diary,

My heart is breaking. My best friend and I are no longer allowed to be together at school because I guess having a best friend is a sin. This morning my dad, (I thought he was on my side?) said to me that the preachers told him to talk to me and if I don't obey, severe action will be taken. After school the 3 preachers made me go upstairs alone in a dark room and they sat and scolded and interrogated me for 45 minutes at least until I cried, and cried.

I'm really scared.

This was not the end of it. After about a year of this, she was once again uprooted and moved into the bush and homeschooled. It should have been perfect, all the beautiful open space. But the financial pressures and stress were too much for her mom, who couldn't take the pressure, and being the oldest at times this frustration and rage was directed at her. She tried to take it with her head down and submission in her eyes, even though many times her stubborn and independent spirit refused to be broken. This resulted many times in a rage-induced beating. Many times, she cried herself to sleep, writing in her diary, being her only relief; her only friend.

Age 13

Dear Diary,

Today, I guess I did something wrong. I don't even know what but I'm being told that my Constitution is not as strong as my sister's. If I were as nice and submissive as her, I wouldn't get so many spankings, I guess. I told them I just want love and understanding, but I just get told that I'm not good enough. That if I want any respect, first of all, I need to show respect. She gets told every day how beautiful she is and when I am asked "Is your sister not the most beautiful cook there is?", I have to say yes or pay the consequences. I am going to try harder tomorrow because my love tank is empty.

Her relationship with her sister was not good. She was filled with jealousy and wished she could receive the same love. This type of conditional love continued for a couple of years. Some days were better than others. Some days were even close to perfect with warm cozy hugs and good visits from everyone. But whenever the day went sour there was always one main reason.

Age 16

Dear Diary,

I am being told today that everything that went wrong today is my fault and that if mom kills herself that it will be my fault for making her life hell. I am so scared. I am so horrible and if something happens I will never be loved or accepted because everyone will know it's my fault. I was told today that God is not pleased with me for not being an obedient daughter and that no one will ever want to marry me. I don't know what I did wrong today. I will try harder tomorrow. I'm going to sleep now because I can't see my paper, I'm crying too hard.

More years went by. Family members and ministers told her parents that if they didn't control her better she would be a rebellious daughter who would cause them much trouble. She didn't understand why being passionate with huge dreams and being a highly sensitive person was punishable. Showing any emotion was forbidden and punished. Having a broken spirit was pushed for and rewarded, and the best way to control this was with fear and conditional love.

"We will sell your horses if you don't start to change." This cut deep, so she began to be a master and faking submission and happiness. About this time her and her family once again moved to another province hoping to leave all the pain behind and remember only the romantic and good memories. She was excited because it would mean being able to hang out with the youth group and be part of this new church that promised unconditional love and she would finally get baptized and belong, and feel included.

Dear Diary,

I think I'm having culture shock. It's been a year since I hung out with anyone my age and how now I'm all of a sudden with people every day since we've moved. It's all most too much for me. I woke up in the kitchen huddled in the corner afraid to move. I was having dreams of men chasing and raping me. I feel like something happened to me that I have pushed out of my mind, but haunts me. Lord, you only know what I'm going through, please help me. Please help me find a husband I can trust, who will protect me and truly just love me for who I am.

She continued to struggle in the mold of conditional love. She was taught and broken down every day that God loves and blesses us only when we follow the rules of the church and our parents. Perverted looks from men at the church confused her as she was asked to wear more modest clothing to hide her body. She was forced to be more submissive to the men around, never saying no to them. She was forced to be submissive to her brothers as they were taught to practice leadership over her. Slowly, but surely her spirit was breaking. She was becoming accustomed to this way of mentality and to join the church, get baptized and find the man she prayed for every day, she would need to be truly ok with this mentality.

Dear Diary,

I feel so useless, and ugly. I hate myself. I need to be more submissive. I had a dream last night of a man in a chair, he was like a King, and he was my husband. He was a love I had never known. I'm scared because it was no one I know, and all the church people didn't like him. It's just a dream.

She was finally baptized into the church of her dreams. It was so beautiful to feel the love of the church people. It felt so unconditional. She felt loved and involved. She got to be included and everyone treated her with love and respect. She had many crushes and close friendships with young men of the church, but as she was part of a church that did not date, she would be crushed every time the young man she was attracted to would be announced to be married Sunday morning after Sunday morning. She decided it was time to just spend the summer doing the best job in the world at the time; training horses. That was when everything changed and her eyes were open and heart began to beat again.

She met the "man in the chair". She did not know it at the time of course but it was he who would spark life into her dead and submissive soul.

Dear Diary,

Today I met an interesting man. He called me "sweet cheeks", and made me smile. Normally, I don't trust any men especially ones with long hair and tattoos, but he makes me feel strangely safe. I rode with him in the combine, I caught him looking as I had one button opened on my shirt. I buttoned up quick. Anyway, he asked a lot of questions about my religion, so I told him. I love my church and maybe he could come sometime, but I was too scared to ask.

Dear Diary,

I went to pick up bales from the guy. His name is Rick, he helped me load. I wasn't wearing my head cover because a horse had bucked me off that morning ripping it off my head. He noticed right away and asked if I was mad at God or something. I didn't know what to say and was embarrassed.

She made sure to never again not show up without her head covering on, as to not attract anymore embarrassing questions. She was following church and God very closely. Every service and church gathering was attended. She had made a close friendship with a young man from church was expecting a proposal, but as she always said, if any man wants to marry her, he will find her in the straw in the barn not on the steps of a church. She had dreams and everyday prayed hard that this young man would find her there., but he never came or even showed any interest in what she did. No one from church seemed to take any interest.

Dear Diary,

I'm confused. I sit here every night at the place I'm house sitting, all alone. I've asked many of the church people to come see me. All they want to know is if I'm living my Christian life out here, but no one bothers to come see me. I'm feeling very lonely.

Her Summer was ending and as she was working two-night shift jobs and one day shift job, she had missed a few church services completely unintentionally, and there again the conditional love reared its ugly head, her family began to shun her, telling her to not bother coming home anymore on Sunday mornings, unless I stopped talking to her "worldly" friends as the door would be locked.

Dear Diary,

Apparently, me not showing up to church has created chaos. They are banging on my doors and windows trying to force me to talk to them, I'm getting texts from my family and church members telling me I'm going to hell, that the devil has taken my soul. My radio that was playing Christian music to my horses went missing from my barn. I found out that my mom took it and threw it away saying she took the devil out of my barn. I better repent on my hands and knees before it's too late. I haven't even done anything wrong. I thought they were different.

She turned to the only person who had ever been truly honest with her, and he was there with a ready ear to listen. She began to hang out on Saturday evenings watching hockey and eating soup, visiting about life in general. She would pour her struggles out to him as she tried to make sense out of it all. Her response to the constant battering was "I need some time to think". She knew she wanted to go back to the church but she needed to get mentally ready for what was to come in terms of punishment, but in response back to her was to harass her even more. This church, the one I thought was perfect, the true church, has asked her to judge and turn her back on the people who had opened their homes to her, had been so kind and unconditional to her, was this the way Jesus would be?

She spent as much time as she could on Saturdays hiding out at Rick's house, as it was the only place no one could find her. He asked her tough life questions about her decisions, and shared his past with her and the things he had gone through in life, and what he had learned from his life experience.

She realized she had a huge decision to make. Take the path in a new unknown life in search of her true love and finding her true purpose, or go back to what she knew, gaining her friends and family back.

She knew to truly make this decision, she would need to leave for a while, let things cool off at home, make her decision and return with her mind made up and a clear blueprint to follow. This was not an easy decision. All the time spent with Rick had slowly warmed her heart towards him. At the thought of him had made her heart start to flutter. She was slowly falling in love and she didn't even know it. His Charm, integrity, and black and white outlook on life had begun to make its mark on her. Now she would have to leave the man she was falling for and learn to fall in love with herself first.

She stood at her door for the last time, her little 9-year-old sister crying as she watched, not understanding where her big sister who had practically raised her was going. The poor little girl had continuously been told over and over that the reason her big sister was leaving was because she no longer loved her family.

Dear Diary,

My heart is broken, my mind is numb, my body is shaking, how do I explain to my little sister what I'm going through, she thinks I don't love her, because of all the brainwashing that she is getting.

Dear Diary,

Today was the day I had to leave. Leaving my little brother and sister and the man I am falling in love with is the hardest thing I have ever done. The look in his eyes says he doesn't believe me when I say I'm coming back. Its wrecking my heart. I had to pullover and cry as my heart is squashed. It's me my dog and everything I own driving 1600 miles down an icy highway going to an unknown world to find myself. If I die no one will even care. I decided to open the gift Rick had given to me with strict instructions to not open till the next town. Now I know why he said that. I would have never left. The gift was so full of love and showed the pain of letting me go. In there were CDs that had handpicked music on it especially for me and my journey, CDs I would spend the next couple months listening to until I knew every song off by heart. There was a letter wishing me the best in life and that where ever I end up to never forget him, as he would never forget me. He also said to please not base my decision on leaving the church on him, as we may never be anything, and then what do you have, he said, Nothing, no me, no church, no family, no friends. That was difficult to hear, but the truth is hurting these days. So why am I leaving, what am I looking for?

That winter and spring was the longest most difficult months she had ever faced. Every conversation with her family or church resulted in anger and fighting followed by preaching and fear tactics.

Dear Diary,

I am so overwhelmed today. My dad told me today that I am going to hell and I better change, and if I ever need help to not bother calling him unless I am ready to repent. It hurts so much more from my dad as all I want is his blessing and his support. Then later today my brother and his friend sent harassing texts telling me to go crawling back on my hands and knees, praying and begging the church for forgiveness. I have stopped answering calls from my mother as they all end the same way with screaming back and forth and her hanging up on me.

I tried to call Rick, he is the only one I can trust at this point but again my remote location has very limited cell service and I couldn't get through. I'm lying here listening to the CDs he gave me, I cried most of the night already. I hope I don't wake up, and if I do I hope it's just a bad dream, I Just want to die. I just want to stop breathing. I even tried a few times. Never have I felt so alone and in need of an understanding and compassionate God. I was taught that God Punishes us for sinning. Am I sinning? Am I wrong?

As the months passed, she began to start with a fresh new slate and she began a fresh and new relationship with God. Learning her bible and the people around her in a whole new light of compassion, humility and kindness. Learning that men did not have control of her, and she needed only answer to God not to man, or to church rules. She learned that God loved us unconditionally, adopting us as his children once and for all once we accept his gift of salvation, and when we slip up or make mistakes, he does not shun or disown us. The fear of dying and hell were slowly leaving, the depression spells and anxiety attacks less frequent, it was slowly being replaced with a sense of peace.

Dear Diary,

I thought I was doing good, but I guess there is another thing I need to address. My boss overheard me swearing and cursing on the phone. Him and his wife pulled me aside and asked me to refrain from that language around their boys. I am cowering with embarrassment. The way they say it was like no one had ever addressed me before. It was and equal feeling full of love and respect. The looks in their eyes was one not of judgment, but one of love and concern, something I had never been admonished with before. He looked at me and said, "you know those words don't suit you at all. You are too full of love to offer without on to so much anger. So, who am I? Is the question.

She Stepped back and looked in the mirror asking herself, what has happened to me? She began to write positive affirmations on the mirror for her to see every day. "I am strong, I am beautiful, I LOVE MYSELF". She forced herself to everyday no matter how hard it was, to repeat them over and over out loud to herself while looking in the mirror.

The profanity stopped all together. She began to read personally uplifting books, building herself up and creating a completely new belief system. She started to let go of the negativity and focus on only the optimistic view, looking at the good in all. She was ready to go home and face the music with her backbone solidified. But where was home? Was it back to the church or a complete new life?

Dear Diary,

I talked to Rick today. He thinks I'm not coming home. So, I gave him a date. One month from now I will be back home. I don't plan to tell anyone but Rick, as I will be staying with him and working on his farm till I find a job. I want to avoid as much drama as possible.

It was hard leaving the family she had grown so close to. They had become family to her. She had watched them as they raised their family and vowed that she too would use that love and discipline for her own family. The inside jokes, the prairie oysters, the midnight overtired laughs. The Thiessan family she had spent so much time with as well gaining so much guidance and insight from, holding her up and always being there for her, supporting her showing her a safe place of love, and showing her the meaning of unconditional love, and leaving her an example of how she wanted to raise her children. She knew that a piece of her heart would always stay here.

Dear Diary,

It was an interesting day. The head covering that I had kept in my drawer for my whole time here awaiting its fate, went into the garbage today. It was liberating and emotional. It was a symbol of a new but scary beginning ahead of me. It is no longer a part of who I am. I have given away my dresses, and I am packed to go back. I am so excited to see him.

Dear Diary,

Well I was about half way home. It was 3 am and I was exhausted and decided to stop at the nearest truck stop and get some rest. I phoned Rick to let him know where I was. He said I should go to the closest hotel and get a room. I told him I didn't want leave my dog in the car so I would just sleep in my car, I was fine, I assured him. He would not let up, insisting that I go find a safe place to sleep saying he would not sleep knowing I was on the side of a road at a truck stop sleeping in my car. I then knew I had to break down and tell him that I had just enough money to get home on. Without missing a beat, he said I should go to the closest hotel walk in and call him from the hotel, and he would use his credit card and pay for the room. What? I couldn't believe my ears. How could someone be so willing and ready to help me and not want anything or any payment in return. It blew my mind. Was this what unconditional love looked and felt like. Why was he showing me something so effortlessly what others had never been able to do?

She had gotten a great sleep and a free breakfast. It was time to head the rest of the way home. The moment she saw him, the feelings began to flood back as she bashfully approached him and embraced him in a hug. She had been gone longer than what she had known him for. It felt like no time had passed. They had just started where they had left off. They even went on a great bonding trip together that summer getting to know each other, spending hours talking and laughing. She wore makeup for the first time. He kept encouraging her and giving his opinion, but never once told her what to do as she learned to make up her own mind making her own decisions. She had come home with only one pair of jeans and two shirts. He took her shopping buying whatever she needed and treating her to the best time she had ever experienced.

Then reality hit. They were home again, she needed a job, and she couldn't go on hiding forever, and avoiding the church people. She would need to break her silence and stand up and take whatever was coming her way.

That summer and fall she spent working for rick on his grain farm enjoying the outdoors. She felt important. She felt like she was respected and had a voice that was finally being heard. For once in her life she felt like she was someone's number one. He built her up, everyday telling her how beautiful and strong she was, and how the way she was just herself blew him away, and how much appreciation between them there was. Her love tank was slowly filling up.

Her family received wind of the relationship and that she was back in the country, once again all hell broke loose.

Dear Diary,

I had another anxiety attack, I felt like I was dying. I talked to mom for the first time since I'm back. The conversation started off ok, but then the bible got thrown in my ear, and I was told how I am living in sin, and that being with a man so much older than me was disgusting. They keep telling me that it's too bad I didn't die in the car accident with my friends cause if I had I would be in a better place than I am now. She said if she could kidnap me right now and take me farm away and put me back in the church and get married to a church boy she would, and in fact wished she had done it sooner. I'm falling apart. Ricks family is so loving and supporting. I don't tell them about these conversations as I don't want them to hate my family. I just hope that it all goes away.

She had gotten a job in a private home caring for an elderly lady, and was finally making her own money again. Then came a shocking surprise.

Dear Diary,

We have just found out that we are going to have a baby. We've never even discussed having children. I assumed he didn't want children, but this has brought on a whole new side to our relationship. He is apparently ecstatic as years ago, the doctor had told him due to a severe accident he would never have children of his own, and as a result he had given up the idea until today. He says it's a boy. I hope it is too. I'm scared but super excited.

Christmas was around the corner and so they decided to wait to announce it until Christmas. She did not realize that there was another surprise for her around the corner.

Dear Diary,

Today is Christmas Eve, wow what a day. After supper with Rick's family, playing cards and overeating on tons of good food, we headed home for the night. We were sitting down on the couch talking about the night. I thought it odd that he was interrogating me about my evening with his family, but I told him how I felt, and how amazing his family was to me. We talked about how amazing it was to not have to spend Christmas alone ever again. I told him it was the happiest I had been in a long time. He got a really weird look on his face at this point and the color drained from his face as he stood up and started walking towards me. He started to stammer as he was fumbling in his pocket something about how happy I made him, and that he wanted me to be in his life forever, if I wanted to be. He said he had something he wanted to give me before Christmas. There it sat in its box in front of my face, a giant big ring. My mouth gaping, I couldn't for life of me in the moment think why he would give me this. Until his words sank in. "Will You Marry Me?". Of course, I would. Then I felt bad, cause for the last couple months I had been telling him that I didn't like jewelry much I didn't ever want diamonds, and when he would test the waters of marriage by telling me he had had a dream about us getting married, I had just brushed him off, so of course the poor guy was nervous and thought I would say no or hate the ring. I was on cloud 9 and overjoyed. The girl no one would ever want? The nothing girl?

Now she was something! Even when ricks mom said she was the best thing that had happened to their family in a long time, and that she couldn't have picked a better daughter-in-law, made her tear up with gratitude.

The winter was passing slowly, she began to start showing. Her belly growing every week. She knew she would need to tell her family before they found out. She decides to email them a picture of the ultrasound and congratulate them on being grandparents. It wasn't an hour later when her mom showed up at her work where she had emailed the letter from. Her heart stopped and the response she received shocked her. She said they wanted to accept the baby with open arms and love him as much as they could. Was this what it took to see that she was serious about her life decision that this was not just a fling and a flirt with the outside world? This was a relief to hear. This feeling did not last long as once again the judgment and criticism began to flow. One day she was called on her lunch break to her parents' house for a "talk". She went. They explained that one day she would severely regret all the decisions she was making and how horrible a life my child would face outside of the church. Her sister promptly informed her that she would no longer be able to visit her, for fear of becoming like her.

Months past with no communication between her and her family. It wasn't worth the negativity. They would just need to love her despite their opinions. The wedding had been put off until the following summer after baby would come.

Dear Diary,

I can't believe the time has finally come for me to be a mommy to an amazing little boy, the fruit of our amazing love for each together, and the proof of God's blessing on our amazing journey together as soul mates. This is the amazing little family god has blessed me with.

The depression came sneaking in again as life tried to return to normal, with an unknown world with a new baby, and a fiancé who had to be out in the field with harvest in full swing. Never before had she been stuck in the house missing everything that was happening outside. She was mom now instead of that energetic farmgirl who had left to the hospital. She began to once again focus inward finding out who she was as a mom, farmwife, and caregiver, while still connecting to the outdoors and the animals or driving a tractor with a little human monkey strapped to her back.

The wedding was finally approaching

Dear Diary,

In a few days, I will be marrying the man of my dreams. Some people ask me. Are you getting cold feet? No!! because the moment we committed ourselves to one another physically and emotionally was the day I gave my heart to him fully before God, and promised him and God that I was committed to the him forever as long as we both were alive. This ceremony was only an official ceremony before our friends and publicly before God to commit to each other.

The days leading up to the wedding were hectic, but not crazy, that was one thing they both loved about their relationship was that there was no fighting, no drama, or arguments.

Dear Diary,

I can't sleep. Tomorrow I marry Rick, it seems so surreal. I'm sleeping at a friend's house tonight, and of course I miss him and am feeling lonely for him.

She was up bright and early getting ready and taking time to reflect.

A few hours later as she stood behind the little bluff of trees, waiting for the signal with her girls behind her. She listened to the soft music as it filtered through the leaves. Her hands were shaking so hard, her eyes were moist. She could see him standing there, he couldn't see her. There he stood, so perfect, so strong, so full of love. How did I come to deserve this man who is so much more than I ever dreamed of, she thought. There he was, her soulmate, her partner, the one who had shown her more unconditional love in their short time together than anyone in her life ever had.

She took a deep breath as she stepped out onto the little path that led to the opening in the wheat field that they had chosen to exchange their vows. As she scanned the crowd looking for faces she recognized, she saw her grandpa and grandma, with proud looks on their faces. It was so good to see them and with them was her brother, sister, and 2 of her uncles. The rest of her family was missing. Her heart gave a little wrench as even the thought of the last conversation with them crossed her mind. She had asked her dad to be there to walk her down the aisle, but the answer had been a flat NO!, and her mom had said they would not even come unless all the guests were uninvited and only immediate family was invited. She gave a little shutter as she realized it was her turn to start down the aisle, alone.

As she made her way slowly down the aisle her eyes locked with his. He began to make hi way down the aisle meeting her half way and offered his arm as he took her the rest of the way to the front. It felt perfect.

She asked her grandpa to do a welcome speech and a prayer before the meal, and he did not disappoint. It was amazing, and full of love, and hope, as he welcomed Rick into the family with open arms. He did it with such unconditional love and humility bringing tears to both bride and groom, and many in the audience. The rest of the evening went by quickly as they enjoyed supper, music, and a fire-pit with their guests

Rick pulled her aside behind the tent away from the craziness for a few moments and pointed up at the sky with his arms around her, he softly whispered, "I have never seen the stars this bright in my life. It's like someone up there is smiling at what happened here today. As they stared at the sky together in silence the feeling of love was intense and in that moment, she knew that as long as she remained in those strong arms that no one would ever hurt her again. She knew she had found an unconditional love that would last forever.

Dear Diary,

I now know what unconditional love is. It is a love that lasts forever. It is a love that is there even when disagreements happen and that even when things get tough there is love prevailing. Even when our children do things we don't approve of, our homes and hearts are always open to them. It means even when there is nothing given in return we do everything we can for that person in our life who deserves all of our love, just because we love them.

I have learned so much on this journey of love. To be humble and kind, to love with all that we have to love. I have learned to be my own voice not saying and doing what I think will get the best attention of the minsters or the church, but to live my life for God and for those I love. To be my own voice in this world helping others find their voice as I found mine. No matter what comes my way. Never will I blame anyone for any deed or any wrong action done to me. Never will I hold a grudge against my parents for they did the best they knew how. They did what they were told and what they believed in their hearts was the right thing to do. I have more love in my heart now than ever before. When you can find true forgiveness and love in your heart towards all then do you truly find freedom of unconditional love.

-    JUDY MARK

Learn more about Judy Mark

God is my guide. Books are my light. Writing is my footprint, and my loved ones are my reason why. I want to leave a path of footprints for others to follow, through writing and through living my life to the fullest with those I love. Leaving the world a better place.

Ariëlle Verwey

<u>Cloud of Doomsday</u>

"She Said I'm Done"

Three *gorgeous* Birch trees in front of a brick wall are close huddled together; their leaves fall down in the cool breeze. Hurried bikers are passing on their way to work or school, the occasional pedestrians walk by, talking and laughing with their companion or they are alone.

I watch behind the tall window where I sit at a big table, all by myself. I am resting and slowly I'm eating my meal. Some faint background noises come from the communal kitchen behind me but mostly it's still and I feel so alone, *I feel emotionally empty, I feel mind-numbingly tired, I feel deeply sad and I'm not sure what to think any more... I'm* in the dining hall of the Ronald McDonald House in Amsterdam. I feel so totally isolated from normal life out there and there's always a heavy cloud of doomsday thread hanging over me.

Behind the Birch trees and the brick wall stands the Amsterdam Medical Center (AMC) eight floors high and on that eight floor in that cloud lays my fourteen-year-old daughter Noëlle, still fighting for her life.

It has been a long fifteen-month journey so far with two relapse since her remissions from Non-Hodgkin Lymphoma. Noëlle is getting her tenth powerful chemo treatment, the first of a series she had twice before to which she responded so well, meaning the inoperable tumor in her belly shrunk.

Her dad and I rotated being with her for a few days and then we usually spend Sundays all together either in the hospital or at home. She and I can't wait to go home again, home is our sanctuary, home is where peace and quiet is, home is where Chico, Noëlle's Border Collie pup is, home is where Noëlle is most delighted. Family and friends have returned to their jobs and school after a long Summer vacation and aren't coming much around these days. The time goes by slowly and is full of pain and uncertainty.

Soon I have to go up and check in with her, to see if she needs anything and to keep her company. Later I go back down, make dinner in the communal kitchen of the Ronald McDonald house, bring it up to her and eat dinner together and spend time with her until bed time. Sometimes I sleep in her room when she needs me the most and wants me very near. It's uncomfortable sleeping in the cod bed and I usually don't get much rest because of the beeps of the pump on the IV pole and the night nurse coming in to check on Noëlle and the machines.

I'm usually exhausted and fully spent when I go back down to my room at Ricky D's as Noëlle calls it. It's nice to get the space and the bed for myself for the days that I'm staying with her. My sleep is usually not refreshing when I wake up in the morning, however I take my time to do my self-care which includes an ingrained habit of stretching and spiritual exercises before I get up.

I'm doing my spiritual exercises in bed as normal and then I feel this incredible joy, I feel peace and love. I woke up after coming out of my spiritual exercise and I was just amazed. "How is this possible?" I was asking myself. Here I'm in this incredible stressful situation with my daughter and I feel this joy and I feel this love and I feel everything is going to work out just fine. I feel I'm protected and Noëlle is protected and all will be fine in the end. I didn't understand where that was coming from. Then later I realized that we as souls are loved because we are soul and no matter what happens in our outside world, we are still pure, safe and loved. No matter what happens, we don't have to react when we just stay focused inside of ourselves and in touch with our higher self, our God like self, we can get through anything.

This realization helped me to continue to completely surrender my trust and my faith no matter what the outcome of Noelle's cancer journey would be. It helped me relax and trust more although the whole experience was taxing me on all levels. Finally, the day has arrived when we go home once more, only to bounce back in the hospital near by our home for morphine the following week. Once home again we travel to AMC for an ultra sound to see whether the tumor has shrunk once more. The technician is vague as what we're seeing on the screen "Wait to talk to you doctor" she says as usual.

It's Friday and Noëlle's fifteen birthday has arrived and she slowly opens her presents in the living room. I see and feel her hesitation and question "What am I going to do with all this stuff?" We're celebrating also in the evening with a party with DJ in the community project house of the special ecological neighborhood we're living in. We're enjoying the time spend with friends and neighbors, holding thoughts far at bay of the impending appointment we have with the oncologist that following Monday. Noëlle is brave, greeting and socializing while she is on pain meds with a kidney drain bag in her cotton cross body bag and she knows that this will be her last birthday.

It's Monday and we sit in a small office as a family with the oncologist and a few other doctors and nurses present. The oncologist tells that unfortunately; Noelle's tumor has not responded to that last chemo treatment. I sit there stunned, although I suspected this outcome, it's still not what I want to hear and I look at Noëlle. She just sits there sadly. The oncologist tells me that's it's okay to wrap my arm around her which I do immediately and the tears roll slowly down her cheek. He tells her that she has two options; the first is to continue treatment thus next chemo but it will be only 1% change that it will work or to just let it be… It's up to her so we let her choose. She says she's done. We ask how long before death is eminent. "About three weeks" he says.

Noëlle is all wrapped up in her pretty warm clothes and blankets and she looks gorgeous half sitting up on the gurney while the ambulance EMT rolls her one last time through the oncology ward hallway towards the open elevator doors. One of the moms says "hello" and asks where we're going. I tell her we're going home for good, there's no more treatment here, it's final. She looks at me in disbelief with tears in her eyes.

Once home I stopped being Noëlle's main nurse and I had the hospice nurses take over. I just wanted to be her mom and not cause her anymore pain. She gets morphine plasters on her arm to control the pain. We celebrate Christmas, Noëlle managed to order us presents online. We take her dressed in her new clothes and boots, wrapped up in a blanket in the wheelchair down the pavement of our street one more time.

Although we were hoping for a miracle, she died few weeks later, a few days after New Year's Day at home (just as she was born at home) in her own bed with her dad, her sister and myself on her side. Right after her last breath we heard bells rings through the open cracked window in the slanted roof. It was magical. Naturally a wake occurs in her room and she lies there peacefully for a few teen friends to visit and say their farewell. We hold a beautiful celebration of her life at the end of the week in the same project house with family, friends and neighbors present.

By consistently putting myself on the VIP list as number one and eat well, exercise and do my stretches and spiritual exercises every day in bed despite that horrible year and a half roller coaster with Noëlle surely made going through the normal stages of loss much easier. I learned to keep my heart open while my heart was broken into a million pieces.

Here I'm eleven year later and I'm whole and I feel happy! Of course, I miss Noëlle, it sucks that she is not here, she was a wonderful girl and she would be twenty-seven almost so I would love to know what she would have done with her life but it is what it is. I just want to let you know this and I help women transform their lives to be better with their hearts and their heart health, even when they go through heart breaking events like I've gone through, there's a way to be whole.

Learn More about ARIËLLE VERWEY

I'm Ariëlle Verwey and I'm a Wellness Lifestyle Coach. My passion is to help women transform their heart health journey on many levels. In addition, I'm a guide to help women create their own wellness business online while improving their own healthy lifestyle and that of others. I was born in Paramaribo in Surinam in South America. I lived there my first five years and then I grew up in The Netherlands. I'm the daughter of illustrator and writer Noni Lichtveld and the granddaughter of Albert Helman (pseudonym of Lou Lichtveld). My dad Ton Verwey was an actor and a director for theater and television. I have one brother who lives in Amsterdam. My oldest daughter lives in Europe as well. My previous publication is *Huis in de Zon (House in the Sun), I.V.K.O. 1977,* which was an assignment for high school. When I was twelve I became vegetarian and I stopped eating white sugar because in those days' cavities were filled without nova cane. Losing my dad to cancer at age fourteen, solidified my path of natural, holistic wellness and I studied and used natural modalities including macrobiotics. I made a pact with myself that I would learn how to take great care of myself so that when I had a family of my own they would be healthy as well.

Thus, I went to the Kushi Institute after finishing high school in Amsterdam. In 1980 I left for America to visit family and to further my studies as a Macrobiotic Health Counselor including getting a certificate cooking for cancer- and heart disease patients. After meeting my husband, we started our family. Besides giving Macrobiotic health consultations and cooking for clients, I taught

Macrobiotic cooking and dance-aerobic classes. I got a diploma in Fitness and Nutrition and taught swimming and creative dance for children. I gave clients ginger compress and barefoot Shiatsu treatments. When our second daughter came along, I became chronically ill myself. Slowly I recuperated using all natural methods and modalities. After losing my youngest daughter to cancer and going through divorce, I decided to become a Certified Wellness Coach and I have also certifications in Holistic Life- and Stress Management Coaching to help my clients get better results. I love preparing and eating organic foods and using natural high quality wellness products. I like nature, dancing, hiking, traveling, animals, reading, writing, creative arts such as sewing, knitting, drawing, painting and creating WordPress sites and graphics. I enjoy meeting people online and at networking events. In my late daughter's honor and her love of her Border Collie Chico, I've been managing the New Mexico Independent Border Collie Rescue website and started the New Mexico Border Collie Club (formerly Santa Fe Border Collie Club). I also created a website for Maine Coon cats called mainecoonies.com. I am the mom of a Border Collie / Springer Spaniel mix named Libby and a Maine Coon cat named Baby Bliss.

Website: www.arielleverwey.com

Facebook: www.fb/arielleverwey.

Dianne Lynn Marling Good

Rose the Saint

We didn't have much in the way of material things growing up but we were never short of unconditional love, rules, morals and family dinner every day and, don't be late!

Mom didn't work outside the home for most of our childhood. Often she didn't even drive so we always knew where to find her. She held prayer meetings at the house, had friends visit and some Saturdays Peggy and Buddy would bring their kids and the adults played Rook in the kitchen while we played loudly everywhere BUT the kitchen.

Life wasn't always easy for mom, she left her home near Boston, MA at 18 and married my dad, an army fellow, to live in a little town where she knew no one. She got involved in church and work and made lifelong friends.

As our family grew to 6, mom learned to make do with $50.00 a week for groceries, pulling out a little each week to save for Christmas and birthday gifts. Though presents weren't many or extravagant there was always a lovely dinner in the dining room with the best china and cloth napkins. We had a happy home.

My mother attends mass every day now and went always on Sundays and every Holy Day when we were growing up. I remember her dragging us to church every Sunday, usually late, but always straight up to the front of the church so we could hear everything and pay attention. One Sunday, I don't remember because I was just little but she tells me often, I had on a new pair of underwear, with ruffles on them, Of course I wanted everyone to see them so I spent most of the mass pulling up my dress and bending over to make sure everyone could see how pretty they were. One mother made a comment about my behavior and to this day, mom gets furious at the woman all over again. A mama bear protecting her cubs.

I learned how strong my mother was and the power of prayer in action throughout my life, always by example and watching how she lived her life. My older brother Jimmy was just 16 and a golden yellow color. The Dr. told my mom it was "a blocked bile duct". She trusted him, she trusted everyone with the trust of a child to all who entered her world. We all inherited it, could be a curse or a blessing but I will count it as the latter because I don't want to question everyone all the time. Turned out my brother had hepatitis, possibly from eating fish from the Ohio River, possibly an unsterilized needle for an allergy shot, we'll never know. Regardless, it had gone on too long and at the young age of 16, my brother had cirrhosis of the liver. I remember waking one night to find my parents praying over Jimmy who was bleeding profusely from his mouth from teeth extractions, he survived and many years later he had a liver transplant on the day his son was born. Two miracles in the same day!

Mom started nursing school in 1979, the year I graduated from BM Spurr school of Practical Nursing. She had dreamed of being a nurse since she was 2 years old. We both worked at OVMC on different floors and shared rides when we were lucky enough to be on the same shift. We started the accelerated RN program together.

By this time almost 30 years in, my parents' marriage was falling apart, mom was heartsick and broken and couldn't continue the nursing program. I couldn't help her, we studied differently, I studied for the test, she had to know everything down to the cell level. After the divorce was final she headed off to Hocking Technical College and lived in a lovely little house and completed her RN training.

My sister Kathy and her husband Randy had moved their little family to Rehoboth Beach, Delaware. Mom needed a change, and her only 2 grandchildren were there so she moved to Delaware and worked several different jobs including being an Ombudsman for the state of Delaware and Director of Nursing at several different facilities all the while going to school. She completed head BSN and graduated with her Masters of Science in Nursing from Wesley College at the young age of 70! She was so proud and we were incredibly proud of her.

Mom's strength in the most difficult times is what makes me most proud of her. Her youngest son, her baby, David, chose to end his life at 42. While it was hard on all of us I have always felt that no mother should ever have to bury her child, regardless of their age. She rose to the occasion with the grace of a Queen doing every reading at the mass on the day of the funeral, arranging and organizing everything even though she was falling apart inside. You see this was her last gift to David, it had to be perfect.

It is funny now to think of some of the things she would say that I now hear coming from my mouth...keep yourself to yourself...don't wash your dirty laundry in public...mind your own business and someday you'll have a business of your own to mind...have fun, but be good...God is, always was, always will be, world without end, amen. I always tell my friends who are struggling, hurting and needing prayers that I will ask my mom to pray, she has a beeline to God, at least in my eyes. I think that as much as I am blessed to have her as a mom, my children are more blessed to have her as their grandma, aka "mucka", she continues to instill the importance of God and family to them and they have been lucky enough to have her for much longer than many children have their grandma. Emily Rose, my daughter has dubbed her "Rose the Saint", it fits her like a glove.

My friends adore her, she can light up a room with her very presence, she can laugh at herself, that is just who she is and if I can be half the wife, mother and friend that she is I will Ok. I call myself blessed that God saw it fit for her to be my mom, my role model and my very best friend. She often says that she just needs to see me, it makes her happy. If she only knew that I need it more than her, she gives me strength, she is a shining example of a Godly woman, I strive every day to be like her, to love, to trust, to have faith. I know the peace that it brings, I see it in her face and her beautiful brown eyes..."Rose the Saint". It fits her perfectly.

More About Diane Lynn Marling Good

Dianne Lynn, born to James and Rose Marling 10/25/1959 in the wee hours of the morning. The third of four children, I, of course, am the favorite child. Graduated from Shadyside High School in 1978 and headed straight to nursing school. Graduated from the BM Spurr School of Nursing in 1979 and went to work at OVMC on a woman's surgical floor. I graduated in 1984 from OVGH School of Registered Nurses with the Ruth S Dunfee award, highest academic average. Married Edward Douglas Good 10/05/1985, we were blessed with 3 children. Hospital, which recently merged with WVU. Expecting my first grandchild in November, living and loving life every day.

Business Leadership

Lisa L. Heintzelman, M.Ed

Investing Our Time

"Time management is really a misnomer – the challenge is not to manage time, but manage ourselves."

In our rapidly-changing, time-conscious world, we are forced to get more done in less time. The quantity of time will not change. There are 60 seconds in a minute, 60 minutes in an hour, and 24 hours in a day. ***What needs to change is our perception and how we invest time, both personally and professionally***.

How many things have you done in the last 24-hours to support your life purpose, your WHY, or your vision? My WHY begins with my curiosity to ask, "Why?" and complementing that with engaging in lifelong learning. I am fascinated by the passion and process of entrepreneurs, business owners, and leaders. Today I invest my time and energy in bridging the gap between education, workforce, business, and entrepreneurship. By engaging with business owners to develop a strategy and sustain a competitive edge, I empower them to work not only "IN" their business, but "ON" their business, while maximizing individual, team, and organizational potential.

What is your WHY? Consider creating a Vision Board with photos, graphics, quotes, and statements that represent your passion, dreams, and goals to discover and articulate your WHY. Utilize your WHY to inspire your Vision, a big picture, aspirational statement of the future. Guide your Vision with Core Values, or absolutes, that drive decision-making. Then unfold your Mission with the WHAT and the HOW of goals and action steps that provide direction to fulfill your Vision. When you develop, and articulate your WHY, Vision, Core Values, and Mission, you provide yourself with a framework to proactively invest your time and energy in activities to achieve the results and outcomes YOU desire!

What moves you, motivates you, or inspires you? As I was growing up, I wondered about the educational process, so I decided to study and engage in early childhood, elementary, teacher preparation, and college education from both the children's and teachers' perspective.

I celebrate having had the opportunity to explore and reflect upon best practices with an emphasis on implementing educational theory into classroom practice.

United with your WHY, motivation drives success!

One of the concepts I wonder about is time. I continue to explore, share, and reflect upon time and productivity. When I engage in something I love, time flies by; that's how I want to live my life every day. Sitting at a desk until 5:00 pm, when the work was already done, was not my favorite thing to do. I was happy when I had more work to do or additions to my responsibilities. Eventually this led to creating my own career and schedule.

Time is an interesting phenomenon. In fact, time management is really an oxymoron. You cannot manage time. You CAN manage yourself and HOW you choose to invest your time. I celebrate Steven Covey's insight, "Time management is really a misnomer – the challenge is not to manage time, but manage ourselves. The key is not to prioritize what's on your schedule, but to schedule your priorities." Time strategies and prioritizing are highly individual and emotional.

In a previous position, I was excited to be assigned the role of completing and submitting the weekly sales report. I remember observing the frustration of my colleague as she worked to the submission deadline. As I began the task, I got in the habit of creating the following week's template because the reporting was progressive. The fun of Fridays, already my favorite day of the week, started in the morning when it was time to work on the reports. Now I realize that was the beginning of my focus on efficiency, effectiveness, and productivity.

These days we are challenged with finding work/life balance. Whether you're a workaholic, have demanding hours, or feel you need to be "on" and "available"

24/7, I celebrate planning time for family, friends, downtime, being unplugged, etc.! Years ago, when I was a child care director, my oldest daughter was entering Kindergarten. I wanted her to only be enrolled in before-school care and come home at the end of her school day, so I planned my work schedule from 7:00 am – 3:00 pm. Unfortunately, if afternoon staff were off, I needed to adjust my schedule. I chose to resign my position at the end of October, after four and one half years with the program.

From that time on, I chose positions where I could work within my daughters' school day. Fortunately, I could engage in a variety of positions where I could pursue my passion in early childhood, professional development, and as an adjunct professor with a focus on exploring and implementing best practices. As I was entering my second year of public school teaching, where I was named the 1999 Sallie Mae First Class Teacher of the Year for facilitating a second grade developmentally appropriate, child-centered classroom, my daughter was trying out for the high school field hockey team.

Because I would have to leave school at student dismissal time for eight games, I talked with my principal about a plan to partner with another teacher to combine students after the initial dismissal. While she liked my plan and wanted me to see my daughter play, she said that the union would never go for it. As I thought hard about my teaching role and the impact I was having, I knew I would regret missing her games, so I decided not to return the following year. I celebrate having coached my younger daughter's softball team, the annual father-daughter fishing adventures with my dad, and the Mediterranean Cruise with my mom for our 70th and 50th birthdays. Whether it's an event, a sports season, or "time" with those you care about, be sure to embrace opportunities to fulfill your Vision, Core Values, and Mission.

During my Master's degree work, I enrolled in an intense weekend course about facilitating workshops and active learning. Before exploring the syllabus, the professor asked us to write what we were thinking about, where we were, and how we were feeling. I quickly wrote how excited I was about the course and was thinking, "Let's get started!" To my surprise other students shared how they had a bad day at work, lost their keys, were worried about their cat, etc. Knowing that my daughters were good to go and I was ready to learn, I was perplexed by their responses and soon realized this was the first lesson of the course.

I was in the here-and-now of time, ready to engage, whereas other students were still thinking about previous tasks or other priorities. This was my introduction to being proactive, rather than reactive and that you must first accomplish something mentally, before you can achieve it physically. Consider planning your time by saying, "Yes" to your life purpose, with a focus on achieving your personal, professional, organizational, and business goals.

All tasks should first begin with your purpose. Figure out what works for you to motivate and manage yourself during the 168 hours in each week. Before you decide "WHAT" is a priority, first embrace your "WHY," and then "HOW" it will drive efficiency, effectiveness, and productivity.

Prioritization sets the tone for being proactive. I began researching the concept of being reactive and proactive by exploring their definitions. I found that reactive and proactive both relate to stress and decision-making. Reactive means force, demand, hasty, and knee-jerk, while conversely, proactive emphasizes importance, initiative, practicality, and down-to-business. While studying the concept of spending and investing time, I found that spend means use up, exhaust, and consume; however, invest means commit with the expectation of satisfaction, gain, or profit.

My takeaway is that when we "spend" time it is gone and when we "invest" time we benefit. These words have inspired my statement of, "Choose to invest your time and energy in activities to achieve the results YOU desire!" It is essential to value ourselves and our time.

Consider these three strategies to prioritize and address your tasks, email, etc.:

Categorize your tasks within the four quadrants of Urgent/Important; Urgent/Not Important; Not Urgent/Important; Not Urgent/Not Important, with the emphasis that Urgent means there is limited time to act and Important refers to how it enhances results.

Make your "To-Do" list become your success list by prioritizing it. Utilize the 3 D's: Do It / Delegate It / Dump It. Should it be done immediately, this week, next month, or when I have time?

Monetize your tasks. Depending upon your focus to increase productivity, sales, or revenue or to save time, energy, or $$$, put a "value" on your "To-Do" list to prioritize your tasks.

I continue my WHY Journey by investing time and energy in empowering individuals and organizations to be successful. How are you investing your time and energy in activities to achieve the results and outcomes YOU desire? It's time to get "busy" with your "busi"ness!

Work Smart . . . Achieve Results . . . Celebrate Often!

More About Lisa L. Heintzelman, M.Ed.

Lisa L. Heintzelman, M.Ed. is the President of Illuminations Consulting, founded in April 2000. She is an expert facilitator with a focus on achieving success through lifelong learning and continuous quality improvement. After graduating on the Dean's list from Harrisburg Area Community College in Early Childhood Education, Cum Laude from Elizabethtown College with a Bachelor of Science degree in Elementary and Early Childhood Education, Lisa obtained her Master's degree in Educational Administration from Temple University. She has been on the adjunct faculty of Bloomsburg University of Pennsylvania, Elizabethtown College, Harrisburg Area Community College, and Penn State University. Lisa celebrates her passion for being a business success consultant with a focus on efficiency, effectiveness, and productivity, facilitating workshops and success processes, while coaching individuals and teams to ultimately "Optimize Your SUCCESS!"

The Journey . . .

We know the words, "Success is a journey, not a destination." My journey started at the age of two in the context of Erik Erikson's developmental theory, "autonomy vs. doubt," when I told my mom, "I will do it mine own self!" Although I was not a stellar student, I decided to pursue a career in education. That's when I realized WHY my schooling didn't work for me, and I was on a mission to provide a quality education for all!

With the opportunity to explore, experience, and reflect upon education through several expert mentors, I learned about child development and how to implement developmentally appropriate practices to successfully engage students in learning. It was time for me to put theory into practice by facilitating opportunities for students to explore relevant topics and curriculum in context. As a measurable result, I could see, hear, and feel students making connections. In 1999, when I was named the Sallie Mae First Class Teacher of the Year for Pennsylvania, a speaker at the award ceremony insightfully encouraged us to reflect upon this question in the future, "Have you taught for 20 years or have you taught your first year 20 times?"

I was inspired to pursue my passion for lifelong learning and expand my facilitation processes within higher education. Through Early Childhood Professional Development and Teacher Preparation, I could live my vision, driven by my values, to "talk-the-talk and walk-the-walk."

In 2006 I was introduced to the world of workforce development, specifically through the Pennsylvania community colleges and statewide workforce development organizations. Having worked from the age of twelve as a babysitter, concession stand worker, pharmacy and fountain clerk, teacher's aide, insurance staff administrator, child care teacher and director, public school teacher, adjunct professor, and director of education and development simultaneously throughout my education, I was surprised to discover a disconnect between education, workforce, business, and entrepreneurship. One might reference that knowledge is power, but knowledge is worthless if not applied; therefore, "Applied Knowledge IS Power!" The Illuminations Consulting Success Processes provide opportunities for individuals and teams to apply knowledge and sustain success.

I would not be where I am today without having the opportunity to learn from leaders and mentors who continually inspire and challenge me. To compete in today's global economy, I have realized that we must focus on leadership and communication to sustain business and organizational success. I am inspired to share my passion and purpose about being an effective and productive leader:

L ~ Listen ~ More specifically, active listening, to ensure authentic communication and understanding!

E ~ Empower ~ Maximizing individual, team, and organizational potential!

A ~ Accountable ~ Creating clear roles and expectations to drive productivity and accountability!

D ~ Dedicated ~ Investing time and energy in activities to achieve the results YOU desire!

E ~ Enthusiasm ~ Exuding passion that's contagious throughout the organization!

R ~ Reflective ~ Reflecting upon a task, project, day, week, or year, to be proactive, grow, develop, expand, and scale!

I have learned that to drive business development and growth, we must work not only "IN" our business, but "ON" our business. As a business owner and entrepreneur, I must strategically develop and sustain a competitive edge to provide the opportunity for customers to buy and clients to engage. Today I celebrate maximizing individual, team, and organizational potential as a business coach. Through Illuminations Consulting, I empower individuals and organizations to be successful.

I primarily engage with entrepreneurs and business owners to develop a strategy and sustain a competitive edge which includes the problems you solve, value you bring, and why do business with you. I also work with organizations to build dynamic management and sales teams focused on efficiency, effectiveness, and productivity to save you time, energy, and dollars. How are you investing your time and energy in activities to achieve the results YOU desire? Work Smart . . . Achieve Results . . . Celebrate Often!

Connect with Lisa

Website: http://www.illuminationsconsulting.com
Email: lisa@illuminationsconsulting.com;
LinkedIn: http://www.linkedin.com/in/lisaheintzelman
Facebook: http://www.facebook.com/illuminationsconsulting

Laura Hopwood Hostetter

True Gratitude for Everything

"It's more than an attitude; it's a way of being'

Gratitude is the quality of being thankful. Are you grateful for every moment, every life experience, no matter how painful or joyous? Many of us are thankful in our lives, our families, our homes, our cars and our jobs. But think about the bad times, the loss of a job, a home or car. Are we thankful for those times too? It is during these times we learn to dig deep and find the courage and the will to overcome. We didn't simply throw our arms up and say I quit. We kept going and we found a solution. It is during these struggles that we grew and changed. But where we thankful for these struggles too?

Think about a child that always earns an A every assignment. They are mastering their lessons, but are they missing an even greater lesson, how to correct a mistake, how to accept imperfection and criticism. Failure is one of the greatest teachers we have. Failure is what taught us to get back up and try again. Sometimes we need to get back up more than once to succeed. Think of a baby learning to walk. They fell over and over until finally, one day they took that first step without falling. Some lessons are easier than others. Some things are easier than others. Some things are easier for others.

Now think about a time when you were struggling, and didn't think you would be able to survive the struggle. You are still here, so I will assume you survived the struggle. Did you look back on the struggle to understand the lesson, or did you simply move on? Take a moment to think about it before we move on.

When my oldest son was seven, I lost my job. I was a single Mom with a mortgage and my income was all we had. I applied for unemployment and was blessed to receive enough to make ends meet. As we all know, that was only a temporary solution that bought me some time. Now that I didn't have to be at the office before my son left for school and I was home when he got off the bus, things started to change and I loved being home with my son. But I knew my unemployment was just a bandage and not a solution.

I decided to change the focus of my job search. Just because I worked in an office before, didn't mean I needed to work in an office again. And what if I didn't have to use daycare or commute an hour one way? The two combined where equal to my mortgage payment. So I started to look into alternatives that would eliminate the two expenses.

I found a job working as a telephone customer service rep. I could work from home about 90% of the time, but more importantly, I was able to make my own schedule. Now I was a stay at home Mom with a paycheck. I was responsible for calling lapsed subscriptions in the US and Canada and because of the time zone differences I could work while my son was in school or after he when to bed. The new job not only allowed me to be the Mom I always want to be, it also allowed me the freedom to come and go when I wanted to. I had as much or little vacation time as I wanted and could afford to take. I loved new freedom I had and wanted more of it. I had solved one problem, but the new job didn't offer benefits. So, a new problem was created.

During my struggle to find a job that paid the bills and allowed me to be a stay at home mom, my wings grew stronger. The fight strengthened the person I was and I knew I was going back. But I needed to find a way to supplement my income so I would can take care of our expenses without benefits or can pay for the benefits myself. I had a roommate during college, so why not give it a try again. After a few failures, I found the perfect roommate.

Everything that life had thrown at me was now handled. Life was good. I was at home with my son, the bills where paid, I was now putting money away each month and I had a new best friend. All because I lost my job, and yes I am truly grateful I lost that job. My new job was now helping me to grow. I was not paid hourly or a salary, but 100% commission. I was learning what it was like to be able to control my income and to be rewarded for effort I put into my work. I was doing more with my son and loving life. But life was not done with me yet.

Remember the roommate who became my best friend? He is still my best friend and we still live under the same roof, but as husband and wife. We have had our share of bumps along the way, but we have grown stronger because of them. After our youngest son was born, I left my job and became a full-time mom and business partner with my husband. We opened our own business. As the business grew, so did the amount of time my husband had to spend away from home. I was home taking care of the boys, the house and the business, but my husband was missing out.

Life had been strengthening my wings and allowing me a small taste of what more was. It was time for me to jump and spread my wings. It was now or never. Learn to fly or accept what we had as enough. And so I jumped. And you don't know how high the mountain is until you jump.

Today life is different. I haven't retired my hubby yet, but he is home more. And we are experiencing life at a whole new level. If you want more from life, you need to be willing to risk the jump. And no one can promise you your wings will open and you will fly at first. Just remember all the struggles you overcame that strengthened your wings. Your wings are strong enough to fly. You just must believe you can. It is because of that belief I am living a life that most won't. Simply wanting it is not enough. You must be willing to jump.

Today we decide the path our lives will take because we are now truly living. There is no easy button or get rich quick fix. But there is a better way and it starts with true gratitude. Remember there is a reason for everything and everyone in your life, and you need to be thankful for all of it. The joyful times in our lives are our rewards for getting back up and trying over and over, until we succeeded. Each struggle we overcome gives new strength to your wings. And the stronger your wings, the higher you can fly. But only if you jump.

If you had told me that losing my job was good thing on the day it happened and I would later be thankful I had, I would never have believed you. But today I am so thankful I lost my job. I know have a beautiful family and I am living a life I never dreamed possible. And with each new struggle, we break through together strong because of it.

There is no limit to how high you can fly, unless you don't jump. Life has brought you to the top of your mountain and given you the strength to fly, but being truly grateful is what allows you to fly. True gratitude is the wind under your wings, lifting you up higher and higher. Are you thankful for all the struggles that are strengthening your wings so that one day you too can fly? Has life brought you to the top of your mountain? Just remember, if you are breathing, life isn't done with you yet. There is more out there waiting for you and it is up to you to get up and go get it. Look back for the lessons life has given you to strengthen your wings. And when life takes you to the top of your mountain spread your wings and feel the wind waiting to carry you higher. Your dreams are waiting for your feet to leave the ground.

Learn More about Laura Hopwood Hostetter

www.LauraHopwoodHostetter.com

Laura is a fun loving, spontaneous and quirky ball of fire. She never waits for life to present her with an opportunity; she just forges ahead and creates it.   As a child, she dreamed of seeing the world, like so many do. And like most, went to college, earning her Bachelor's Degree at Elmira College in International Business, and started building a life of her own.

After marrying, Laura became a stay at home Mom with her two sons and office support for the trucking company she and her husband own. She is implacably dedicated to her family, work and dreams. Like her own Dad was, her husband is gone days at a time and often misses out on events their sons are involved in. Deep in her heart she knew there was a better way and the world was still calling her. Laura made it her mission to find a better way.

This is where her story began building its own path. She believed there was a way to earn a living, while living. To experience life and not just watch it go by. Today Laura is running her own business helping other live a better life and slowly retiring her husband from the road. She is exploring the world with her family and friends one destination at a time. But don't ask her for her favorite destination because she will respond with, "I don't know. I haven't seen them all yet". Those that know her best, describe her as giving, loving, caring, a go getter, a no-nonsense woman with strong opinions, a role model and team player. If you them where to finder her most of the time they just shrug their shoulders and say, "I'm sure see is somewhere" or "see where she checked in last on Facebook".

Laura was born in Waverly, New York, and grew up in the small farming community of North Norwich, New York. She currently resides in Martinsburg, WV with her husband and 2 sons. When she is not exploring the world, she enjoys spending time with her family and friends, a good latte, cheering for her favorite driver, her hubby, at semi pulls and playing aggravation with her boys.

Shari Brandt

<u>Embracing What I Want in Life</u>

Knowing what I want in life and who I want to become, developed as I made the decisions to let go of things and relationships that were not serving me. It wasn't easy at first, but my choices became clearer as time went on.

I helped my husband with his financial services business and I gave until I had no more to give. I had five children over ten years and I gave up my own interests to raise and educate my children. I stayed married for sixteen years before I was not only suffering from emotional abuse, I could see the effects on my children as well. My self-esteem was suffering because I could not do anything to make my husband happy and when I saw that he was displeased with the children, too, I knew this could have devastating consequences in their lives. I had to decide.

I began to earn money on my own. This wasn't a decision, it was a response to him saying that *if we lose our house, it was meant to be*. We had five children and would not have could find an apartment with lower rent than our mortgage so this did not even make sense. I began to serve at a local restaurant. It wasn't my dream job, but when I began to pay close attention to how much money I was making I realized that I was making enough money to pay all the bills of our home. This gave me a little bit of power.

After I got him out of the house and gained some strength emotionally, I went to work in Financial Services on my own. I felt courageous and hopeful.

I met my second husband. He was my "Knight and Shining Armor" at that time. My children were even in awe of how this man, who was not their father, wanting to spend time with all of us and help us to make our home a beautiful place. He lived with us for two years before I married him. I wanted to be sure he was who

I thought he was. He even stayed with me when we found out that I had cancer and I had to go through surgery. Many people were amazed since this is a time when relationships often end. We were married about a year after my surgery and had only one good year when things went south. Within two more years, it was over and he was gone. I was shocked and disappointed that what I thought was a healthy relationship that would be a good example for my children to see, had turned into a relationship that lost communication and lost love. I could not expect more from an alcoholic.

So, I asked myself, "Who am I?" Have you ever asked yourself that question? Are you your job? Are you the things you do? Are you your role of spouse or parent? What was I doing? I was now running a gallery, I was making stained glass jewelry, I was raising children, I was serving, I was no longer working in Financial Services afraid of the stress and cancer. I was gardening, not keeping my house very well, and I was trying to stay afloat.

When I asked myself, "What do I love?" That was easy. I love my children; I love helping people and I love art of all kinds. I want to paint, create pottery, jewelry and mosaics, take pictures and write. One of my children at this same time was struggling with school and getting his schoolwork done. I was trying to figure out how to spend more time at home instead of working, so I went back to school.

I decided to get a Bachelor degree in Graphic Design. My previous Associate Degree in Visual Communication would help me a little bit towards that goal and there was a school not too far away where I could study. This time off, rekindled my creativity. I was feeling more alive than I had in a long time. I had ideas that I will be working on creating for years to come. And when I got a job in the field, I had a little bit of security.

Around the time that I got this job, we found out that my brother had cancer. It was bad enough when I had cancer, but I was never sick and I was determined that I would survive. It helped that my cancer was slow growing and carcinoid. My brother's cancer was aggressive. By the time the doctors found it, his bones were like lace. My family and I watched him die over the next eight months. We were in denial the entire time, hoping for a miracle until the very end. But a miracle did occur and my brother began to proclaim, "I have never been so happy in all my life, God has healed my soul."

He wrote a poem he called a song and my friend turned it into a real song. My brother heard it two weeks before he died and loved it! I have had the honor of helping my brother, Train, live on through the words of his poem by illustrating the song as a series of three children's books. I had been writing about my own experiences and had hoped to turn them into encouraging books, but his books have come first. This was serving myself while I am serving others. A new direction and something even better than I had imagined.

I worked in my job over a year after my brother's death. I worked on his children's books too. The company was growing and the person who hired me left me believing that there would be opportunities for advancement. I had some security and even a little bit of comfort for a little while. Then it became evident a change was necessary. Those opportunities for advancement went to younger people and when I lost my child support and was no longer making enough money to cover my bills. This was when an opportunity in Financial Services came my way.

I have come to a place a peace. A place where I am creating what I want in my life and at the same time following what comes easily if it seems to be my highest good at the time. I have a sense of knowing that the Universe wants what is best for me and is bringing it to me. Learning that what I want doesn't always come as fast as I might like, was probably my biggest challenge. Part of my resolve has become that I decided to live longer. I research how to make that happen and how to maintain a high level of energy. Being present, positive, forgiving, grateful and clear of limiting beliefs is my constant intention.

I also gave myself permission to do more than one thing. I used to hear, "Just do one thing and do it really well." But I couldn't stick to it and would become distracted by other interests. Then I would feel guilty. Guilt is a low vibration and will hinder everything you are trying to achieve. Now I do several things. My highest priority is what will pay my bills and provide me with the benefits I am now required by law to maintain. But I take time to do other things that I enjoy and I incorporate people into my life who have similar interests. When I want to accomplish something that is important to me, I hire a coach or collaborator to help keep me on task.

The bottom line is that no matter what I do, I will enjoy it. I will be happy during the good and the bad. If something isn't what I want, I try to identify that quickly and make a new choice. Life sometimes leads us in directions we never imagined. It is all okay and it can all lead us to our ultimate passion if we just enjoy the ride adjusting the reigns now and then. I have come to believe that there are no mistakes and everything that I experience is for learning, if not another purpose. So as I design my life, it is with the intention that what I do brings myself and others happiness. If there is something better for me than what I can imagine, I am open to receiving that into my life. As I design art it is what will bring me joy and inspire and create joy in the lives of whom my art reaches. In biz, my intention is to share what I have learned in a way that helps others to improve their lives in some, this is my greatest purpose. Love yourself, know yourself and trust yourself while you live, learn and love others.

Learn More about Shari Brandt

I am an Artist, Writer and Entrepreneur living life in AWE of creation with the intention of bringing more happiness to the world through presence and various media. I didn't always know this but I learn more and more each day about myself and my goals. One of the first decisions I made to create change in my life was that I wanted to live a long and healthy life. The first thing that happened after I made that decision was I found out that I had cancer. Surgery was not only a cure, but a catalyst into my study of alternatives which led me to energy healing. I learned about many alternatives including energy psychology and Taoism which I believe will enhance my longevity.

Having cancer led me to look at my life and seek out tools which could help me make the changes I desperately desired to bring into my life in significant ways. I am thankful that the Universe has provided me with the teachers that I needed to get to a place of peace and happiness regardless of my circumstances. While healing from cancer and emotional distress, I have learned how to make improvements in my life, my actions, my thoughts, and my words. Your thoughts are the blueprint of what your life will become. Your words are the framework of what you will experience and your actions are the evidence of your thoughts and words. I hope that I can effectively share how I have learned to change my thoughts, words and actions in a way that will be beneficial to those who are ready to make their life what they want it to be.

I have enjoyed illustrating books including <u>The Sock Monkey Train Song</u> which was written by my brother before he passed. This song is a happy song about traveling with friends which I hope to do more of in the future. As an entrepreneur, I work as a Financial Professional helping people experience happiness in retirement. In addition, I run a nonprofit and am working on producing educational interactive websites where people can learn more about loving life, art, and being in a biz that supports how you want to live your life. This didn't happen overnight. Life is not a right or wrong practice, it's about discovery and change and is different for every person. When I try something and it doesn't work out, I now know that I have the freedom to make a different decision. It may not look perfect, but I am happy and hopeful that the best is yet to come. That is my experience.

The ongoing roller coaster ride is much more under control now and the loops don't take me back too far. I am propelled into the future I desire at greater speeds and with greater ease. I know what I want. I don't know how to get all of it at once and I am not sure that I have shared the BIG picture with anyone. The benefit of that is I do not have to hear that my dream may be impossible. The suspense of how my dreams will come true isn't killing me, it is increasing my life force and my desire to live fully.

I received an Associate Degree in Visual Communication right out of high school and for my 50th birthday I earned a BS in Graphic Design. I didn't give myself permission to do many things for a long time and a phrase I used frequently was, "I can't." I had a rather large list of excuses to go along with it. Now I am working on an MFA in Web and New Media while working a full-time business, illustrating and writing books, and making jewelry on the side. There is nothing that I would say "I can't" about. I may say, "I don't know how I would find time or how I could accomplish that," then I ask the Universe and others for help and trust what happens next. When you have a desire, and add some determination, you can accomplish anything.

Maureen Williams

A Metamorphosis in Progress

"Without change, there would be no butterflies." ~ *Anonymous*

Life isn't easy. In fact, sometimes it can just downright stink. Everyone will have difficulties and challenges in their lives and change is a part of life. It's how we deal with those challenges during pivotal moments that determine whether we sink or swim. We can let it overtake our lives spinning us into a spiral of darkness and depression or we can choose to pick up the pieces of our shattered selves and go onward and upward. I always choose the latter.

My family didn't have riches when I was growing up but we had love, a solid roof over our heads and parents who instilled in us a strong faith and belief system as well as a respect for others. I credit my mother and my maternal grandmother for giving me my inner strength and the belief that there is something larger than me in control of my life.

Even with that solid upbringing, if someone had told me all those years ago that I would endure what I have endured and rise to become an entrepreneur running my own business; I would have laughed right in their face.

Me...a business owner? How could I ever run my own business when I didn't have a college degree? Although I did well in high school surely I wasn't good enough or smart enough. At least that's what I was lead to believe during the fourteen years I was married to a controlling husband whose cruel remarks and undermining demeanor over the years slowly eroded any sense of the real me that had once existed.

Until, that is, I began on the path to my metamorphosis. There were many moments in time that took me down this circuitous route to where I am today.

I am the youngest of eight children and was raised in a crazy yet loving Irish Catholic family of five boys and three girls. No family is perfect but my childhood was one that I look back upon with fond memories of large family dinners filled with lively discussions and holiday gatherings that included those blinding lights Dad used as he filmed us tearing our way through our Christmas gifts.

My Dad worked long, grueling hours so that my Mom could provide a home for us. My maternal Grandmother also lived with us and helped raise me to be a strong, independent young woman who could do anything she put her mind to. She encouraged me to read at an early age, broadening my imagination through the written words on the pages I read.

During my early teen years, I experienced some very emotional upheavals. First was the death of my Grandmother in our home. Years later, I suffered a date rape at the age of fourteen by a boy older than me who by rights should have been arrested if I hadn't been so ashamed and allowed myself to be controlled by my fear.

And then just a few months later, the murder of my brother's girlfriend that shocked our sleepy little town and led me into a mode of self-destruction and bad decisions. I was fortunate enough to survive before losing my way completely.

I learned early on that if I wanted something, I would have to work hard for it. I took my first job at the age of 15 as a waitress in a small diner for a pittance. After high school, I picked up a second job in retail. I was making my own money and I felt empowered to be able to help pay for the things I wanted so that my parents wouldn't have to.

I had met my future husband just before my seventeenth birthday. He was six years older than I was and had traveled the world while in the military. I was enthralled with the stories he told and was amazed to be the one he chose to be 'his'. He doted on me and wanted to spend all his time with me taking me to or from school and work most days. He said I was so beautiful that I didn't need make up or fancy clothes. And he kept me so busy that I had less and less time with my friends and family.

I didn't see it then and ignored friends or family who told me that ours wasn't a healthy relationship. I took it as their jealousy. He wasn't abusive. He loved me and never laid a finger on me. I didn't go on to college because, naturally, he didn't want me to. I quit waitressing because he wanted me to only work my one part-time job so that I could spend more time with him. My cocoon spun tighter and tighter, cutting me off from those around me.

Looking back now I can see it all for what it was. He controlled how I looked, who I spent time with and what I did. He kept me under his thumb and destroyed my self-esteem piece by piece. I was caught up in a cycle of verbal and emotional abuse that would take me years to escape and overcome. I was held back from making any moves due to my pride and couldn't accept the fact that I had failed. I wanted that idyllic marriage that my parents had.

As life went on I learned to choose my battles and I found solace in my work at a women's retail store. I was given several promotions over the next few years that led me into management positions. In my job, I found the one place where I was appreciated and respected for my skills and slowly gained some of the confidence I had been missing.

When my father passed away suddenly it was at a time in my life where I had begun doing a lot of soul searching. I realized that life was too short and change happens when you least expect it.

I had been in my unhealthy marriage for almost ten years. We hadn't been able to have any children and I had suffered a miscarriage that left me feeling empty and inadequate believing it must have been my fault. I was almost thirty years old. What was I doing? Why was I doing it? Was there something more out there for me?

A year after my father's passing I was given a golden opportunity. My company offered me a job promotion that required a transfer to a city almost two-hundred miles from our home. Surprisingly enough, my husband decided we should take the offer as he was unhappy in his job and this would hopefully give us a fresh new start.

What was not surprising, however, was that my husband had made it abundantly clear to anyone who would listen just how much I ruined his life by making us move. One day after being reminded of all the things I did wrong and how he hated it in our new place, it was as if someone had flipped on a light switch for me. I made the decision right then and there to separate and send him back to his family and friends.

Gone was the constricting feeling in my chest. For the first time in fourteen years I felt as if I could breathe. It was the beginning of my new life and I slowly emerged from a cocoon of insecurities, self-doubt and a marriage that suffocated my every being.

And then suddenly, the job I had relocated for was eliminated. Not only was I living alone in a town far from home without the security of another income, but now I was without a job for the first time since I was fifteen years old. It was like I was literally living a country music song; lost my husband, lost my car, lost my job, lost my company paid insurance. Poof...gone.

Using my mother as my role model and her strength to survive alone as my beacon, I had a decision to make. The option of going back home with my tail between my legs may have entered my mind but never for long. I didn't care if I scraped, scrounged, borrowed or begged. Ultimately, that choice helped me reinvent myself for the first time.

It wasn't long before I had created my new life, found my new love and had a new profitable career in media sales. For over eight years I continued to blossom but eventually I became unfulfilled by the corporate world. I was ready for a new challenge and change was again on my horizon.

When I chose to work for a new small media agency I traded making a lot of money for peace of mind. Being able to do what I loved to do, work hands on helping customers grow their business, and being able to enjoy life were worth far more to me at that point. I knew that with hard work the money would eventually follow.

After four years, I was both happy and devastated to see the company grow. With an impending change in leadership, it saddened me that our values were no longer in sync.

'But what should I do?' I thought to myself. Do I try to start my own business or find another job? All my old insecurities bubbled to the surface and I felt unsure that I could do it on my own. I opted instead to go work for another upstart advertising agency with the hopes of it being my last career move.

Have you ever felt like a square peg trying to fit in? I struggled to make this move work because yet again my pride and fear of failure froze me in place.

I came to the realization that I had to take responsibility for my own happiness despite the fear in the pit of my stomach. I literally had an epiphany one weekend where I heard the words escape from my mouth, 'I'm quitting my job and starting my own business.' Once the genie was out of the bottle I talked it over with friends, colleagues and a few clients and of course, my husband Tom, who had been a huge supporter of the idea.

The chrysalis covering me all those years finally began to dissolve. It was time for me to stretch my wings on my own. My agency, Monarch Media

Solutions, was borne in July 2012. It has not, however, been without struggles or sacrifices.

Just as the three-year mark of my growing company approached, my Mom passed away. Six weeks later, my husband Tom, whom I had been with for twenty-one years, was diagnosed with Stage IV Lung Cancer with metastasis on his brain. As my world tilted and spun off its axis, I did my best to continue to function in a world that I no longer understood.

Whenever I would start to feel overwhelmed with my problems and worries I thought back to this saying that both my mother and mother-in-law would say, "If everyone threw their problems into the street, you would be scrambling to get your own back."

None of us is alone in having problems and there are many who have more problems than I do. I needed to accept my challenges and count my blessings.

I'll admit there have been many days that I've thought I'd like to leave my worries in the street to grab someone else's, but then I smile as I think back to those two strong and loving women and forge ahead.

After a remarkably courageous fight, Tom lost his battle suddenly on June 1, 2016, just shy of one year since his diagnosis. To say my heart was on my business would be foolish. My heart was ripped in half and I felt like just a shell of who I was supposed to be.

I'm so thankful for the people in my life that have helped me the first days and months immediately following his death. For my friends who helped me emotionally and even financially with a myriad of expenses. For my clients who have been loyal and understanding during this transitional period, and for the grace of God. I'm not sure where I would be today without any of them.

Although I'm still adapting to life without my husband and finding a balance with work as I rebuild again, I know I will survive and thrive. How does my story end? It doesn't. It only has a new beginning. You see, I am still a metamorphosis in progress.

Learn More about Maureen Williams

Maureen Williams considers herself a media junky with a mind full of useless trivia as well as a budding business owner who thrives on fun gum (bubble gum) and fire drill deadlines. Being the last of eight children in a large and loving Irish Catholic family, she quickly developed the determination and ability to fight hard for what she wanted and believed in. This same determination has now become Maureen's skillful ability to adapt and thrive today through a myriad of life's changes. Williams developed a love for reading books at an early age and always felt in her heart that there was a book in her somewhere just waiting to get out. Today's environment of blogging and journaling have fed that desire and being a part of this book is her first attempt to tell her story on an international level. years of being raised in front of the television, growing up with the ever-changing media environment and a natural desire to solve puzzles have played a part in fulfilling her destiny of owning her own media buying advertising agency in 2012. Although media buying was not her original career path, pivotal changes in her life forced her to continue to change and grow. Events that may have broken another's spirit only fueled her determination to stretch her wings and become successful. She is a volunteer for Sertoma, Inc., a non-profit service organization based in Kansas City, MO where she previously served as a Director on their board. Currently, she enjoys being a Certified Trainer for Sertoma and an active charter member of the Carlisle (PA) Sertoma club. She is also active in her local community by way of business groups, the Chamber of Commerce and volunteering as a Director/Secretary for her Credit Union's Board.

Recently widowed, she lives in South Central Pennsylvania just outside of the state Capitol with her trusted fur baby, Bella the Wonder Dog. Her passions in life extend to her company philosophy and values. Her story is one of adaptation, one of a metamorphosis and a continual desire to serve others as a servant leader.

Website: http://www.maureenwilliamsauthor.com

Email: maureen@monarchmediasolutions.com

Jillian Williams

Professional Photographer

<u>CHOOSE your voice</u>

{How helping others can impact your personal voice}

Each one of us has a voice. An individual way that we see the world, that is portrayed every day through our speech and personality. This voice affects how we are perceived by others, and is depicted daily through our words and actions.

This voice affects how we feel about ourselves, and others around us. It affects our choices, our mood, and our decisions. This voice, whether internal or external, is the single best indicator of our personal health and happiness. Sadly, so many of us have let negativity impact that voice. Whether it be outside influences, like the media, or someone close to us making a negative comment, we are choosing to allow others to impact how we feel about ourselves, and our place in this world.

The good news, is that we each get to CHOOSE our voice. Regardless of the things that have happened to us, or what we have done in the past, our voice belongs to us, and us alone. We have the choice of what we want it to sound like. I know my personal voice can be sugary sweet (when I want it to be!), or in momma mode (when no one is listening), downright scary! Regardless of which voice you are hearing, it is a direct result of what I am choosing to portray.

So many of us are trapped by our past experiences, and think that defines who we are, or that our current situation is a marker of all that we can be. I have found through my personal experience, that we are putting out in terms of our voice, is exactly what we will receive. Ultimately choosing a voice that is uplifting, kind, helpful, and encouraging will not only help you, but also everyone around you!

The term empower, means to "give power" to others, to give them the authority to do something. So many of us spend our lives waiting for someone to give us the power to make change, instead of realizing that the power comes from within us. We are waiting for someone else to give us the power to speak, and to use our voice, instead of speaking our truth. Once we can harness our individual power, and make real change in our own lives, we can help ourselves and ultimately others. My journey to this realization was not as succinct as a couple paragraphs, but most good things don't come easy.

Have you ever felt like you were missing something? Like your life wasn't what you thought it would be? I felt that way for many years, because I was believing what others had said to me, or about me, instead of what I knew to be true. I found that through helping other women to realize their beauty, both inside and out, I found myself!

Although I have been a professional photographer for many years, a couple years ago a friend approached me, and asked me to start photographing women with her. Her reasoning was simple- every woman should have a photo she loves, and feels beautiful in. Although it sounded like a fantastic idea, I wasn't sure I would be able to commit- since I didn't have a photo of myself that I loved! Immediately I was flooded with voices, that screamed all sorts of things with negativity. "You aren't good enough." "You will never be able to do that." "Your photography isn't even that great!" "No one will want that." The negativity went on and on. Instead of letting her know how I felt, I just smiled and said casually, "Maybe." Over the next couple weeks, she continued to ask, and I reluctantly agreed to give it a try. We began our business in earnest, and could find plenty of women who were willing to help us build a portfolio. As they began to come into the studio one by one, I realized just how much my voice, and my words had an impact on them.

Sadly, the majority of the sessions started in a similar way- with apologies and insecurities. Although they were so excited to be photographed, with the hope that they would finally have a photo they were proud to use, most women didn't fully believe that was a reality. We have all suffered from a photo that was taken at a horrible angle, or a bad time, and those are the ones we remember. Our negative voice files that as truth, and we assume that the person in the photo was to blame and not the person behind the camera. These women, who were amazing business leaders, CEO's, Owners, and entrepreneurs, were believing the negative voices that said they were not good enough. Instead of being able to choose the positive, they were focused on a negative feeling based on the past, and I was very familiar!

Then throughout the session, as they had their hair and makeup done, and were shown how to pose, and laughed with me, they could relax, and show off their best selves. By the time they left after spending a couple hours together, they usually said things like, "That wasn't as bad as I thought it would be!" or "I actually really had fun!" I was paying close attention to these ladies, and realized just how much the experience was starting to change them, and the power that positivity can have on our personal voice. Instead of putting out things that were negative, they were starting to shift into a more positive way of talking about the experience and themselves.

Statistics say that it takes 20 positive comments to outweigh 1 negative. Is it any wonder that so many of us feel negatively about ourselves? That boy who made a mean comment in 4th grade wasn't replaced by 20 kind things we said to ourselves. Instead that negativity grew, and became the foundation of how we speak to ourselves. Most of us are carrying around years of negativity, and whether we realize it or not, that is affecting our personal voice.

I realized the power of positivity clearly when the ladies came back to see the images. Being able to see yourself in a way that makes you proud and happy is a powerful thing. As the images flashed across the screen, and they held them in their hands, I could speak positivity into them, and help to change their voice. Instead of the comments they made in the beginning, they were choosing to look at what they loved! They were seeing the best parts of themselves, and could feel proud and excited. By giving them a photo to be proud of, and tangible proof that they were beautiful, it could change how they felt about the world and their place in it. I have had many women cry, and I love that sessions have been called, "visual therapy." Being able to spend time with these women, be a positive influence, and then give them visual proof of their beauty was truly changing their lives.

Not only was I changing their lives, but they had drastically changed mine! I realized while photographing these women how much power our voice has. The quote, "Be kind to yourself, because you are listening," is a profound example of what I have learned in my time of empowering women and myself! When we spend most our time with the negative voice, it begins to be what we believe! We need to speak to ourselves in a positive way, and focus on the best parts of who we are. By focusing on the positive in my women, it changed my personal outlook. I challenge you to spend time each day searching for the positive, so that you can improve your voice. If initially it is difficult for you to find the positive within yourself, start by finding it within others.

Try to genuinely compliment someone each day, even if it is a total stranger. By including that type of positivity in your day, you will put yourself in a different mindset and start to see the world in a more positive light. As I mentioned, your voice is not only how you interact with the world, but how others perceive you.

Start now, and make the change! You alone get to CHOOSE your voice.

Learn More about Jillian Williams

My name is Jillian. I find it hard to describe myself, so instead I will share what I love. I love my four beautiful children, and have been married for 12 years. I love Starbucks, Disney, and Star Wars. I have been a newborn photographer for the last 8 years, and 2 years ago started a boutique photography business called Bevrore. I love owning a luxury brand, and I specialize in women. I love being able to remind women how beautiful they are, and to make a new friend every day that I have a session. It never feels like work, and I am lucky to love what I do. I have a thing for beautiful shoes, and I love a good bubble bath. I truly believe one can never have too many friends. Oh, and diamonds…. I love diamonds. :)

Website: http://www.bevrore.com

Email: jillian@bevrore.com

Facebook: https://www.facebook.com/Bevrore/

Zara Broadenax

Starting with Vulnerability and Moving Forward

Hurt. Betrayal. Broken trust. Used. These are just a few types of pain you feel when someone has taken advantage of you. These are the emotional states you face when you are and have been vulnerable. How do I know? Because I've been vulnerable. It saddens me to say that all too often in life, I have been vulnerable. I have been vulnerable in school. I have been vulnerable at work. I have been vulnerable with family members. I have been vulnerable with friends. I have been vulnerable with members of the church. I have been vulnerable with members of other organizations that I participate in. I have been vulnerable in relationships. But I'm not alone! At some point in our lives, we all have been vulnerable. Vulnerability is a very difficult lesson to learn and yet, it is one where I find myself continuing to push through in hopes of one day mastering the lesson.

Merriam-Webster online dictionary defines vulnerable as "easily hurt or harmed physically, mentally, or emotionally; and open to attack, harm, or damage". The definition almost screams "victim" to me and yet, even though it may scream "victim", I know that it's not. Vulnerability is really a state. It is a state of mind and emotions that leaves one open to be led into something or taken advantage of. Unfortunately, I have personally experienced both. I have been led to the fire to be burned and I have been so misused and taken advantage of that at times my heart still breaks.

My quest to have close relationships has left me vulnerable one too many times. My desire to share love and friendship with others has left me hurt. My concern for family and friends has left me broken. My generosity for the people I care deeply about has left me damaged. Let's face facts, not everyone has access to me or can affect me. Only a small percentage of people have access to me while I am vulnerable and an even smaller percentage can take advantage of me or use me. Truth be told, it is those that I'm the most open and comfortable with that I'm extremely vulnerable with.

What's amazing about vulnerability is not the fact that you are vulnerable but it's who you are vulnerable with. Not everyone has the ability or access to see me vulnerable or be around me when I am vulnerable. The world doesn't get to see me at my lowest of lowest. The world doesn't get to see me vulnerable. It's the people I trust and rely on the most that I'm most vulnerable with. The people I do life with. The ones that know my deepest and darkest secrets. My family sees me vulnerable. My friends see me vulnerable. Unfortunately, these are the ones that are close enough to do bodily harm and fatal damage.

I am the epitome of the saying, "don't take my kindness for weakness". It seems that I have a tracking device for the manipulator, user, or con artist. I cross paths with so many that have hidden agendas and ill-will towards me. I'm looking for friendship and there are looking at what they can get from me. I have been a revolving ATM. I have been a take-out restaurant. I have been the rebound girl. I have been a hotel manager. I have been a taxi driver. I have been everything under the sun but what I crave.....friend!

This constant path of people planning on using me, being used, and vulnerable has me not only being cautious but also build walls. I will only let you get so close until you prove no wrong intentions towards me. Does this work? Most of the time. Every now and then someone of low regard for me, my feelings, my well-being sneaks in and that's the most damaging.

After being heart broken by the fact that it has happened again, I then shut down from the people that do care. But when I do see or interact with them, I'm not really me. I'm wearing a mask. The mask that says all is well. The one that displays that life is wonderful. I'm whispering that I have no issues or problems while all the while I'm screaming for help. But I masked my pain and frustration so well that only a slight few can peel away the hurt. Those are the ones I avoid!

I avoid them because I am ashamed or embarrassed. I avoid them because I don't want to face the truth and deal with the pain and the issue. I avoid them because they won't allow me to wallow in my dismay. I avoid them because they want not let me have an extended pity-party. I avoid them because I don't want to heal.

Ironically, as I try my hardest and best to avoid them, the love they have for me pushes them to seek me more. It appears that the more I run, the more they pursue. They search for me to help me. They will allow me to feel the pain and the emotions that go along with it. They will give me a shoulder to cry on. They will offer ears to listen. They will offer open arms that are ready, willing, and able to embrace me.

For me, the road to recovery is long and difficult. My road to recovery starts me off as a prisoner to my mind. It forces me to revisit every interaction. I start by reflecting on every conversation held to see if I could have changed a word here or a sentence there. I deeply analysis and pick apart every text message, every email, every phone call, and every moment of time spent doing something. I replay every happy item and every day starting at day one. All-in-all, I relive the toxic relationship countless times trying desperately to make sense of what happened. I constantly repeat and pose the questions of why and how! Why me? Why now? How this happen, again? How do I learn to trust again?

After countless hours and numerous months of beating myself up, I step back, exhale, and declare the painful truth to heal and move forward. I admit that I was used, played, conned, hurt! I admit that I'm human! I admit that I have compassion for my fellow man; more so, my family and friends. I want to help. I desire to help. Helping is how I am made. Vulnerable, at times, is who and what I am. Every experience.....good, bad or indifferent makes me who I am.

Yes, if you prick me I will bleed. Depending on the wound, blood will flow for a second, a minute, a hour, a day, a month, a year, or even longer. But once the scab is gone and the wound heals, my scar becomes the door within the wall. It reminds me of the people whom I trust and who I can truly be vulnerable with.

I don't like the process of these "life lessons" but who does. But going through a low point and rising out of the ashes like a phoenix says something about me and my resiliency. I'm greater than any battle. I better than every war. I'm an overcomer. I'm more than a conqueror. I'm worth far more than rubies. These life lessons help develop and form me into the person I am.

Learn more about Zara Broadenax

Zara R. Broadenax was born and raised in New Orleans, LA. She is a contributing author in the #1 International Best Seller, Beyond the Woman. Zara dabbles with creating Creole/Cajun cuisine cookbooks and is placing the finishing touches to her first children's book designed to inform preschoolers on the fun awaiting them at school.

As a licensed minister, ordained elder, and founder of WELLWoman Ministries, Zara specializes in Christian inspirational and Christian urban novels. She is currently writing a Christian inspirational book showcasing the journey of spiritual birthing concepts and ideas designed to pursue purpose and fulfill destiny. Weekly, Zara can be found on Blab.com hosting "A Virtuous Life"; her webcast which takes everyday issues/situations and implements Christian application towards resolutions.

An entrepreneur at heart, Zara is the CEO and owner of Gathering House Publishing or GHP. GHP helps ordinary people create, produce, market, publish, and distribute high quality and extraordinary books. GHP does publishing services, self-publishing, and traditional publishing.

True to her life's mantra of "glad to serve and to be of service," Zara's servant hood extends beyond her personal life. Zara is a retired Soldier from the United States Army. She serves as a Girl Scout Troop Leader. She also is a member of various organizations with a community service and scholarship focus.

Zara is married and the mother of two beautiful daughters.

zararbroadenax@gmail.com
www.facebook.com/zararbroadenax
www.twitter.com/zararbroadenax
www.instragram.com/zararbroadenax
www.linkedin.com/in/zararbroadenax
www.flickr.com/zararbroadenax
www.tumblr.com/zararbroadenax

Yvonne Dvita

The Wayward Girl Creates a Verse in the Powerful Play

This is timeless story, I think. About a little girl who wished for a better life. A story of me, and maybe of you, because I believe all stories are both personal and universal. There was no one more wayward than I, as a child. Yes, I spent too much time alone. I wrote stories and lived in my own little world. Over the years, I grew to understand that it wasn't a bad thing, to be wayward. And one day, in a flea market, I discovered this sign...and it now hangs in my foyer.

Just imagine the wayward young women who must have passed through its doors, back in the day! I might have been one. I do wonder how they made them better? It all reminds me of a favorite quote, from Professor Laurel Thatcher Ulrich, which says: "Well behaved women seldom make history." And so, I will not be well behaved! I am here to make history! I am going to create magic out of hope and desire and battered boxes full of crazy ideas! It's who I am. There is no room for failure...thank you, Susan B. Anthony.

But, we must go back in time, to the history of little Yvonne and how she (I) became wayward. Growing up in the 1950s, living with a divorced mother struggling to pay the bills on a waitress's salary, I was a lost and lonely little girl. I had two older sisters who mysteriously disappeared from my life. I had been placed in a foster home with them early on, and I have awful memories of it. When I finally got back to my mother, it was me...just me, and her. I know now that my sisters went to live with my father, but I only knew they were gone, back then. And my mother, in her struggle to work and pay bills, was less than happy to be saddled with a small child who cried all the time.

There was no happiness in my early childhood. I never smiled. Still, smiling is a human kind of thing. We all smile. A smile is an invitation into someone's heart, don't you think?

And so, I created something to smile about. I created stories to make myself feel better. I almost failed second grade because I would sit at my desk and write all day long, instead of doing schoolwork. I wrote with my treasured lead-tipped pencils until the point of each one was dull, and then I would stop to sharpen them ...and admire them as if they were the most amazing tools ever invented. Because, of course, they were.

I embraced my inner Virginia Woolf - a woman as wayward as they come. Virginia Woolf said, "We write, not with the fingers, but with the whole person. The nerve which controls the pen winds itself about every fiber of our being, threads the heart, pierces the liver."

All my stories were about a little girl who had a dog and a cat. I drew the faces of this little girl and her pets, writing in my simple second grade way how pets made everything better, day after day. And it made me smile.

In 5th Grade, my teacher, Mrs. Mutz, smiled at me after reading one of my stories and said, "You're quite the writer, aren't you?" I will never forget her! She made me feel like a writer, a real writer. I was inspired by her words to continue writing. I wrote, and was praised, throughout my school years. The memory sticks with me because I am passionate about the concept of stories and how our stories make us real.

And then I also remember how reading stories written by others lifted me up out of my sadness, year after year. I remember the window seat at my old home - where I spent many a long afternoon, reading. I lost myself in my books but every now and then, I would pause and gaze through the window at a great tree that reached across the yard next door and touched the glass, as if waving at me with its brilliant green leaves and gnarled gray branches.

I loved that tree. I would pretend to sit beneath the green boughs, lean against that sturdy bark, eyes closed in peace. It was a place of safety; a place of refuge.

In fact, my first dog came to me, at that house with the window seat, and I think of her when I remember that tree. Missy was my life and my love and she made me smile, a lot. It was truly a "love me, love my dog" kind of life I lived. I took her everywhere and if you didn't want her there, well, then I didn't visit you.

Missy lay by me, as I read on the window seat. She listened when I would put my book down and talk to the tree. After all, it was my friend. It would waive its branches and I could hear it say, "You can write a story like that." But I would shake my head, no, no, tree, I can't. "You're very talented," it would tell me. But I would shake my head and say, no, no, I don't think so.

"Being wayward is not a bad thing," it would say. But I would shake my head and say, no, no, it is a bad thing, my mother says so! Over the years, I've spent a good bit of time thinking about Missy and my tree. I remember the joy I felt with her by my side. And I remember the tree and how I felt safe under its canopy. Together, they tapped into my waywardness, in a good way.

They supported the girl who liked being alone, who wrote constantly and dreamed of being a published writer. The comfort of Missy and the tree held me together, despite dreadful trial and tribulation. And yet, because of the trial and tribulation, I learned independence and self-awareness. Perhaps being so alone made me more wayward, perhaps it just brought out the waywardness. You see, just as I had trouble, as a young girl, learning to smile, I had trouble relating to other people and so I became more and more introverted.

I know other women are the same way, because they've told me so. We seem vivacious, we seem extroverted - and yet, in our hearts, we want to go hide in our rooms, all by ourselves! I was delighted to discover, recently, that back when I was considered a wayward, unfriendly girl, who spent too much time alone, I was really learning to be a great storyteller. My solitude allowed me to observe myself, and others, from a place of safety. Which, per a story in the Harvard Business Review, by Bronwyn Fryer, is a good thing. She says,

"Self-knowledge is the root of all great storytelling."

Sadly, as a young woman, the story I was telling was full of criticism, self-doubt and unhappiness. The kind of story that comes with constantly telling yourself you're not good enough! Not smart enough. Not talented enough. Not tall enough...or thin enough! It's more a woman thing than a man thing, I know!

I think I spent so much time worrying, that the door to my future and my happiness was always there in front of me. I just couldn't see it. I spent so much time worrying, I lost sight of my own talents! While perusing the net, one day, I came across a writer named Dan Zadra, who says, "Worry is a misuse of imagination." How awesome is that? And true!

My imagination, my waywardness defines me - in so many ways! It's been brought home to my very heart by this Walt Whitman poem, O me! O life!

This marvelous poem speaks to my very soul! Embracing it has opened so many doors for me! The lament of the poem, Oh Me! Oh life! asks the eternal question: Why are we here? In the middle of chaos and unrest, Whitman asks, why are we (why am I) here? His answer is profound. He writes, "The question, Oh Me! So Sad, recurring, What good amid these, O me O life? Is answered by...

That you are here - that life exists and identity;

That the POWERFUL PLAY goes on, and YOU MAY CONTRIBUTE A VERSE."

He wrote this in 1892. He expressed the angst and worry of the human condition.

He inspired me to recognize the power of contributing a verse in a bigger story, making poetry out the work I do. The sad little girl is a happy woman today.

There is no "making bad girls better" about it. I am but a verse in the powerful play; wayward and proud of it.

Learn More about Yvonne DiVita

Creating stronger women's voice to enrich and expand our businesses worldwide."

People ask me, "What is The Lipsticking Society all about?"

The answer is easy, "It's about the power of a woman's voice. It's about allowing women to bring their waywardness forward, building strength, purpose, and poise in communication at all levels."

Harriet Beecher Stowe wrote, "Women are the true architects of society." This one sentence sums up the heart of what I am about. I believe it wholeheartedly. I support it with everything I have and everything I am. It is my desire to work with strong, determined, focused and yes, stubborn, women who are out there putting the time and effort into their work. Women I call wayward because it's the right way to be in today's challenging business environment.

Dictionary.com says wayward folk are a little stubborn, independent, determined to find their own way.

The idea of wayward women and the need to be 'better' came to me a year ago, when I discovered this sign at a local flea market. It was too perfect to pass up. I want The Lipsticking Society to celebrate women's waywardness! I am purposely creating a place for business women everywhere to build stronger, more successful business ventures by improving their writing, speaking, and communicating skills.

We are all wayward. I submit that wayward women will not be silent. We will embrace our determination and stubbornness, and we always get "it" done, *whatever it is*, at the time.

Women are too important in today's business world to be ignored. We cannot allow silence or softness to hold us back from competing on a level playing field. It's not women trying to take over the world; it's women deciding to stand up and be heard!

Why would you work with me to improve your speaking, writing and communication skills? Because I bring more than 20 years of writing and speaking via my study of the written word; my work with other women in small business; and my speaking/presenting to a variety of professionals, in a variety of industries, over the last 12 years. During that time, I've been a professional blogger, I've written two books, and worked with a strong team helping clients learn to use social media and other web tools effectively.

In my previous company, Windsor Media Enterprises, LLC, I coached authors in a print-on-demand focus. Helping people create fantastic books for and about them, and their business, was and is a major passion in my life. Print or eBook, books promote a higher level of expertise than a website, a blog, or a company brochure. At WME we called it "Book as Business Card".

If you're writing a book and need coaching, at any level – beginning, middle, or end – I've worked with women and men to create successful business books that would represent them in their industry, as experts with more authority than their competitors. I am eager to work with you to turn your book and/or idea into a masterpiece.

The Lipsticking Society exists to support a growing community of strong, independent women who embrace their waywardness as they compete in a global marketplace, with a focus on making sure they have the tools and the support to amplify their voice across all disciplines to build stronger, more successful business ventures this year and every year to come.

You can find me online at:

Website: http://lipstickingsociety.com/
Twitter: https://twitter.com/lipsticking
Facebook Page: https://www.facebook.com/thelipstickingsociety/

Meet the Bellard Family who wrote as a team with us this year.

Family Writers

Jessica Ledet- Bellard (Mom)

Go and be Great

I can do all things through Christ that strengthens me..

Philippians 4:13

You have been called, chosen and set aside for a time such as this, so why do you sit in fear? The strength has been provided for you you just need to tap into it and go forth. We tend to easily find reasons to not do something but it's much harder when you are challenged to come up with solutions. To many a solution would mean we have to put in hard work or we must stay up long hours. We all want to have that instant gratification by doing as little work as possible and then we are upset when that doesn't happen- we are quick to throw in the towel or fault someone else for us not doing what we need to. Now is the time for you to step into your greatness and start reaching your highest potential.

I'm just a simple girl born and raised in a small town in Louisiana, nothing spectacular about me I'm just like you. I've endured many setbacks, failures, loss and upsets but what sets me a part is that I am not willing to give up and I don't allow anyone or anything stop me. I'm a girl of great faith and movement. I believe where there is a will there is a way and that is why I am unstoppable. I refuse to continue in the curses that have been set before me and the lies that I have been taught to believe. You see growing up I were taught to believe certain things, live on a limited mindset and mediocre was good enough. I don't think it was done to hurt me but this was all my family knew. Know that I have grown up I have learned better and I realize the choice is mine. So, are you trapped in the limited mindset that you were taught as a kid?

You remember those things, like go to school get an education and get a good job. Yes, I'm sure we can all relate. I did all those things graduated from college worked numerous years in corporate America but what I realized was I was not fulfilled. I was doing what my family wanted and what I was taught. In this process, I could have made thousands of excuses from I have kids or my health is not the best and so on but I chose to make solutions. I realized that all I had to endure was not for me but for me to be able to share my testimony. You see I've been saved and set free and I am determined for others to experience the same joy that I now do. Living in bondage, working 3 jobs and just merely existing was not the plan that was intended for us. It is time to break loose and LIVE and not just exist.

Excuses have become outdated it is now time to find a way, find a solution and began living the desires of your heart. I am a mother of four with one on the way, I homeschool, own multiple businesses, speak, travel and put a lot of support into my kids that are also business owners. That's A LOT, right? But, let me tell you honestly, it's not easy but it is doable and it is worth every minute of it. To be transparent with you my businesses was developed from the confines of a hotel room with a crying baby in one arm and two toddlers on the other arm, I was at my optimal health and my kids weren't as well. I suffer with a chronic illness that causes excruciating pain, my baby has epilepsy, my oldest has asthma and my second child is allergic to almost everything that exist. I could have sat and soaked that all in and complained or griped all day but what would that have done for the situation? So, when I hear stories of I CAN'T I can't help but think how could you not.

My why was great, it stood out to me more than my how. I knew someone was relying on me, I knew I was an example for some little eyes that were watching and I knew someone was waiting to hear my voice, my story, my testimony. Remember that whatever life gives you it's not for you it is for you to help someone along the way. Now my story may not be your story, my pain may not be yours but one thing that is for certain that it is for someone, someone was waiting on me to show up and now they are waiting on you to do the same. You have already been equipped to walk in greatness so own your greatness and go forth because someone is waiting for you.

Au'Ryanna Bellard (Age 12)

Life As A Young Entrepreneur

As a little girl walking with my parents through neighborhoods and cities, I watched as business men and women rushed from place to place. I was fascinated by the way they carried themselves, and how professional they were. Being the curious young person I was, I decided to ask my mother why those men and women acted and looked different from other people. She told me that they were entrepreneurs. At that time, I was very young, maybe about 3 or 4 years old. I asked her, "What is an entrepreneur?" She told me, "An entrepreneur is a person who owns a business." I then started to ask more questions and learn more about what it meant to be in business.

As I got older, I watched my mother and father work hard and stay up late formulating ideas, business plans, and goals. Sometimes, they would even let me help them write and help them with their ideas. One day, my family and I went to a McDonald's restaurant. As we went inside, one thing caught my eye. I ran over and looked at a big red and yellow compensation chart. I read and analyzed everything that I saw and started to do the math. My mom walked over and started to read it with me. I figured out that I would make more money in a couple of hours than I would make in 10 hours working at a physical job. I sat down with my parents and we talked about how I could make money.

Every successful entrepreneur has a total of 7 or more streams of income. Before I could even talk I would hum and tap my fingers while my favorite songs played.

At the age of 3, I started to sing and play instruments. I was always outspoken and confident, so speaking and performing came easily to me.

But, I had to make money for my needs. I had to find my passion! One summer, I was bored and couldn't think or anything else to do, so I picked up a piece of paper and a pencil. I started to draw designs for dresses and watching How-To-Draw tutorials on YouTube. At first, my drawings were bad. I got frustrated and angry because I couldn't get them to look right. I reminded herself that practice makes perfect. After long months, days, hours, and minutes of practice, I eventually got better. After showing my illustrations to others and thinking of some ideas, I decided to start my own businesses. But of course, I still had to go to school, and do other things, so I had to learn how to balance life and work.

Balancing may seem hard for some, but it's easy when you get the hang of it. If you think of some creative ways to schedule and keep track of the things you need to do, it will help you in the future. For example, you can use neon-colored sticky notes, and color code them based on what you do or your goals. For instance, you can use blue for business, orange for academics, and green for other activities. Another example is that you can set alarms or reminders on your device. For example, if you forget things easily or are not good with time management, you can use a device such as a computer or cell phone to set an alarm/reminder. Some ways might work better for others, but you can get as creative as you would like.

Being a young entrepreneur means lots of things. You must make many sacrifices to be successful. Owning a business means that you would have to stay up late, miss out on activities that you wanted to do with your friends, and taking risks. You must breathe, eat, and sleep entrepreneurship! You should be hungry and willing to put in the work even when you don't feel like it. Even when people tell you that you're crazy, you still should push and strive to be the best! Believing in yourself is the key to your success! Every single day will be hard, but think about what you've been through and let that motivate you to be the best that you can be!

Many people don't understand what life is like for entrepreneurs in general. When you first become an entrepreneur, your family and friends might say you're crazy, too young, or that you don't know what you're getting into. One of the biggest struggles we face today as young entrepreneurs is getting our friends and families to understand what you do and that you want to change your life for the better.

To be honest, I have tried many times to tell relatives about being in business and that they could make more money, but I have heard countless excuses as to why they didn't want to do anything with their lives. See, most people only see what you post on social media, the car you drive, and your clothing. But have they thought about what you had to go through? Sorry, the answer is obviously no! They don't understand the struggle! Behind closed doors no one knows how many nights you had to eat a hotdog instead of steak and potatoes, how many hard decisions you had to make, or the risks you had to take.

Besides all the negative points of being a young entrepreneur, there are many positive reasons. For example, being young is a big advantage. No matter what kind of business you own, it will be much easier for you to sell your products or services. If you are confident, and outspoken, you will be successful!

Instead of having Christmas only once a year, you can have it every month! Another good advantage of young entrepreneurship is that your imagination will come in handy when you are thinking of new ideas and products. Young people tend to have very vivid imaginations, so their ideas will help them make more money. Also, being as though child business owners have a lot of time, and are willing to learn new things and take risks.

Watching older people such as a famous entrepreneur, a parent, or anyone you look up to will teach you skills that will be helpful. For example, if your parent owns a business and you watch them talk to their clients, send invoices, or anything else they may do will help you in the future.

Most importantly, in every deal or sale you make, you must be professional. Even when you're going to the store you must behave the right way. You never know who's watching you! When you are speaking with a client, using proper etiquette will attract them. Always remember to be polite, even when something frustrates or makes you angry. One of the biggest lessons I have learned from my mother Is that when someone says something that frustrates you or does anything else that can make you angry, don't show it. Never show that you are angry no matter what!

As a young entrepreneur, I go through lots of ups and downs. Everyone will at some point. However, your life would be more flexible. Having many people supporting you can help you in the long end. I am very grateful for the people I have in my life, because without them I wouldn't be in business. I am especially thankful that God helps me every day and that he gives me the strength to run my businesses and do what I do. My motto is 'I can do all things through Christ who strengthens me'. What that motto says to me is that through prayer and seeking God, I can do anything I put my mind to. Most importantly, believing in yourself and having the drive, motivation, and passion is the key to your success. I don't know about you, but I'm starving! Are you hungry or are you starving?

Learn More about Au'Ryanna Bellard

Au'Ryanna Bellard is a 12 year old entrepreneur, author, speaker, and artist. She is the CEO of Dope Digitalz By AB, Blinged Out Bosses, and she is also the Co Founder of Young Entrepreneurs In Position. She is very passionate about helping other young people reach their goals. Au'Ryanna has always had an entrepreneurial mindset. She has always been a force to reckon with, she is not only a multi business owner but she is a speaker, psalmist, radio host and magazine editor and contributor. Au'Ryanna has recently received the Unstoppable Award Young Female Entrepreneur of the Year and was a finalist for Start-Up Business of the Year. She loves to empower, motivate, and inspire other young people. She is ready to help you reach your highest potential.

Take a Look at My Work!

If you would like a digital drawing of you or

Nedrick Bellard (Dad)

This thing called Life

T his thing we call life is not as difficult as we make them out to be. Often, we as human beings convince ourselves that our problems are greater than we believe they are. Ninety-nine percent of the time we worry and stress ourselves out for no apparent reason. It's not much required to be happy and live a very successful and stress free lifestyle. There's only a few simple guidelines you have to follow. First, you have to learn to live your life according to the word of God. If you have read the holy bible, then I am sure you have noticed that every man that has obeyed and kept God's command has always lived a prosperous and joyous life.

The bible says when you trust, love, and obey God's word he will give you happiness and meet all of your needs. Think about some of the significant men in the bible like Abraham for instance. He was so obedient that he was willing to offer his son as a sacrifice to God. For his obedience, God made sure he was very prosperous and his children's children were prosperous as well. God's word is meant to encourage and empower you through everything. Remember the story of Job? Here is a man who lost it all, was disease stricken, and still never cursed the name of God

. Job knew that God would deliver him from the troubles he faced. And for his obedience, God blessed Job with more than he ever had. There is nothing far more greater than the power of God, especially when you believe in it and apply it to everyday life. Also, we have to stop making excuses for everything. It's not always someone else's fault for our own misfortunes. I went to the laundromat one day and I met a man who had been homeless. Being as though I hated to see the man sleeping outside in cold weather, I started making suggestions of where he could seek shelter. I started noticing that for each and every suggestion I came up with, he had an excuse to follow up with. After a while, I saw I could not help him because he had barricaded himself behind an impenetrable wall of excuses.

I bring this to your attention because I want you to realize that excuses are hurdles placed in your way to make you come to a standstill. You cannot allow anything to bring you to a screeching halt no matter what the situation is. You have to know and understand that there is always a solution for everything and there is always a way around problems. Excuses are used when people have given up and are tired fighting. Always trust that God will keep you in his grace and mercy just as long as you believe and keep pushing. Remember, if the enemy make you carry his load for a mile, then you carry his load for two, and show him you do not give up. You have to understand that you were not created to have such a give up spirit. You were not created to move in the backwards direction, but you were created to move forward. You were built to be tough and able to handle anything.

What person do you know has gained success by being weak. God wants people with strong backbones because the road to success is not for the softhearted. One of my favorite stories is about the bamboo plant. One day a monsoon made landfall and ripped everything apart. The landowner noticed afterwards that the only thing left standing was a four feet tall skinny bamboo plant. It moved and bent back and forth in the strong winds, but it never broke. The bamboo plant is a very good example of staying strong during hard times. It does not matter how rough the wind gets, you might bend but you must never break down or give up. Sometimes we as people give up because we cannot accept failure. Most of your successful people have failed many times over. They are only successful because they found the courage to get back up and keep on pushing.

You have no other choice but to believe that God will give you the strength to overcome any odds placed against you. You cannot allow anything to stop you from achieving your goals. Cultivate and renew your mind daily for the daily grind. Have faith that you will overcome all of the odds stacked against you. Always remember that faith without works is dead.

Michael Bensley

The Power of Trust and an Unbreakable Bond

Sometimes being a brother is even better than being a superhero – Marc Brown

The power of trust out weights any other emotion. I have trust in my brother that will never fade, no matter what happens. I remember a time when my brother and I went through the hell that felt like forever. We were summoned to wrestle under the will of my ex step-dad. At first, we were excited to wrestle because both of use loved to watch WWE. All of that changed when we had to drop everything. Every other sport we played, we even dropped school basically. We were forced to be held back and homeschooled just so we could wrestle 24/7. During that year my brother and I endured mental abuse. My ex step-dad told us every day how much of a failure we both were. He would yell at us to run harder, train harder, wrestle harder, but we never broke.

We trained everyday all day, we would wake up run five miles, then go to triple practice sessions. While this active nightmare was occurring I found trust in my brother. We did everything together even the dumbest things like, taking the trash out, feeding the dogs, or doing laundry. I only had him and he only had me. I remember we would stay up for hours at night just talking.

Most of the time we would be interrupted at 12 o'clock at night because my ex step-dad would make us go run five more miles. During our late talks we would talk about how we were going to run away on one of our midnight runs. We had a whole plan for how it was going to go down too. We were going to run to the local market and call my grandmother, may she rest in peace, to come pick us up. The mental abuse got to the point where my brother and I planned take things into our own hands.

We decided the only way to get our self's out and our mom away from this monstrosity was to kill him. This plan never came to fruition of course. Throughout everything my brother and I never broke, there were times when we wanted too but we knew if we did our mom would have been lost.

It got so bad that I wanted to give up on life, I didn't want to live anymore because I wasn't even living my life. I told my brother on one of our talks, and I remember exactly what he said to me, "Mike you can't." That night I realized that if my brother wasn't there for me when I needed him most I don't think I would be here today. If the tides changed and he was the one that wanted to give up on life, I would have been lost.

Without him I would have never made it through everything. It wouldn't have been fair to just leave him to fend for himself. I knew that I needed to stay to be there for him. I would bet my life that he would have done the same for me. When my ex step-dad found out that I wanted to quit on life. He made me go run five miles in the middle of the night to "rethink." Guess who came to run with me that night? My brother came to run with me that night, he didn't let me go through it alone. Just has I never made him go through anything alone. I owe everything to my brother. Even though nothing could good could have possibly came out of that. Well something came out of it, and that something is trust. My brother and I formed a bond that can never and will never be broken.

My brother and I have grown up to be driven and head strong young men. We are both high achievers in our academics and our sports. Although we have our arguments there is not a day that goes by that we aren't thankful for each other and the bond we share. We toss ideas about college around with each other. We talk about our futures and what we want to be when we grow up. Me, I have big dreams of becoming a top chef and maybe own my own restaurant one day. My brother, he has big dreams of playing in the NFL. Are either of us happy that we went thru that hell? Absolutely not, but what we know is everything happens for a reason and because of that hell we are stronger and wiser and we will rise to the top.

Learn more about Michael Bensley

Michael Bensley is a student currently in his Sophomore year of high school. He attends a culinary program and works as a prep cook at a local family diner. He is a fantastic artist and loves to play baseball. He is a son and brother and a role model to the kids he coaches in the youth baseball program. An honor roll student, ranked in the top 25% of his class, he hopes to attend the Culinary Institute of America and open his own restaurant on day. In his down time, he likes to watch Netflix, play video games with his brother or teach his mom some new skills in the kitchen.

Relationship Rehab

Shantell Gutrick

<u>Growing Up as A Fatherless Child</u>

"Growing up without a father can damage future relationships if you don't go through the healing and forgiveness process."

"My dad broke my heart way before a man had a chance to." - Unknown

One summer day a little girl was anxiously waiting for her father to pick her up so that they could finally spend quality time together. This is something the little girl dreamed about, and hoped for her entire five years of living. She knew of her father, but only recalled seeing her father once. She kept a lasting memory of her father, who she could describe as slender build, long beautiful black hair, beautiful brown eyes, and a light brown complexion. She felt her father was a very handsome man, even from the one visit with her father.

As she waited for her father to arrive, she played with the neighborhood friends and happily expressed that her father was on his way to pick her up. This information was very important, as a majority of the neighborhood kids didn't have fathers in their lives either.

The little girl even had a special gift she wanted to give her dad. It was an extremely large candy cane. Her father would know how much she loved and cared for him, regardless if he hadn't been a part of her life for the first five years.

As the hours ticked away, and the day turned to dark, the little girl quickly realized that her father wasn't coming.

This broke the little girl's heart, and from that moment on, she realized that her father was only a thought and not a reality. The little girl in this story is me. I grew up without my biological father.

Sure, there were spotting of him, here and there. If I was at his parent's home for the summer and he decided to stop by, and/or we happened to go visit a female's house, only to learn he was the female's boyfriend at that time. Honestly, if I put a number to how many times I spotted or recall ever seeing my father, it would only be five; perhaps less. This number is throughout my entire 41 years of living.

Initially, I didn't think "not having a relationship with my father" impacted my life at all. However, after personally experiencing numerous bad relationships with men, I quickly realized that not having a relationship with my father placed me in the category of women who didn't have the knowledge required to select decent men and/or to grasp the understanding of what a healthy male resembled.

If my father was in my life, I would've learned about the characteristics of a man and what to look for and what to avoid. The players, the cheaters, the users, the manipulators, and the abusers.

Because I wasn't taught those things, because I was fatherless, I experienced everything you can imagine. I had to learn about relationships and men the hard way. I can't count how many times I've been hurt by a man because either I was looking for them to love me the way my father should've, or I simply didn't understand the male species. Men are unique from the way they think to the way they love, and as a young woman you need a man in your life to give you the pointers.

Unfortunately, because of his lack of desire to be a father and a role model, I spent many years hating the very air that my father breathed. In fact, I don't call him "father" or "dad", for many years he was simply considered a "sperm donor".

I recall telling my mother, as teenager, that if I received a call informing me that he was dead, that I would attend the funeral, but it was to only spit on his grave. This should provide a clear understanding of how much I detested the man.

I didn't want anything to do with him, and I didn't have a desire to speak to him ever again. For many years, I longed to have a father in my life. I wanted someone to love me as their daughter. For many years, I felt rejected and unwanted by my father. This caused me to feel rejected when a man didn't show me the love the way I felt it should've been shown and/or the relationship didn't work out. I believe, even when I married the first time, there was always a void there.

This huge void, I tried to fill but it was never filled, not until I started counseling. I reached a point in my life that I needed to figure out why I continued to get into bad relationships and selected bad men. I needed to know why I tolerated certain things from men, and why it took me so long to leave them alone. At first, I used the excuse of having a good heart and didn't want to hurt anyone but, honestly, I didn't want the men to feel rejected like I did as a child.

I didn't want to hurt anyone the same way that my father hurt me. Why should anyone experience such hurt and pain? I thought more about their emotions and feelings more than I thought about my own. It wasn't until I took the time to identify the deep seeded issue of being a fatherless child was I able to connect the lack of relationship with the quality and standard of men I was selecting and/or allowing to select me.

Now, I must go on the record to say that not all the men I dated or was married to were bad men. In all honesty, there were one or two who genuinely loved me, but it was very difficult for me to love them back. At least not in the same manner they loved me.

I didn't know how to recognize genuine love from a man. Again, that wasn't shown to me by my father. I do believe daughters date based on what they learned from their father, what they thought they should've learned from their father or someone who could be or resemble the father figure in her life.

Tragically, this is not the right way to feel or date. You need to date someone based on compatibility and not someone who can fill the father role. In counseling, I learned that for me to have a healthy romantic relationship with a man, I need to have a healthy understanding of my father. This allow me to be strategic, and honest with myself regarding what type of man I would be willing to date. As well as, I developed a voice and will happily express my discontent in a relationship.

Now, let me make sure you clearly understand what I am saying. After going through the healing process, I realized that I needed to make a change and I needed to forgive my father. Forgiveness wasn't for him, but it was for me. I was ready to heal and meet the man that was destined to be in my life.

I was whole and so I was ready to meet a "whole" man. But for me to do so, I had to forgive. I learned that I can forgive my father, but I didn't have to forget. I started on the journey of forgiveness. It took months to reach the point that I knew deep down in my heart that I forgave him.

I recall my sister asked me if my father could have my telephone number. I politely told her no. Over the years, I communicated with my father, and he wasn't truthful about attending my wedding, and a few other issues, that I knew I had to cut him out of my life and my heart. He had inflicted enough pain, hurt and damage, and I no longer desired to be a broken little girl, but a healed woman.

He wasn't allowed in that space anymore. I was in my right to protect my emotions and establish a boundary when it came to him. There was absolutely nothing wrong with it. In my healing process, I learned that I am responsible for Shantell, and I can't worry about how others may or may not respond to my personal boundary. I made the decision to forgive my father, but I no longer had a desire to have a relationship with him. I discovered, not having a relationship with him didn't prevent me from being in a healthy romantic relationship. As long as I was healthy and whole, there was no reason for me to not be in a healthy relationship.

While I was in counseling, I learned there were two men in my life who stepped up and became fathers to me: my step-father Bonnie Richardson and my children's grandfather, Rozia "Pop" Armstrong. Both men taught and showed different characters of a man and I learned from both of them. They both equally loved me as their daughter, and I trusted them as my father. Although my biological father and I had no relationship, I did have a relationship with the two father figures in my life, and I am forever grateful to the both of them.

If you didn't or don't have a father in your life, it's okay to recognize another father figure that you feel worthy. Especially if you are a young girl or raising a young girl. The early years of a young girl's life is very important, and her relationship with her father is equally as important. His role in his daughter's life is valuable. Is in the early years that her father explains to her that she is a Queen. He sits her down to discuss how she should be treated, and he is the first to treat her with respect and dignity so any man she deals with romantically, would know that she has a father in her life that taught her well.

Her father discussed the games that men can sometimes play, and if a man only has intentions to have sex, to be a user, or to manipulate her heart and emotions. He has the innate ability to recognize if the man pursuing his daughter has a genuine heart to love her, and again he can spot a player, user or abuser a mile away.

Honestly, even as a young woman or an older woman, with experience, it is wise to have a father or a father figure you can introduce your potential "man" to, and seek advice, guidance or counseling during the dating process. This is wisdom, and after being in a few unhealthy relationships, I wish I practiced what I am currently preaching, as I am sure I would've avoided several relationship catastrophes.

If you are a fatherless child, I encourage you to seek counseling to help you navigate your emotions. If you fail to heal, it's possible you will struggle emotionally, and in your romantic relationship with men.

You must remember that healing is for you, and not for them. You need to heal so you can have a free life. You need to heal so the remainder of your life can be a happy one. Don't allow another day, moment, hour, second or minute go by that you allow this situation of not having a father in your life to steal your joy and happiness. No matter what, you are still worth a healthy relationship. You still deserve to be loved and appreciated.

You are worth more than you think. Your lack of relationship with your father doesn't define who you are as a person and what you deserve. Don't make the same mistake I made by blaming myself for my father not having a relationship with me. It wasn't my fault. In fact, he missed out on a beautiful woman. He missed out on having a relationship with my children. However, it's not my responsibility to make him understand the magnitude of his lack of being available, it's my job to remain healthy and to not blame all men for my father's lack of love, for my father's rejection, for my father's unwillingness to be the man that he was supposed to be. It's not my fault and I need for you to know and understand that it's not your fault either. You continue to live your life, and if you need to get help; get help.

Don't worry about what someone else might think about you if you decide to get counseling -- YOU NEED TO HEAL FATHERLESS CHILD! Healing starts the process of a healthy life. Don't you want healthy relationships? Don't you want to heal from the brokenness caused by the man who was supposed to love and protect you? Don't you want to love your husband or boyfriend the way you desire? In my early years, there was no way I could truly and deeply love the man the way I wanted to because I was so afraid of that man leaving or being hurt.

However, I didn't recognize any of this until I started counseling. Don't allow your fatherless relationship to steal away your romantic relationships. Don't give the relationship that much power. Take your life back. Take your love back! You are not a rejected "child", you are loved and there is someone out there who will love you for who you are. There is someone out there who will not reject you, but first I need for you to heal. It's time for REHAB!!

Dr. G Davis Jr.

[Ladies] Build a Bear and Not Your Man!

Several weeks ago, a video clip of a man crying at his wedding as his beautiful bride made her way down the aisle went crazy viral. While it's not incredibly uncommon for a man to tear up at his ceremony, this clip quickly made rounds throughout numerous social media sites because of its raw and unfiltered emotion. Most of us who have seen this clip know little to nothing about these newlyweds, their chemistry, or their back story. But the 1-minute and 47-second sudden eruption of passion speaks volumes, and reinforces my long-held belief that for a man, there's possibly no greater feeling than experiencing a great, transformative, world-changing love. The type of love that makes him crave to know his woman's very essence. The type of love that makes him love a woman's "core." The type of love that makes him want to be a better man for her.

Let's be clear, when a man is deeply in love with a woman he truly feels blessed to have her in his life, it's almost second nature to want to give her everything she deserves, because he's sees the queen in her. He loves her without compromise or reservations, because her price is beyond rubies and precious diamonds, she's more than a woman... she's kingdom royalty! However, no matter how much we may love ourselves, we'll happily demand far more from our body, mind and soul in order to be the best possible version of ourselves for her. Unfortunately, we are always in a silent competition to be better than her last ex or previous lover.

And this is where the problem comes in.

Lately, I've been watching a lot of my homegirls enter into relationships with men they really like, whom they feel are just one or two "improvements" away from being the best him. Whether it's something so minor as "expanding" his dress code, or even more substantial like "coaching" him to go back to school or asking for a raise/promotion at work, these women are out here effectively molding men into better versions of themselves. And once they're task is completed, I find myself caught up in a lot of emotionally distraught conversations with these women who've found themselves covered in horrific breakups with the same dudes they helped improve.

Please understand, these women simply don't understand why he would dismiss her suggestion to maximize his being, just to turn around and leave her. The despair of having to honestly answer that question is only surpassed by the despair of hearing it. Let's be clear, even if you awake my desire for self-improvement, just because I want to be a better man doesn't mean I want to be a better man for you.

This is a hard pill to swallow for most women, but it's the awkward truth. Let's forget the cheap rosy belief that you may only experience real love once in your lifetime; the reality is you may never experience it in a lifetime at all, if your never in stay in a position to receive. While love may be a choice, a truly undeniable and metamorphic chemistry invading our emotional, mental and physical capacities is a rare cosmic incident, anything is possible. In fact, many of us have said the words, "I love you" to more than one partner, many times we find ourselves in relationships of comfort and convenience. We like the person we're with and we may even care about them, but that like isn't going to drive us to improve our most intrinsic being for their benefit because, well, they don't really mean that much to us.

So when a woman approaches a man and starts talking happily confident logic about what he can do to improve himself, it is very possible that her words can penetrate a part of his brain and his heart that motivates him to set out on that path of personal growth. Unfortunately, far too many times women make the mistake of believing that the better him will obviously want her, and that's just not the case in all situations.

When a man changes, his entire composition undergoes an all-encompassing shift that alters him in ways even he couldn't predict. How he views life, how he views work, and how he views love can all change very quickly, including how he views you and your relationship. The external push will almost always render a different reaction from an internal thrust because when it's done internally, it's focused and goal-oriented with her directly in mind.

When done externally on purpose, we place ourselves as the sole focus. That's the big difference!

Look, I'm not saying women should not attempt to make their men face the possibility of self-improvement, but please know that it's not your job to make him a better man. He has to want to become better for himself. So why settle for an another "project" or fixer- upper", when you deserve a designer masterpiece! However, if you make it your duty to force your man to change or to magically customize him in anyway, you will eventually see an incredible resistance that you could have never prepare for. Then you will be back at the drawing board again! So the next time you feel inspire to help and create, ask yourself how bad do you want to build a man? Happy Dating!

Rebecca Hart

The Unliberated Woman: My Relationship With Myself.

"Madness need not be all breakdown. It may also be breakthrough."
- R.D. Laing

"The truth will set you free."
- Jesús

The "Un-Liberated" women has very little sense of self. She does not know that she lacks boundaries: clarity about where she ends and others begin. She is truly never content because she doesn't know what she truly needs or wants. She can be controlling because she has no sense of self and needs to get it from others opinions, and she slaves away to make sure those opinions are good. She, nor others, can ever satisfy her unrecognized expectations. She is isolated from her own feelings because she spends all her time trying to figure out and provide what she thinks others want. She pats herself on the back for giving and giving without understanding how her giving hurts. Her giving hurts those that need to step up and solve their own problems to be whole. She hurts herself by not allowing herself to ask or receive.

When I was young I believed I was a liberated woman. I moved out at 19 and worked 3 jobs while going to University full time. I said "yes" to all my friends, all the time. I was proud of all the different 'circles' I could hang with, molding myself to whomever I was around to fit seamlessly into their world. I had every minute of my calendar booked from sunrise to sundown. It seemed everyone loved me, and when it didn't I worked tirelessly to correct that. I was what they wanted me to be. Everyone looked to me if they needed advice; if they wanted a charming, beautiful, lively gal at their party; if they wanted a youth leader in church. When a friend said, "you always know what to say, and never ask for anything," it was a compliment falling on my ears, a deceptive notch of pride in my opinion of myself.

She can be controlling because she has no sense of self and needs to get it from others opinions, and she slaves away to make sure those opinions are good.

I was a woman in control. I made myself unattainable. I smiled sympathetically at fellas in my life as they were ushered into the friend zone (I had a collection). The blonde Italian from the jazz club who invited me for a private homemade-meal was dismayed that I showed up with my housemate. My no's were always disguised as yes's. I had fellas I grew up in church with and band boys in my college neighborhood, all floating around in possibility. I had endless possible husbands in my mind and I relied on this mask to feel powerful.

She, nor others, can ever satisfy her unrecognized expectations.

I was a woman of perfection. I paid my own way and others too (sometimes I ate ramen for a month when my credit cards secretly snuck up on me, but it was my "special ramen," with sautéed carrots and onion and an egg dropped in, and no one needed know about that). The neighborhood kids came over when they were hungry and I gave them big art supplies to create on the floor. I started a reading program. I wrote thank you notes. I rescued a dog. I committed to being a vegan for a year, and not one of the fake ones that cheat all the time. I went to church and volunteered and said yes, yes, yes. I was nice to my drug dealer neighbors & the shut-in across the street. There was a neighbor around the corner who kept his turntables at our house so he had an excuse to come over all the time. He always had food in his beard, talked too much about math, held obnoxiously strong opinions, and commandeered our time. I said yes to him too because I was "nice."

She hurts herself by not allowing herself to ask or receive.

It's hard to know where each path to liberation begins, it's somewhere between learning and unlearning. I'll start mine with 'him.' He looked just like this boy Shawn from one of my classes, the quiet one who walked through my neighborhood on his way home with kindness and a hope deferred. He looked just like him from across the way, the only difference was how he locked eyes with me so boldly. I called out, "Shawn!" But the man who came to me wasn't my classmate, it was coincidentally another man named Shawn, but this one, a stranger. What were the chances of that? He kept up with my walking pace and invited himself to accompany me to the campus fashion show I was late for. *She does not know that she lacks boundaries.*

We became friends. He pursued me with a confidence I'd never known before, but I knew better then to get involved with him. I said no to his daily advances, but not to his presence in my life. I said my weak unpracticed "no's" until the day I didn't. He must not have ever believed them. Then he was mine, or perhaps I was his.

She is truly never content because she doesn't know what she truly needs or wants.

He wasn't enrolled in my university (or any). He had been there that day, the day I called his name meaning to attract someone else, to play in a basketball tournament with the hope of winning some money. He never had any money. I always paid. He always drove my car, when we were together, and when he took it out at night to go the studio until 4 or 6 a.m. He was often at my house, then he was always at my house. His mom died that first summer. I went to his little brothers wrestling matches. I fed him. When I went out with friends I saved half my meal and brought it back for him. My housemates tolerated him because of his charm. He came to my church and everyone was going to help get him on track.

She is isolated from her own feelings because she spends all her time trying to figure out and provide what she thinks others want.

He always had my stuff. He kept my camcorder so he and his friends could film something and "make it" one day. Well, one day I watched the camcorder tape he left sitting in my living room. I watched it beyond the intended recording, as he tossed the camcorder into his backpack, still rolling, listening, left on by accident, documenting sound. I heard him talking in a pizza place. The same pizza place he once bought a slice from and believed there was glass in it that got caught in his throat. The ER released him with instructions to gargle salt water for a scratch. He insisted to me, with the convicting passion that he did everything with, that something was stuck in his throat despite what the hospital said. In my bathroom with flashlight, tweezers and his mouth wide open, I delicately scraped back some tissue and cells and pulled out a sliver of metal from the back of his throat. From that same throat I heard him on the camcorder tape tell a stranger about "his girl," and the baby on the way, and his plans to move. I thought to myself as I listened, "but I'm not pregnant? I'm not moving?" I listened 3 times before I really got it.

Her giving hurts those that need to step up and solve their own problems to be whole.

One day I found jewelry receipts for gifts I never received. One day he slept with me and then got a call his baby was being born with another woman. That day he borrowed my car and crashed it. One day I found the slit cut in my cars carpet floorboard that he hid his other life in. One day we broke up. One day I went to a clinic to find I was pregnant. One day I started bleeding. One day I stopped paying my credit card bills and pretended they weren't there. One day I stopped going to school.

The un-liberated women has very little sense of self. She hurts herself.

I continued to deceive myself for years. I walked away from him into an arms of another like him, one much craftier. After each fall I believed I was better and wiser, until one day when I whole-heartedly realized, I was not a liberated woman. My relationship with myself was based on self-deception. How can a deception be free, be liberated? I opened my eyes and began my climb out the prison of appearances, perfection, and pleasing I had put myself in, the victim position I chose. I climbed through books, therapy, break-ups and even an actual 6 month climb across the country on the Appalachian Trail. I climbed through the web I wove and into truthfulness with myself. I accepted I could not liberate myself and climbed into God's arms. I climbed into the mental health profession and many other women's lives. Giving and giving, but this time receiving too. Receiving lessons about myself, from each person I work with, each soul I encounter-- gifts. I climbed, I'm always climbing, into a liberated woman, into God's design, into myself.

Kadiatou E. Traore'

<u>Liberation from Domestic Abuse</u>

Domestic Violence became part of my reality when I was a young girl of 17 I was talking to this guy and we were having a conversation about something. I remember that he wanted me to do something that I was totally against. I disagreed with him. The next thing I knew, he slapped me! Right away, I told him to take me home. He immediately apologized. There was no need for any apologies. It was over right then and there. No man had ever put his hand on me and this was something I knew at that age that it was not something that I was going to put up with.

In college, I dated another guy who I thought I was crazy about. As athletes, we had a lot in common and he made me laugh. Things were going great until one day out of nowhere he confronted me on campus when I was headed back to my dorm and slapped the crap of me. Someone caught me as I was falling on the ground.

I was shocked like everyone else because we had never ever argued. Of course, the guys nearby subdued him but the damage was done. Once again, I had been hit by another guy! Security was called and I had to make a report and was asked if I wanted to press charges. Not wanting to ruin his college goals, I decided not to press charges. He was barred from coming anywhere near my dorm or me. Once again, there was no apology needed because that was the deal breaker of our relationship.

When I started dating again, I established the rules of deal breakers from the beginning and shared what I had been through. My dates knew that abuse of any kind would not be tolerated. When I would see signs in their actions, I would let them know that the relationship wasn't going to work and I would move on. I didn't care about their money, car, houses or status. I cannot and will not be controlled by another individual!

As I grew older, I became more informed about domestic abuse/violence and learned that it happens more frequently than we realized because it is often not reported. Most victims never say anything and often blame themselves while they provide an excuse for the perpetrator. Domestic violence is often thought to be just a physical act but it can also be mental, emotional, verbal, and/or financial. It doesn't happen overnight; it is an ordeal that is done by someone that you deeply love, care for and trust. They are often the primary breadwinner and decision maker in your life.

Throughout my life, I have had various relationships where I have experienced every form of domestic violence there is. Every abuse did not occur in every relationship. A lot of times, I minimized the situation by pretending that it was not as bad as I thought. I made excuses and often silent when the abuse occurred. Let me share a few signs of each one so that you can get a picture of how you might be going through domestic abuse.

Everyone is familiar with physical abuse because it involves interaction where a person is hit, slapped, pushed, shoved, grabbed, or forced to do things. When the bruises appear, victims will hide their scars due to being embarrassed or feeling like it was their fault for making the perpetrator upset. They will lie to cover the incident by saying that they fell or walked into the door to avoid being questioned. Mental abuse involves psychology manipulation. A person tells you that if you leave them that they will follow you where you go and you will never be able to get rid of them. They threaten harm to you, your children, friends, family, and even your pets to the point that you are too scared to leave.

They do not want you to be around your family and friends fearing their influence on you. They do not use the word "fear" but come up with reasons why you should not go around others. Emotional abuse comes by negative comments about your weight, health, your looks, the clothes you wear, and anything that can be said that will diminish your self-esteem and self-worth. You start to second guess your decisions and look for validation from the perpetrator instead of those who really care about you. They put a wedge between you and your children by gaining their trust and seal of approval while condemning you to the children, undermining your rules, and forming an alliance that condemns you every opportunity they can while overtly praising you.

They will accuse you of cheating when you are not in their presence. They will sulk when you go places with family and friends to make you feel guilty for leaving them at home. They will guilt you into having sex with them when you don't want to or force themselves on you saying that it is part of your duty to them. Verbal abuse comes in the form of putting you down, calling you names, and making you the butt of jokes in front of family, friends, and children. They tell you are not good at anything or that you are a bad parent. They emphasize how they are a better parent than you are especially when things happen beyond your control like missing school programs due to work. Financial abuse occurs when they take control of your finances by making you hand over your money and tell you what you can or cannot buy. You essentially have no access to the money you earn. You must constantly ask for money to do the smallest things like buy food or gas.

I was involved in a long-term relationship where I was I thought the guy loved me and was serious about making our relationship work. Little did I know that even though he cared for me, he did not love me in the true sense of real love. Feeling that the relationship was not going in the direction I felt it should be, I started doing my own thing in preparation for my future just in case things did not work out. This did not sit well with my partner. One day, we got into a heated argument and everything went downhill. During the argument, it got physical!

While I was never punched, or slapped in my face, he put his hand on me. Flashback!! My instinct was call the police before it got bad. I called my daughter who heard the altercation and told her to call the police. Once they arrived, a report was made and I had to go to court to get a restraining order. He was very upset about that because he did not feel that it warranted the judicial intervention and that it would now be on his record. I told him that it was best that we part ways because for me, it was a serious matter that I did not take lightly. He knew about my past domestic abuse experiences and this was a line that he should not have crossed.

I realized in a relationship where you think you have everything under control and have laid down the rules that things can still go wrong. People always think that as long as you say you love someone, it should never be questioned. Wrong!!! Always listen to your instinct! Luckily for me, I had family and friends who I listened to and I begin to see the signs for myself. Most people do not have the support they need to make the hard decisions to live. Find that support group, open up your eyes, listen with your ears, and let your instinct guide you even when your heart wants you to stay. You deserve better.

The reality is you cannot change someone unless they want to change. People can and will change when someone becomes important enough to them to make that change or risk losing them. When you realized that you are not the catalyst that inspires that change, it is time to move on. It is a hard pill to swallow but we must accept the truth as it is presented. Maya Angelou stated, "When someone shows you who they are, believe them the first time." Once you begin to truly love yourself, you will go in the other direction when what you see is not what you want.

If someone does not accept who you are, or the way that you are, send him or her on their merry way. Wait for someone that will give you unconditional love, accept your flaws, respect you always and show you that you are needed and wanted.

Love is a process that takes time to develop and should never be rushed or abused in a relationship. Love should be natural and forth coming. You should never make someone express their feelings for you; either they feel it or they don't. You are able to tell by how they make you feel, the things they do for you unprompted and how well they communicate their feelings to and for you. When you can accept that, you will take the first step of staying out of an abusive relationship.

Dig deep within yourself and bring out the courage that has been dormant. Fight for who you are meant to be and for the relationship you deserve to have. When you get sick and tired of being sick and tired, you will formulate an exit plan. Never ever do it alone or tell your perpetrator your plans; always have a support group and a backup plan. There is so much information on the Internet about domestic abuse that goes into more details than I have provided. There are organizations that will guide you through the steps of gaining your independence and consultants and counselor that will assist you from the prison within yourself. Research your resources, and get support from family and friends to help you transition.

Finally, know that it is not your fault!!! Do not blame yourself. Forgive yourself. Love yourself unconditionally. Know that you are loved and lovable. You are desirable, smart, funny, and intelligent. Take control of your life and do not allow fear to keep you from taking that first step toward happiness and love. I have faith in you and know that you have the power, with some help, to set yourself free. Liberate yourself from domestic abuse!

Awakening & Empowerment

Binu Alag

<u>My Anger, My Greatest Teacher</u>

"Holding onto Anger is like grasping a hot coal with the intent of throwing it at someone else; you are the one who gets burned." Buddha.

I sat on the kitchen floor, leaning against the dishwasher as tears streamed down my face. Pieces of broken dishes lay scattered on the floor. My three-year-old daughter stood about fifteen feet in the distance, staring at me. She was clutching her favorite blanket and sucking her thumb.

A loud, scary crashing sound had woken her up.

These anger spells used to hit me out of nowhere. I'd throw things, scream, and punch my kitchen counter. When I got like this, I became afraid of myself.

That evening, however, my daughter's innocent little eyes melted my heart. She was too scared to come any closer. She knew something was wrong. The moment she saw me crying on the kitchen floor changed me forever. It made me realize I had to do something about this battle within.

After my angry spells, I'd feel deeply guilty for my behavior. Part of me knew that angry person was not who I was. I'm generally a very happy, calm, and a positive person.

The more I thought about it, the more I realized about this battle within I was suffering from. There was the pleasant, angelic side of me, and then this horrible, diabolic side. I was so angry, frustrated, confused and lost.

I came across this quote, **"Holding onto Anger is like grasping a hot coal with the intent of throwing it at someone else; you are the one who gets burned."** **Buddha.** Oh, boy, did that ever hit home.

My journey began to seek answers for my Anger. On the outside, I had everything, a husband who deeply cares for me, two beautiful daughters, a corporate job, a house, a car-- pretty much everything a woman needs. Why was I so angry?

One thing lead to another; the universal synchronicity has worked phenomenal to get me connected with lovely mentors and teachers I needed in perfect Divine timing. After many self-development courses, reading loads of books and a whole lot of soul searching I've been able to tap into the higher version of myself. Today, I'm grateful for my anger.

Through my transformational journey I learned that my horrible, diabolic side was my "Rebellious" teenage self. A part of me I left behind and she was yearning to be re-claimed.

I was about 15 years old when I heard an ugly truth about my birth.

I overheard a conversation between my mother and my sister. My mother was talking about the day of my birth. They had no idea I was listening.

In a small village of northern India, the minute I was born - a doula held me in her hands and asked my mother, "it's a girl – do you want to keep her?"

Of course, my mother decided to keep me but in this moment, she was regretting her choice. This was devastating for me. I remember I was standing at the bottom of the staircase and hoping the ground underneath my feet would open so I could vanish. I was ashamed to be alive.

From this point forward my life was forever changed. I felt a myriad of emotions; guilt, devastation, shame, abandonment, and unworthiness. I felt unlovable. There was this feeling of being "less than" *just because I'm female.*

I made choices in my life to seek approval from others, to feel loved again. I put on many masks, trying to fit in these societal traditions and expectations. My free spirit, however, was suffocating. I was at a very low point in my life with suicidal thoughts and I was only 17 years old. I had a whole life ahead of me, yet it felt like no one understood me. My needs and desires were judged and criticized. In this world of over 7 billion people, I felt extremely lonely. I used to talk to God as my friend.

When enough was enough, I decided to live. Things shifted inside of me. I got this inner power to get myself out of this landscape. I put on my warrior armor and fought for my rights and truth. This is where my angry persona took over to protect me, to get me the heck out of this ugly landscape.

What I learned is that our body often reacts to situations from our past experiences and programming through my EFT training. This is often the source of fight, flight or freeze response. I realized I was still in fight response. It was time to take off the warrior armor suit.

I took a Master Empowerment Coaching course for my personal development with the S.W.A.T Institute. I learned about the map of consciousness in this wonderful book titled, "Power vs. Force" written by Dr. David Hawkins.

I learned that lower emotional points such as shame, guilt, hatred, grief, fear and anger are at the bottom end of the scale. They keep us stuck, make us feel contracted. Higher emotional points such as courage, willingness, acceptance, love, joy and peace are at the top end of the scale. This is a conscious awakening. This is expansiveness.

I've been on a magnificent journey to "heal" all my heavy stuck emotions. I used EFT tapping, an energy modality to tap out my heavy emotions. I learned the power of forgiveness. I learned to forgive myself and those who played a role in my growth in ways that seemed harsh at the time. I love my mother from the bottom of my heart.

I started peeling all these layers and feeling much lighter. I learned that my emotions are not who I am. I started believing that I'm not my story, I'm not my pain, I'm not my struggles, I'm not my anger, I'm not my shame or guilt, I'm not any of these things. There is a higher version of me that is magnificent, brilliant, golden, who has a calling and purpose to bring positive change in the world.

In August 2014, I listened to my inner calling and left my corporate job, working as a Business Advisor with one of the top Financial Institutions of Canada, to launch my own coaching business. I'm so passionate about helping women become financially free. I believe so many women stay stuck in toxic jobs, relationships and environment because of their financial situation. I work with conscious entrepreneurs such as transformational leaders, coaches and intuitive healers, who all have callings and want to share their gifts and talents to make a difference in the world. I help them heal their story, master their message, and fall in love with money conversations with their potential clients so they can create wealth through their meaningful work and impact the world.

In February, 2016, I faced the most awkward challenge of my life. I was asked to waive my rights to inheritance after my father's passing. This is an eons old tradition in India that disqualifies women for inheritance due to gender. EEK!

Since I'm committed to improving my relationship with money and helping my clients to do the same, there was absolutely no other way than to ask for my fair share. I was nervous and felt so much anxiety in my gut. My inner dialogue was telling me it makes me seem greedy to ask my fair share, my family will think I'm all about money, and people will judge me for doing something against the norm.

Making this phone call was totally out of my comfort zone, but deep down I knew it was time to make a change. Before dialing the number, I used EFT tapping to literally tap out all my fears and installed new beliefs for the outcome I desired. I made the call and it went better than I expected!

Two weeks later I get the news that I was now an owner of a piece of land in India. I was thrilled that I manifested my desired outcome. Beyond that I'm over the moon ecstatic even today for the opportunity to have paved the path for so many women. This literally has changed the legacy in my family. This victory has given me so much fuel for my passion to help women become financially savvy because we deserve it!

Today, I'm more connected with the source, and trust that the universe is on my side. Even the events of my life that weren't so pleasant and almost felt like complete disasters at the time, has given me the experiences necessary for my evolution.

Reflecting back, I'm in awe of all that has conspired to bring me here. All these "Universal Interventions" were expansive, beyond the thinkable form, and outside of my scope of comfort. The more I became available to play in this "unknown zone" the more miraculous results I received.

My triggers have been my greatest teachers. I'm thankful for my Anger!

Learn More about Binu Alag

Binu Alag is a Business Coach with her expertise in Money Mindset. She is the author of the upcoming book, Your Time To Play Big – 8 Keys To Sky Rocket Your Success. Binu mentors conscious leaders and entrepreneurs overcome personal barriers, build confidence, find their voice & master their heartfelt money conversations so they can magnetize their ideal clients to create wealth and impact in the world. She pulls from her extensive knowledge and training in coaching, sales communications, leadership and various energy modalities to achieve optimum results for her clients.

Along her journey, Binu has been a Police Officer and helped thousands build their wealth as a Business Advisor with one of the top five Financial Institutions in Canada. After 3 career changes and a whole lot of soul searching, she left her corporate career in the financial industry to launch her dream and follow her passion. She has had the honor of sharing the stage with well-known authors and speakers such as Crystal Andrus Morissette and Collette-Baron Reid.

Website: http://www.binualag.com

Email: binu@binualag.com

Facebook: https://www.facebook.com/BinuAlag

Fruit Grace Mauzy

The Issue of Esteem is Monumental for Anyone's Wellbeing

The issue of esteem is monumental for anyone's wellbeing. Most people pay attention to what they think are two forms of esteem, high self-esteem and low self-esteem. But what they are not realizing is that both high and low self-esteem are on the same line. They are a continuation of self-esteem. They are not two forms. What most people don't understand is there is self-esteem and there is other-esteem. Esteem alone is defined as "to consider as of a certain value or of a certain type" (Dictionary.com).

Self-esteem pertains to how you esteem yourself. As defined by the Merriam-Webster dictionary, self-esteem is "a reasonable or justifiable sense of one's worth or importance." When you hear about people talking about their low self-esteem you get it. They don't value themselves highly. They feel they are inferior to others. When you hear about someone who has high self-esteem you know that type also. They value who they are. They have their life together. They are often prominent in their community.

Other-esteem, therefore, is how you are valued and typed by others. In our society, there is tremendous pressure to pay attention to other-esteem. We wear brand names, follow fashions, eat trending foods. Why? Is it truly because one can of soda is significantly better than the no name brand? Or have we been so indoctrinated with needing other-esteem that we can't consume the no name brand? The reason we are all so desperate to gain high self-esteem isn't because we are all walking around with incredible low self-esteem, it's because we live in a world mass pressured, mass produced, and mass processed to value what others think of us, how we fit into the mold, and what we can do to be valued and recognized by others.

I believe that we are taught from infancy to be more concerned with other-esteem than any form of self-esteem. Let's go back to that friend you know with high self-esteem. When you get to really talking with that person what do you find out? In my case, I find out they are great cover uppers. They can hide the fact that they are totally nervous and anxious about fitting in. They put out a strong message that they are above the other-esteem, and yet they will deny many aspects of true high self-esteem to be valued highly by others. Most people prefer being highly valued by others at the expense of being highly valued by them self.

A couple of weeks ago one of my daughters and I were going to a barbeque for the Toastmasters group she is a member of. She wanted me to join her because most of the members are closer to my age and she thought I'd like them. I dressed in what I thought was barbeque clothes for the part of town I understood we were going to (other-esteem). I asked my daughter if she thought what I was wearing was ok (other-esteem). Actually, after she said it was fine, I decided I didn't feel comfortable in that outfit, so I changed (self-esteem). And off we went to the party.

Now my understanding of where the party was and where the party truly was were very different. We headed to the mansion side of town. Some jitters in my tummy (other-esteem). We were some of the first arrive. I was ready to just high tail it out of there. I'd just come back to pick up my daughter, rather than go in with my shorts and t-shirt (other-esteem). But then I knew. I had no choice. I chose my clothes for my comfort. Not to be concerned with anyone else's opinion of me (self-esteem). I grabbed myself from the back of my neck and shook me all over. I shook off my desire to be favorably judged by others and went into that party feeling pretty awesome (self-esteem). Everyone was eager to chat with me.

I've often wondered why people are attracted to me. What sets me apart from others. Why people say I have an energy and presence that makes them want to get to know me better. What I have figured out is I attend to my self-esteem. It's what I do for others and it's what I do for myself. When I have my self-esteem, intact I am ultimately me. I don't need to impress them. I don't need to get their approval. This sets me apart. It allows me to genuinely attend to others for their own self. No one has to put on a pretense for me. Because they realize that it doesn't matter to me. I'm not impressed with the pretense. I'm impressed only with them at their essence.

Now don't get me wrong. I can fall into the need for other-esteem just like anyone else, as I've already shown you. The difference is I know when I fall into it and can decide if what I truly want is other-esteem, to be valued by others. Or, if what I truly want is to be highly valued by myself. You may be asking, "Aren't there times when other-esteem is beneficial?" And the answer is twofold. Yes, there are times when other-esteem is not only beneficial but necessary. A student works for the grade and approval by the instructor. An employee works for the paycheck and approval of the boss. A spouse compromises for the joy of the husband or wife. But if this other-esteem completely undermines your self-esteem, then you are studying with the wrong professor, you have the wrong employer, or your relationship with your spouse may have migrated into an abusive situation.

It's a crazy thought to think that we can get stuck in other- esteem. Isn't our whole system all about purchasing things, doing things, and going to things for the sheer purpose of our self-empowerment, self-learning, self-esteem? I'd say one hundred percent not. Women are molded and trained to be conscious of and needing other-esteem above and beyond all else.

Many years ago when I was In college I took a course, women's studies and the influence of the mass media". I was totally taken off guard when I learned how purposefully magazines, advertisements, and even the plots and conversations in all kinds of movies and shows created the need for women to live and feel a need to gain other-esteem. Even forty years ago, the mass media was fully aware and totally engaged in making their entire female audience become indoctrinated in to think they need the approval of others to feel satisfied and complete. And yet the mass media also structured things so that women never actually gain inner strength because there is always another product better than what's been available, keeping women trapped in vulnerability.

I've had goals and plans, intentions and desires. And honestly not one single one of them has ever happened. But- and it's a HUGE one- I am happy to my core. Grateful for all that has come my way because I let myself flow with what arrives. I know I have absolutely no control of any solitary thing in my life. Although I've had some hard, awful and truly deeply stressful events in my life, I always find the silver lining to everything. The thing is that my goals and plans were completely set to get approval from my family. My intentions and desires were set within the bounds of social norms. Somehow, even as a child, I quietly skirted around the social norms. I played and followed my heart, even during the excruciating ages of being a middle school girl.

Rather than being a time when the mass media could use its strength to empower girls to be magnificent, strong, and potent, mass media chose this vulnerable time to do whatever possible to capture girls to never be satisfied. To always be striving to find peace just beyond their reach. To notice that other girls always have more, are better adjusted, and more accepted than what ever place and stage the girl is in.

And now these girls are mothers and grandmothers. We are these women. We are raising our daughters with more insecurities and needs than existed when women couldn't vote, own property, or even have a higher education. It's time to value yourself. To actually take the plunge and realize how you are controlled by your deep need for other-esteem. Know when, and particularly, why you want other-esteem. If it's at all connected to thinking you will raise your self-esteem scrap it. Know it will only bind you tighter, make you feel even more inadequate, keep you from your own personal best. Instead, find the joy in your heart, the calm in your gut, and the peace of mind that sets you free from other-esteem and guides you to the elevation of pure and genuine high self-esteem.

Learn more about Fruit Grace Mauzy

First and foremost, I am an incredible mom. I love life and live love. I have taken my daughters to a level and life that many can't even think is a possibility. By giving my daughters the gift of true inner high self-esteem and believing in them, I have set them free to pursue their dreams with absolute freedom. Now that my daughters are incredible young woman pursuing their ultimate dreams, I am resuming giving my time and energy to help and support other women to free themselves from their shackles and live with inner high self-esteem, to not care or worry about societal norms. To help these women live with inner peace and glow with the wellness that comes from with in. My dream is to be an author-done thank you Carla, be a public speaker-done, and an event leader- planning that one to still happen

A lifetime of wellness, a lifetime of happiness sums me, "Fruit" Grace Mauzy, up. I have devoted my life to creating wellness for myself, my world class athlete daughters, my extended family and friends, and to the many thousands of people i engage with personally and professionally. Through my almost quirky lifestyle and my exuberant energy I practically explode with my information, skills, and magic. "Fruit brings the sparkle and fun to everything including helping get me in shape, to love my body, the activities I can do with it, and the way I feel". For the recovery of my daughter Jamie's gnarly almost deathly ski accident during the Association of Free Skiing Professionals World Tour Finals April 11, 2015, in Whistler, Canada, I brought all my love and skills to the forefront to bring Jamie from her coma back to her full self in an unbelievably quick time. Magic and miracles happen with love.

Master's Degree- Counseling Psychology and Education
Certified Personal Fitness Instructor
Certified Fitness Nutrition Specialist
Certified PSIA Level II Ski Instructor
Certified Reiki Master
Certified Aroma Touch/ essential oils Therapist

Vonda Morrison

The Gift of an Awakening

You know you're in love when you can't fall asleep because reality is finally better than your dreams

~Dr. Seuss~

As a little girl growing up in my house the thing that I wanted the most was to feel important and to feel loved. I was extremely shy and sensitive and by the age of 9 I was already wrestling with the issue of personal self-worth. I struggled in school but was always afraid to ask my parents for help. My mother's patent response was always to tell me to ask my father for help. You see, my mother was homed schooled by my grandmother and she only completed grade 8 so personally I think that she was just scared that she wouldn't be able to explain or answer my grade 6 questions.

Fear would literally course through my veins whenever my mother would holler at my dad to come and help me with my homework. I could always tell from his sharp response and body language as he forced himself to get up from the comfort of his living room chair that he really didn't want to be interrupted.

Take for example something as simple as asking him to help me learn my times tables. I still remember that simple exercise turning into a terrifying experience in my father's presence. His impatience and anger would quickly flair up at me when I didn't know the right answer.

I bet you can guess what happened next when my dad would ask me my times tables. My initial response was to just be frozen with panic, but eventually I would blurt out an answer, any answer, just to appease my dad. I had already took too much time coming up with nothing. What's the worst thing that could happen I thought? "Wrong, he would shout in my direction with his teeth clenched and his stare fixated on me." "What is wrong with you?" He always made a point of making sure that I knew he was very angry and disappointed and it was all at my expense. "How come you can't get this? I never had any trouble learning my times tables" he would say.

The scenario always ended the same way. I would cry and not want to do any more questions and my dad would simply return to the comforts of his chair and his evening news paper.

That same fear carried over into the class room. Like at home I was petrified that the teacher would ask me a question in class and I would feel stupid if I didn't know the right answer. So, my solution was simple. I just didn't participate in class and I would hide as much as I could at my desk, never making eye contact with my teachers in case they asked me something.

This feeling of being stupid and of low self-worth carried over into my choice of friends, relationships, career, and eventually the person I would choose to marry.

I wanted to be a Veterinarian in the worst way. Not only would I help animals that I loved so much but they never made me feel stupid. My animals were always there for me and their love was always unconditional. I spent much of my childhood playing with my cat and two dogs as we lived a very isolated life on the shores of Lake Superior. If only I had some encouragement from someone early on I thought. I wish I could go back in time and tell that little girl how smart she really is and always was, and that she always had the ability to become whomever and whatever she wanted to be. I realize now that that little girl simply needed a mentor in life. Someone who would help her believe in herself and overcome her irrational fears of feeling stupid and not good enough. One caring soul can change the whole outcome of someone's future.

My dream early on was to own my own riding stables. Not that I was around horses a lot growing up but my love for horses was a driving force on its own and it's all I could think about. My Cousin and I at an early age had planned our stables in its entirety right down to the names for all our lesson horses. Hers were names from characters from the Star Wars Movies and mine just sounded like a weather forecast. You guessed it, names like Sunny, Stormy, Thunder and Lightning just to name a few.

At 18 I was engaged and was planning a summer wedding so I would be married before I entered college in the fall. Then three months before the wedding my fiancé who is now my ex-husband got cold feet and called off the wedding. I was filled with so much embarrassment that I just wanted to run away and hide.

When I moved to London Ontario that fall my he followed me there, as he still convinced me that we were still good friends. How crazy is that! I get dumped before I even get to the wedding alter the first time yet I should still see us as good friends! I see now looking back at time in my life just how much my self-worth was in the gutter. Hell, we weren't really in love or crazy about each other in the least but he was funny and he made me laugh and I felt safe.

So I made an adult decision and let him move in with me but very early on my past upbringing and moral compass began to leave me feeling unsettled internally, that living together and not being married was wrong. I feared being judged by my parents for living in sin, so to speak, so when my family would come down for a visit he would move out and literally live on the streets until my family had left. I told him I couldn't keep living this way. I felt horrible and ashamed so that following summer of 1985 we got married. I remember walking down the aisle, in a state of perpetual numbness with no emotions or feelings at all. I felt like I was watching a car crash in slow motion and there was nothing you could do to stop it. My low self-worth and my inner shyness was paralyzing as I listened to myself saying my wedding vows in a zombie like state. In that moment I believed that being in love and happy was just an illusion, and this was the best I was ever going to get. But at least I would now be free of the judgement of others and what else really mattered.

In 1984 when I first moved to London one of the first things I did was look up a local horse stable. I was so desperate to have a horse of my own that I took some of my school money and bought a yearling. I couldn't afford one but I didn't care. I was a true animal lover. I spent every spare minute that I wasn't working or going to school with him. I had no idea how to train him, since I couldn't afford to buy a broke horse or pay someone else to train him.

So, I bought a book on how to train a horse from the ground up and that's how it started. I finally finished school with a few career changes and I became an Animal Health Technician and I had worked eight years in a Veterinary clinic which I really did enjoy.

By the end of eighties I was riding pretty well and so I started showing my self-trained horse at club level, knowing nothing about showing other than from trial and error, and believe me there were plenty of errors. Which in the end made me even a better teacher.

I wanted to learn all I could about horses and riding so I started apprenticing at a nearby stables in 1987 and within a year I was teaching my own classes. I was a natural teacher. I figured most things out on my own as I read books and listened very carefully to what my teacher were saying and by watching how each horse and rider would react together. I also watched other trainers work their horses and practiced what I saw with my horse. I was driven to learn as much as I could so I decided to take all the Provincial equestrian coaching levels.

In 1993 my dream came true to own my own riding stable with a partnership of one of my riding students. With my drive, knowledge and love of horses and my gift of teaching others the whole world opened for me. I could train and show many talented horses and my students were also excelling winning many Provincial year end awards and awards recognized by The American Quarter Horse Association.

Then it happened:

It was a Monday night in May of 2001, just after a successful spring show weekend had wrapped up. Almost everyone there from the barn had left. I had asked my then husband to help me with this three year old horse. The horse wasn't show quality but it was what I needed to boost my income enough to pay for full time child care of my 4 year old son.

I'd been working with this horse on the ground for almost 6 weeks. This was far longer than any horse I've ever worked with without getting on their back. That little inner voice in my head had kept nagging at me and stopping me from getting on. I felt pressured to get this horse riding. I had already worked this horse earlier that day, so I saddled him up and put him in the round pen and worked him both ways doing the Pernell Roberts, John Lyon, and Clinton Anderson type techniques for those of you who know the lingo of horse trainers.

I believed I knew what was going on in this horses mind or at least that's what I was telling myself. Like my wedding day that inner voice began screaming in my head saying," OMG what are you doing! Pushing my inner voice a side I stepped up into the stirrup anyway and cautiously swung my leg over and just sat there talking to the horse as my husband held the lead rope. I was caressing the top of his shoulders and talking to him sweetly, and before I knew it I was laying on the ground on my side. The only thought in my mind was "how did I get here"? It all happened so fast that I couldn't believe I was lying on the ground. Then the unimaginable happened!, It was bad enough that this horse had initially reared up so hard and fast that I had no time to react to the sensation of flying off his back onto the ground below. He then hovered for a split second above me as he hit the end of the lead rope, and then proceeded to lose his balance and fall straight on top of me crushing my pelvis. I heard every break that occurred as his body slammed into mine and the intense pain as he struggled to lift his entire weight off my now severely broken body.

After a long rehab and much determination, I not only rode again but after a few years I continued to train horses for a living. Unfortunately, as the years went by the pain in my pelvis never subsided. It was relentless. The cold damp weather in the winter was depressing and only intensified the pain. Some days it felt like I was broken all over again.

I started to dread riding horses the more my mind replayed the memories of all the pain I had endured at the hands of that horse. It's no different than the race car driver who is attempting to overcome his emotional demons and get back to racing while still suffering physically and emotionally from the memories of a horrific car crash. As the years went by the demon that began to take root within me was fear. Every time after the accident, whenever I came off a horse I would revisit the memories of pain, which would re-stimulate the fear in my mind to the point that I felt emotionally crippled. Life wasn't worth living at this point.

As you can probably guess depression had set in by this time as well. Depression is simply fear turned inwards. I would put on a happy face and pretend I was doing fine, but inside I was dying. I knew I had to do something. Depression pills were not the answer. I had given those medications five years of my life just to stay in a continual state of numbness. I tried all types of pain relief medications and treatments but nothing seemed to keep the pain away for long. I didn't sleep either and I tried everything from prescription meds, homeopathic meds and Gravel. I even doped myself up with Benadryl just to feel groggy and even more depressed the following day.

I stayed in this numb depressed state for a decade but eventually my soul cried out as I had enough and I started looking towards finding an answer and a permanent solution to my pain. In 2009 after a very successful show season I had a falling out with my business partner at the biggest horse show of our life. After we got home I told my husband I was unhappy and didn't want this life anymore. Something had to change. I knew in my heart that I was done with the horses and with this whole business. He looked up from his bowl of chips, took a sip of his rye and coke and said without emotion or any inflection in his voice," Well, I can't make you happy." That was it and then he went back to watching

TV. Like in our relationship in the past I had simply been dismissed without any discussion or compassion that one would expect from a spouse.

That's was my lightbulb moment. That's when I took charge of my own happiness, for the first time in my life and made the decision that it was up to me, and no-one else, to change the outcome of my life. I then happened to have an insightful talk with a good friend who was our farrier in the barn. He handed me a book on emotional healing. It talked about how emotions, which are simply energy, can become trapped at a cellar level within our body. These trapped emotions ultimately become expressed in the external body as symptoms of disease of which physical pain is the most prominent.

I was really excited for the first time in years and I needed to know more. I read the book voraciously from cover to cover and thought that I would really like to take this course. I finally had a new fire, purpose and passion in my life, but unfortunately I wasn't strong enough yet to stand in my own power and I allowed myself to be pulled back down once more. Before I knew it another year was upon us and we were back showing horses the following spring. I felt trapped. I had no other way to make an income. By this time I had let my skills as far as going back to work as a Veterinary technician become outdated.

I went home that father's day weekend in 2010 and talked to my mom about my marriage and what I should do about my career. When I left I decided to finally attend the "I Can Do it" Conference hosted by Louis Hay in Florida. I thought that I would like to become what is known as a Life Coach. My life was definitely full of worldly experiences that I felt others could learn from. Along with the fact that I had been a natural teacher and advisor to so many students as a riding coach got me excited about what my future could become with a little hard work.

Fast forward. Another year slipped by and I hadn't accomplished anything of the goals that I had envisioned for myself in my dreams. So back I go for another" I Can Do It" Conference, this time in New York City. I knew in my heart that this was the time for action and not the time for excuses anymore. I could feel in my Soul that my future happiness depended on it. As Wayne Dyer once said, "Don't let yourself leave this earth with your music still inside of you." I was now more determined than ever that I was going to take this course on emotional healing.

The first thing I did was I started praying and ask for guidance. I wasn't what you'd call a church goer but I did believe in an energy higher than myself. I also believed in the art of manifesting my goals and dreams.

From my own life experiences, I came to believe in the spirit world around us as I myself had on numerous occasions felt the presents of spirt around me quite clearly. Once I gave a deceased friend a hug because I felt so strongly that her energy was present right there with me in the horse area with me while I was teaching. She used to teach for us and she had died in her sleep from complications of diabetes. I gave her a one arm hug as I didn't want my students thinking that I was losing it.

I also felt and saw one of my favorite deceased horses trotting in the field next to me while I was riding at the back of our property. My horse appeared so real to me in broad daylight that I felt impelled to talk to her as she looked so free and happy. I also once saw the soul of one of my dogs leave her crippled body right after we had put her to sleep and watched her run 30 feet away and from us and bounce around like she was her young self again.

I felt for me at least that I needed to do more than simply pray in order to manifest a new life for myself. I started by writing out what I wanted in a relationship in every detail. I wanted someone who was honest, who really loved me and was romantic and made me feel like a woman. I continued the exercise by writing out how I wanted my new life to look in every detail including something as ordinary as being able to walk my dog on a side walk. At the time I wrote this list I would have to load up our truck at the farm and drive our dogs somewhere quiet to walk. If I wanted to be able to ride our bikes safely I would have to take our bikes into town to a public park because our paved country road was too fast and dangerous for either myself, my son or for my dogs.

After I wrote everything that I desired to manifest within my life I took these letters outside and burnt them. Sending the energy contained within those words out to God, heaven or whomever or whatever exists beyond the physical bounds of our world to answer my prayers.

One morning shortly after waking and after having previously burning the letters, I heard an audible voice that said that I was going to meet my twin flame that very day. Hearing that voice when I was clearly alone in the house caused me to sit up with a startle and look around. That voice sounded so real! I chocked it up to simply being the tail end of a dream I must have been coming out of so I flopped back down on the bed not thinking much about it.

Later that morning I got on the internet and investigated what a twin flame was. What I read left me saying wow! I only had women for students that day and the only other thing I had going on was my Chiropractic appointment. Nothing out of the ordinary occurred that day until the moment I was sitting in the reception area waiting for my business partner to finish her Chiropractic appointment. Dr. Morrison then came out of his office to talk with both of us as we were about to leave his home practice. As he stood there talking and looking ahead through the glass windows on either side of his front door I saw it. I could look into his soul through his eyes. In that moment I had soul reconnection. Still to this day I can't even explain what I felt emanating from him energetically, or this unexplainable feeling that I felt of instantaneously knowing in detail everything life we had shared together in the past as well as knowing what he was meant to mean to me within this lifetime. I was dumb struck. I stared out the window all the way back home. What the hell just happened, and what was I supposed to do with this information? I had never experienced anything like this before nor have I since. I started to question myself if what I thought had happened had actually occurred? Was that real? How do I know that was real? I just buried the experience as I didn't know what else to do with this information and new level of clarity and knowing.

I wasn't even going to share this previous information with the readers as part of my story but just recently during a radio interview on a New York based radio talk show with my Mentor and good friend she told me that she wanted me to share this story with her listeners, I was hesitant at first as I had only shared my story with a few of my closest friends and relatives as I was afraid of others judging me. But after the show aired I decided that this was one of the most important spiritual parts of my life story. And as I have always said and believed right to my core, "We are here having a spiritual experience in our human bodies, not the other way around."

Some time went by but I eventually did talk with Dr. Kevin my Chiropractor about this emotional healing technique I had read about earlier, because he had used to do a similar technique in his big office before he had moved his practice into his house. I explained the technique and its similarities to his. Like with the emotional technique I had read about he also used a form of Muscle Testing or Applied Kinesiology as it more known as, to assess his patients both physically and emotionally. On top of that I had known Dr. Morrison for many years as an extremely gifted and passionate Intuitive Chiropractor who would routinely uncover people's health issues without the need of words from the patient.

I told him that with his intuitive skills he was a natural and should take the course on emotional healing with me that I had been reading so much about. Unfortunately, just a few months earlier the woman who he was living with and had dedicated his life to suddenly died of cancer which left him sad and withdrawn. At first he said he wasn't interested in furthering his emotional intuitive abilities simply because he was in a dark place, but I was persistent. I told him that I needed him to go with me to Chicago as my train buddy, as I was afraid to go alone.

Dr. Kevin and I travelled to Chicago to learn the healing modality for emotional healing which ultimately would start me on a path that was destined to change my life forever. With what we learned together in that course along with Dr. Morrison's many years of past experience with emotional healing with his own clients we were able to ultimately create our very own unique and very powerful emotional healing technique called, "The Awakenings Technique."

By the third trip to Chicago in April of that year we were to become certified in this technique of healing that we were learning. All the time I was learning with Dr. Kevin I never told him about my twin flame experience or anything about what I had experienced that day in his office. I was still asking myself," If this was real or if it was not simply a figment of my imagination? I felt close to Dr. Kevin but not on a romantic level. We had done many levels of this course together, practiced the technique so much together and had healed so much of each other's past hurts that we had become very close as friends.

While at course I had asked myself again how I know for sure this is real and then I heard very clearly "your body will let you know this is real". Wow I thought what does that mean? That afternoon when I was playing with some pendulums that were for sale at the coarse we were attending. I was simply checking out which one I liked the best.

When Kevin as I now felt ok in calling him, walked up behind me. Touched my shoulder and said something to me. I felt a shiver go up my spine right to the back of my head which blew me away. I couldn't shake the feeling of love like I've never ever felt before that moment but I can tell you that it was overpowering. The following day preceded by the worst sleep of my life. That night as I tried everything to sleep, a voice kept telling me that I wouldn't sleep a wink that night until I promised to tell Kevin how I felt about him that following morning. To this day, I think it was my angel guides speaking to me, but whatever it was it worked. I got the guts that next morning to tell him my story and how I felt and in that same instant he told me that he had felt the same feelings for me.

Once I knew that all of my feelings, knowing and intuition was real I decided that my new life was going to start from that moment onwards. But as the spiritualists like to say, in order for one to get to the calm in life, experience it and really appreciate it one must first weather some storms. Was that ever true. I felt like I was crucified by most of my friends and riding students from that part of my life for going home and finally putting my needs first and actually walking away from the horse business forever, which up to that point had been the only thing I had known. I finally cared enough about my body, my wellbeing and my own health and happiness.

 I told my husband in March of that year and before I went to Chicago with Kevin that our marriage was over. I needed to have happiness in my life and he didn't even ask me if there was anything we could do to change that. We went on that last summer as if nothing had change and within that six months I had told no one as I struggled with how I was going to tell my son, who was 15 at the time and was my priority. What was he going to think or do? Will he hate me for leaving his dad? I was now working hard at building my emotional based business so I could support myself and my son. In September of that year I had asked for a divorce. The only two things he asked me was if there was someone else and secondly if I would still teach him riding lessons.

I moved in with Kevin just before New Year's Eve of that year as there was no money for me to get a place of my own and I felt I had no choice as my Emotional Healing business was still in its infancy. I didn't even ask Kevin. I just told him that I needed to move in and thank God he didn't say no because I already told my ex that I was moving out. I talked to my son who was understanding at the time and said he loved me. I care about was my son and I always told myself that if I could just hold on within my marriage, no matter how unhappy and unfulfilled I was, that my new life would somehow manifest itself once my son turned 18 and he was well on his way to becoming an adult but life just seems to have a way of just happening.

After I had moved out my ex with a couple of others went as far as to report Kevin to the College of Chiropractors for sexual misconduct to see if he would be successful in getting him to lose his license to practice. Thank goodness he dismissed me as a patient all most a year earlier when we started working together. I believe he just wanted to hurt me and ruin Kevin's main livelihood and means of making an income. Thankfully, nothing ever came of it.

Since working with Kevin and "The Awakenings Technique" I am totally pain free for the first time in my life since my accident. I mean both physically and emotionally. And my passion for Life has returned even better than before!

On September the 10th of 2016 I walked down the aisle feeling excited and overwhelmed with joyous emotions to marry the love of my life. Looking back I think that everything that I have put on my list not so long ago has come true.

My son after a short separation which made all three of our relationships even better and stronger than before, is now playing a big part in my life again.

I'm now an author, I've been on numerous radio shows and TV interviews, I do public speaking and I work in the office with Kevin each day changing lives. I've taken my Masters in NLP (Neuro Linguistic Programming) and I help others on a daily basis get over the same fears, anxieties, and past traumas that once plagued my life. But most of all I help others find and nurture that seed of greatness that lives within each of us. I work every day to help instill confidence in those that yearn to feel it within their life and I help to ignite the light of joy in those who once could only see darkness. That is my calling. I am like all of you. I was once lost but now I am found. If you keep shining your own light of faith in life your purpose and path for being here is destined to appear.

Walt Disney once said, "Dreams do come true." I am a testament to his vision. I am now confident, happy and I walk my dog every day on the sidewalk hand in hand in love with Kevin.

Miranda Popen

<u>Empowerment fueled by Self love</u>

It all started back to the spice girl days.

When women shinned of independence and girl power. Those days led me to being completely independent at the glorious age of 5 years old when I told my mother I did not need her to do my hair anymore. I was a proud hair braider by the age of 8 and creator of my own line of hair extensions by the age of 14. I could not keep my hands off my own head. You might think I was crafty young lady but the intention of the crafts had much more meaning. I was a determined little girl who wanted to be anything but the ugly curly-head-clown-look-alike-duckling she saw in the mirror.

At the wee age of 10 years old, my mornings consisted of soaking my hair in the bathroom stalls and evenings of braiding my head. There was no way I could leave my house with curly hair! Fast forward to high school, I was in the halls of hair extension lovers and influenced by social media prospectors pushing girls with straight, long hair girls have "it all" This idea powered over me in several ways. Constant jealousy, hatred towards myself, self-doubt and ultimately what led to eating disorder behaviors. To put it simply, yes it started with hair, and unfolded into a much greater problem. I ached to feel good enough day in and day out so my actions and behaviors focused on that.

Looking back at it now, I denied myself from love, respect, and approval, searching for it from others. There was no place of self-sufficiency. I was constantly putting conditions on everything I did. Once I am liked by my peers, or if I lose this weight, if I win this competition, if my coach says I did a good job, then I will be happy. This prevented me from feeling any joy in the moment. I did not have any self-respect and always measured my success against some outside standard. The truth is, if you're waiting for happiness to come to you, you're putting conditions on your own joy. That's real happiness.

You see, self-love is completely unconditional. Real love has nothing to prove. Sometimes we put conditions on the love we give and receive. We say things like, When I get the raise, then I will be happy. When I hit my goal weight, then I can find The One. When I x and y, then I can z. This prevents you from feeling joy in the moment. With the innocence of the little child that lives in us all, we ask again and again through our actions, "*Now do I deserve love?*" "*Am I worthy?*" Only we often can't hear it because we're so busy doing the next "great thing" and calling it self-improvement. Can you imagine this simple motion had power over you're eating habits, weight gain, mood, energy, behavior and so much more? I sure didn't.

My self-empowerment became very clear to me when I started my own personal health journey. During this path, I had discovered my self-worth which ultimately turned into self-love. I was in foreign territory. As I struggled on this new-found path, there were many surprising negatives that came along with it. Losing friends, being judged, feeling resentment, confusion by others and even from myself. My thought process turned very quickly from bettering myself to what's the point? This grief was not worth it. It's funny though. This thing called self-love gets a bad rap because some folks often think it's selfish.

Real self-love is of service to others. But if self-love is opportunistic, greedy, inconsiderate and self-seeking, it's a false representation of real love. Don't be fooled by the inconsiderate one who puts their needs first, sacrificing everyone else. Women across the world are struggling day in and day out being female and yet, still, some women continue to turn against one another. In the developed world, we may forget the difference that small gestures and connections can make. There was no article I had read, no class or lessons taught to me, but there was a feeling I have felt. When someone smiles at us, we naturally smile back; when someone is in pain, our bodies also reflect that emotion and physical sensation. Our wiring for empathy is so deep that, just by observing someone else in pain, the "pain matrix" in our brain is activated. The worst circumstances seem to bring out the best in us. But we shouldn't wait for a catastrophe to help others.

Too many women haven't learned yet how to be effective supporters of each other, but that's changing rapidly. There is this incredibly magic out there; when you show someone that you think she has value, you can transform her life. What I didn't know is that our existence is the self-evident proof that you matter in every moment. You are needed. And you are more than enough. This self-hatred and negativity in my life not only vanished when I found my worth, but I became the woman who I never thought I could be. I could run fast, I could pick up heavy weights, I learned to sculpt my body, and I learned how it worked. I faced my fear, left my amazing job, opened up my own business and thriving! Here was a girl that was completely imbalanced physically, mentally and emotionally seeing for the first time, that she can be strong inside and out. I knew there had to be more to it. I kept moving forward, finding out I could improve my moods. No, this was not just a mental change of being a self-proclaimed positive person, I didn't just turn on my 'positive switch' or as you think, so it shall be. I did not need any of that, because I had started experimenting from what I put around me to what I put inside me. People who love themselves also respect themselves enough to know they deserve better. From the people that were around me, to filling my body up with as many organic foods as possible, my life started to change.

You could say I was starting to feel high on life. As if there was a whole new matrix of life I have just stepped into. I didn't know than that digestion played the biggest role in mood, immune, hormone balance, energy-pretty much everything. So, I experimented by eliminating with my diet. My IBS symptoms improved and so did my attitude. I mean, it's not easy being Little Miss Sunshine when your insides are tied in knots. I then eliminated gluten. After a few weeks, I distinctly remember thinking to myself: "Is this what happy feels like?" This was my 'aha' moment, realizing if I sought out further information, there is another way to my goals that isn't so hurtful to my mind and body to get there.

I no longer suffer from debilitating dizzy spells. Symptoms of IBS have vanished, acne went away, ulcers disappeared, and I became hungry throughout the day. Oh and hello metabolism! The weight was FINALLY coming off! I continue to look to my diet and self-care to stay balanced. I wake up in the morning ready to take on the world. These cool things were happening to my body and to my life when I began to love myself. I still make mistakes and am far from perfect.

"I am a masterpiece but also a work in progress." There is still a fight, more days than others, to keep moving forward, especially when it is so easy to go downhill, but what keeps me going is that everlasting taste, feeling, and moment of true self-love that could take me where ever I wanted to go. It's a type of love that liberates you to be the best you can be.

This type of love allows you to exceed previous limitations and become limitless in your dreams, hopes, and desires, and limitless in the actions you take to achieve them. From a state of total self-love and acceptance you're generating the most effective energy of love. Nothing is forced, and all is natural. This love has a powerful impact on everyone you deal with throughout your day. This power naturally magnifies your tribe members to you, asking for you to act upon the job you are here to do to help one another. Women empowering women makes amazing stuff happen. Women empowering women can change the world. From a state of total self-love and acceptance you're generating the most effective energy of love. In my opinion, it doesn't start, but simply ends with empowering one another and begins with self-love. We must love ourselves first.

Inspiration & Gratitude

Jane Duncan Rogers

<u>Embracing Death</u>

Tears sprung to my eyes as I read the words on the page. The author had written the following:

'A few weeks later when Jean knew the time had come, she asked me for the drugs. As wrenching as it was, I had to agree. We spent the morning reminiscing about our twenty-two years together. Then, after dissolving the pills in some coffee, we said our last good-byes. I watched as Jean picked up the coffee and drank it down. She barely had time to murmur 'Goodbye, my love' before falling asleep. Fifty minutes later she stopped breathing'. From Final Exit by Derek Humphry)

My tears were there because I wished, so wished, that my husband and I could have that kind of ending together. It didn't happen though, not least because he was afraid of dying.

When you're afraid of death, naturally enough you turn away from it, like we do with anything of which we are afraid. However, having been diagnosed with stomach cancer, and while my husband thought there was still hope, he did turn to face it fully, even after the first shock. I wrote about it in *Gifted By Grief: A True Story of Cancer, Loss and Rebirth:*

Philip didn't soften the blow. "It's stomach cancer."

"What?" I felt my body go cold all over, and sat down suddenly. I wished I was with him at home, instead of on the end of a phone, miles away in London. "No. Really?"

"Yes. The consultant told me they found traces of it in the lining of my stomach."

"Oh, God. What happens next then?" Immediately, I was into trying to get the problem solved, even though I was so shocked that I didn't really take it all in. This kind of announcement is one of those things you think only ever happens to other people. But, devastatingly, here it was now, in our own lives.

Later that night, I came through the gate at Inverness airport, and saw Philip waiting for me. "Is it really true?" I whispered, nestling into his tall, strong body. It didn't seem possible.

"I'm afraid so."

"I can't believe it." Somewhere, on that plane trip, I'd been desperately hoping it was all a dream. Philip told me he knew, really, when he got a letter from the hospital earlier that week, saying he should contact them immediately. He'd spoken right away to his daughter, Jackie, a nurse. The hospital simply confirmed his worst fear.

It confirmed my worst fear, too; that he would die and abandon me, leaving me all alone in the world with no husband and no children.

One of the things Philip did on diagnosis was to agree to medical intervention, in the form of chemotherapy and an operation to remove the cancer from his stomach. However, he also embarked on a variety of different types of complementary medicine, including mistletoe treatment. When you're ingesting poison in the form of chemo pills, it's an excellent support to be also taking something like mistletoe, which at best can drive out the cancer, and at least be supportive to a body going through chemotherapy.

But after the operation didn't work, and he chose to not have the second bout of chemo, things were different. This was an active decision that we both knew would mean his life was limited to months rather than years. And so we were forced into living a week at a time and then a day at a time. Nothing like cancer to force you to live in the moment! (Thought I can't honestly say I recommend that as a strategy – much better to practice being here now without that kind of kick up the ass).

When someone is dealing with a terminal illness, no-one knows when they will actually die. Not even the doctors. There are plenty of people who confound the medical profession with their longevity even in the face of extreme illness. When you don't know when you're going to die, you are living. Living right in the moment, on that day, that week, wondering what will happen, just like you usually do. It's just that the moments become more and more precious.

So when Philip was admitted to hospital for radiotherapy treatment (suggested in order to buy him a few more possible months) and then was kept there due to his dramatic weight loss and inability to swallow, no-one addressed the fact that this might be time to simply face up to the fact that he was going to die, sooner than later, and to think about what that might mean.

Now, I was following Philip's desire, which was to hold onto life for as long as he possibly could, no matter how he felt physically. This meant he ended up spending the last six weeks of his life in a hospital bed. When he was finally told there was no more could be done, he was too ill to be driven the 200 miles home.

But going home would have meant him admitting a lot earlier that he was dying. He would have been going home to die, as for various reasons he couldn't be fed by intravenous drip at home. This he was unable to accept, and so ended up contracting pneumonia in the hospital, and having a final ending that was not in the environment he loved.

If he had could accept it, maybe we could have had the conversation that the author above obviously had with his wife. Whether we could have found a health professional willing to give drugs in the way that this man's doctor did is another matter entirely.

But I have long been appalled at how we treat those in our society who have a terminal illness, are finding it unbearable, and yet we continue to 'try to make them better'. For instance, when Philip got pneumonia the first time round, would it not have been kinder to administer no antibiotics, and let nature take its course? It's not called 'the old man's friend' for nothing. Instead, we (including health professionals) keep people alive in circumstances which we would not wish upon our dearly beloved pets. And yet, in a similar situation, we 'put our pets down', acknowledging this is the kindest thing to do.

So, what has happened to kindness when it comes to our human loved ones? It apparently flies out the window, and we have situations where the family members witness sometimes great suffering before the body finally gives up the ghost and let's go.

But we cannot express the compassion we give to our pets and could give to our loved ones until we face up to our fear of death. Nowadays, with the medical profession, nursing homes, crematoriums and funeral directors having 'taken over' the business of death and dying, it's no wonder we are fearful. It's rare for a grown adult to have seen a dying person, let alone a dead body. It's time for this to change; time to choose to have the end of life we wish to have. To do that, we need to bravely educate ourselves about the one thing that is going to happen to us.

We need to prepare in advance by becoming aware of our values, of what life means to us, when attended to in the context that it *will* come to an end. We need to prepare for the practicalities of what is to happen to our body after we no longer inhabit it. And we need to prepare our families for this by being willing to have a conversation with them, and to encourage them to boldly face this topic that has, so sadly, become taboo.

After Philip died, I never for one moment believed that I would be become an educator in the field of life and death issues. Never would I have imagined the enormity of the blessing his death gave me (which was the secret to life itself – that's what I wrote about in *Gifted By Grief*). Not once did I think I would be conducting workshops and online courses to help people face up to end of life issues, and the moral, ethical, emotional, spiritual and practical challenges this brings.

But that's what I've been called to do. It's not an easy journey, by any means. But it is one that allows me to honour what my husband went through; what another friend of mine is going through as I write; and what I want to have a choice about when it comes nearer to the end of my life. What about you? Where are you in relation to all end of life issues? Be brave and face them now, while you're alive and healthy.

Learn more about Jane Duncan Rodgers

Jane Duncan Rogers, and award winning coach and author, is committed to enabling a world where dying, death and grief are considered a natural, normal and nourishing part of conversation.

Having been in the field of psychotherapy and personal growth for most of her life, she now helps those who wish to prepare well for their own death by having them complete their own copy of her book *Before I Go: Practical Questions to Ask and Answer Before You Die* – a priceless document that brings relief to the dying, and is of invaluable help to those left behind.

This has all been inspired by the events that happened to her after her husband died in 2011, and her book *Gifted By Grief: A True Story of Cancer, Loss and Rebirth,* was published in 2015.

Visit her site: http://www.giftedbygrief.com to take the free Before I Go quiz and discover how well prepared you are for your own end of life.

Marta Stanczyk

<u>Half Orphan</u>

A Story of Empowerment through Self-Awareness

"You don't have a father anymore," said my mother as she walked through the door returning from the hospital with the devastating news. In that moment, the story of who I believed I was, its newest version, began to form. "You are half-orphan now," I heard at the tender age of five years old.

"Half-orphan?", I questioned.

Yes. Sadly, in the world I lived in, it meant a child with only one living parent, and that's all it meant. But to my young, innocent mind, over time, it came to mean so much more.

~ If you don't know who you are people will tell you who you should be and you will believe them. ~

Losing my dad, meant losing my protector. It meant losing my security. It also meant losing deep fatherly love, devotion, and laughter; he was so very funny. I lost the life I knew and with that, I lost my identity. I began hearing comments about what happens to lives of 'poor little girls' without daddies. I learned that life becomes hard and people treat you differently. Because of all that, life also became scary. Fear, uncertainty, and sorrow entered my heart and made it its home.

~ Life becomes what you believe it is. ~

It took many years to become aware of the beliefs I had created to go along with my new identity of 'half-orphan'. One day, when I was forced to look back over my life, I realized the meaning I gave to that title assigned long ago. *Half* was the defining word of the story I had no idea I was living. Half as good. Half as smart. Half as capable. Half as worthy. Half as important. Half as accepted. Half as deserving. All painfully reflected in my life thus far. It's as if I was living only half of what was possible as I could not receive fully.

We all, as I did at just five years old, formulate beliefs about who we are and perceptions about the world we live in. That is what we all do in our formative years – without exception. It becomes the story we tell ourselves; the story of our life, the beliefs, and assumptions as they inform us of how to fit in. That story is the backdrop of all our experiences as it was in mine.

~ Change starts with awareness. ~

Then, one terrible day, I saw the truth of who I thought I was and how I saw myself. The door to my awareness had opened. That day, I found myself sobbing on my kitchen floor. I was on my hands and knees unable to stand up to make a sandwich. I had to use the floor because, following a car accident, my lower back was too damaged and in too much pain to hold up my torso.

So there I was, on the floor, broken spiritually, physically, financially, emotionally, and mentally. Depleted to a point of resignation. Alone. In pain. Terrified. Abandoned. Sobbing. Lacking comprehension of how all that happened could happen to one person, to me! I lost my job and lost my health. I lost a relationship and friends. I lost so much in less than a year. How could this happen? Why did this happen? Why was Life so unfair! Why me, again?

All the unfairness, mistreatment, feeling unworthy and unimportant – discarded even. Yes, discarded like a piece of trash is how I felt after I was relieved of my duties in a supervisory position two weeks before Christmas. Then, after a car accident, incredibly, the doctor representing the insurance company and without all the required testing, declared me healthy enough to go back to work. The pain of not being believed, heard, understood, respected, accepted, cared for and, instead, rejected and abandoned in my most desperate hour was unbearable. It was worse than the physical pain of the spinal cord nerve compression I was suffering. In all the loss I had already endured, I was so very close to losing hope as well.

The pain of that moment on my kitchen floor was indescribable. It was what some call hitting rock bottom. I refer to it as the shattering of my foundation, the foundation of my beliefs from which all my experiences stemmed. It was also a necessary moment of breaking open. The door to self-awareness opened just enough for me to begin my journey to truth. The truth of my beliefs about myself, my life, and everyone and everything in it.

Gradually, I began to see the meaning of all that happened in my life. I was beginning to realize that Life was reflecting ME back to me. It's as if it held up a mirror so I could see who I thought I was, how I saw myself and life, and how I blamed it for so much. No wonder I was feeling like a victim of circumstance; this life that was so hard and unfair. That 'poor little girl' was ever present; the constant survival mode, fear, and uncertainty flavored so many of my experiences.

~ You see what you believe. You are what you believe you are. You have what you believe you can have. ~

Eventually, I realized that until I changed my beliefs about life, life would keep showing up as unfair and hard to show me what I believed and to give me an opportunity to change my mind. At last, I knew I had to free myself from who I thought I was so I could resume BEING who I was always meant to be.

~ Our wounds contain our Purpose. Our 'story' is the path to who we are meant to become. ~

Empowerment came with yet another level of clarity. I began to see the other truth of my old beliefs. I began to see the deeper meaning of everything that my life contained, from birth to that exact moment. I finally understood the purpose of all that happened; it was all part of my Purpose.

This is the truth of life, anyone's life, as I know it now: the story of your life does not create your Purpose. It is the Purpose that calls the story into being. To be a great teacher, I had to first learn deeply the lessons I am meant to teach. And I have.

I spent decades working on the whys of my own behavior unaware that I was already fulfilling my Purpose – a deep inner dive into who I was, why I was, and how I was, and everything else you can think of. I THOUGHT about it! I was acquiring profound expertise in the discipline of self-awareness. My life's design, my 'story', is in support of this intense inner journey, part of which is not being married and not having children. I can clearly see all the reasons why.

~ Let the Journey take you to where your Purpose awaits you. ~

One of my most empowering beliefs is knowing that everything I have been through was part of my Purpose. I embrace my 'story' and I understand its importance and divinity. I am working toward loving all parts of it completely. I now know with certainty life was not unfair and I was not being punished. I was evolving and preparing for the rest of my Life. My story is the essence of my becoming.

Our story and everything in it unfolds so we can experience the journey back to innocence. First, we are born, then life brings about a defining moment. A moment that comes for all of us, in which we lose our innocence. Thus our story is created. We then live the story until it's time to begin to understand it, to extract the lessons we were meant to learn, provided we are brave enough to do it. Those brave enough get to partake in life fully by understanding and expressing their Purpose. But, most importantly and simultaneously, they get to partake in the divine evolution of themselves and the collective Human Spirit.

My defining moment was when I lost my dad; when I lost the innocence of a happy, joy-filled life. I went from a happy-go-lucky, care-free little girl to someone completely different. It's only recently I grasped the profound impact his death had on me. It's been a long, hard, lonely journey back to the child I used to be, but I think I found her again, right where I lost her.

I went back to the place where I saw my dad well for the last time. The same place where I saw him struggle to breathe and be taken away by ambulance never to return. I've been near that place, the green space near the apartment block we lived in, many times since he died. I lived in the same area for years after. But this time was the first time I went there to BE THERE with myself and my sorrow. I sat in that space, felt my pain, cried, prayed, and cried some more. I finally let myself grieve the biggest loss of my life.

I had to go back to that place because I left a little piece of myself there and I had to retrieve to be whole again. It wasn't as bad as you may think. I started to feel relief as soon as I connected to my sorrow and I felt them both at the same time as tears fell down my face....it was beautiful. The next level of healing had started. I chose to allow it to continue, so I and my life could begin again.

~ Own your thoughts. Own your choices. Own your life. ~

Empowerment is knowing we have a choice. I chose to examine all the pieces of my shattered foundation – my beliefs, perceptions, and assumptions. I chose to recreate them all and to reassemble my foundation anew. I now understand I get to choose how I feel so I choose to believe I am no longer the victim of an unfair life, or circumstance, or hardship. And in my most courageous step, as I chose to face my sorrow I found my strength.

We are most disempowered when we thinking we have no choice in whatever it is we are experiencing. We may not always be able to choose our circumstances, but we always have the power to choose how we experience those circumstances. We do that by choosing what we think and how we feel about them. That I know for certain.

To illustrate this point, I will share with you a process and a story I often use in my coaching practice to help my clients understand how they experience their journey:

Imagine a rainy day. It can be perceived as 'bad' by a bride who planned a garden wedding or as 'good' by a farmer with dry fields. It's the same event but the people experiencing this even have different expectations and ideas of what the day 'should be' like. Based on their expectations they create different judgements or opinions of that event. Their opinion creates emotions which, in turn, create feelings. The result is the flavor of their individual experience of the same day.

As part of our intrinsic human need to assess anything that happens in our lives we judge, asses, everything we experience. Every event or person is an experience. Our brain takes in the event and makes an assessment based on many variables, most related to safety and survival. Then, it sends signals, patterns of recognition defined as emotions, to inform us how to feel about the event and what behavior is necessary or appropriate to react to or handle this event.

Here is the part we often miss: the space between the 'happening' of the event and our judgement of it is what I call the Moment of Creation; the space of neutrality, before the judgment, in which anything can happen. A moment in which we create our experience of that event in that moment. How you judge anything is how you'll experience it. Period.

And here is the beauty of knowing you have the power to choose: You can go back to that Moment of Creation and change your choice in judgement. Any time you choose to do so, you can. Herein lies your emPOWERment.

Learn more about Marta Stanczyk

Marta Stanczyk, founder of Woman to Woman Empowerment, is a certified Master Empowerment Coach and graduate of a Canadian coaching program exclusively for women, where she now serves as a Student Advisor contributing to the learning platform. Marta is also an honours graduate of Applied Counselling Certification program at Red River College in Winnipeg, Manitoba, where she currently resides. Marta is also eligible to be a member of American Association of Drugless Practitioners.

Marta is an intuitive self-awareness expert, who's passion and purpose is to empower women so they can live inspired and fulfilling lives powered by their individual Purpose and by sharing their unique gifts and talents. She works internationally with women who want to create lasting change in their personal and professional lives. She teaches women how to live their highest potential while emphasising the importance and power of self-awareness.

Marta's other passion is to work with women in her community by teaching workshops and extending her services to those less fortunate. She is a creative writer and a poet and is currently involved in collaborative endeavours with women in her industry as well as developing new projects. Her work was featured in local publications and in online magazines.

Marta is a lifelong learner and has dedicated much of her time to study the subjects of spirituality, human consciousness, psychology, quantum theories, and energy healing modalities by learning from top leaders in the industry. In 2015, she had the privilege to take part in a year-long mentoring program with Marci Shimoff and Debra Poneman that featured experts like Jack Canfield, Lisa Nichols, Sonia Choquette, Panache Desi, and Marian Williamson.

Marta affectionately refers to her life's challenging experiences as earning a "Ph.D." from the School of Life and says she is working on her "Master's Degree" indulging her curiosity and deep desire to understand the complexity and beauty of human behaviour - including her own. As her inner light shines brightly, Marta hopes to be the sparkle that ignites the light in those who come to know her.

Learn more about Marta at:

www.womantowoman.ca

www.MartaStanczyk.com

Cami E. Ferry

Emerging from the Shadows, Stepping into the Spotlight:

Choosing to live as a Visionary, Empowering and Inspiring Others

"I am a Committed, Focused, Worthy, and Abundant Woman. I am Joyful and Free!!" This is a contract statement that I repeat aloud to myself several times each day regardless of what is going on in my life, regardless of how hard I am being hit by life's circumstances and, believe me, I have been hit hard lately. I do this because I honestly believe that we can create our own reality, we can manifest our successes, and our lives are not limited nor controlled by the challenges that are sent our way no matter how overwhelming they may seem at the time. They are nothing compared to the power of Love that we hold within us that can flow through us if we open ourselves like conduits to allow that highest vibration energy of Love to flow from the original source, the Creator, through us and out to everyone with whom we come in contact.

Our challenges become Opportunities to Grow, to Learn, and to Empower and Inspire Others!

Every day I am choosing to emerge from the shadows of my passed and step into the spotlight of my greatness to live as a Visionary so I can Empower, Inspire, and bring Benefit to those who are open to receiving. My vision for the future is to build a performing arts center where my theatre company, In Motion Theatre Company, can produce professional live theatrical productions on a regular basis giving countless people, especially those who have never experienced a live production before, the chance to enjoy high quality entertainment and thus fulfill it's mission statement of giving back to the local community by providing fund-raising opportunities for caused based organizations and individuals through live theatrical events and performances. But the vision doesn't stop there. You see, I want to eventually franchise In Motion Theatre so that the good it does can multiply and reach countless communities. My vision is not limited to just a theatre company putting on plays where a portion of the net proceeds goes to a beneficiary such as a local charity or an individual who needs funds, but expands to all kinds of other activities that benefit and fulfill a need within local communities.

My vision for the future includes Brains In Motion which will offer people a chance to take part in Brain Health activities and seminars, Kick Cancer to the Curb In Motion which will provide specific performances and events to create funds and awareness for cancer survivors, warriors, and the victims' families, Training In Motion which will provide community members of all ages the opportunity to grow in every aspect of their lives through learning and improving skills in every aspect of theatre arts and live performance, and there is so much more in the works like the Murder In Motion Series of Murder Mystery Dinner Theatre Events, Singing Telegrams In Motion, Children's Theatrical Parties In Motion, and Topsy Turvy's Flying Circus Comedy Improv Troupe!! My vision for the future is not limited, it is a Legacy in Motion!!

My vision is one of win/win scenarios for everyone who chooses to be involved in any aspect of In Motion Theatre Company, the Performing Arts Center, and every future IMT that opens in every community and neighborhood. My vision includes events and platforms which will benefit and promote local businesses and anyone who has a cause or a message to get out to the community. My vision is one of continued CREATIVITY that is Growing and Evolving and Multiplying. My vision is one that will in some way some how reach throughout the world whether that is through Missions In Motion digging wells of clean water for villages in third world countries and sending groups to physically and practically help people in need around the world or simply by providing the foundation for that one special person who takes that leap of faith from some aspect of In Motion Theatre Company that gives them the freedom to dream a huge dream and make it a reality.

My vision includes the Rush Hour For Success radio show on Money 105.5FM where I am known as the radio personality, The Theatre Queen. My vision includes the Rush Hour For Success becoming syndicated and expanding to provide an even larger platform where those with a humble heart to serve through their own mission and passion in life can step into their power and spread their message to a greater listening audience for the greater good. I envision connecting, partnering, promoting, and creating with so many wonderful visionaries to empower and inspire countless listeners.

My vision includes The Theatre Queen Publications, Productions, and Media Broadcasting Company where local authors and playwrights can get their work published and promoted, where business owners, entrepreneurs, film makers, and those who are on a mission to get a message out to the public can find the tools and services they need to be produced and aired on a weekly TV network reaching millions of viewers.

My vision includes Cami's Cardio and becoming a certified Health and Fitness coach so I can empower others who are looking to better their lives by improving their health to become the best versions of themselves.

My vision also includes rising to leadership in Exertus Financial Partners which is headed up by some of the humblest leaders filled with integrity and compassion as they strive to empower people to live their dreams and help people create legacies for their loved ones. People need to put things in place for themselves and their families to prepare for life's unexpected events and challenges and that is exactly what we are doing at EFP.

Every aspect of my vision is geared toward helping others, building legacies, and creating win/win scenarios because I believe that the highest vibration energy of Love compels us to do so when we are open to it's movement within our souls. Our brains, our minds, our imaginations, and our voices possess power beyond our comprehension. We simply must open ourselves to the flow of energy surging through us and focus our power on positive creativity. We need to acknowledge and respect our connectivity to every human being and every living creature so we can accept and receive the beauty around and within us that sets us free to live and move and have our being within the Source of all Life and all Creativity that is Love Itself Personified. Can you, for one moment, imagine a world where all people chose the power and freedom of Love over the binding restricting chains of fear and hatred? Imagine, if you will, a world where each one of us could see every single human being as our beloved brother or sister to be valued, cherished, and loved.

Of course, in our fallen world, there will always be those who can't or won't comprehend the wisdom of this vision but I do believe that the more of us who choose to step out of the shadows of fear, hatred, abuse, and oppression and step into the spotlight of our power and greatness illuminated by Love and Creativity, the better our world will become. I am Committed to doing this and moving forward with creating my vision as well as helping you to create your vision, I am Focused on persistently staying the course, finding the mechanisms that work, and taking the action necessary, I am Worthy of the Blessings that will flow to me, within me, and through me to Bless others, and I am Abundant in the Power of Love, Creative Energy, and Financial Blessings so that I can not only create a legacy that will inspire my children and my grandchildren and continue to give back to them throughout their entire lives but also for a multitude of others for generations to come.

You, my precious reader, are also Worthy of this Flow of Blessings and if you desire to join me in this pursuit, I urge you and encourage you to contact me. You can find my contact information within my bio. Come! Let us Emerge from the Shadows and Step into the Spotlight to Create, to Empower, and to Inspire each other and everyone who meets us. Let us Live, Move, Dance, and have our Being within that Source of Light and Love for as Gene Wilder said while performing the role of Willie Wonka during the 1971 film, Willie Wonka and the Chocolate Factory, "We are the Music Makers and We are the Dreamers of Dreams."

Come! Let us Dream Big Dreams! Let us Envision, Manifest, and Speak into existence a Legacy of Creativity and Love!

Learn more about Cami E. Ferry

Cami Ferry - Founder/Artistic Director of In Motion Theatre Company, Founder of Cami's Cardio for which she is currently completing her certification as a Health and Fitness Coach, Co-Host and Partner of Rush Hour for Success Radio show as The Theatre Queen on Money 105.5FM Thursdays and Fridays at 2pm PST, Founder and CTQ (Chief Theatre Queen) of The Theatre Queen Publications, Productions, and Media Broadcasting Company, an executive team member of the Solutions4Life program, a Committed, Focused, Worthy, and Abundant Woman. Cami is the mother of six wonderful children, three boys/three girls, and Grandma to her Grandbabies, Nathan & Cassy. Cami was also very blessed to be the caregiver to her mom who has positively influenced her life in many ways and was her biggest fan until her recent passing on Oct. 11, 2016.

Cami is an actress, singer, and dancer with 30 years of professional training and experience in classical theatre, opera & voice, as well as ballet, jazz, and contemporary dance in London, England and the U.S. She is currently pursuing training and partnership for professional and competitive Latin and Ballroom Dance. Through her company, In Motion Theatre, she has not only performed in high quality professional productions but has also co-produced, directed, and starred in award winning Independent films.

She is an author having written several articles for various publications and co-authored three anthology books including Women On A Mission, From Fear to Freedom, and Echoes in the Darkness. She is participating in other anthology books that are in the works including 100 Voices, Breaking Barriers, Women on a Mission Sisterhood of Stories, and Chocolate & Diamonds for the Woman's Soul. Cami is passionate about Creating, Becoming the Best Version of Herself, Loving, Respecting, & Valuing Each Human Being, and Promoting, Empowering, Inspiring, and Positively Influencing the Hearts, Minds, and Lives of Everyone she encounters.

Cami Ferry
2133 W. Pine Street, Lodi, CA 95242
209-663-9953
cferry@InMotionTheatre.org
www.InMotionTheatre.org
https://www.facebook.com/cami.e.ferry
https://www.facebook.com/InMotionTheatreCompany/
https://www.facebook.com/rushhourforsuccess/

Penny Norkett

Empowerment through my son's healing journey

December 1st, 2015, funny how certain dates stick out in my mind. That was the date I began to journal, the start of my daily gratitude practice, the start of my daily intentions, the start of my journey to empowerment.

I had finally decided to invest in myself. I invested in a mindset business coach. I began to create dreams and goals for myself like I had never done before. I now knew what I wanted to do with my life. I wanted to become an empowerment coach. I wanted to share my experiences to assist others in creating the life of their dreams.

I began stepping out of my comfort zone. I began to expand my mind, my body and my soul. I was ready to heal my past, expand my mind and achieve my life purpose. The how was still to be revealed. I just had to have faith. God would not have given me a dream without there being a way for me to achieve it. I researched some coaching schools and at the age of 57, one day before the anniversary of my sister's death, I enrolled in the personal empowerment coaching certification program at The Simply Women Accredited Trainer Institute.

My life has not been the same since. I learnt how to process the grief I had been carrying around with me for over 39 years. I became self-aware. I no longer numbed my pain with Facebook games. I started to listen to my heart. I began to examine my thoughts, my beliefs, my values and my emotions. I analyzed my intentions.

I felt the fog had been lifted from my brain. My life did have a purpose. Feeling guilty for my son's health was no longer serving me. I have a voice and needed to use it. I needed to share my story.

It is only now that I realize the significance of me beginning to journal on December 1st. The biggest challenge of my life as a parent began five years earlier on December 1st, 2010. My then 14-year-old son, Kyle developed a migraine headache that never went away. My son's healing journey began my own healing journey.

Kyle's healing journey began at his birth. At 9 lbs., 13 oz. there was an issue during birth. The doctor saved his life by pushing and turning his shoulder. Digestive issues were noticed, but passed off as insignificant as he was thriving as an infant and reaching all his milestones. I listened to the professionals even though in my heart something did not feel right.

An intelligent fast learning child, he surprised me by learning how to read at the age of 4. In junior kindergarten Kyle was outstanding in all areas. He was asked to count as high as he could – expecting him to stop before 20, Kyle's teacher was happy when he stumbled near 115, the highest number by any of the students. By Grade 2, he was practicing spelling words from the Grade 7 and 8 vocabulary lists.

Frequently bouts of the flu interrupted his childhood. School trips, birthday parties, and Halloween were missed. Kyle was always a trooper; he pushed past his pain and continued his life as best he could. He was wise beyond his years, always concerned about others and how they were feeling.

Kyle made friends easily the year my husband, Glenn's company closed and we relocated to a new city, for a new job. Kyle's symptoms were getting worse so we were pleased when we were referred to a digestive specialist who diagnosed Kyle with possible cyclical vomiting syndrome and chronic functional constipation. Missing over 45 days of school academically, although concerning to the principal, did not affect Kyle's marks. He could attend his 6th grade graduation. By High School he was not so lucky.

As Kyle's stomach issues seemed to get better, Kyle was now experiencing headaches. At first they only lasted an hour or two. Over the course of two years they steadily increased in intensity and duration. We tracked their frequency. A referral was sent in for a neurologist. The long wait for the appointment began. It was early fall when Kyle had his first 5-day migraine. Two weeks later he had one that lasted 7 days. I was beside myself. I had never heard of a migraine that lasted that long. Little did I know the journey we were about to embark on.

My husband Glenn and I researched causes and solutions on the Internet. We read books. We spent our time together discussing Kyle. Nothing else seemed to matter. I was shocked to read stories of other children suffering chronic migraines. The unfortunate part was no one seemed to have found a remedy. I just couldn't imagine a migraine that lasted a week, let alone a year. My brain was not ready for this. I would get a headache and feel even worse knowing the pain my son was in. I worried Kyle had inherited migraines from me.

The long-awaited neurologist appointment finally arrived. We had so much hope. A new medication was offered. Was this the solution? Side effects were getting worse. Kyle tried another, and another without success until we heard the crushing words; there is nothing more I can do for your son. He needs to be seen by a pediatric neurologist. The waiting began again.

As a family, we learned the ins and outs of the medical system. We persevered. I knew in my heart there had to be a solution.

Determined to find a solution for my son's migraines we explored new therapies. His diet was revised. Tests were taken. We investigated massage therapy, physiotherapy, athletic therapist, naturopathic medicine, acupuncture, eastern medicine, osteopath, cranial sacral, and energy work to name a few. Nothing was off limits. We were grateful for the health benefits but soon realized how little of the therapies were covered. We were fortunate to be able to afford the treatments. I couldn't imagine someone having to deny their child treatment due to lack of funds.

Acupuncture was Kyle's saving grace. Kyle began to function again. Limitations were huge but lowering the pain even for a few hours was welcomed. Kyle attempted attending school in person again. It was a daily struggle.

Conflicting advice led to some stumbles. Throughout it all Kyle remained positive. I think I was more devastated when he could no longer attend High School than he was. Every credit Kyle earned was a struggle. Although highly intelligent, Kyle's pain prevented him from thinking clear enough to do his assignments. Countless hours were spent devoted to medical appointments. I was embarrassed that my super smart child was incapable of graduating with his peers.

As a parent, I experienced tremendous guilt. Why couldn't I stop his pain? Why was this happening to Kyle, to me? I put my life on hold. We stopped celebrating. We stopped having fun. I didn't even realize I was suffering. I neglected myself to provide for him. My happiness was co-dependent on his health. I did not even realize my unhappiness was creating more stress for Kyle. It wasn't until the two-year mark in Kyle's healing journey that I realized I needed to take care of myself. My guilt lessened. We adapted our expectations. I began to live my life again.

I believe things happen for a reason. My son began to improve. Life got easier. We had setbacks along the way but always looked to the future with hope. My worrying was not helping anyone – most importantly me. Sometimes the solution is right in front of you and you do not see it. I asked my son if he was ready to seek a new solution. He stated he was ready. The synchronicity of events was amazing.

I had been working for an occupational therapy company and had been requesting appointments for our clients for binocular vision testing. Although not injured from a motor vehicle accident, Kyle demonstrated some of the same symptoms. I made Kyle an appointment and the results were amazing. That specialist was a member of a local team of health care professionals that collaborated to find solutions for their patients. We eventually connected with a pioneer in post-concussion treatment. We finally had a diagnosis. In non-medical terms, Kyle suffered from a pinched nerve in his neck. There was a solution. There was hope.

Kyle began his therapy. New technology had been developed that could be used to cure Kyle. Results were noticed within a month of treatment. Setbacks occurred along the way but he persevered. We celebrate all his successes. He is now well on his way in his healing journey.

Obtaining his driver's license has given Kyle freedom. He is in control of his appointments. He can now drive to visit his girlfriend four hours away. He is no longer tied down by acupuncture treatments. He can travel. For the first time, ever this Fall, Kyle enrolled in University with a full load of in-class courses. He has a part-time job. His opportunities are now limitless. Miracles do happen. Kyle is healthy! Having graduated from my coaching program, I realize how empowered I was during Kyle's journey. I advocated on his behalf. I listened to my heart and knew deep down that there was a solution. I was determined. I never gave up. I was empowered! Today I empower women worldwide to connect with their heart, to follow their truth and become the best possible version of themselves.

Learn More about Penny Norkett

Penny Norkett is a Personal Empowerment Coach & Success Strategist. She is the co-author of International Bestselling book 100 Voices of Inspiration, Awakening, and Empowerment. She is also the co-author of the upcoming book My Fondest Memories.

Penny assists professional women to process their emotions and remove blocks so they can skyrocket their life and business success.

She has published inspiring articles in The Mompreneur, The Huffington Post and Simply Woman online magazine. Penny is a rising Speaker inspiring many women around the globe. She is leading a community of like-minded women in a closed Facebook group Claiming Your Brilliance.

She can be reached at: pennynorkett.com

Joanne Feather

<u>Children should be "Seen not Heard"</u>

My Voice from the "Children should be seen and not heard" Proverb

Dome may be familiar with the Olde English Proverb "Children should be seen and not heard", to others this may be your first time hearing it. The origin is from circa 1450 when the opinion of an Augustinian clergyman was shared in a collection of homilies titled "Mirk's Festial".

It read; "A mayde schuld be seen, but not herd." In doing this research I see how such a proverb has rooted even deeper in my life patterns, as the original expression was aimed at young single females (it is said also denotes celibate males) and therefore as it accounted for both young genders through time the saying became that of children.

In any event this saying was repeated to me many times as I grew up in my typical English home. Although my parents, both born in England immigrated to Canada and my sister and I were born here in Canada our home and household rules were very British, right down to the Sunday tea of liver and onions and if we were good roast beef and Yorkshire pudding.

Now, this chapter is not to blame my parents or to complain about them and my childhood. I simply mention this for perspective as I accept full responsibility for my choices as I am now an adult and mother myself. As parents we do our best with what we have and know and that is exactly what my parents did for our family. What I wish to illustrate is how one simple saying, a grouping of words can stick with us and create an impression within us that can affect us in many circumstances. I also find it suitable that for an anthology of short stories titled 100 Voices that my contribution is about finding my voice.

Growing up I remember the evening parties, dinners, "Get Togethers" my parents would host. It was the late 1970's and the socializing of that time involved neighbours and friend's families coming over for drinks, appetizers, and dinner. Husbands, wives and children would all show up usually with a bottle of wine in hand or some flowers for the hostess gift.

Everyone was so happy and ready to enjoy the weekend after the men had had a stressful week working in the city and the women needed to release their anxiety of staying at home with other women that understood. This was the social time. There was no texting or other forms of social media for people to vent their frustrations and so these weekend soirees became that time and place. No wonder the alcohol flowed so freely.

The children also enjoyed seeing each other because usually someone had a new toy they would bring and share and we could all experience. However not until the formalities of sitting in the formal living room took place.

All the children would sit together in the corner of the room as their parents enjoyed some wine or scotch and all spoke about their week, or bragged about a bonus they had earned. The words "children should be seen and not heard" was commonplace during this time as we were shushed to stop giggling or whispering in our excitement to see each other. Our parents expected us to sit there cross legged on the floor, neat and tidy, prim and proper in silence. As soon as a noise was heard from our corner dependent on who it was from the parent of that child would place their finger to their lips and "shhhhh, children should be seen and not heard".

I was a shy introverted child to begin with, add this into my programming and I was set to be quiet for life. I am a rule follower and if you tell me to be quiet, I would be. The cone of silence did not last all night. As the women moved to the kitchen to drink some more and "help" in the preparation of dinner also known as "take me away so we can commiserate together", we kids got to take off as well and play either outside or downstairs dependent on the weather. This was the start of my programming into "speak until spoken to", "be seen and not heard", "stay silent", and "you don't have a voice that matters".

How did that play out into my life? My first memory of being silent was in Kindergarten. I interacted with the other kids, but I didn't speak. When the teacher asked a question and I knew the answer I would raise my hand and approach her and whisper it in her ear. I remember her excitement whether I got the answer correct or not she would always raise her voice in appreciation to the whole class "Very good Joanne, yes an apple is red." This was all to boost my confidence so I would speak out in class. I could speak. I had a broad vocabulary and knew how to explain things quite well for a child in kindergarten per my report card.

However, I never felt like I could speak up in front of people. I would approach the teacher and whisper in her ear asking permission to go use the washroom. Everything I spoke was in a whisper to the teacher's ear. When I think back on this now I find this very sad and yet so very happy that that Kindergarten teacher treated me with compassion and care over my fright and shyness.

As the years went by in middle school and high school it was standard good behaviour to raise your hand to answer a question or to be excused, and so following protocol allowed me to maintain my shyness in being selective in when I spoke. I answered questions when I knew the answer 100% and I rarely asked to be excused, using recess and lunch to use the washroom and avoid having to speak. I attended an "Girls Only" private school and we were shown so many strong, independent outspoken women it still surprises me today that I didn't fully feel accepted with my voice.

School is only one area of life that I adapted my way of being for fear of using my voice. That was quite simple compared to the remaining life experiences that were coming my way in which if I had my voice I feel I would triumphed more. Not feeling like I could speak up for myself, nor even share my voice with anyone I became a victim.

I was sexually assaulted at a young age and my voice screamed "no" but that didn't stop him. It also stopped me from going to the police and pressing charges. It also stopped me from telling anyone in my family or friends, and most will be finding out for the first time by reading this chapter.

I survived domestic violence as a young mother and my voice screamed "stop". I had no choice in going to the police as my life and my daughter's was in danger. But as soon as I got there I said I didn't want to press charges. It was ingrained in my mind that this causes problems and issues, and lays a large spotlight on a very private matter. I joined a women's domestic violence support group via the women's shelter and I became an advocate within that group. I knew what happened was wrong and those women gave me strength to have a voice. That voice soon got squashed by the perpetrator and the court system. This was in the early 2000's when domestic violence and women's issues, and in particular women having a voice was still not socially acceptable in my opinion.

I have gone through and survived a multitude of things which I didn't consider needing a voice a fractured spine, a near death experience, divorce, the family court system, relationship break ups, job loss, financial loss, diagnosis of depression, chronic fatigue, fibromyalgia and so much more. Many people take one experience and make them their new platform and become advocates and warriors for the cause and I applaud them. Instead I sat quietly and accepted the verdict, the outcome, the diagnosis. But today, today I found my voice.

Today I have my platform. My platform is to have your voice and tell your story. Speak up and out. Children and adults should play and be heard for all they must say and share for we all have something to learn from everyone. My voice is rising and there are many more chapters to be written and shared.

Today, I encourage all parents, grandparents and teachers to not enforce the "Children should be seen and not heard" mindset as it sets in place a tendency to not speak up among girls. Let's all rally behind them so they start out with a voice.

Learn More about Joanne Feather

Chief Energy Officer and Founder of Aurora Lifestyle

www.auroralifestyle.com

Joanne is a born empath committed to helping and guiding people to create the lives that they desire in healthy ways. Joanne has always been a natural compassionate spirit who people have turned to for advice and ultimately healing from life troubles and difficulties. Joanne's journey with energy began as a child. Spirit and angel communication was natural to her and she openly discussed what she saw, heard and knew much to the amazement of friends and family. Joanne taps into her four clairs - Clairvoyance, Claircognizance, Clairaudience, Clairsentience. Many consider these "psychic" abilities, whereas Joanne's school of thought is these are gifts of the spirit which we all can develop and attain some more naturally than others.

Joanne has been learning and practicing non-traditional energetic and therapeutic methods to heal and change stuck mindsets, disease, illness and seeing fast results in those she helps. Joanne is skilled in many areas and has helped her clients open and cleanse their minds and spirits of past hurt, trauma and stress therefore easing their effect on the mind and body.

Joanne has taken her studies in biological science specializing in physiology to heightened levels and developed a new method of therapy and guidance in energy medicine, The Feather Touch (TM).

Through the guidance of spirit and angels Joanne works with them and tools of life coaching and mentoring combined with tailored energy modalities to connect with you. This process is a true awakening. Clients discover who they truly are, receiving messages and validation they long for moving them a step forward into a more passionate life.

Joanne spent half her career in veterinary science and holds a Bachelor of Science degree in Zoology as well as a degree in Veterinary Technology. This education and her years of experience working directly with all species of animals lends her to be a natural animal communicator. Joanne is the real life Doctor Doolittle. Animals come to Joanne freely and speak to her providing messages their owners need to hear regarding their health, their personality and favorite things. Such a connection leads to a more compassionate relationship between pets and their owners.

Joanne's work has led to many calling her "The Compassionate Coach" ™ for her guidance leads those she touches down a more compassionate, heart centered path.

To connect with Joanne visit her at www.auroralifestyle.com

Donna Keeley

My Life Transformation at "Soul Camp"

"How my whole life changed when I changed."

This is a part of my life's journey that I want to share with others on how I went from being a victim my entire life and how one brave action started a massive transformation of me leading a life I love.

At this time in my life, I was being bullied for approximately 4 years at work and I was exhausted from having anxiety and panic attacks for many years. I had anxiety as a child and for much of my adult life but masked it with alcohol and distractions. This lasted much into my late forties and I came to a point where I knew something had to change, but I didn't know what or how to change. Then one day sitting in front of my computer at work completely exhausted, depleted and depressed I saw a post on Facebook that said "you should go to this". It was an event called "Soul Camp" posted on Facebook.

It was a message from a friend and I wasn't sure what this thing called Soul Camp was but I knew that message was meant for me and I needed to go. The life I was currently leading was one of people pleasing, not having any boundaries, not expressing myself, not doing what I wanted and I knew something had to change.

I was committed to a friend's birthday gathering that same weekend and I was torn from pleasing my friends or choosing what I wanted to do for myself. I decided to not attend the birthday party that weekend where I was expected to be the life of the party (as usual) but instead I decided to take care of myself and go to Soul Camp. Little did I know; this would be one of the best decisions of my life.

I was looking forward to stepping out of my chaotic life and trying something way out of my comfort zone. The fact that I was going alone to something that I had no idea what it even was, no money to even pay for the trip and it was during the most anxious time of my life this really was close to a miracle that I even decided to invest in myself. On the bus ride to Pennsylvania it was peaceful and I met a few nice people but when we pulled in and I saw all the camp counselors in their tye-dye shirts jumping up and down to greet us, my heart smiled.

As we got off the bus, each counselor hugged us and welcomed us and gave us instruction on how to check in. I walked into my bunk and saw about 20 beds and was terrified that I had to sleep with so many people since I was used to living in my apartment that I called my cocoon where no one bothered me and I could handle my anxieties behind closed doors.

The first person I met in the bunk was a thin woman with black hair and a sweet smile anxiously walking around trying to find a place to make her home. We became instant friends and are best friends to this day. With each woman that showed up in the bunk, friendships just organically blossomed and to this day most of these women are my close friends. They are my support system, they see me and love me exactly as I am and I feel the same way about them.

Each day I was at Soul Camp I realized that I wasn't someone with all this anxiety, instead I was living a life with people and situations that were creating anxiety in my life. With each passing moment, hour and day I was so high on life and happy for every new experience there. I loved eating meals with others and having intimate conversations and bonding with all the women in the bunk. I went to lectures, yoga, blessings and breath work and with each passing day I fell in love with this feeling of peace, fun and bliss.

I knew my soul longed for this and I had to figure out how to take this home with me. Everywhere I turned there were the most amazing people who wanted to connect and go deep and know you, truly know you. At night we had fear burning bonfires, dance parties under the stars and talent shows that made you laugh and cry. This place gave me the most magical experience of my entire life and I was so grateful that I listened to that inner voice and went against what others wanted from me and did what I wanted for the first time in a long time.

I grew up not feeling like I belonged or not sure what my purpose in life was but I knew that this trip was going to bring me something, I just wasn't sure what it would be. This was the first time that I felt like I belonged in a group of people. I felt like I just walked into my tribe of 150 people and it never felt so good.

There was one day I walked down to the lake with my journal and it was a sunny perfect kind of day. I meditated, prayed and wrote in my journal that from the day forward, I would not abandon myself to please others and that I would commit to myself to change my stressful, miserable existence of a life that I created. I knew this needed to happen or the stress would take me out. It had been too many years of high level stress and pain for my body to endure much more. I closed the journal put my hand over my heard and I spoke the words out loud that I love you Donna and I will never abandon you again and I meant it.

It was the last night at Soul Camp and we had our talent show. I was dreading going home for the first time ever but I knew that when I went home there was work do to and I was committing to myself that I would do whatever it took to have more peace in my life. I remember sitting next to Natalia an instructor at Soul Camp and she told me her life story. She was a police officer and was ready to be promoted to Sergeant and she let it all go to create a life she loved and she has succeeded.

As I cried in my hands that my life was too painful and I didn't want to go home, she told me set your intention and go home and act (take Action). The one action will start the Universe in motion and start to bring you what you need and want. Those words stayed with me and they were my mantra. I went home and the first thing I did was got rid of my 14-year-old truck that broke down every few weeks and for the first time ever bought myself a new car.

I had a lot of money fear at the time and lived paycheck to paycheck but I knew I had to start giving myself things that made me feel worthy and those bold moves of action were a necessary part of my growth. The next thing I released was a lingering 10-year toxic relationship with a man who never was meant for me but fear kept me hanging onto something I believed was better than nothing. Slowly I released five fifteen year friendships with women who were nice but my time with them was over, it was time to attract what I needed in my life so I could be lifted and supported in a way that would heal me.

Later I would also release the job that I was miserable at for 10 years and move from a home that no longer served me into a home with my spiritual boyfriend.

Every time I let go of what no longer served me, something bigger and better came along which gave me the strength and faith to keep shifting out of a life that I was unhappy in to one that I love.

I am now in a place of my life where I feel that I have made so many bold moves, that I have healed enough to a hold space for other women who are ready to shift out of their depleted, exhausting lives to one that feels good and makes them happy. I am holding Goddess Circles for women to have a place to be supported and share their everyday struggles and learn tools in moving through life with more ease. I am in the process of writing a book that I hope will inspire other women.

I come from a difficult childhood where I learned behaviors that kept me a victim for most my life and attracted situations that perpetuated a victim lifestyle. I can say with confidence that no matter where you come from or where you are in your life today, if you are willing to be bold, brave and fierce, you can have a life you love too.

Carol Davies

Canada

Failing to Plan is Planning to Fail

Starting your own business can be a daunting task for many women. I think back to my own experiences in 2007 when I wanted to start a business I could run from my home, leaving me with lots of time to be there for my family as well. I thought it was going to be easy, since I knew I wanted to be a life coach and help other women find their way to a balanced life with a great job they loved, suited to their talents and making great money. Guess what, it wasn't so easy!

I think, as women, we have been trained emotionally and culturally to be the nurturers capable of doing everything and taking a back seat to our own needs. This leads to a set of impossible standards to achieve. Often we morph into overdrive, go around exhausted, nervous, not having enough time for friends, family, or business. Nothing ever seems to get done right, nothing is ever enough. Does this sound like you?

This was me after 6 months of trying to implement a coaching and energy healing practice. I'd read lots of books and took some on-line courses for creating a successful business. I thought I knew exactly what to do, but it wasn't working. I got so down and discouraged. I felt like a big failure. I told everyone things were going great because I thought I would be a great success immediately. I was doing all the "right" things and kept hitting a brick wall. Why wasn't I succeeding? I was a trained business coach with so much enthusiasm and knowledge. So, what was holding me back?

I realized I needed to do some basic energy healing on myself to get to the core of why I was not getting ahead. I am a trained EFT (Emotional Healing Technique) practitioner who uses "tapping" on basic meridians on the upper body to clear emotional blockages. So, I did some basic work on myself. I discovered I was emotionally and mentally holding my "self" from success. I was surprised to find out I "did not feel worthy" because of low self-esteem issues rooted back in my childhood.

I was unconsciously not allowing myself to succeed. I was uncomfortable doing things for myself, such as establishing a successful business. I was doing too much and not asking for help. I got overwhelmed. I thought I could do everything myself. This mind-set was a product of unproductive beliefs instilled in me unknowingly as a child. This realization gave me a big wake-up moment. Once I understood this, I knew I could change my unconscious beliefs and go forward to become the best I could be. I consulted another EFT expert and did a lot of work with her to help me clear through blockages I needed to eliminate. I wasn't able to do that on my own. I was still hiding out in my comfort zone and not taking risks. I was tolerating being in overwhelm and not able to go forward.

Another thing that helped me was to focus on all the strengths I have, not negative aspects. A work colleague once said to me I was the most positive person she knew. I was astounded as I had never seen that view of myself. That colleague never knew what a profound affect her words had on me. It was another "aha" moment in my life.

It took time to figure out what my strengths were, but I took that time. I asked family and former colleagues what they thought my top 3 strengths were. I wrote all their ideas down in a list. I thought long and hard about what I thought I was good at. Then I compared the two lists to choose words that resonated with me, things like: organized, creative, diligent, logical and so on. I also focused on what was my passion in life, what got me fired up and excited. It turned out I liked to help people find a better way to live their lives successfully.

So, what did this mean for me? What kind of business could I start where I would feel excited, of value, focused and successful and make a viable living to support myself? I found out that life coaching was perfect for me. It was a career that formalized all the skills I had done informally in previous jobs where I worked for someone else. Now, I was going to work for myself and I needed to find a way to make that succeed for me with joy and ease. It was going to be a period of my life filled with change and relying on myself. I took several training courses and became a certified life and success coach. Now I was on my way.

Change used to be uncomfortable and scary for me. It's often hard to release "the old" when I haven't met "the new" yet. However, I've learned that I need to let go of the past to get a better life that's aligned with the inner me. Life's about growth, not safety, especially when I am planning things for my business.

Transformation is a constant basis in life. I never used to like change, as it made me feel off base, not cantered in my life. I like to feel safe, but that is not a luxury I could afford when deciding to go into business for myself. I know now how important it is for me to develop strategies to deal successfully with change.

When I was planning my business, I knew big change was on the way. I was going to be responsible for creating a new chapter in my life, not working for someone else. Planning a business called for all MY creativity. It was all good, even though it did not feel like it right then.

I know when something is going to change in my life. I start having odd dreams, my stomach has butterflies, and I feel jumpy. I usually get an intuitive sense that something wonderful is on the way. The tenser I feel, the elder habits I've outgrown start to become attractive again. I want to hold on to what's familiar. I question myself – my thinking, intentions, and ability to make decisions.

I like to plan with logical steps. This activity frees my mental processes from worrying about "what if". It leads me to contemplate the "why not". I hover on the edge between what I know now and what I secretly desire. You can do this too.

I lived with a lot of uncertainty for a while. I experienced self-doubt, that little voice telling me I couldn't possibly start a coaching business, I had never done it before, I didn't have the skills, I didn't have the money and so on. The doubting voices in my head were trying to undermine me to stay in my comfort zone. I used to be happy in my comfort zone, but I couldn't stay there and start a business I loved. I knew I had to break free of my old thoughts and take the steps to go into the unknown.

I deserve to be a success in my life, both personally and in business. When I was starting out as a solo woman entrepreneur, I felt scared and alone. I realized one way to feel less alone is to create strong relationships with other women entrepreneurs. I do this by participating regularly in business network groups in my area or in on-line social media groups such as Facebook and Twitter.

Each one has policies for users that make them unique. Networking with other entrepreneurs does take time and effort. When I went to local networking meetings, I tried out a few to see if they were a good match for me personally and for my business interests. I feel it's better to go to those meetings where I feel inspired, uplifted and making valuable business connections.

The same is true for social media groups. I use Facebook and Twitter as I find the interactions with other people and business owners give me an avenue to promote my business and make good contacts with prospective clients. Try a couple and see how it feels to participate in them. It will take dedication to schedule time to learn about different groups in Facebook and how much time to plan to join in these. Get recommendations from friends and business associates on what groups they find to be valuable. Choose what groups will be a good fit for you and then start out to participate actively.

Ever heard the saying "Failing to plan is planning to fail?" That old but wise adage often rings true when it comes to social media marketing. Creating a detailed, goal-oriented social media strategy is just as important as having a rock-solid business plan. I use Facebook in my on-line marketing by participating in the groups hosted by my local networking groups. I regularly read the posts, "like" posts by other women entrepreneurs and exchange information where I can. I've made a lot of valuable connections through Facebook as well as attracted clients for my services and programs. I schedule time each week to plan the posts I wish to put up, especially when I have special offers or a new program to announce.

Being a woman entrepreneur is a wonderful choice. It will take a lot of work to prepare you for the journey. Have a clear understanding of the lifestyle that YOU want. Be confident to pursue and nurture the kinds of relationships that work for YOU. Renew your commitment to nurture your body, mind and soul. Understand the relationship between self-care and the ability to care for others. Develop a support network as you can't do it all.

Above all, I wish you joy, ease and happiness in becoming a successful woman entrepreneur.

More about Carol Davies M.A., CCP, EFT-Adv.

Ms. Davies is a certified professional coach whose passion is to assist individuals and groups to achieve Better Life Performance. She uses a variety of methods and practices including lifestyle success coaching, EFT (Emotional Freedom Techniques), Matrix Re-imprinting, BSFF (Be Set Free Fast), NLP (neuro-linguistic programming), guided visualizations, mindfulness, meditation, and positive self-talk among others. These help clients resolve issues around personal and professional challenges in their lives.

Having worked abroad for more than twenty years in large international organizations including the United Nations, her considerable management and coaching experience, combined with her recent training and expertise in holistic healing and energy therapies, give her a unique approach. Her extensive work with women entrepreneurs from different cultural backgrounds has given her a deep insight into the diverse ways that people can approach life. She considers the woman her life in context, not just focusing on isolated goals or behaviors.

Together with her clients she helps design strategies for success for them to achieve emotional and work/life balance. Clients learn to manage life's challenges more easily by defining a plan to deal with an issue, breaking it down into manageable components on which to work towards habits of success. For her, this is what makes her work thrilling: Helping women unravel old stories that are running their lives… and create new possibilities, in a moment. She is a well-known writer and speaker who also facilitates seminars and workshops using EFT and Matrix Re-imprinting for issues, such as Weight Loss, Motivation, Lack of confidence, Decision Making, Dealing with Difficult People, Social Phobia/Anxiety, Smoking Cessation, Compulsions, Interview and Presentation Nerves, Phobias, Stress Reduction and other topics upon request. With EFT, you can effectively resolve emotional, physical, and mental distress at the source, often within minutes. By combining her skills of coaching and energy work, Carol can serve and empower others.

Ms. Davies encourages women to take their lives into their own hands. She firmly believes "Happiness is a choice". Be it relationship issues or problems with your health or confusion in your career, her comprehensive approach will help you bring your life into alignment, ensuring that you live a life of balance and happiness. She is the founder of the Passion Motivator Coaching HOPE

http://www.caroldavies.com

Personality Leadership

Cheryl Miller "Sponsor"

Direct Sales Saved Me

"The company I work for today, had the platform, compassion and message I needed to get out of a very painful situation in life."

Despite all we have endured throughout our lives up until this point, we finally feel there is a sliver of a chance that life is about to change for the better. Why would this time be any different than all the rest? We've already learned there is no sense trying because, good is never good enough. Do any of these things sound familiar to you?

Here is my story.

My past circumstances have already shown me I am not supposed to be happy, find true love, live an abundant life that is filled with loving people, amazing family and friends or can just travel the world as I would like to. Nope! I am supposed to endure my pains bravely. While I may feel despondent to life around me, I shall never question its framework because as fate has it, this is the life I deserve. By the time I reach my forties, life had already refined me to believe that despite what my inner womanhood wanted in life, it would never eventuate in my lifetime.

Throughout my childhood, I endured episodes of bullying, molestation, rape, physical and mental abuse and more. Don't get me wrong here, in high school I had some super sweet friends but, ashamed of my life- I never revealed any of this to them. Through the traumas my innocence, self-worth and identity were stripped from me. I longed to fit into a society that hadn't been very accepting of me. Life taught me that I should stop dreaming of a better life because, dreams bring pain. You are not worthy of happiness in life! Somehow, dreaming of a better life feels like a mortal sin. Considering the fact that I had been forced to put the needs of others ahead of my own for as long as I could remember, it was only fair to assume, the future would be the same way.

I married at the tender age of seventeen-not out of love but, more an escape from the life I had been living. With respect to my children and grandchildren, I will not go into details of this next eight years but, I will disclose that by the end of the ninth year of our marriage, I realized that I was tired of being the victim of my circumstances. It was time for me to reclaim my place in life and provide a life for my children that they deserved. I knew it wasn't going to be easy but, I was determined to make things happen. The problem was, I would spend the next twenty some years navigating life uncertain as to how to accomplish all I set out to do.

Over the course of my lifetime thus far, I had held many jobs that ranged from assistant manager in a small convenient store, direct sales rep, plant manager in a small plastics plant, meat cutter in a hog slaughtering plant, all the way to being a nurse aide in a variety of nursing homes. Throughout my employment years, I found the work as a nurse's aide to be the most rewarding for me. I was caring for residents who accepted me as a piece of their family without my enduring abuse from them.

Through this employment, I developed empathy, compassion, acceptance, and most of all that through my own perseverance, life can be rewarding. It was during this time where the universe revealed to me my passion was to help other people and my purpose was to use every ounce of my being to make a difference in the lives of those I encounter. The truth is, we all have dreams and somewhere along the way, I became a dream weaver. My goal was to slide into my grave sideways knowing I had exhausted every ounce of talent and capacity within me for the sake of humanity.

One morning as I was sipping my coffee and hanging out on social media, I came across a post for a new direct sales company. Remembering I had sworn to never do another direct sales company, because they just don't work, I scrolled on. It was too late! The images of those beautiful nails had been ingrained in my subconscious mind and had triggered thoughts in my conscious mind that said, "unlike all those other companies you tried in the past, this company has a product that screams "GIRL TIME" all over it.

Having spent most of my life being abused, raped, beaten, broken and more; I had finally met the man of my dreams and eventually moved in together. We shared five children, none together. After living together for several years, we obtained custody of my first born grandson. Shortly before his second birthday, he was diagnosed with Autism Spectrum Disorder. Sometime after this diagnosis, we decided I would stay home to get him the help he needed. Life was going great, our grandson was thriving, and we were getting married!

Despite all those horrible years of abuse, assault and more; life had finally taken a turn in the right direction. My husband and I married in May of 2009 and was enjoying the new home we had just put in. It was so nice to finally have the life I had only once dreamt of. However, that feeling came to a screeching halt in February, 2010. While we had planned our whole future together, life had different plans. My husband was not only diagnosed with Meniere's disease but, we were told that he had one of the worse cases doctors have ever seen in a man. Determined to overcome the odds, my husband underwent surgery to minimize or stabilize the attacks he was having three to five times a day. The man I had waited all my life to meet, was now confined to a bed.

Somewhere in all of this, I tried to stay positive but, deep inside I could feel all the emotions slowly creeping back in. Refusing to allow my husband to see the pain I was feeling, I would take long showers with the radio on so I could scream to the heavens. My soul ached from the mere thoughts of everything that was transpiring around us yet, there was nothing I could do to control it. I found myself feeling like it didn't matter what I wanted out of life because my true purpose was merely nothing more than always caring for people.

Knowing how much stress had just been added to my full plate, in March of 2012, I jumped back over to that website, paid the enrollment fee and bought me a business. If anything made sense to me, it was the fact that with everything life had placed upon my shoulders, I needed to find an outlet for the sake of my own sanity. Earning an extra income would be helpful considering we were about to embark on a long disability process that would leave us broke.

Having received my new business kit, I was ready to get those parties booked so I could hang out with other women. Over the next couple of days, I could get a few bookings and then it happened. Anxiety consumed me because throughout the years, I was never given time to hang out with friends. Determined to preserve my sanity, I packed up my bags and off to that first party I went. I had the mindset that these women would be so engaged in the beauty of my nail wraps that they wouldn't even realize just how socially awkward I was feeling.

Boy, was I wrong! Thank goodness conference was coming because, I needed to learn from the professionals.

I arrived in Salt Lake City, ready to learn from these amazing ladies; yet, found myself retreating to the corners of my being because again, I do not know how to approach other women, little on to engage in conversation. I never developed the skill sets needed to carry on a conversation in a reciprocating action; little on how to add humor to a statement. Another hard task for me was maintaining acceptable body posture. I had no clue how to hold myself while talking to others face to face. Who the heck had time to focus on smiling or making eye contact while talking when you are just merely trying to survive through the entire ambience of being in a crowded room of women you have never met.

General training session is about to begin! I have claimed my seat at the front table with two of the first ladies to join my team, as well as, my upline/sponsors. I knew I wanted parties, I wasn't sure how to get them, and I wanted a paycheck!

About that time, Belinda Elsworth took the stage. Belinda is a motivational speaker and let me tell you, by the time her first twenty minutes were up, I was ready to catch a flight home because I had parties to book! Over the next few months, I wasn't doing so hot on the parties but, I sure had me a rock star team going! I was up to almost a hundred and fifty girls in my downline and hadn't hit my first anniversary.

Over the next year, I watched these women achieving their goals by hitting top ranks in the company. Sitting in the audience at conference the next year, I remember saying to myself, "I'm going to hit that rank next year!" Well, the next year came and went and there were no new ranks.

Finding myself in tears, I began soul searching. What does this woman have that I don't and how is she able to do all that magic but, I can't? Instantly, I blamed it on my circumstances. She doesn't have to be home caring for two disabled people like I do. Another good one was well, her husband is wealthy so they don't have to worry about not being able to afford food, little on gas to leave the drive way.

As you can recognize, it was my own patterns of self-sabotage that kept coming in my way. It was only me and always only me. Determined to make my little girl time out business work in more ways than one, I began networking with top leaders in my Jamberry company, as well as, consuming as many free training webinars as I could.

Dana Wilde kept telling me to "change my mind and change my life" while Belinda was telling me to "Step into Success."

Little did either of these ladies know I had already bought new shoes and was determined to step into the role of that lady who claimed her spot on stage that first year at conference. What I didn't realize was that I was comparing myself and my journey to the lives of those around me.

Two years later, not only did I wake up but, I WOKE UP!!!!! For the first time in my life, I realized that to have the life I have always dreamt of, I had to make the conscious choice to walk out of the body I once held and claim my spot in this new body. I had to make a mental transformation before anything else would happen. I was no longer a victim of my past, and my past did not define who I am today. I had to own it with intention! I had to conceptualize the fact that I was now steering the ship and it was up to me to adjust the sails. Having always felt like my purpose in life was to take care of people, I never fully embraced that my true life calling was to take care of people. Whilst most are not comfortable sharing their weaknesses, the truth is- everyone has needs, and everyone has a story to tell. Here I was given the opportunity through Jamberry to not only help families in need but, I could help people heal emotionally by sharing their stories through my nail wraps.

Remembering that when tears flow from our eyes, the soul heals. The same is true in that when we tell our stories, we heal from the inside out. Without realizing it until now, my life has been blessed in ways I would have never imagined. Through the grace of my God, my faith has been restored and I am now able to visualize the opportunity he has blessed me with through Jamberry. Today I am changing lives of others by helping them tell their story through my products, or helping them provide an income for their own families by coaching them to their successes.

Through my journey in direct sales I have found that our lives are nothing more than what we make of them. If we allow the negatives in daily life to pierce our spirit and consume our mindset, we will remain a victim for life. The true key to success is measured by your capacity to overcome the obstacles life places in your way. When you change the way you think, your entire life changes and in doing so, you will see yourself impacting lives of others in a positive fashion. If you want something bad enough, you have to have determination, perseverance, and self-discipline and make the conscious choice to never allow yourself to be succumbed to your circumstances again without a fight.

Until then, you are confined to the prison of our mind.

Terry Dika Volchoff

The Truth is Within

As I have walked on this earth, I have had many adventures, but none more important than the inner journeys I have taken to discover who I am, my life's passion and purpose and my innate power to create the life I want and assist others to do the same.

There had always been struggles, there had been signals but I was not prepared for the biggest struggle of my life of not being able to walk or stand for more than 5 minutes at a time. This is what brought me to the ground I stand and move freely on today, this one event in my life.

I had to allow the solutions to come in and through me in ways that were never expected. .... the solutions to all life's problems I found were not out there in the world, in a container, in a workshop or a book nor in another person but in ME, INSIDE me I found how I created my problems and how too uncreated them.

It was me, all me, totally responsible for the outcomes in my life for the reality I live in now and for the reality I occupied when I was stopped in my tracks, prevented from living the physical life I took for granted.

Some of you will find this hard to understand, I was there I didn't fully understand either. I was angry, I felt betrayed by my body and my mind If ever there was a time that I was in over my head it was now and I needed to be strong and I only felt powerless.

I had been doing all the right things. I was meditating, I was positive, teaching meditation to others, I had been in the personal development field for 15yrs. I had always given back; I was doing it all the right way.

Or so I thought!

I had to find a way, I had no choice I would find a way out of this trap, no doctors could help, so I had no choice! The old ways of being positive were not working anymore and so it would seem, I was called on a new journey. I searched, I listened to expert after expert, tell me there was no cure, or this would work and didn't!

I was on a mission! I tried so many things that failed! I would have gone on and on and on until I found the answers until I could walk again and get my life back and I did. And you know what happens when you have this kind of deep conviction inside of you? You know what happens when you decide something? It happens. I kept trusting myself to choose the wrong thing, follow the wrong advice, get worse before I get better, I just kept going until I understood how I had attracted this into my life.

I had no idea! One of my teachers, said it this way! If you knew what your problem was you wouldn't have a problem! Now this may get you riled up, that part of you inside that say's, that's not true, I was the same. But it's true! Time after time, it's true! You see what I found is we have 2 minds and most of us are only in touch with one of them, our conscious mind and it doesn't know all the answers, this is the part of the mind that analyzes, it is your objective or thinking mind. It has no memory, but it triggers memories!

Things started to make sense. I didn't know how I created this, if I did attract this into my life, then it was not my conscious mind the part of me that wanted health, wealth and happiness, the part of me that had so much more to do, it was my unconscious mind the part of my mind that I was unaware of.

This part of the mind that stored my memories! My unconscious mind wanted to be sick? But wait a minute the unconscious mind is also me! The unconscious mind describes itself to a tee! You are not conscious of its power, its treasures or its motives. *The unconscious mind is the storehouse of all memories and past experiences, both those that have been repressed through unresolved life experiences and those that have simply been forgotten and no longer seem important to us.* It's from these memories and experiences that our beliefs, habits, and behaviors and our life results are formed.

Everything we do in life is decided initially by your conscious thought and then referenced or compared to the files of information and memories in the unconscious mind! If the unconscious storage and files have the right memories to line up with your decisions and desires then it's all good, full steam ahead, but if they don't this is when the memories signal fear, and fire you up with physiological sensations signaling this is not a good idea whether in fact it is!

My mind was accessing memories and bringing them to fruition? My body stopped moving forward and until I listened within it would not move forward. So, I set out on a journey, an inner journey into the memories of my unconscious mind!

I was excited, I couldn't wait to get started, the fear of staying where I was so strong, for once fear wouldn't stop me, it would push me forward! On this inner journey, I encountered many parts of myself that held the secrets to my freedom and I began to have a compassionate understanding of myself! This would eventually set me free to walk again and help others find their true-life path and thrive. What you might be thinking did I discover in this inner world of mine?

I found all the memories, thoughts, emotions and decisions and that had brought me to a standstill.

So what was I thinking deep inside my unconscious mind?

How did I lose my footing!

I had to face what was distorting my vision of my life and my part in it!

I found aspects of me that we're POWERLESS, and unable to express what they were thinking or feeling.

Powerless and afraid! Afraid to live fully and move forward in life, afraid to speak, afraid of making a mistake afraid of living. This is what I found, the truth from within! As a child, it was not ok to be me, in fact I had experienced being made wrong so many times that now I was totally efficient at making myself wrong This is not a formula for success. I found so many memories frozen in time of me small, weak and powerless unable to defend myself, unable to feel safe, afraid, unable to move!

And here I was now a grown woman a mother living alone and now I began to understand comprehend what had happened, I was once again unable to move, but now I knew why. Through my inner journey and subsequent trainings, I was educated on the workings of the mind. The power I had within to restore myself to rewrite those stories to grow up the rejected aspect of myself and allow a process of reintegration!

Long ago aspects of me hid, shut down and, decidedly disallowed any power, unpermitted to be! Once they finally got my attention, I was fully resurrected, fully alive again, to enjoy the wonders of life, to not just manage a life but to truly live and thrive again! To allow all of me to be fully expressed for the first time in decades and to walk again.

My body slowly started to mend, each day I became a little more like the woman I remembered! My inward travels to me, to the unexpressed, unacknowledged aspects of me that were hidden were now revealed. Once allowed to have their say they no longer took over my desires but merged from within into wholeness, no longer in conflict, but self-sovereign. When this happens the changes, you want have permanency! I had been returned/reunited to my true form of confidence and strength!

I have travelled to India to meet the most angelic gurus, to the amazon rain forest of Ecuador to drink their ancient medicine and four continents but no journey on earth was as fascinating or life altering as the journeys I have taken into the inner world of my own mind and the mind of my clients.

There I found all the answers, and as I was strategically guided to asked the right questions, I was able to release all of the pent-up emotions and stories and now I could hear the whispers from within guiding me back to the path of health, wealth, happiness and conscious, purposeful living. I had been taught to turn my power off and now I was finally allowed to be me! I was turned on to living! Today I fearlessly take risk after risk to play my part in creating a better world one mind at a time! Terry is a Transformational Catalyst who loves journeying with her clients to the inner realms of their minds to discover what they are thinking and believing and guiding them to unleash their innate genius to transform their lives and influence world change!

Dr. Jo Anne White

Free To Be Me

As a child, when I began writing letters and words, what showed up was mirror writing, which meant that the only way anyone could read what was written on each page was to hold it up to a mirror. Only then, reversed words and letters magically corrected themselves. Great, if your teachers had mirrors handy— unfortunately mine didn't.

That was the first signal that my brain was wired differently, and may or may not be attributed to my left-handedness; the jury is still out. *Mirror writing only occurs in about 1 out of 6500 people*; Leonardo da Vinci being one, although his could have been by choice.

People who mirror write may have 2 language centers: one in each hemisphere of the brain, and these language centers may be connected, which is suggested by some researchers, as a form of heightened intelligence. Other research suggests something entirely different: a neurological problem, dyslexia or something else that needs to be fixed. I chose the first hypothesis so not to berate myself.

From early on, I had to cope with and understand what being atypical was all about. I taught myself how to learn things differently because I discovered that conventional methods of teaching didn't always work for me. Perhaps that's why after I worked in a day camp program with special needs children and 'fell in love' with them, I shifted my college career goals from English Literature to Education and Special Education, yet my journey never stopped there.

I believe that our experiences also guide us and aren't random. A dance injury temporarily debilitated me in my late twenty's, but pressed me to seek out alternative ways of healing to help myself because traditional methods weren't easing the agonizing pain or helping me to sit and walk. I remember a vision/dream I had that was my catalyst to look beyond the medical interventions that weren't offering me relief.

I was resting due to intense pain and feeling sorry for myself, hopeless and alone. I dreamt I was in a white room, lying down on a table, clad in hospital garb, but it was no ordinary hospital. There were celestial beings that looked human-like dressed in white: white gloves, traditional protective white masks over their mouths.

They began working on me and the message I received was that I was going to heal! I woke from the dream/vision, feeling upbeat and hopeful. As strange as it seems, from that moment I knew and believed that I was going to be alright.

Roused by that conviction, my journey to find what would heal me accelerated. What a blessing, whether from my inner guidance or a message from beyond, it moved me forward and I am eternally grateful.

Once I was successfully out of pain and again ambulatory, I wanted to help others heal, grow and transform. Thus, I become certified in different techniques such as energy healing, hypnotherapy, Alexander Technique, Reconnective Healing, Life and Business Coaching and more! This was resilience at work in my life, picking myself back up from a knee and back injury I never thought would heal. Ultimately finding meaning in the circumstances so I could weave them successfully into my business to help other people.

My senses and empathic knowledge are also heightened so that I receive information in many ways which is wonderful now that I understand it as a gift and can rely on that information. I also teach others how to connect more intuitively and psychically, and use the information they've received to their advantage. As a young child, it was all very confusing to me and without a lot of answers. Other messages, outside of the realm of ordinary were my norm, such as heightened perception, acute sensing, knowing things and knowing information about people, yet not knowing how and why I knew—I just did.

Another challenge was my left-handedness; my handwriting was an early source of embarrassment. Nevertheless, I was determined to succeed; giving up was never an option. It often took me longer to learn than others. Even in my graduate statistics course, I taught myself how to solve equations by starting at the answers and working my way backwards to the beginning.

That determination to overcome what I initially saw as flaws and differences in myself that not too many people shared at the time is what pushed me to strive and work even harder. I was resolute about getting ahead and succeeding. There have been times that fear and doubt plagued me with their commanding and insistent tones, often drowning out everything else, including reason! If I had listened attentively to them, I'd never be driving a car, owning my own business, walking, standing and dancing—which I love!

I took on my mother's fear for my safety when I got my auto license. She drilled into me that driving was dangerous with the potential of car crashes and aggressive drivers racing down the roadways. When the time came and I was in the driver's seat, my hands shook and my legs trembled so badly that my right foot couldn't stop bobbing up and down uncontrollably. I couldn't move and just sat there, glued to the seat.

In the windshield, I saw my smashed image in a fatal accident; it wasn't pretty— it was violent and loud. I had to figure out fast, how not to allow my fear to literally stop me from moving ahead and I did. I decided what I wanted to do was far more powerful than the fear. I wanted to drive and had a place to go and a friend to meet and more life to be lived.

From necessity, a way out was born. I had to develop a strategy so I could function and operate and drive a car safely and without the horrible visions. It's a powerful strategy that I teach my clients even now because it works! I still use it myself if the need arises. It's helped change the images in my head from catastrophe to celebration which is resilience at work.

When I look back at some of the challenges I've had (and we all have different ones), I believe my saving grace and what powerfully contributes to my success is my tenacity, perseverance and resilience. I think perseverance is an important habit to adopt. I say habit because it's to be developed with conscious awareness.

Over time it becomes second nature, keeping you steadily on course. You don't waiver, give up or back down, despite difficulties, obstacles, discouragement or even naysayers that tell you no, or try to steer you away from your goal, vision or dream. Instead, you move forward relentlessly toward your goal. If doubts surface, as they sometimes do, I remind myself of the importance of the project at hand and the necessary steps along the way leading me to the finish line; this jumpstarts my energy and enthusiasm.

For me, resilience is the mental and emotional ability to recover quickly from depression, illness, misfortune or something painful unexpectedly showing up in our lives. I've had to work hard at this recently by reframing and seeing the events that showed up in a more positive and meaningful light rather than things falling apart.

Here are three examples:

My car's steering going haywire: Once fixed, I viewed the outcome as creating clear steering in all areas of my life. My furnace going kaput: Replacing it infused me with a new energy source for my life and work. For my recent emails and computer glitches, I chose to envision them as transforming and restructuring just to keep up with my own continuous transformation happening right now!

I'm also guided by my passion; being passionate about the work I do for myself or others is important to me. I'll turn down assignments I feel don't resonate with me. My heart, mind and soul must be engaged in what I do igniting my commitment and passion and keeping it constantly fueled.

Strong values are essential in my work: Being aligned with the job, people and businesses I serve, their vision and message as well as my own messages and values are necessary. I'm grateful for the family values I embraced throughout my life: justice, empathy, helping and respecting others regardless of differences and standing up for my beliefs.

Service has always been front and center for me. First with children with autism and special needs and their families, then teaching undergraduate and graduate students at Temple University, and subsequently as the executive director of an educational, vocational, clinical, residential and community program, and now through coaching and training.

Helping my clients successfully envision and realize their personal, business and spiritual goals and dreams is gratifying. Sharing in their joy, fulfillment and success is a gift I'm blessed with and cherish as a sacred opportunity. Thankfully, the love and necessity of writing wasn't extinguished by my career choices, it was amplified.

Learn more About Dr. Jo Anne White

International Bestselling and Award Winning Author, Certified Professional Coach and Speaker, Dr. Jo Anne White is living her dream of helping others live their dreams and thrive. She's CEO/ Founder of the Power Your Life Network and the Power U Online University: Guiding individuals, families, businesses and professionals to grow and succeed. Dedicated to excellence and service, Jo Anne enhanced her client support as a lead generation expert, image and branding specialist and Energy Healer.

"We can manifest our gifts and talents to fulfill our desires and pressing goals, and make a difference in other's lives," Jo Anne said.

She's also the Executive Director and Host of the popular Power Your Life TV & Radio Shows, and CEO/President of Dr. Jo Anne White Consulting Services, LLC. Featured online and in national and international media outlets: (CNN.com, Good Housekeeping, More, WebMD), Jo Anne's appeared frequently on Radio and Television Networks as NBC, CBS, FOX, and Voice America. Dr. White authored and co-authored numerous books including: Amazon International Bestsellers Keys to Conscious Business Growth, Bully Free, More Heaven: Because Every Child Is Special (Mom's Choice Award for Excellence), Mastering the Art of Success, JOY, and The Self Architect.

Website: http://www.drjoannewhite.com

Website: http://www.poweredbysuccess.biz

Website: www.poweryourlifenetwork.com

Elizabeth Harper

<u>Dancing with the Energy of the Storm</u>

"Letting go of fear and replacing it with trust opened a world of synchronicities that started appearing to me."

There is a saying, "... the calm before the storm," that eerie stillness right before an approaching storm, although this isn't always the truth. Some people can feel it in their bones and some are oblivious. Seldom do warning signs appear when our lives are about to change drastically. I compare it to an unexpected storm in the middle of a calm, beautiful summer's day; catching one off-guard. Some people, fearing the downpour, run for cover and safety and others allow it to cleanse and renew them. Still, others may see it as a beautiful chance to dance in it. Either way, eventually, the rain subsides, gray clouds disappear; the earth is renewed again and so are we.

We go through storms in our lives that seem ominous and the dust may take a little longer to clear out, yet it pushes us in a direction we often need to go; mine came in the summer.

I am a mother of two children working towards a better life and healthy. I don't have any big life plans, other than paying the bills and raising my children the best I can. I painted my nails the night before a minor surgery, anticipating my life would continue as usual. Only, that wasn't the universe's plan; a storm was coming- just for me. The next day I find myself waking up from surgery; hallucinating, fearful, ill and wanting to crawl out of my skin literally, only I cannot run away from myself. I was told these feelings would subside, yet months later, still lingering and growing in intensity, my mind and body felt shattered.

The downpour came; panic attacks, extreme anxiety, depression; thoughts I seldom knew a person could experience, much less myself, and feeling so absolutely, physically sick I cannot eat or sit still. Tidal waves of impending doom overcome me, the same feeling I finally fall asleep to. I found myself in an endless cycle of hopelessness, as I never experienced these physical or emotional reactions before. Lost in my own personal hell, I find myself wishing I could do the little things I found so burdensome before, such as cooking a meal, to be bittersweet. I spend months laying down watching my heartbeat violently in my chest; that is all I can do. My body and mind relentlessly feel this primal fear stuck in a state of hyper vigilance that I cannot control, despite myself trying to rationalize it all.

Trips to the ER with doctors handing out prescription tranquilizers, while turning a deaf ear to my story, only added to my continual state of despair. I become stigmatized as another irrational, weak woman who lacks the common sense to control her body's and mind responses. Knowing this, I feel demoralized, disempowered, vulnerable, and ashamed of myself and take on that burden internally. I hear the nurse remark "She better get that under control!" Those words hung like daggers in the air finally hitting their aim when I was alone in the dark that night. I felt it. Never mind, that a drug induced this agony, a drug for nausea during surgery that also acts as an anti-psychotic. Months pass by in slow motion and I finally realize these medications are making me worse, so I quit suddenly, not realizing the dangers of withdrawal, but that is another story.

I cannot honestly and adequately describe in words how I persevered through that year. I recovered, although I still felt some physical illness, and so did my self-worth when I was hired by the county as a family advocate. I also returned to school to obtain a BS in Psychology so I could eventually help others going through what I had experienced. The last time I attended college we used index cards and microfiche; this was a whole new world. And although I felt my education didn't honestly address issues in real-life, with two classes left to graduate, I am content and hopeful riding up that roller coaster of life.

There are no guarantees in life, one moment, I am experiencing an incredible feeling reaching the highest point of that roller coaster and then comes the descent rushing down and not being able to stop it- that's how illness insidiously rushed back into my life. Instead of choosing to fly back up, I stepped off and just sat terrified in one spot for a long time; fear will do that to you, if you let it.

Despite doing the right things, I was somehow felt punished and basically lost faith in everything. What was the point?

Comprehending that events happen in one's life to change a person's path and sometimes it takes a monumental one was not a realization of mine in that moment. Alternately, I am being re-directed to a higher path that resonates with me, but that is a difficult concept to internalize. I read somewhere that we tend to cling to an idea of reality rather than the reality itself. Taking the path of least resistance, even if it's not what our souls crave, seems easier in a moment of struggle. Fortunately, I finally awakened and knew I had to take my health into my own hands and moved forward.

I became obsessed with that one focus, spending years studying holistic health, mind-body connection; how both are interconnected. I studied online and eventually received a BS in Health and Wellness, became certified as a Holistic Health Practitioner, Life Coach and a Law of Attraction Practitioner. If I could learn anything from this life, it was going to be how to heal myself and others by sharing the tools to empower ourselves. Perhaps I believed that all my training, degrees and certifications would finally solidify my knowledge was something tangible I could hold in my hands that declare "See, now I know the way, I have the proof!". This perfectly illustrates that we don't always know it all and never will. Life is a learning process and I had more to learn.

Although I began helping others, changing my diet and taking supplements, I had spent almost a decade feeling as if I was a disease and not a person. I completely lost my self-identity as a person, a mother, a woman and my power, energy, self-esteem and identity were endlessly and completely wrapped up in a desperation to eradicate myself of any semblance of illness. Yet, the irony was I was directing my energy on eradicating myself of illness and negative thoughts. That is exactly what I was focusing on and creating in my life. I realized most my thoughts and energy were focused on fighting against being sick on many levels. I was focusing on what I did not want; not what I wanted in life. Knowing now we tend to create more of what we focus on in life whether we desire to or not is invaluable.

I felt as if something was missing, although consciously I had no idea what it was. This knowing, in quiet moments, was tugging gently at me to take notice. It's in all of us, believe me. It our Higher Selves, the Universe, our intuition, the name is irrelevant, but I believe we know when something is not quite right. There is more to us than what occurs in our physical bodies. Eventually, it becomes the feeling of knowing and trusting that everything will be alright in our life; easier said than done I know.

There are times when fear will stop us dead in our tracks; fear paralyzes, we are biologically wired that way in real danger, but our conscious mind does not know the difference between false and real fear. When driving we usually know our destinations and how to reach it. We may get lost along the way, must back track, take another route, be temporarily stopped by road blocks, traffic or a storm or just cruise along. It would be pointless and distracting to focus on where we don't want to go because the possibilities are endless. If your only desire is avoiding an accident, then the journey (if there is one) becomes slow and painful. A year from now, in the same place, you will continue to wonder what lies beyond your hesitancies. I lived in this mindset for many years; even though I had tangible reasons, I am and we are so much stronger and capable than we realize.

Most of the time it doesn't take strength to let go of certain ideologies that we hold on to that hold us back. It takes just letting go and opening our eyes to the possibilities that exist all around us. Peel away the layers of fear, self-doubt and insecurity and we have our core ess-ence, the real you that exits without all the false attachments and illusions that hold us in bondage. Focusing our energy and running closer to what makes us feel alive shouldn't be avoided; we might ignore our calling but it doesn't mean it isn't there. Realizing that focusing my energy and intent on raising my vibration so the Universe (call it what you like) receives this intention was a revelation. Everything has energy that vibrates, just at different speeds. Nothing is static, everything changes and energy transforms-it never dies.

I felt an inner calling to learn more about this concept and how we are interconnected with the Earth and the Universe, about women healers and shamans in history, rituals, chakras, herbs, using crystals, all the good stuff I call it. So, I enrolled in a school to learn and practice more. Yes, I know, I'm laughing too, more schooling, but this time I did this for myself and I felt a peace and empowerment like I had not previously known. I am not saying that I miraculously was healed, but my life began to unfold in ways that I had been blind to before. Letting go of fear and replacing it with trust opened a world of opportunities and synchronicities that started appearing to me. I become more acutely aware of events, people and situations in my life happening for a reason and a connectedness to bring about what I needed. Some of these events I honestly have no explanation for other than it was magical. It's also about giving gratitude for what we do have and the people in our lives.

I am still on this journey along with everyone reading these words. We are all interconnected and each of us have our stories to share and inspire one another.

I am ever transforming, learning and evolving as each day brings a new experience. My biggest desire is sharing the transformative insights learned along the way. I am creating courses to empower women into harnessing personal and Universal energy; being more receptive and open to opportunities, synchronicities, and manifestations in life; to become more of who we are and less of who we are not. In doing so, I have begun the next chapter of my life. What will be yours?

Learn more About Elizabeth Harper

Elizabeth J. Harper is a LOA Practitioner who resides in Southern California where she has found her passion for writing and inspiring women through her own life transforming experiences. She is currently writing courses to empower women in finding their authenticity, spirituality, and inner Goddess by connecting to Universal and personal energy. Her education includes a BS in Health and Wellness, Psychology, and Certifications as a Holistic Health Practitioner and Life Coach as well as taking classes in Goddess/women's history and metaphysical studies. She is a passionate activist for environmental and social causes and enjoys traveling, music, being in nature, playing chess, and discovering everyday magic in life.

Website: http://www.elizabethjharperauthor.com

Email: elizabeth@elizabethjharperauthor.com

Debbie Tax

Learning to Walk in the Light

"Anything I wish, I create, I become, I do."

I learned at a very young age that you cannot make someone love you---they either do or they don't. My parents were not parents by choice. They were a couple of young people who double dated with some friends and decided they would try dating each other.

In a short time, they found out they were pregnant. Of course, over 50 years ago, you either got married or you were sent away to have and leave the child elsewhere. My parents opted to get married. They had a love-hate relationship from the beginning...my birth did not change anything.

I remember as a young child the fighting and rage and trying to become as small as possible so that maybe, if I wasn't there they would stop fighting. Neither one of them wanted or were ready to be responsible for another life. They both felt that the other should be the primary caretaker.

So, as it happens in most cases where both parties feel the other is responsible, no one truly took care of me. As a baby, I was left in the foreign country where I was born. My father was deployed and my mother felt abandoned and decided she wanted to go back to the States.

She tried to collect military support and obtain housing, but when the Commanding Officer found out she did not actually have her child with her she was denied those benefits. I got to read this in a letter from the Commanding

Officer of an Arizona Military Base that I found at the time of my mother's death. I still have a copy of the order for my passport showing I was still in Europe while she was in the States. My parents separated after my father was deployed.

My mother eventually moved back to the East Coast to be closer to her family. It was at that time, my Grandmother decided for me to come to the States. I didn't meet my father again until I was a junior in high school. My mother had remarried and divorced during my childhood. I did get a sibling from her second marriage.

I raised my ½ sister from the time she was 6 weeks old, after my mother threw her screaming little naked and soiled body across the room, stating, "I never want to see that again unless it is quiet and clean." I am still here because of that little one—without her I would have given up long ago. My mother had such painful resentment toward my little sister.

My childhood was the stuff of nightmares. I never knew what would set off my mother. Mostly, she was very angry I was alive—sometimes, she just needed a place to release all her frustrations and failures. I always told my sister to close her eyes and sleep, it would all be over when she woke up. I know now that that was the wrong choice, but I thought I was protecting her from seeing the ugliness that was my life. I truly didn't want her to be jaded by our mother's anger. Today I have done a lot of work on myself to get to a place of forgiveness.

Instead, somehow, it made her believe that what happened was trivial or just a dream I made up and that I must have deserved it. As I grew older, I learned to keep the both of us safe and out of harm's way. There was a time when my mother was quite ill, that we had peace.

We never had much, if any, food and I wore the same clothes I had from age 9 to 16, but I always tried to teach her that there were good people and amazing experiences in the world. I was an excellent student and I loved teaching her to read and write...she was and is brilliant and absorbed everything like a little sponge.

During all of this, I was very blessed to have my Grandmother. She was a pure Italian spitfire-- all 4'11" of her. She was also one of the most loving souls I have ever met. She faced all challenges head on with grace and fire. She loved me but was never soft with me. She knew if I was to survive, I would need a backbone, will of steel, and a heart of fire. Grandma never minced words—she told you like it was period. If you didn't agree, that was your problem.

She spent a great deal of time with my Great Grandmother...the two of them loved each other as I have never seen in a mother and daughter—it was almost like they were twins—I firmly believe they were twin souls. Grandma was the local "healer". Both she and Great Grandma knew which herbs, spices, soups, or concoctions were needed to heal any ill. Grandma was a ribbon winning cook and baker. Her chicken corn soup was famous and people would come to the local Firehouse whenever there was a cook-off just to have a bowl of her soup.

This proud, loving woman took care of me. She taught me to cook, clean, and be self-sufficient. She taught me to look for the good in any situation, to work hard, and to always leave a place and/or person better or more than when I got there. She told me the kind of childhood I would have and it would be up to me to determine the color of my soul.

I developed a mantra for me –one that I shared with my children--- Anything I wish, I create, I become, I do—the key is that it is anything I wish......that means whatever I focus on, hold onto, carry anger towards I will manifest. Through the years, this has become quite evident to me—this manifesting people, things, challenges I do Not want---until I realized what I was focusing on was the reason these manifestations occurred. I believe I chose the parents I had to begin that process—to start that journey towards learning unconditional love for myself and my ability to manifest the things I want and need. I am not excusing the behavior in any way just acknowledging that in the end those experiences helped me to create the color of my soul.

I understand how it feels to be lost—to be so alone that no one sees you in the room. I spent the early part of my life trying to please everyone so that someone would see me and love me. I learned that lesson finally that you cannot make someone love you, you must love yourself. I have been so blessed to have 5 amazing children, each one a miracle as I was told I would never have or can carry children. They are such beautiful souls, so full of light and love. They care for each other and will always be there for each other, I am so thankful they chose me to be their Mom. I understand what it means to feel as if there is no hope and yet holding on until there is. I am still learning so much about myself and others.

I love being of service to others—now I do so without the worry of trying to please everyone—honestly, it just makes me happy and brightens the color of my soul. From those dark days, I am learning to walk in the light...to acknowledge my gifts as blessings....to be of service when needed...always encouraging...always believing in and finding the good in others. I have always used my "gifts" to help and heal others—I now do so without hesitation.

I am focusing on manifesting what I truly desire—a spouse that loves me as I am, friends who are not afraid of the things I know and can do, being of service to others in life and business, and being a success using my definition of what that means. Coming from being in the arms of darkness, I am learning to walk in the Light.

Gail Dixon

Living the *I Life*

"There is nothing wrong with taking the best care of yourself first."

I am living life with different pronouns these days. Pronouns might not seem like a big deal to you, but they make all the difference! I haven't always realized how important pronouns can be. Over time, though, it has finally dawned on me that the pronouns I use control the reality and the rhythm of my days. This story chronicles my journey to the life I am leading today – "The I Life."

I am, in all respects, my mother's daughter. My mother Joan, was the cherished only child in a household of five British immigrant adults. In her home, there were heavy expectations about who and how you had to be in life in order to be loved and accepted. Polite, proper, refined and self-contained are all things that come to mind when I think about that family expectation. And oh, my mother was good at it!

As the first born, I was the chief inheritor of this expectation, this way of being. In Joan's world, the world I inherited, the two dominant pronouns were *you* and *they*. There were, of course, the very occasional *he, she*, and *we*, but, make no mistake about it, *you* and *they* reigned supreme. As in "what do you want, what do you need, what is your dream, intention, rule, expectation," for what happens in our relationship? I can still hear my Nanny, my great grandmother and matriarch of my mother's side of the family, telling me as a little girl, "A real lady never expresses a personal wish or desire, because that might infringe on the wish or desire of another." I took that admonition as gospel during my growing up years and well into my adulthood.

Even when asked what I wanted, often my response took the tone of, "whatever you say," or "I don't have a preference." It took me a long time before I questioned how the heck anything would ever get done if the world were made up only of "real ladies!"

So, how did the *you*- and *they*-driven life play out? For starters, I was the ultimate good girl. No smoking, no drinking, no cutting school. Mostly on my best behavior and constantly aware of what the neighbors might think. I pleased my teachers and was a favorite among my friends' parents. I got good grades and participated in all the "right" clubs and extra-curricular activities. Up until high school, I was doing well with living up to the expectations *they* (meaning my parents, grandparents, teachers and any other adult who might be in the picture) had of me.

A few minor things cropped up that tarnished my perfect record. I was severely scalded as a toddler, which left some ugly scars on both my legs and then burned again when I was about seven, leaving a deep and unattractive scar under my left arm. Everything was okay for the most part if I didn't draw attention to the scars. You'd know how well that worked, though, if you could see the photograph of me on the beach with my family – in my long-sleeved sweater in the middle of August! Even so, life went on and I continued to make my life about pleasing *them*. And then I hit a major bump in the road.

When I was a freshman in high school, we discovered that I had a heart arrhythmia. It was a serious enough problem that it severely restricted my activity. I could no longer take PE classes, gave up dance class, limited the distance I could walk and heard that I might never be able to "please a man in that way." Oh, boy, hold the phone! Now I had the whole male gender as a *you* or *them* who would judge me and find me lacking. And, of course, my parents worried about who might love me, who might think of me as unacceptable and all sorts of other awful scenarios. It didn't stop there. The lack of physical activity created some weight issues for me, issues that my mother lamented until the day she died.

Add to that the fact that I am a lesbian and by the time I was 25 chose to acknowledge and live that identity. My parents, some of my siblings, and a great big segment of society had big black check marks next to my name for that one.

I had a lot of compensating to do to make up for these big flaws and compensate I did! Every relationship – work, church, friendship, intimate partnership – all became places where I needed to fade to the background so that the other person or people took precedence. I believed that I needed to constantly earn my space and place in the world by being so loving, giving, capable, competent and unselfish that I was filling others' every need. I believed that I needed to be a bottomless well of giving and I poured out all I had over and over until I had no more to give.

Fortunately, some of the people I worked hard at pleasing were kind, generous and loving and my connection with them helped to replenish the well from time to time. It's a good thing or I'd have collapsed in a heap long ago! Don't get me wrong – my life was not all suffering and sacrifice. In fact, I have considered myself, for the most part, to be fortunate and successful and happy. And, if I stayed focused on everyone else, it worked.

Then along came retirement and suddenly, my day-to-day life was no longer going to be governed by my organization's needs and agenda. I was without a parent, a partner or a child whose needs take precedence over my own. There was a big question looming on the horizon –"Gail, what do YOU want?" Whew! Who knew that saying "I want this," would be so hard? But, I had to say it because there was nobody else whose needs were at the top of list, nobody to fill in the space where I ought to be.

There began the adventure of living the I Life, the life where what is real, true, important and authentic for me is the most important consideration. It took some getting used to – I admit that. At first, I kept looking around for someone or something to consider first, but the weird thing is, nothing quite fit the bill. Try as I might, I couldn't get me out of the center of my life.

I worked hard to blame myself as selfish or inconsiderate, but there was a stubborn truth trying to poke its way into my consciousness – a truth that I could no longer ignore. That when I live the *I Life,* there is more for everyone!

Living in the space where I take responsibility for making sure that my needs are taken care of, that the reservoir of loving, caring and energy get replenished, means that there is always enough. Enough for me, for you, for them. When I live "*The I Life,*" we all win.

Petalyn Albert

THE ART OF FINDING HOME:
Pilgrimage to Belonging after Divorce

"When we belong, we believe. When we separate, we doubt." R. A. Delmonico

If home is where the heart is, then where do we belong after divorce? My pilgrimage to belonging began many years before I met either of my two husbands. Coming to grips with what it means for me to belong (anywhere) has proven to be a priceless if, as in my case, lengthy road. Like so many of us, when I was a child, I used to wonder why everyone else seemed to know where they belonged while I only pretended to.

Every year or two I became the new girl at school, and I didn't easily make friends among kids my own age. I suppose that after a while they became like three dimensional ghosts passing through the screen of my mind. I remember how much I craved conversation and social interaction though. Enjoying meaningful connections with others is still one of my primary values.

A natural curiosity about human nature fueled my fascination with adults and ideas which were by far more interesting than the drudgery of homework or learning to sew. I was pretty sure that other grownups could help me see myself differently and interject more hope about the future. Both my mom and stepdad had their own businesses, and as long as I was living under their roof it was my job to stay home and help out. When I wasn't doing that or avoiding homework, I spent a lot of time alone drawing quietly or writing terrible poetry filled with the lamentations and longings of an only child.

People have often said, "You are so lucky that you got to travel so much." From their perspective, living in eight countries by the time I was twenty was nothing to complain about. Even my parents used to say that living in so many places would provide a richer education than most children were able to have. Therefore, to suggest that it wasn't as romantic as others imagined was seen as being unappreciative of the advantages I had. However, after nearly two decades of such a nomadic lifestyle I felt increasingly isolated. This exacerbated the growing gap I felt between who I was and who I could stand to become; the dream of who I wanted to be when I grew up seemed to be floating farther away from me and anything I could achieve on my own.

As a little girl I intuitively knew that I would need people to help me create the life I wanted, and yet after so many years of living everywhere, and nowhere in particular for very long, I felt connected to no one but my mother. I gradually accepted the belief that I was alone. I wasn't aware of when exactly I began to feel underserving of the life I dreamed of, or of feeling undeserving of feeling alone and underserving. But I felt them nonetheless, and whilst I still lived for the distant dream of another life, the overriding mood of my youth was that of melancholy. Living felt heavy and increasingly hopeless the older I got.

Later I looked back and realized it was impossible for me to cultivate an enduring friendship; to learn how to get passed the humiliation of making mistakes, how to reconcile and trust that a friend would still love me, and how to move forward confidently into many years of making memories that we could one day recall together. And to me, that was the real prize really. Years of collective celebrations and recollections between many people through whom I might have come to understand myself better, and the opportunities to learn how to trust in the positive influence I might one day grow up to have in the world; this is what I craved above all things. A sneak peek into how I might uniquely help to create a happier world, and in a way that allowed me to feel happy as well. This mirroring we seek as children contributes to how we come to know and differentiate ourselves from others, particularly in a world where extraordinary success requires that we know exactly who we are!

Nevertheless, this is also true: The circumstances of my youth and my reaction to them gave me a keen understanding of how we perpetuate isolation without meaning to, and what it's like to really know that we belong. In the movie, I AM NOT YOUR GURU, international life coach Tony Robbins said that if we're going to blame our parents for the bad stuff, we'd better also blame them for the gold we manage to sift out of the shale. You and I have been able to take what we remember as pure crap and turn it into fertilizer. Yup! The fact is, we learned how to do that also from our parents.

Because my early years seemed to take me 180 degrees away from the life I imagined I'd grow up to have, I gained an extraordinary level of insight and intuition about how we humans respond to early impressions and deep conditioning. I also developed an enduring resilience. And I am intimately acquainted with the unconscious behaviors that keep us searching (out there) for the person we might yet become and the life we yearn to have.

Crossing the Thirsty Desert

"Home is where you go when you run out of homes."
John le Carré,

Fast forward now to the question, (after we have been pre-conditioned to look for 'belonging' almost anywhere we can find something resembling it) where do we belong when our marriage ends and everything is different? Your friends have dwindled, the house you live in now feels strange, and the 'someday soon' dreams you suspended for so long in deference to the family you nurtured, have fallen like faded petals cast to the side of the road.

Perhaps you've lost track of the person you used to be or now you scarcely know your own mind without the pronoun we to describe what's in it. (Some women don't have an issue with this, but for many we is a hard habit to break).

Home becomes a desert. Even after a year or two, the lead in your feet often persists. Despite periodic weekends away or yummy cocktails with friends, the acrid routine of dry logistics dominates the landscape. As far as home is concerned, there is no hint of what that might look like, when you will have one, where it might be, or whether it will ever exist again.

Nonetheless, even in this drained and thirsty state, you still yearn to belong. You ache all over for that place you can crawl into, curl up, and just rest. The womb of your bed with a pint of ice-cream, or the arms of a stand-in lover might do. And even then, even if you could do all those things, eventually you must strike out on your own like you want to, though your wounds are still unhealed. You know you must ready yourself to grow up—again—by yourself, although for your-self this time. At this point, nothing could sound lonelier, because you cannot yet see that a happy life awaits you and that it is closer than you think. Indeed it begins by healing the relationship you have with yourself. It's time, in fact, to stop and pick up that beautiful, broken, and neglected beggar you've walked past so often and who's cup you've tossed mere pennies into year after year. I speak to countless women, who are very high earners, but who never get their nails or hair done professionally because on some level they believe that denying themselves that level of personal care would show their husbands they are conscientious and caring wives. For you it may be something else. While this may seem a trifling thing, over time it conditions the mind (and others) to believe that we are, indeed, worth less than we are.

The parts of you that have been tossed out or judged must be reclaimed. This begins the most fulfilling relationship of your life, and it is the only one by which all other relationships will be defined. No one else has the answers you seek. Even if in your inertia all you want is to have someone tell you what to do, and gently say that everything will be alright and that you will – beyond a shadow of a doubt – never die alone, you must be resolved that the only thing that matters right now is rebirth; bringing yourself back to life.

The Mountain between You and Belonging

"...our sense of belonging can never be greater than our level of self-acceptance." Brené Brown,

Do we ever stop to ask ourselves what, precisely, is home? We almost never consider that perhaps it isn't a place, a house, a country, a person or a group of people. Perhaps it isn't even a state of mind.

I've asked hundreds of women what home is for them, and after an few moments to pause and reflect, they all say roughly the same things; my kids, my house, my town, my business, my friends, my art, my husband, my lover. And despite these traditional definitions, they acknowledge having undertones of restlessness; a dull uncertainty offset by cautious self-assurance. And like most of us, they are still searching for Home without actually knowing what it really and truly is; what it ought to be if it could be anything at all. What if home was never meant to be a noun? What if it is actually a verb? What if we belong less to a place or a person than we do to a way of living our life?

This is a question we must each ponder and explore for ourselves. If we do not, the question remains an active unknown, destabilizing the foundation of all our relationships. The subtle dis-ease it creates is emboldened by our predilection for ignoring it and for instant gratification to distract us. All too often we anchor our underdeveloped definition of home to a man who appears to be a good provider, a home that is in the right neighborhood, to people who know the right people, and to the children we hope will fill our gaps of purpose. Alas, we forget that even our kids will leave home one day.

What if long ago, when we were young enough for our brain to absorb anything fast, someone taught us that home is created and maintained through vitality? What if we grew up with the concept that home is a verb rather than a noun? What if we grasped in our bones that while other people, places, and beautiful things richly add to our experience of belonging, they cannot stand in for home because home is an expression, a movement that rises from within.

"How do I do that? How do I begin with me when I feel so tired and weary from my fight?" you may ask. It is understandable that when we feel emotionally fatigued, just imagining the feelings of being truly at home again seems herculean - pure fantasy at best. So how do we begin?

It really does start with a sincere effort to accept the miracle that is you, and it continues best by an attitude of adventure for exploring that miracle. You are a lovingly created cosmic secret that was designed to explode onto the scene of your life, and to develop in partnership with the divine drive that moves within you. You belong to you. You are all yours. You are exquisite. There is no other like you in existence or in history. You were made with love, you were constructed out of love; despite your parents or your current relationship with them. You activate yourself and find the right path by the radical quest of remembering who you are. Exploring the wonder of your labyrinth leads inevitably to the center of true belonging.

In an unhealthy marriage, a prolonged divorce, or the many events along life's way, we can acquire an unconscious idea that it isn't safe to be ourselves, that we are insufficient, or that we need to correct our ideas so that we don't get ahead of ourselves and entertain unrealistic expectation for our lives. We learn to frustrate the natural course of our dreaming from a young age so as to save ourselves from rejection later. But what also happens, without our ever noticing, is we dilute our central (and intuitive) understanding of how to naturally move the mountains in our way. The tragedy is that we learn to doubt our unique capacity to create our very own reality. A reality that is most often unlike that which our loved ones, standing right next to us, can conceive or perceive.

Excavate Your Gifts – the Ones You Didn't Realize You Had

"Nothing can dim the light which shines from within."

— Maya Angelou

The extraordinary and utterly rewarding journey to knowing what it means to genuinely belong to yourself, begins with the first of a thousand steps back in your own direction. One of my favorite excavation tools for helping to repossess our natural and true-self is StrengthsFinders 2.0. It's important to work with an intuitive expert to fully identify how the results apply to you personally, and to develop and use your natural strengths for your benefit in real time. While the evaluation results will make sense, they will not suddenly compel you into the person you want to be. For that you need hands-on guidance. Harry Potter had to go to school to learn how to develop his natural abilities, didn't he? Consider doing the same for your own exceptional talents, because an informed and personally customized approach will get you where you want to go, skyrocket your self-confidence and rapidly clear up the fog of how to be really you again, an inspired and effective leader moving forward.

Although it took your entire life to refine your current opinions of yourself, you can correct them in an extremely short amount of time with the right professional. Why? Because the real you is alive and well and waiting to be released by the right key. The world very much needs – requires – all your gifts, just as they are, and waiting to be polished.

The Speed of Light is yours

"Whenever you see a successful business, someone once made a courageous decision."

— Peter F. Drucker

Many of my own clients come to shorten the time it would otherwise take them to recover well and rebuild their life again after divorce. They are busy, stressed, extremely high achieving, and they don't want to be someone who still feels stuck two years later. Through our work together, they come to profoundly know who they are today, and an unprecedented level of self-confidence follows. Sure these women all came with moxie built in. Moxie and a dogged determination. But smarts and moxie are not the same as confidence or true belonging, and they all knew it. They knew that in order to make that leap with certainty and safety, they must give themselves the opportunity to have what they never allowed themselves to have before. A professional thinking partner.

For some it was a business decision. For others it was for their health, but for all it was a decision not unlike those they make every day. They always look for the return on any investment they make. So for them investing in a coach or mentor was an investment in a future they were determined to have and they were not about to let their own resistance stand in their way.

They made an executive decision on their behalf, the same way they make other decisions that succeed every day. I too have had at least one coach, and as many as three at a time for different areas of my life, ever since I first became a professional coach many years ago. And this has been key to my own personal breakthroughs and public successes. It's what I do for me and for the life I am able to create despite my formative years. Real confidence that stands up to both regular and irregular challenges, and generates momentum (even when others encourage us to quit) rises from cultivating an intimate if objective relationship with ourselves. The price of self-confidence is the courage to take risks on your own behalf.

It takes a bit of courage to look at the parts of ourselves that we discarded, and it takes courage to reclaim them. But we must be willing to welcome them home again. Find a mentor or a coach who is willing to work with you on what you need, and who will be an efficient guide. With the right thinking-partner you will make stunning progress and see the changes you want to see in yourself quickly. The successes that were intended for you from birth will rapidly become your experience.

More Food For Thought

"If you care about what people think about you, you will end up being their slave. Reject and pull your own rope."

— Auliq Ice

The word confidence comes from the Latin word confidere. 'Con', meaning intense force, and 'fidere', meaning in trust. To embody an intense force of trust in oneself is to have personal power like no other. It is the necessary and inevitable reward of knowing who we are and what it truly means to belong. Having such trust in oneself is to possess agency. And this is what it means to belong to yourself. This is Home. This is the seat of our most sacred YES in 3D form. In you!

I have been divorced twice from men I adored. At one time I had thought they each were home for me. And yet, both of those relationships ended. But thanks to my amazing mother, the exact way I grew up, and the mass of valuable experiences I've learned from so far, I became exceptionally resilient, skilled at personal-reinvention, and intensified my first dream to help people get over the hump that holds them back from releasing the marvel that they are. It turns out that 180 degrees away from the life I dreamed of as a child was nary one-degree off course after all. I know what home is for me and I want every person who was once a little person with a big vision to know it also.

True belonging is so much closer than you can easily imagine when you find yourself adrift; when an era or a long love has ended. And yet if left to mere hope or a prayer, it can remain the journey of another thousand miles. That's right, the choice is always and only yours to make. I hope you will choose happiness AND choose you, every time.

"In general, young women seem bent on finding their next husband. I work with women in their 40s and 50s because they have the mettle and the experience to see themselves as whole."

Petalyn Albert

Brenda Pearce

<u>Lovingly Letting You Go</u>

Ours was not a marriage of convenience, or a merger of wealth and privilege. Ours was one of those everyday miracles where one touch leads to spontaneous combustion. Like looking for air and finally taking a breath ... together. Some people call it finding your soul mate. Others call it chemistry, kismet, or fate.

Irrevocably entwining hearts and lives, and taking a leap into the future together. Sandwiched by rituals, families, jobs, responsibilities, and culture, love needs to be strong to stand the pressures of modern day life. It all didn't matter, because my prince had come. The magic of a first touch, the spark of life, had ignited dreams that were slumbering, now come true.

A dreamer and believer in love, I always believed that love is forever, and love can overcome any obstacle. I believed in *for better or worse, for richer or poorer, till death do us part*. I believed in my Religious upbringing, The Sacraments, the commitment. Little did I know that beyond my beliefs, there was something so painful, that there was little to gain. There needn't be any wounds or physical assaults necessary to destroy something so sacred as love and commitment, than the destruction that illness can bring and the need to lovingly let the love of your life go.

Mental illness is around us. Every day we see and hear stories of people who ended it all, sometimes seemingly over nothing at all, although it felt huge to them at the time. Streets are filled with homeless people, who may have been very successful to all accounts at another time in their life. What is it that helps some people overcome life's struggles, yet for others it can do them under? As a nurse, I have dealt with life's triumphs and great tragedies for those whom I have cared for. The birth of a child for some can be such a great joy and for others, just another mouth to feed.

Watching a vital person succumb to the ravages of dementia and cognitive decline is truly a tragedy that makes me cry inside. Their loved one bleeds with coming to terms that their spouse no longer recognizes them. Those situations, as hard as they are, were part of the job I could walk away from. However, coming home to a situation that was my life – the life filled with a spouse's delusions, paranoia and pain – was so painful and inescapable. To watch our beautiful children hide in their rooms to escape the irrational parent, robbed us all of the life I and my husband dreamed of when we conceived them. It was frustrating, to say the least, to awaken in the middle of the night to an accusatory call from a loved husband who believed I wasn't home in bed, when in reality, I was trying to get my precious sleep so as to get up and go to work. Awakened and worried for the remainder of the night, I spent countless nights crying.

Mental illness touches so many, many lives throughout the world. In this time, when life should be so much "easier," more and more mental anguish is present. We have fast food, social media and advanced communication tools, fuel efficient cars, warm homes and many luxuries in our lives that even 20 years ago did not exist. Why? Why do lives have to be ripped apart so much by it? Why do families need to succumb to divorce and despair because of it? Why do people need to walk around in physical, mental and emotional pain? Pain so real and debilitating that even modern medical science, to its best efforts, cannot treat or cure? Why? Why? Why?

Why did the wonderful, magical man that I hitched my star on, succumb to the ravages? He was cycling every six years into a deeper spiral – his new normal – always lower than the last. The man I deeply loved, honored and slowly lost, and lost respect for due to the frustrations, the bad thoughts and decisions. Still I knew that he couldn't help it. Trying so hard to hang on, and hold on and keep on keeping on.

Was our life, our marriage, our family so difficult that he felt it necessary to hide into false thoughts and beliefs? To mentally check out to a world so very different than the reality of what it was. Normal. Two working parents and three beautiful children. A lovely home in the country, dogs, birds and cats. To all intents and purposes the dream!

Many times I was hurt as I watched my husband not express himself or share his thoughts. Yet when he did, it was as if the door opened to an entirely different perspective that was deep and dark and yucky. Still I was living with a person who could not express himself, or when he did, it ended up in arguments and yelling and screaming. Who was crazier, the person with the problem or the person dealing with it? Sometimes I would think that I was the crazy one for even trying to live with it, trying to get my spouse to deal with it or even understand that his beliefs were not correct, but real to him. Trying to justify why his thoughts were not correct and trying to get him to shed wrong thinking that was really not of the collective consciousness of what the rest of us were living.

I couldn't love him enough, do enough or be enough to make him better. In the end it was a process of trying and surviving in a web of lies & delusions. Our life was not filled with joy at the end of 26 years of marriage. We never celebrated our Silver Anniversary as we were actually going through the throes of divorce at what should have been a happy time of life, a time of celebrating with friends and family, of getting through the difficult years. In trying to hold it together for so long, to protect and create a facade of a family, trying to hold it together out of desperation of maintaining a family for the children, it became increasingly impossible to keep honoring vows. Keeping a memory of young love and the spark that ignited this inferno.

Mental illness ravages lives, creates looks of suspicion. Casts suspicion. Is he/she taking their meds? Maintaining their appointments? Following through on the doctor's recommendations? Is there a better medication, or cocktail? Is there a specialist? Is hospitalization needed, will it be accepted? Will the doctor look at the marriage and the spouse with judgment? How to cope with the sideways looks, the doubts, the fears, the uncertainties? What is the underlying cause of this illness?

If there is a cause, there must be a cure!

After the last hospitalization that occurred within the marriage, I remember one poignant moment. He had been home for a few days and suddenly got up and left. No word. Just left through the back stairs and took off. I remember hearing the door close and went to follow, and found a note on the floor. It had obviously fallen out of a pocket, or did it? It was a note written by a fellow inpatient at the time who I had met during a visit with family one Sunday afternoon. She was very disheveled and obviously was in for some severe psychosis. She had flight of thought and seemed to be throwing herself verbally at every male. What did it, for me, were the words on the note, written by her and inviting my husband to leave me and take up with her and the promises she made to him including her phone number and address. Did he act on this? Had anything happened during the hospitalization to help him gain insight, or was it another futile ruse into the entrapment of illness?

Will they recover? Will life get better? Will this be a phase that will pass? When to pull the plug? How much can I endure? How much can he endure? How much can we endure? Is it better to stay in the marriage and not have to worry about custody issues, spousal support, lawyers? To struggle with new ways of getting him help? Will he cooperate? Does he understand? Will he think less of me for going about behind his back to get him help? Not telling others about what is going on, so they don't look at you differently, or think of you and your family differently. So they don't look at your spouse differently. Who can you trust, where can you go? Will your Church family be able to help? Once the label of the illness is exposed, what will people think? How will people treat your children? Will this hold your children back from living their fullest life experience? Will they continue to love and respect their father? Will they feel loved?

The myriad of issues that have run through my mind in my marriage have now quietened out of the marriage. It took time though. Now I seek to assist those who have lived through the journey, to know that the pain of love hurts. To watch someone loved and beloved journey a different dimension than what we perceive to be ordinary and every day.

I remember it was after the event of finding the note, realizing that the marriage was killed in that moment. What was I hanging on for so tightly? I was tired, a wreck and now I had to survive. It was in reaching out for support that a friend emailed me a Prayer of Release, which I have included at the end of this chapter. It was a prayer asking for the chords, chains, contracts and obligations to be severed once and for all and for God, his Angels and Archangels to guide and support me, and that I was not alone and was loved. This situation was over and now would be released.

I do know that when one turns to God and asks with all their heart, God delivers the answers we need. For me it was that prayer. However, I do since know that when we seek that work, Archangel Michael stands ever ready with his sword to sever through those connections that no longer serve us. The results may not automatically occur, but you will start to see the effects of that plea take shape and form. Do not despair, but believe without attachment to an immediate result, and when you relax into the knowing that the process is in motion, it will be done for the highest good of all parties.

My husband, of his own accord, walked out of our home, our family, our heart May 10, 2010. He painlessly arranged for a place to live, and on Mother's Day

Weekend of that year left us for his new life and journey alone. Leaving us to heal, pack and leave into our own futures. The circle closed one person closer, snuggling our family stronger from five to four. Safe in knowing the nights of confusion, upset and pain were over.

Into the future I go, hand in hand with the fruits of our marriage. Rebuilding, rebranding, re-creating ourselves knowing that when he left, he took a piece of each of our hearts with him, and those pieces over time have been lovingly let go. His thoughts unchanged, and so tattered have been released. No healthy person can continue to deal with the innuendos, even casually.

The practice of the Prayer of Release and finding the benefits of Reiki and subsequently other connections of higher consciousness, have helped me to endure and heal. I found my voice and am now speaking out in many amazing ways. During the final years of the marriage, I found the human potential world, and understood that what we think about we bring about. I became a telesummit junkie. My drug of choice was listening to various seminars by people, who experienced their own difficulties, and the truths that transformed them to living peacefully and at their fullest potential. This was my therapy, and I drank in each technique. I worked on doing EFT (Emotional Freedom Technique) from the free manual I downloaded online. I learned Reiki. The feel of Universal Life Force flowing through me consciously enlivened me. I worked on myself and others, as I stepped out of the way.

Like a jump start from another car battery to my own, elevating my personal view of the world to greater possibilities has been the manna my heart was searching for during and now beyond the marriage. Since the divorce, I have developed outward outlets of expression. Finding my voice and helping others through the sharing of words, wisdom, and the wisdom of others whom I held dear during my telesummit junkie years, has led to great connections, opportunity and directions I never dreamed possible.

I have even hosted a telesummit series! Yes! It was a giving back to all those who had filled my cup of life, that I was able to host them in grateful thanks. I now host a broadcasting network online, allowing a space for others to house their podcasts. I am also in the process of setting up online radio to further broadcast those transformational podcasts in other forms of enlightenment. Hoping and helping those out there, like me, to find the answers their hearts and minds are looking for. Creating community to embrace and know that you can live a life of value, non-judgmentally. My hope is that you do not feel alone, no matter what your story is. I do know that what does not serve you is painful, and that lovingly letting it go may open the door to the rest of your life.

*The views expressed are that of the author, and based on her true life experiences and do not reflect those of the co-authors of this book.

Releasing Agreement Prayer (Use cautiously, it is very powerful.)

I call upon Jesus Christ,
Lord Sananda and Divine Mother
To cancel, release and dissolve,
Any contracts, agreements, commitments,
Exchanges, trades, or relationships
That I may have made at any time
In my multidimensional existence
Which are limiting my Wholeness in any way.
These commitments, contracts, trades
Exchanges, agreements and relationships
Are now dissolved, released, cancelled, let go,
Made null and void on every level
Of my multidimensional existence.
In the name and through the power of Jesus Christ,
In the name and in the power of Divine Mother,
In the name and in the power of Lord Sananda,
I know that I am free.
All frameworks, structures, circuitry,
And multidimensional matrices
That have developed as a result
Of these now canceled contracts
Are now dissolved, collapsed, let go,
Released on every level of my energy field now,
And I am opening fully in Wholeness of Divine Love,
Aligning with Wholeness of Divine Truth,
Allowing Wholeness of Divine Grace,
Thank you God, and So It IS.

Learn More about Brenda Pearce

Brenda Pearce (Canada) is a Registered Nurse, author, artist, broadcaster, speaker, teacher, CEO E Factor Live Broadcasting. She is also co-producer of The Breast Show In Town, which is raising awareness that "Breast Cancer Is Preventable" You can find out more by visiting www.breastshowintown.ca along with Holistic Hot Talk Media www.holistichottalk.com

Facebook: www.facebook.com/efactorbrendapearce

Amazon Author Page http://www.amazon.com/-/e/B00KPQGFVW

My Free Gift To You.. Visit www.yourreikibreakthrough.com

Rebecca Leonardes

The Power of I Am

I was reminded recently that two most powerful words in the human language are "I AM". These words are so incredible because whatever words you place after them will begin to manifest into reality. When you stop to consider this for a minute or two you become aware of the true power of your mind. As I continue to learn so much from my family, friends and mentors I am certain that the things I think about, the emotions that I exude and the belief system that I carry with me are responsible for the people that I attract into my life and for the experiences that I'm having.

I am a very grateful person. I have great relationships with the people I know and I have a career that lights me up and sets my soul on fire. I spend my professional life educating people on integrative health. I have the honor of speaking in front of audiences of varying sizes (sometimes just one on one) about the options that exist to take their health and that of their loved ones to all time high. I support people in reaching new goals and align myself with them as they discover the powerful ways they can live an optimal life. The unique thing about this is that I do not have a health background. No formal education.

In fact, I didn't take a single class in my university career that even came close to the topic of health. At one point, I assumed I would never be successful in my new professional endeavors. I let the fear of being "found out" or the fear of "not being enough", "not knowing enough" limit what I knew in my heart I could do. You see I had a reached a pivot point in my life where I knew beyond the shadow of a doubt that things needed to change. We all have a pivot point. Some of us will embrace it and others will allow the fear of change and uncertainty to dictate what we do next.

My pivot point came in September of 2011. I *gave birth to my daughter* Gabriella and in that same month my *mother was diagnosed with cancer*. Either one of those events was sure to have a profound effect on who I was as a person but the combination of the two have turned out to be the most significant events in my life in terms of inspiring change. I had beautiful support all around me. I have a wonderful husband and two incredible stepsons.

My network of friends and family is outstanding and I knew that relying on them would be a must as I navigated through a whole host of emotions but more importantly I recognized that I had reached a point in my life where I was going to need to dig deep. I needed to re-evaluate what was important to me and allow myself to evolve into a new version of myself. I started to recognized small moments where things just didn't feel "right". Let me give an example: the thought of returning to work after my maternity leave was something that brought about the highest level of anxiety I had ever experienced before. I would sweat, feel nauseous and my heart would ache.

Originally, I thought it must be exactly what every new mom goes through but as I allowed myself to sink deeper into the possibility of not returning to that line of work; which including a lot of travel. I began to feel happy and relaxed before it was even a reality. The job that had once been a coveted role in my life no longer had the same meaning. Despite having worked so hard to attain the position I had, the importance of it seemed to vanish.

This is one example but there are many where I let myself just listen to my heart without judgement. I allowed myself to follow something new. I won't lie and say I didn't worry about what everyone would think but I knew the people I surrounded myself with would soon see my "why" which fueled the change.

So, I began dabbling in holistic health research. I felt excited. I felt strong and I felt like I had the heart to share what I knew even if I did not have a degree hanging on the wall that confirmed I knew what I was talking about. The more I learned the more I became hungry for additional information. Nutrition, exercise, integrative medicine, alternative therapies, new age modalities…. I couldn't get enough. I was very aware that I had landed in a space where I was meant to be.

Now, how could I translate that into a lifestyle and career that contributes in every way including financially to my family? This would be the key question to solve, but before long the concept of manifestation began to show me what it is capable of.

Inspired by my mom and my daughter I stepped out of my comfort zone and signed up for some holistic health programs as a participant. This took some serious encouraging from my husband who believed in me long before I believed in myself. This is where I began to meet the like-minded souls who have become such an integral part of my life. I realized through the encouragement I received, that what I truly desired was empowerment. My mom's illness and the birth of my daughter both put me in a position where I felt I had lost control. I didn't trust myself enough to know what to do next. I was seeking the opportunity to feel like I had regained some of that control. I was looking for options and to solve the question I had about whether there was a better way of living.

I knew there would be no magic bullet but I also knew that having a toolkit full of options was something I needed and wanted. In giving myself permission to explore the unknown I found the lifestyle, the people and the experiences that gave me that power source. I still search for answers on many things but the difference now is that I have equipped myself with the resources to find what I need. Now I am the person who helps others identify what life changes are necessary for them to regain their power and live an optimal life. I am without the formal education, yes. However, I am relatable, compassionate and vibrant. I share what I know to inspire others to find their source of power. I believe in the work I do because I've witnessed the profound effect it has had on me and my family.

I continue to attract abundance into my life through the work I love, and the way my family and I live our lives. I have lost a few people along the way though too. Not everyone was ready to see the evolved version of me. They were comfortable with the old me and what I've learned in that process is that our paths are not meant to be perfectly aligned with others for our entire life. Our paths will cross and run parallel from time to time and the rest of the time it is necessary to just let go. I pride myself on dedicating a lot of time on my work because it fills me up. I dedicate a lot of time to taking care of myself because it fills me up.

It is only in taking care of yourself that you can take care of others. My mentor has always reminded me to fill my own cup first so that I can pour myself into others. I recommend it to everyone. I am a grateful person. I am grateful that five years after diagnosis I still have my mom. She is an advocate for holistic health now too and believes in the power of proactive healthcare. I am grateful for my daughter who in her short life has taught me everything about priorities.

The power of those two little words is beyond measure. Just listen when you hear them...what follows next is whatever you make it to be. Be amazing. I am.

Artists on Call

Artist development through community contribution

www.artistsoncall.org
artistsoncall1@gmail.com
PH: 740.815.8842

Nikki Fleming

Every Child is an Artist

John Lennon is quoted as saying "Every child is an artist until he's told he's not an artist."

As a little girl, I found countless hours of pleasure making up and staging shows with my younger sister Lori in a tiny little white wooden shed in our backyard. I don't recall what we did in our original little made up shows, but what I do remember is that I had fun...tons of fun!

Lori and I worked for what seemed like forever to clean up that little shed to make it presentable for our very special audiences – our neighbors. After we readied our little "theater," we practiced like crazy and then canvassed the neighborhood – walking door-to-door up and down our block, asking our neighbors to purchase tickets to attend our shows. Our wonderful neighbors were always so gracious to us, as we were always knocking on their doors for something. You see, we not only staged shows, we also made and sold potholders too. Every neighbor opened their door with a smile and always welcomed us – and most made a purchase or two. Looking back at those days, I chuckle to think what must have been going through their minds as they saw my little sister and me coming up their walks every other week.

Looking back on these days, Lori and I were little entrepreneurs. Who knew?! We surely didn't at the time, as that word wasn't something we ever heard in those days. In fact, we didn't think our future could hold anything outside of being wives and moms when we grew up. Now, I am not saying there is anything wrong with that – it's just that a working profession of any type wasn't something ever discussed in our home when we were growing up. We were just happy little girls having a great time doing things we loved to do – never thinking there could be a future in this somewhere down the line.

Fast-forward nearly 50 years later and my life feels as though it's coming full circle. To explain, this past year, I founded a new handcraft business featuring Swarovski Elements jewelry and accessories known as "Nikki Nakks" and a nonprofit organization that supports artistry and the community alike called "Artists On Call." With that, I am now again staging shows and selling my wares, though my shows and the scope of my wares have grown exponentially since those days in my backyard so long ago. In fact, the beautiful historic Capitol Theater in Wheeling, WV and other wonderful venues have provided me with a stage and my wares have been making their way across the country – to even being included in gift bags for the Emmy's and the Golden Globes.

With my ventures of today, I am most certainly having the time of my life – doing what I love and helping others to do the same. What I can also tell you is that it took me nearly 50 years to get to this point. Why you ask? Well…

My dad Nick was a professional musician and my mom Sandy is a very talented handcraft artist/seamstress/decorator. I am quite blessed in that I received the love for music from my father and my love of handmade/visual arts from my mother. With respect to my dad and his music, he learned to play the accordion in his early teens and, in turn, started his own band while still in high school. He played music throughout our home area of the Ohio Valley from the 1950's until his passing in 2016. He and his music were very well known and, as a young girl, I looked to him as the authority on all things music. Around the age of 10, I started asking my dad if I could sing with his band. I wanted so badly to sing with him but every time I'd ask, he'd tell me no – always saying people would say the only reason I was up on the stage singing was because I was his daughter. Now…as a young girl, you might imagine what that said to me – that I just wasn't good enough.

No matter how many times my dad said no to me, my passion and love for music/performance never waned. In fact, when I was in 5th grade, I started singing professionally with my first group – a trio of girls. We sang for many hometown parent club meetings and our classmates' parties. I loved singing with those girls and our time together formed the basis of my love of singing harmony.

As a freshman in high school, I earned the spot to sing my first solo in our school's minstrel show. I was so nervous but so very excited to sing! After the show, I couldn't wait to ask my dad what he thought of my performance, which I did. His answer - "typical high school girl." He also told me that if I had to ask how I did, then I could have done better. I was crushed to say the least. Again, my young mind thought – I wasn't good enough.

There are those of you who might say my dad was attempting to inspire me to work harder in order to make me better. There are also those of you who might see it from my young-mind perspective – I just wasn't good enough and perhaps never would or could be. I'm sad to say the thought of never being good enough has subsequently plagued me throughout my life - in nearly every aspect of my life.

My mom, on the other hand, really didn't have much input into my musical journey. She left that aspect to my dad. She's always joked that she's tone deaf. I'm not so sure that's the case, but either way, my mom deferred to my dad in all things music. I was obviously looking for some encouragement on that front, however I didn't feel I got that. Now, none of this is to lay blame anywhere. It simply provides the background as to how my confidence could have been lacking.

When I was 25 years old, my mom and dad divorced. At that time, I was already a wife and a mother (two toddler boys) and their separation was the awakening in me that my parents were just human beings too – with shortcomings just like everyone else – but always just doing the best they could. I also began to question a lot of things in my own life – including my musical talents. In turn, I sought the assistance of a vocal coach, who did encourage me, and thus my journey back into performance began. I joined a local band for a few years, starred in many local musical theater shows and even started my own band in 1990.

I have been on stage several times at Jamboree In the Hills, the Superbowl of Country Music, performed as a backup singer for Bobby Vinton and have sung in Nashville, TN during the CMA festival. Through the course of these wonderful opportunities, there was still that little nagging voice inside of me that kept telling me I still wasn't good enough. I always loved being there, but just never felt worthy. This all changed in the latter part of 2015.

This past year, for whatever reason, I had an epiphany – at least one for me. I came to realize that we can only please ourselves. Yes, I know we hear this all the time – that we can't please everyone, but I couldn't seem to even please myself. I was constantly comparing everything I did to a standard that probably nobody could ever achieve. And, especially with music and art in general, it's very subjective. Everyone has an opinion. But really, whose opinion is the right one?

One day I woke up and realized it just didn't matter what "everyone else" thought. The main thing was I needed to please myself in my performances – be true and always share from my heart. I may hit a sour note from time to time, but I ALWAYS sing from my heart. For me, that's what's most important. I can say the same thing about everything I do. I may not be the best at it, but I always attempt to do the best I can do in completing it.

Until this past year, I would never have called myself an artist, but that's exactly what I am! I finally found my voice, so to speak, and I have been so excited about doing so, that I want to help others do the same. Thus, the birth of the nonprofit I founded. "Artists On Call" is truly my calling in life – and my passion.

"Artists On Call" is basically a non-profit artist agency. We have artists of all types on our juried roster. Our mission is artist development through community contribution and we are organized to partner with anyone in need. I KNOW God put this wonderful organization in my heart and mind, as it's a way to pool all of my artistic endeavors into one single focus – and, the BEST PART is I get to help other artists AND the community as well. It's truly a win-win for all! Through this organization, I hope to encourage other artists along in their journey – have them understand that they CAN achieve their dreams.

All of this brings me right back to my opening statement with the quote by John Lennon. My hope is that nobody lives their lives in question as to whether they are an artist or not. We are ALL artists and it's my every intention through "Artists On Call" that this becomes the normal way of thinking in moving forward.

By Nikki Fleming

Learn More about Nikki Fleming "Nikki Naks"

Nikki Fleming is a professional artist, an entrepreneur, the founder of a nonprofit artists' organization and a 1st-time published author from Ohio. Nikki is best known for her many years of musical performances in a variety of venues across the Ohio Valley. She was a regular performer on the WWVA's Jamboree USA (Wheeling, WV), the lead singer of her own band "Nik of Time" and a backup singer for Bobby Vinton. Nikki also appeared many times on the stage of the "Superbowl of Country Music" – Jamboree In the Hills – and has held leading roles in a variety of local musical theater productions, including: "Nunsense," "Li'l Abner," "Little Shop of Horrors," "Oklahoma," and "Wizard of Oz."

Nikki's most recent accomplishments include the founding of her own handcrafted Swarovski Elements jewelry and accessories line – (Nikki Nakks, www.nikkinakks.com) - and a nonprofit organization that supports artists and the community alike called "Artists On Call" (www.artistsoncall.org). "Artists On Call" is Nikki's passion and calling in life – a way in which artists of all types can become all they wish to be in conjunction with service to their communities.

Beverly Ramsay

True Love & Quilting

I am the type of person who tries to find the good in everyone and every situation. I know that sounds cliché but I truly believe I am an optimistic person at heart. I grew up living next door to my Grandma, who was my Mom's Mom. She was the greatest person that I have ever known. She worked hard all her life and she taught me so many things about life.

I was young, but I never missed a story or recipe that she told me. She was such an amazing woman and I know that I get my kindness and love of life from her. She passed away when I was a senior in high school. Oh, how I wish she was still here now that I am an adult so she could see how she molded me into the woman I am today.

Today, I can extend the love I have in my heart, the optimism I inherited from a loving family and the dreams I have for my future, into a hobby; I love to quilt. Quilting is what makes me come alive.

My parents were the greatest. Yes, I know that everyone thinks that, but I was truly blessed with a mommy who loved me no matter what and my daddy who loved me even more. My mom was a stay at home mom and my dad worked so very hard to make sure our family had everything we needed. My parents were married for 54 years.

They taught me what true love is. My mommy passed away going on 5 years now and she was not only a fabulous Mom, but she was my best friend. When she died, it was the worst thing that has ever happened to me in my life. I think about her each day and I miss her sweet smile, her friendship and her never ending love. I am still blessed to have my Daddy. He is the sweetest man and I love him to death. I see him almost every day and if I don't I at least talk to him. He will always be my first love.

I do have one older brother who of course tormented me to death and a sister who was a good bit younger than me. My brother and I were always close and had great times growing up. My sister, being so much younger, but the time I was a teenager, I didn't want much to do with her. I do regret that now that I am older. But we are still a very close family that talks to each other as often as we can, and we see each other when we can.

I had a lot of friends growing up and I was very spoiled and so very loved. Many of my friends have not left the small town we grew up in either. It is a very small town with no street lights and very few street signs because we had "the loop". It is one continuous loop around the main street in town that everyone just rode around for fun. It was great. No worries about being out after dark or being by yourself because everyone knew you or your family.

I met the most amazing man in 1979. I knew the first time I met him that I wanted to spend the rest of my life with him. We have been married for 34 years. He is such a hard worker and wonderful, loving man. He has given me the most amazing life. These have been the absolute best years of my life. He has always been my rock, my love and the most wonderful father to our two girls. My oldest daughter, Jess lives in NYC. She has been there for 10 years now. She went there for grad school and she never left. She is a true New Yorker now.

I am so proud of her. She is a very successful woman. Strong and independent and talented in so many ways. My other daughter Alison, lives in Savannah. She moved there 8 years ago to pursue a career teaching deaf children. She now teaches 5th grade special needs children. She was Teacher of the Year in her county this past year. I am so proud of her and all that she does inside the class and out.

She met and married her husband Ross 4 years ago. He is the love of her life and we think of him as our son. As you can tell, I am proud of my family. My daughters and my husband have been and are the single most important people in my life.

Being a mother has been the highlight of my entire life. I am so proud of the strong, independent and loving women they are today.

I have never been one to sit around and do nothing. I have had a few jobs that I didn't like, but I still did them to the best of my ability. I have had jobs that I loved. I was the owner of a children's and women's consignment Shoppe in my small town for 15 years. In those years, I have met some interesting and wonderful people who have changed my life by just knowing them and I have made deep and lasting friendships. I am now a pharmacy technician. It is a very challenging job and my friends there are fabulous.

Quilting!!!!!! My love of quilts started long ago when I was quite a bit younger. I have done a lot of crafting in my day but the first time I took a quilting class, I was hooked. It was in August of 2001 and I have been quilting ever since. I think it is kind of a therapy.

Quilts are like life, I would say. The different patches can represent different times in life.

I get lost in time when I am working on a quilt. I have made numerous quilts, probably 200 or more. Belonging to a small quilt group has been amazing. There are women of all ages there who have taught me not only how to improve my quilting, but about life. Sitting around a quilt, quilting, you can learn about the "old days" as they call them. I think sometimes I should have been born back then. I have a love of old junk and I treasure keepsakes from my Grandma and my Mommy. They are irreplaceable to me.

Every day I get up I am so ready to face the day with all the gusto I can. I try to plan each day to include my morning walk to clear my head for the day. I am an early riser so I get things done early. Did I mention I am a serious coffee drinker? Yes, it's true. You can ask anyone who knows me that I have a love of coffee.

What I want people to understand is that each day is a gift that we are given. We can choose to be happy, sad or grumpy. Whatever you want you can get out of it. I just know that I start everyday happy knowing that I have the love of my family and that I can do anything if I try. As I get older, I realize that I am not good at everything, heck I am bad at some things, but I love to at least give it a shot and see what happens. It's like a recipe. You add all the good ingredients and hope it turns out, but if it doesn't, make some adjustments and try it again.

Remember, you are blessed to be alive and that you are who you are because you have been molded by all the adventures, sorrows, joys and the people you meet every day. Just listen and open you heart and see what happens.

Love life and sparkle when you can!

LEARN MORE ABOUT BEVERLY RAMSAY

I have been a lifelong resident of a small town in Shadyside, Ohio. I have always been an artisan. Growing up, I was surrounded by creative family member, and loved learning new techniques from a very young age. I love cook, craft, read, and most of all quilt. As a quilt artist and avid crafter, I have spent the greater part of my life mastering traditional textile arts and immersing myself in a dynamic, vibrant community of creative professional

I have filled many shoes in my life. I have been a sales rep for Elizabeth Arden, a paralegal, a bank teller, sales person in home interiors, a sole owner of a children's consignment shop for 15 years, and now a certified pharmacy technician and now an author. But most of all I have been a wife and mother to the most amazing husband and daughters. It has been the best thing ever in my life. I am also a self -taught quilter who never stops learning, I began quilting in 2001 and am a founding member of a local quilt group. I travel the east coast throughout the year attending retreats, lectures and quilt venues. I have made countless charity quilts and fundraising events over the years with my quilting friends.

But most of all I am proud of my family. My husband Randy (Buck) and I have been married for 34 years. He is the absolute love of my life. He has always encouraged me to do whatever I wanted and the love and support he gives me is endless and amazing. My oldest Daughter, Jessica, has lived in NYC for 10 years now. She is an amazing woman. She is works for Spotify and is a DJ and fabulous artist. My youngest daughter Alison lives in Savannah with her husband Ross. She teaches special need children and is a fantastic teacher. She is an avid crafter and a fantastic gardener. So, as you can see, I have been very blessed in my life. I hope everyone will at least try things they never thought they would. You will be amazed at what you can do!

Jacquie Jochumsen

<u>Passing the Matriarch Torch</u>

I am the youngest of 5 children, 3 girls and 2 boys. My mother and father were raised during the Great Depression. My father worked in the coal mines of the Ohio Valley, underground for over 42 years. Mom was a homemaker for most of her married life of 52 years before my father passed away.

Although times were financially tough, we children never knew it. Mom could do anything; cook, sew, hang wallpaper, fix anything. You name it, she single handedly could make it happen. She was the glue that held us all together.

So growing up, Mom and Dad made sure there was ALWAYS enough food in the house. Several shelving units lined the basement walls with a case after case of each vegetable, even ones that I had never heard of...hominy? Who eats that? She always said it was better to have it and not need it.

We also had a 22-cubic foot freezer loaded up each year with a side of beef and a half of pig. And they still went to the grocery store every week. We children finally figured out in our later years that this behavior was a product of our parents being raised during the Great Depression. In my eyes, I could never figure out why they referred to it as the "Great" depression, as there was nothing great about it.

So, my story is rooted deep with my mother, she was the family matriarch. She ruled the roost. My father was the provider, a tall man, one would say scary looking with his 6'3" frame, but he was a gentle giant. He never had to discipline us kids, although mom would try to use that age-old expression, "just wait until your father gets home"! We all thought that was so funny (behind her back of course).

As mentioned earlier, I am the youngest of the five, with the oldest being sixteen years my senior. That's my brother Butch. He use to take me uptown in the stroller to show off with all the young girls at the city park, he called me the "best chick magnet there was"!

Eighteen months separated him with my sister Nancy, she was the "vice-mother". She stepped in and helped mom raise us all, even when she married and moved away, the three younger siblings would spend the summers with her and her husband. When we were blessed with the first grandchild, I was only 7 years old! How awesome was that, I was an AUNT.

We lost my sister Nancy, 5 months almost to the day that her husband passed. Very heartbreaking.

My sister Barbara was the middle child; she was the only one that inherited my father's blond hair and blue eyes. We lost her at the young age of 57 to breast cancer, 7 months after losing our sister Nancy.

Eighteen months separates my brother Chester and sister Barbara. Chester is just like my mom. He can do anything. I am not even kidding. He is a great cook, he has taught me how to can, we have exchanged recipes throughout the years, and he is an excellent hunter, and has passed that passion down to his only son.

So, that leaves me to bring up the rear. I was born 4 years after my brother Chester. I was called the baby, or lovingly "Boo Boo". Some people think that nickname was given because I was number 5 and not expected, but that's not the case. I am named after my mother. When she was born in 1927, the umbilical cord was wrapped around her neck she was blue, her aunt helped deliver her and promptly named her 'Jackie Blue". So when I was born, my Godparents son, pronounced "blue" as "boo boo" and it stuck! From then on there, I was crowned "Jacquie BooBoo". My family and close friends still call me that.

Time has its way of making people old, taking my father away peacefully on December 9th, 1999, 17 days short of his 77th birthday. He lived a hard life and it took its toll on his body, between the coal mine, diabetes, and Alzheimer's, he had a tough fight.

Mom continued to live on her own, she had her own beautiful three-bedroom apartment located in a private senior center high-rise. She was very happy living on her own, she often said, "The first time in my life that I do not have to take care of someone, other than myself." I never understood that until now.

In May of 2010, Mom started having some stomach pains, doctor visit after doctor visit, emergency room after emergency visit, nothing. I was not going to sit by and watch her suffer. I just kept taking her back, looking for answers. One doctor was convinced she was "simply constipated" and sent her home with some medication, that in turn was the cause of an intestinal rupture, which led to an emergency surgery. Then problem after problem, which meant I led a, before work, during lunch then back until midnight vigil by her bedside for over 4 months.

A new doctor discovered the day before she passed that mom had advanced stages of pancreatic cancer and it was just a matter of weeks if not days. Unbelievingly my mom was settled with the news. She had known there was something gravely wrong with her and she was seemingly at peace with finally getting the confirmation.

With that said, there was still some things that she wanted to "pass on". Earlier that day, with all of my siblings surrounding her, there was lots of laughing, storytelling, and crying, she made the announcement that "when I go, this one here is in charge". She was pointing at me! What? Wait, I am the baby, surely you cannot be referring to me! Yes, I AM she said. At that moment, she had passed the torch, even if I wasn't ready or willing, the deed was done, in front of everyone. Now what am I going to do?

The evening before my mom died, she and I had time to ourselves, the rest of the family had left the hospital, and I curled up into her bed, lay my head in the crook of her shoulder and drifted back 50 years. Mom proceeded to giving me her secrets of life. And what she expected to see once she was no longer here. She assured me that she was not afraid to die, that she ready to be with Our Lord and she was looking forward to seeing dad and her dear mother who had passed away when my mom was only 9. My poor mother had lived a lifetime without a mom, heartbreaking. And seeing all of her relatives and friends that had passed on before her, she was actually excited.

Mom passed 24 hours later. All five of her children were with her, holding vigil, praying, crying. With all of her children there, she took her last breath, it was like an invisible power of strength had been passed on to me. In the hours and days that followed, I handled everything, with my devoted husband at my side, and my devoted son, we spent days emptying out her three-bedroom apartment, sorting, boxing, crying at the memories, joys of finding things we had all forgot about, donating clothes to the women's shelter that my mother had handmade, etc.

Mom had taught all three of her girls how to sew, but I was the only one that kept it up into my adult years. I had inherited all her sewing equipment, and "stuff" which filled a complete bedroom. I still cherish each item.

With only 3 years under my belt of losing my (our) mother, the year of 2013 was a very dark year, I personally had 5 family members pass and a co-worker of 12 years. I am not sure how my heart survived all the pain. I am certain that most my hearts strings were broken that year.

It was during these times of heartache that remember the things that my mother shared with me the day before she died. **One being, you must stay strong, protect your heart and know that God has it all planned and that we are only on this earth for a short amount of time.**

Since my mother's passing, I have immersed myself in the teachings of love, kindness and forgiveness. I had to do something, I always had my mom to lean on, now she is gone, it was my turn to step up and step into my mother's shoes. I had a family to look after, to be the voice of reason, to help in anyway. With losing my two sisters so close after the passing of my mother, I was extremely

heartbroken. But I still had my two brothers to look after and to be that rock for them.

You see, I have learned that one cannot heal if we still hold resentment against another. The energy that it takes to hold a grudge, or even dislike, takes so much more than love. I strive to hold true in that statement every day. There are times when it becomes tough, but then I remember her words. "God has it all planned

out." I get it now Mom. I have grown profoundly since losing my mother. I embraced the torch that was passed and I carry it with pride. Thank you, Mom, for everything. I will continue to take care of your legacy.

More About Jacquie Jochumsen

Jacquie Jochumsen takes sweet success to the next level. Founder of *Unique Treats by Jacquie*, she started baking at age 9 and hasn't stopped since. She comes from a family of 5 children with her being the youngest. Her mother passed on her passion of "being in the kitchen" to not only Jacquie, but her brother Chester, who is a master Gardner and an avid canner. After the passing of their mother, brother Chester took on the role of teaching Jacquie the one thing that she hadn't learned her from her mother, how to can. Brother Chester also gave up his Apple Pie filling recipe, which Jacquie has refined and it has become award winning!

Her signature gourmet caramel apples have become an Ohio Valley culinary sensation, in part due to the many scrumptious toppings Jacquie concocts, but mostly thanks to the 'certain' apple that's in limited season and which she and her husband individually hand select.

Jacquie loves to cook and shares her passion by teaching others; she hopes to launch a home cooking class party series. She has catered weddings, graduations, anniversaries and other large events. She recently hosted her daughter's wedding for 200, not only preparing dinner, but also baking 250 dozen assorted cookies so guests would have a nice assortment to take home from the reception.

Passionate, driven and creative, Jacquie knows the way to every person's heart is through the stomach. You only must meet her and you'll understand! Jacquie and her husband Mike live in St. Clairsville, OH. She has two grown children and a granddaughter/apprentice who shares Jacquie's passion for all things culinary and she is also a skilled dancer.

https://www.facebook.com/UniqueTreatsByJacquie/?fref=ts

The Honky Tonk Sweethearts

Artists Doing their Thing

Laurie Labishak

It's Never Too Late

"Wow!" I heard myself say out loud. Here I was sitting in The Strand Theatre listening to a rehearsal for an upcoming fundraiser. The proceeds would benefit the Wheeling Jamboree, the second oldest country music broadcast in America. The radio show had been broadcast from the historic Capitol Theatre in Wheeling, West Virginia for a very long time.

Since the theatre had been sold and closed, the Jamboree no longer had a home. This event was organized to raise funds to help continue the tradition in another location. I had been invited to perform with other individuals who had spent time on the Jamboree shows. One after another, they made their way on the stage to rehearse with the five-piece house band

What talent! I found myself especially in awe of three talented ladies. One of them, Joylene, I had worked with before. She was a beauty! Dark hair, short in stature, poised and professional. Her voice had a rich tone reminiscent of Patsy Cline. We had worked together in another theatre in town years ago before she relocated to Nashville, TN to pursue music on the big stage. I knew she had moved back but had only seen her once or twice in the past couple of years.

Then there was Nikki. She had helped organize this event and was the one who contacted me. She was blond and spunky! She had a lot of energy on and off stage. I knew who she was but had never met her. We were in competing country bands back in the mid '90s and to be honest, I never really liked her. I know, I just said I didn't "know" her, but there was something about her stage presence back in those days that just rubbed me the wrong way. Maybe I was jealous. She was quite talented.

The third female singer was Lois. She was tall and brunette and sang soulful and sweet. I had no idea who she was, but I heard people around me talking about her father, an icon on the Jamboree stage. They also talked about her sisters, who sang with Lois in a group called Sweet Harmony that performed all over the world. She had a way about her that commanded attention. She owned the stage when she performed and you couldn't take your eyes off her.

As I sat there and listened to these talented ladies, all I could think was, "If we could all four sing together, that would be some pretty harmony for sure!" I began to plot an idea of putting together another fundraiser for our beloved Jamboree. We could do a show in tribute to the women of country music, the ones who paved the way so that the four of us could do what we love! I pulled the director of the Jamboree aside and asked him if we could put this show together, would he let us perform on the "live" broadcast of the Jamboree? He offered me half of the two-hour broadcast. Now to convince the ladies!

Through Facebook, I messaged the three girls, laid my idea out there and waited for feedback. Joylene was the first to reply with a yes. Then Lois. Finally, Nikki. We got together to see what we would sound like as a group, and the harmony was incredible. All four of us naturally went to our parts without hesitation, as if we had sung together for years. Excitement followed and then the planning of the show. Whom do we honor? What songs do we sing? And most importantly, **WHAT TO WEAR!**

The show took shape over the following months, and we ran into a small problem. There was too much material for just an hour show. We went back to the Jamboree director and asked for the whole two hours of one of the broadcasts. He gave us a date in April of 2013.

We planned our show right down to the minute. We put together a band of some of the best local musicians who had also played the Jamboree at one time or another. The songs had to be just right, filled with two-, three- and four-part harmony. They had to include the women who inspired each of us, from Patsy Montana to Chickie Williams, Tammy Wynette to Loretta Lynn and Patty Loveless to Pam Tillis. We invited former Jamboree star JoAnn Davis to be our hostess and MC for the evening. Our script that told the story of the women we were honoring. We coordinated our outfits for each song and arranged the set list during the hours of weekly rehearsals leading up to the April date. Finally, the day arrived!

Here we were, four former Jamboree performers, ranging in age from 48 to 58 and with more than 125 years of performing between us. We had opened individually for some of the biggest stars in country music on the stage of the Capitol Theatre. Now, we had our own show, honoring the women who made it possible, being staged in the ballroom at the local casino. The place was packed! Over 500 tickets sold and more people coming to the door!

Do you remember your wedding or another event that you planned for months? The excitement and anxiety leading up to it keep you on edge for months. Then when the day arrives, everything goes off without a hitch, and it's over in the blink of an eye. That's how the show felt. Two hours of great music, great history, great fun and then BAM! It was over!

We were thrilled with what we had accomplished. Four old gals who love sharing the gift of music that God had given each of us. We all agreed that it was God that brought us together to do something wonderful with our gifts. Was this it? One show? Months of getting to know each other and learning songs and parts and sharing laughter and tears and two hours on stage and that's it?

Little did we know! When we walked out to meet the crowd of people who were waiting for our autographs—yes, autographs! —we were met with lots of questions like "When is your next show?", "What will you do next?" and "Would you think about a Christmas show?"

We didn't even have a name for our group. We simply got together to plan one show to pay tribute to our heroines in country music. But the people wanted more!

So we gave it to them! We named our group The Honky Tonk Sweethearts and began planning a fall variety show for the Jamboree. We would include family, faith and America in the show. We paid tribute to our fallen soldiers and the victims of 9-11. We all agreed that our shows should benefit a charity if we were to move forward with this endeavor.

After the fall show, we planned a Christmas show, this time in the ballroom of the historic Capitol Theatre, which had recently reopened. We partnered with a local charity that helps needy families at Christmas and donated the show's proceeds to their efforts. We also had concert attendees bring new, unwrapped toys. It was a huge success. The ballroom was standing room only and everyone enjoyed the Christmas selections.

In the months following our Christmas show, we would perform in Ohio, West Virginia, Pennsylvania, New York, North Carolina, South Carolina and Georgia. We auditioned for America's Got Talent in Indiana, and the judges called us "intriguing" and "awesome"! Although we didn't make it on the show, we learned from the experience and broadened our musical choices to include more than just country. We now sing a variety of music from the Beatles to Miley Cyrus and, of course, our beloved country music favorites!

After a couple of years, Lois left the group to pursue her own musical dreams. Nikki, Joylene and I continued our mission, and in the Spring of 2015, we opened a show for the group Shenandoah on their comeback tour. What a highlight for all of us!

Fast forward to today, we have added a fourth Sweetheart, and we are still making music and donating to charities. This year will mark our fourth annual Christmas Homecoming Show and the third year that we have partnered with a local veteran organization. We now produce our show on the historic stage of the 2200-seat Capitol Theatre where it all began! This family-friendly show is fast becoming an Ohio Valley tradition for the holidays!

Although we are all "seasoned" women in the field, we are empowered to continue this mission to share our gifts with others and to donate much-needed funds to local nonprofit organizations who help our communities thrive. We have all four been reawakened by this group and feel empowered to make an impact!

We hope to inspire other women of a certain age to wake up to your talents and gifts and find a way to share them with others! You just might be surprised what you can accomplish. After all, it's never too late to live your dreams!

For more information about the Honky Tonk Sweethearts, please visit us on Facebook or at www.honkytonksweethearts.com.

LEARN MORE ABOUT LAURIE LABISHAK

Laurie Labishak is a God-made successful business woman who shares her life experience in a unique way. With no formal college education, she has risen to the heights of National Membership Director for an international nonprofit, Vice President of Marketing for a hospital system as well as Executive Director of a nonprofit foundation. <u>As a songwriter and talented vocalist, she uses music to evoke emotion in her audiences as she shares "real-life" experiences to empower women to live their lives to the fullest.</u> Throughout her life, Laurie's faith has been her stronghold. Her stories of challenges, pitfalls and the abundance in life when you truly accept God's grace and His will for your life, is inspiring and uplifting women from every walk of life. Learning to live by the "Simple-Truth" is priceless!

Laurie is a Christian and believes that God expects her life to reflect that she belongs to Him and that she is pursuing a Holy life. She believes that the Bible is the truth and the anointed Word of God. She believes in the Holy Trinity and that God, the creator of all things, is our heavenly Father and that He came to earth and became man for one purpose and that was and is to save the souls of His people and that He is the object of our worship and the subject of our praise. She believes that God's gift of salvation through the resurrection of Jesus Christ is offered to ALL and those who accept it by faith and not works become new creatures in Christ. She believes God commands us to Love one another and to share the gifts that He has given us to bring glory to Him. She believes that now is the time for people to stand up and "Give Thanks" to God for all He has provided and continues to provide.

Susan K. Schmelick

<u>Finding a Love for Making Jewelry</u>

B eing a child born in 1956, I was one of the few exceptions in my high-school graduating class. My parents were divorced!! (Not many of my classmates shared my situation. I knew I was different, and I never felt like I truly fit in anywhere.) Mom was a nurse and worked full time, and Daddy was busy with his work, too, so at times I felt like an orphan.

I was very young and can't recall details, but I lived in my grandparents' home until I was 9. Grandma Annie, Papa and my Mema (Grandma Annie's mother) were my saving grace. They loved me and cared for me when, I am quite certain, I was not very lovable! God blessed me abundantly.

When I was 9, Mom married a widower with four children. Oh, My God! How would I survive THIS?!? I went from being a spoiled, only child to one of 5, and soon 6 children. What a rude awakening!! These 4 children (ages 8 to 15) had lost their mother. They were still grieving for her, and here we came... A step-mother who had no clue what she faced in her new role, and a step-sister, who they thought was Satan's spawn! (This is true; the girls told me so!). It was not easy for any of us. My life was turned upside down. I was afraid. I was selfish. I shared a bedroom with 2 strangers. But it didn't take long until I knew I belonged.

It was late December. Our only heat source was a coal furnace, so we were cold, a lot! I remember all of us huddling together on the one register in the hallway after Bill (my step-father) fed the furnace in the mornings. I was surrounded by love, and it felt good. There were many nights when the fire must have gone out, and we girls would cuddle together in their double bed as my twin size was cold and lonely. I learned to share. I learned to be patient, and I learned to be kind. It took a long time, but in the end, we are closer than many "blood" families. God blessed me abundantly.

Fast forward to high-school. I met a boy. Steve was a year ahead of me in school; he was cute, he had a car, and he had a job; and he thought I was pretty. He was sweet to me and we fell in love my Junior year. In a nut shell, we married in '78, had our first son in '80, and our second son was born in '82. We raised our boys the best we knew how. We loved them and spent time with them and helped them as much as we could. I believe we did o.k.; David and Daniel are both nice people, happily married, and honest, hardworking fellows. God blessed me abundantly.

I have been a working mom since the boys were young. I am the Administrative Secretary at a 99-bed nursing home in our hometown. I have been working there for 30 years. I have always enjoyed working with the elderly, probably because of my grandparents. About 11 years ago, the boys were leaving the nest, and I was searching for something to do with my extra time. I discovered that I love making jewelry! It makes me feel good to create beautiful things that others can enjoy.

Lord knows, I have a pretty large personal collection, and I give handmade gifts away every chance I get!! My family and friends probably dread holidays and birthdays, but I continue to create unique, personalized pieces for people that I love.

Early this year, an acquaintance asked me to join her artisan group, and become a part of a great opportunity. I was given the chance to do what I enjoy most, and help others through charitable contributions while I do it!! It was like a light went on inside me. I am 60 years old, so I thought I'd better jump in with both feet!! If not now, when?!? The project is in the infant stages, but already I can see I am once again surrounded by love and support. Love has lifted me once again, and I am in the position to lift others up. New friendships have blossomed and the possibilities are amazing! From my childhood to the present, I can see that God blessed me abundantly, every day, in all circumstances.

ABOUT SUSAN SCHMELICK

Susan Schmelick is a wife, mother, former LPN, and the Administrative Secretary (for 30 years!) at the 99-bed nursing home in her little home town of Shadyside, Ohio. She and her husband, Steve, were high school sweethearts. They have been married for 38 years and they have 2 grown sons and 2 beautiful daughters in law. (There are no grandchildren yet, but hopefully it won't be much longer.). Susan feels fortunate that her sons graduated from the same high school as she and Steve did. They continue to make their home in Shadyside.

Susan enjoys boating with her husband and their little "river dog", Dunkin. About 12 years ago, she went to a 'Bead Retreat' home party. She made a bracelet there and immediately became hooked! Since then, Susan has made hundreds of beaded bracelets, earrings and necklaces, for special occasions and everyday wear. She has many regular customers, and she enjoys setting up and selling her unique creations at local craft fairs in her area. Susan hopes to retire from the nursing home soon, and make her "Beadz By Suz" her full time 'hobby job'. Susan's story is the first writing she has done. She enjoyed reflecting on her life and sharing it with the readers. Quite often, it takes many years to understand and appreciate circumstances and lessons in life.

Shelly Nichole Lester

Home "The Good Stuff"

"Momma always made us eat breakfast before getting into the cookie jar but at my Nanny's house you could be elbow deep in the cookie jar any hour of the day."

If you've ever been to Oklahoma, then you know that the dirt is red. I can remember as a child always having red dirt stains on my clothes from where I sat and played in a big pile of it. I was never the girly type, I would much prefer to sit in the dirt driving my hot wheels pretending to be Smoky and the Bandit with my little brother than sit in the bedroom playing house with Barbie dolls with my sister. For the most part of my childhood I grew up on my grandparents' piece of land located at 18th & Eastern in Oklahoma City.

My grandpa raised rolling pigeons, chickens, goats and he even added an old donkey named Joey once. There were pigs and English bulldogs at one time also, but that was all before my time. He kept a huge garden also. All of us kids were included in the feeding and watering of the animals as well as the planting and harvesting of the vegetables. I can remember walking behind my grandpa in that ole red dirt as he plowed up rows to plant corn. I would be under my toe nails, in the cracks of my neck, which my grandma always called "Granny's Beads." I wore granny's beads a lot in those days.

I enjoyed helping him pick up eggs and toss chicken scratch out for the hens, always keeping one eye on that big red rooster he had. I learned early that was not the bird to turn your back on for fear he'd flog you as soon as you did, thus the reason I carried a big stick for good measure.

To this day, I don't care much for roosters. It was then, in the early 80's in southeast Oklahoma City, on that little farm that my love affair with having my own farm one day - first began. I wanted to grow up to be just like him, from his old worn out cowboy boots to the raggedy red flannel jacket he wore.

As I got a little older, my parents moved us off that old place and into the neighborhood up the road. I still had access to my grandparents often but it wasn't the same as getting up each morning and being able to walk barefoot from our house to their house on that old private red dirt road. I can remember being in a big hurry to go barging in the backdoor to their house to perch myself at that old cedar table in their dining room.

These were the days "the good stuff" was made.

Momma always made us eat breakfast before getting into the cookie jar but at my Nanny's house you could be elbow deep in the cookie jar any hour of the day. As the teenage years came, riding bicycles with the neighborhood kids, playing football in the street and shooting pool in the garage took the place of feeding chickens and shucking corn.

The only time I visited my grandparents in those days was after I had gotten in trouble at school and been sent home for a few days. My punishment would be to go work for my grandpa in the wood yard all day, and ricking wood was no easy task, especially on those cold bitter winter days.

He got to sit and split the wood but I had to be the one to toss the wood out of the truck and then *rick it up* after he had it split. A rick of wood is a carefully measured stack of wood that stacks up to be 4-feet-tall and 8-feet-wide. That was a lot of bending and tossing even for a healthy 15-year-old girl. But as time wore on, life took me away from that old place where many of my fondest memories were made. As the years flew by, that old place began to wither away. My grandpa wasn't the young man he once was, the heat got to him much faster than it did in his younger days.

He could no longer climb the tallest tree to hang a tire swing for me, although he continued to hang the moon long after his climbing days were over. Then with the death of my grandmother, also came a "For Sale" sign.

I drove by once after the home place sold to new owners, I guess for one last glance at the house where it all took place. I'm always reminded of that old house when I hear the song "The House that Built Me." As I looked through the windshield of my truck, I will never forget the feeling that came over me when I saw the blackened wood where the house has almost burnt to the ground.

I'm not sure how that happened but it took place after it sold. I parked my truck and walked down that old familiar hill. I sat down on a cinder block under that big tree where my tire swing had hung and cried for what seemed like forever. As I sat there looking at the ground, I reached down and grabbed a handful of dirt and watched as it sifted back out of my hand and back onto the ground. I then reached down and wrote my name in the dirt with my finger, just like my grandpa has taught me more than 30 years earlier.

As I walked away that day, I got the strangest feeling as I glanced back one last time. I realized that my love for that place had much less to do with dirt and chickens and old raggedy red flannel jackets as I had originally thought. I didn't just miss the place and the people that I love but more than anything else, I missed the person that I was during the time I spent growing up there.

I knew deep down that no matter how much I wished my grandmother back, she simply would not come back just like no matter how much I missed that little girl I once was, I would never see her again either. That girl played hard, dreamed big, loved without hesitation and the dirt meant something to her. I had left that little girl behind somewhere along the way. *Life forced her out when I had gone from a girl who never wanted to leave home to a woman who couldn't wait to get gone.*

Against my family's wishes, I saddled up with a traveling man. Actually, it wasn't him my family had a problem with, it was more about how I had never recovered from the first husband before marrying another.

They knew the agony I had just gone through and they were left to pick up the pieces of this dark soul he left in his wake. I understood where they were coming from but they also understood that I was never a very good listener. And with almost no warning at all and with only what I could fit inside my Excursion along with 7 kids and a big dog, I drove away from Oklahoma and didn't stop until we reached the panhandle of West Virginia.

West Virginia truly was a wild and wonderful place. I fell in love with everything about the hills of West Virginia. What was supposed to be a summer away from everything and everyone, quickly turned into almost four years. I never dreamed in a million years that I would have spent that amount of time there or become as engrained into the community as I did.

I was surrounded by beauty and some of the most wonderful people I've ever met in my life. I felt at home there and at times wondered if I had finally found the place where I belonged. I don't think I've ever been happier and I could write an entire book on my adventures in West Virginia.

I honestly believed that I could have spent the rest of my years there. I even stood on a few porches of houses for sale and imagined myself living there and raising my family in those amazing hills. But my thoughts were always abruptly interrupted with the thoughts of Oklahoma.

I entertained the thought of staying there for good and many times asked myself could WV drown out all those childhood dreams of owning my own piece of red dirt someday? They say if you keep looking back, you never left in the first place. So, after much discussion and prayer, Tommy (my husband) and I made the decision to get back to our roots. Mine being the dirt and his being a hammer and nails.

You see, before the pipeline came along he used to swing a hammer for a living. He's had numerous oilfield jobs through the years, but through the first few years we struggled he framed houses for a living. I can remember during those years we'd lay in bed late at night and talk about what our cabin would look like someday.

All hours of the night, both of us having to be at work early the next morning. I believe those dreams got us through the hard times. But I think somewhere along the line we gave up on that dream, forgot it even existed. The more kids we had, the more income it required. The struggle just became too hard.

But in retrospect, the years of struggle were the most beautiful. At the time, it just seemed easier to dream of being a gypsy on the open road and seeing the world. It sounded so wild and wonderful, and was much easier to attain. The need to feel accomplished over-rode the need to fulfill our dreams. I can always tell of our adventures in unfamiliar places, the bravery it took to just up and leave without looking back. But at the end of the day, the lack of fulfillment will haunt you. It robs you of your sleep and it leaves a void that nothing else can fill.

Truth is, I couldn't let go of that "old" dream to dream something new. It would never work, I would always long for those red dirt roads. They say home is where the heart is… I never agreed with that but it's because I didn't understand it. You want to know where your heart is? You heart is where your mind goes when it wanders.

And my mind, always kept returning to him and there. Tommy and Oklahoma. Any time spent away from either, my mind would drift off searching for ways to have both. I know you've all heard the old saying, "You can take the girl out of Oklahoma, but you can't take Oklahoma out of the girl." It is true. Whether it be Oklahoma or wherever your home may be, it will remain…. All the days of your life.

I've spent my life looking for that girl that sat sifting dirt through her fingers just to pass time. She was a dreamer, a believer and her faith in those she loved was unbreakable. She felt safe. No one could hurt her there.

That was long before life had torn her to pieces. *Her grandpa once told her that if it hurts, rub a little dirt on it to make it all better.* She once believed that with all her heart, the dirt could heal any wound. As Tommy and I hammered four stakes into the ground to mark where our house will go… I can literally hear that little girl whisper, "Don't give up. Keep pushing forward. Sometimes life is about risking everything for a dream no one can see but you. With each passing day, remember you are one day closer than you were yesterday. When things get hard, have faith that it's going to work out. Never let anyone talk you out of your dream or beat it out of you. And if you do happen to get skinned up along the way, rub a little dirt on it."

I will see this through. In less than a month, we will see our house come together all nestled amongst some tress in southeastern Oklahoma. I only wish I could go back and tell myself all those times that I wanted to give up that this day WOULD arrive. A new chapter has begun for our family.

The process has taken much longer than planned and we've had to jump through quite a few fiery hoops, but through some of the darkest moments of my life, I can honestly say God was there to see me through. He never left my side, even when I shook my fists at the sky. He remained. And just today, I saw that little girl from so long ago. She is a blue eyed blonde haired child and she wore a little pink plaid sundress with no shoes. She sat in a pile of red dirt and looked up at me and said, "Momma, will you play with me?" I bent down and took her finger and showed her how to write her name in the dirt.

Wendy Black

Survival of the Bayou Bride

An Inspirational Story as told by a Widowed at 21-Single Mother in 1978

Before I can begin my story, you need to understand my hometown. Bayou La Batre lies along the Mississippi Sound on the Gulf of Mexico in south Alabama. It is a charming community steeped in Southern history and a heritage with a distinct French impression.

Known in the late 1800s and early 1900s as a resort town with medicinal spring water, Bayou La Batre is known as the *Seafood Capital of Alabama.*

We commemorate our fishing industry with annual events such as the Blessing of the Fleet and Taste of the Bayou. You can take a ride down scenic byway 188 as century old oaks graciously welcome you to our city, and in case you don't hear before you get here, we call home "By-luh-ba-tree."

As part of the French settlement of the Gulf Coast, the bayou was originally called "Riviere D'Erbane" and acquired the present name from the French-maintained battery of artillery on the west bank ("bayou of the battery"). Bayou La Batre was the first permanent settlement of the south Mobile County mainland and was founded in 1786, when Joseph Bouzage (Bosarge) [1733-95] moved into the area and was awarded a 1,259-acre Spanish land grant on the bayou's west bank.

Bayou La Batre is mentioned in the 1994 film *Forrest Gump* and in Winston Broom's book on which the movie is based as the home of Forrest's army buddy, Benjamin Buford "Bubba" Blue, and later as the home of Forrest Gump himself during his time as a shrimp boat captain.

I have always been proud of being from the Bayou. It states that in the census count the population of 1980 was 2,005. In other words, everyone knew each other where I grew up. We all attended church and school together. As a student, I excelled academically, socially and morally. When most of the local teenagers were hanging out smoking pot, taking drugs and having sex, I was working after school, at local restaurant, Catalina as a waitress and sewing my own cheerleading outfits.

My story probably sounds like every other ordinary small town girl, but in honesty, the direction my life would take was going to be anything but ordinary. As a cheerleader, I was popular and knew every guy in the Bayou. Many of my friends were guys. After graduating from the class of 1976, which consisted of a 101, I was anxious to save money and begin my life. I was working at one of the local fish houses.

On a cold December day in 1977, an extremely handsome guy with shoulder length silky blonde hair walked in. Without realizing it, my breath had caught in my throat, I wasn't breathing. I was hypnotized by his dazzling green eyes and brilliant sparkling smile that melted my heart. His name was Clint, he started work that day. The only other man in the world, who was as handsome as him, was Elvis Presley. I was hopelessly in love.

Clint and I dated for a few months. He was adventurous and exciting to be around. His parents lived in Grand Bay but they were originally from somewhere in Texas. He was unlike any other guy I had ever known. It wasn't hard to be in love with him.

He and I were married in May of 1978. Our marriage was a rocky one, but we were young and very much in love. Clint and I moved from place to place. He had a wandering, roving spirit. At 19, he would work on a job for a few days or weeks and then we would be off going somewhere else. This wasn't anything unusual for young couples to do in those days.

On one weekend, I had gone to visit my aunt in Port St. Joe, Florida. Remember, this was before cell phones were affordable. My mother drove to my aunts to break the most horrible news to me that would cause my ordinary world to come crashing down around me. Clint had been killed in a horrific automobile accident.

Remembering those events are still painful. My family surrounded me with love and protection. On the other hand, his family had never accepted me as his wife. I would not learn how deep their resentment for me ran until a week after the funeral. Mystery surrounded his death. As it goes in a small town, rumors were flying the accident was really a murder. I was so devastated and distraught I became physically ill.

Two days after Clint's burial I found out I was seven weeks pregnant. He and I had wanted children, but now he was gone. I began to wonder, how am I going to make ends meet with a baby to take care of? I believe in your darkest hours of anguish God is closer to you than you can ever imagine.

Faith should never be confused or mistaken with feelings. At the time of my despair, I could only feel numbness. It was as if I was looking through a window at someone else's life events unfolding before me. However, deep in my soul I knew I was not alone.

I believed and knew as a young girl I had accepted Jesus Christ as my Savior. I had committed my life to Him. Clint was my first experience at everything. I thought we would be together forever. After only 14 short months, nothing but a flood of uncertainty lay before me. However, I had faith in God, my family and a willingness to live because of my baby. I was determined to take things "One Day at a Time". This was a very popular song, which gave me great comfort.

One week after Clint was buried in the local cemetery, word spread through the Bayou his grave was empty. I quickly went to see for myself and sure enough, his casket was gone. Nothing was there but a deep hole and wilting flowers. It was obvious a truck had been there because of the tracks it left. Who would steal my husband's body? Why?

With the help of my family, I could hire an attorney. The case went to trial. It was a heated battle and I learned his parents had moved Clint's body to another state. I was granted the right to move his body back to the original burial site, but I would have to pay for it. I was not told where he was buried. I was given a price but unable to raise the exorbitant amount. It would be 15 years before his burial site would be revealed.

At the time of Clint's death, I was not working and there was no life insurance. I lost everything we had. I moved back home with my wonderful parents. I was a pregnant single-mother, homeless and a widow before I was 21 years old. I am grateful for my family, but I was so alone and scared. During this time, my best guy friend also died, from a brain tumor. Death and sorrow had engulfed me from every side. I know God understood my plight and my pregnancy went well.

On a beautiful day in March 1980, the most beautiful healthy baby girl was born. I did not know at the time of her birth, she would be my only child. Finally, some joy had entered my life. Truly, God works in mysterious ways. For every time you are blessed from above, evil lurks to trap you up! This would prove to be true very soon.

I recovered well and ran into an old guy friend one day while out in town. We began to date. He was a commercial fisherman and was gone much of the time. I was lonely, no job, no father for my daughter and only drawing $147 a month social security. Within a few months we decided to get married. In not much time at all, I began to realize this marriage was not working. He was cruel, mentally, emotionally and physically abusive. I began to hate him so much; I took down the bed and sold it. We only had a sofa to sleep on. This was not good for my daughter.

I decided to go to work for a direct sales company called "Home Interiors". Within two years I had built a business that would become my career, I was able to get out of this abusive marriage. I bought a new car and our first house, for my daughter and me.

We were happy and doing fine a year or so later. We were out skating, when couples skate time came up, this nice, charming guy (so I thought) asked me to couples skates.

After a year, we were married. He became **very** abusive, physically, mentally and emotionally. He made my self-esteem so low, he made me feel fat, ugly and no one else wanted me. He cheated, lied, used and sold drugs. He threatened to kill me, my daughter and my mother if I were to leave. I was stuck.

My daughter so wanted a sibling. I did conceive once and was not far along when I miscarried. The Lord so knew I did not need to be tied to him.

One day, after 8 years of abuse, he decided "We needed a break", he left. When he did, I changed the locks, put in an alarm system and put burglar bars on my house. I was still scared, but I had him out and he could not get back in.

We got a quick divorce, nothing to fight over, it all belonged to me. He went on to stalk me for 4 years. I can't begin to delve into the confrontations, heightened sense of danger I lived in for myself and my daughter. However, God had a plan in the works. It was better than what I had ever longed for. Truly, God loves us more than we can fathom.

The church I attended, the minister's wife and I were very good friends. With all the bad relationships, I'd had in my life, we prayed for God to send the Right person to me that I could spend the rest of my life with.

Then, in March of 1997, on a blind date, I met that man, Gary. When, we met, I was not impressed with him at first. He worked shift work and after a few weeks of getting to know each other over the phone, we had our first real date. In no time, we fell in love.

He confessed, he had been praying for God to send him that Right woman. By September we were engaged. We were planning our wedding for February. Then, one day we were out riding, the song "It's Your Love" by Tim McGraw, came on the radio. Tears swelled up in his eyes, he looked at me and said, "That is our song, I want it sang at our wedding, because you have changed my life and that's how I feel about you". I had chills and tears streamed down my cheeks. Moments like this in your life are few and far between.

Later that day, Gary asked me what I wanted for my birthday, November 13th. I told him, "All I want is you". Then we decided to change the wedding date. We were married the day after my birthday!

This year we will celebrate our 19th Anniversary. Like all marriages, we've had our ups and downs, but we have a fabulous loving marriage. He has been a wonderful father to my daughter. He has been there for her and loves her as his own. I regret the mistakes I have made in my life. Regrettably, my daughter had to share in these trials and struggles, as well. Even though the devil meant to destroy me, God made a way out of every hopeless situation. Through faith, hope and trust we have overcome all adversities and this is the fiber that has made us the women we are today!

The End

Terry Sutton Hammond

A Letter of Love to my Father

"Dad, there have been so many times I needed to talk to you, and I can feel you with me."

Now, almost 5 years later, I still try to call you; I still try to imagine our last dinner together talking about our day, our last phone conversation, and our last laugh.

The hurt and feeling of hopelessness of losing your father is so strong. As your baby girl, I was spoiled. My husband would be the first to agree with that statement. As an adult that never changed. You were my hero, my boss, my friend, but most important, my dad. I know that I am not alone in going through this agony, but my pain still feels so real so strong. A song on the radio, a commercial on TV, it only takes one thing, one second to throw me back to when you were here with me.

I would love to be back in our office making plans for the next business day or you asking me if I was planning on working instead of talking on the phone. I remember you helping me with my college final project by letting me survey your empty lots. You were my boss but I always knew you were my daddy first.

So many things to capture, so many times you didn't realize it would be the last time. I can still see the tears in your eyes when each of your grandsons was born. I still remember waking up to the words "You should see the feet on that boy" after an emergency C-section, wondering what in the world was wrong with my first born child's feet, only to hear your next words of "He has blue eyes like mine".

I laid there thinking "his father has blue eyes too Dad", but I never said a word.

I let you have your proud Grandpa moment and was just happy that you were there beside me when I woke up, to eventually tell me everything was fine. You and mom were there every day and Rob was there every day until I got home.

I remember that first Christmas as I walked through the door and you looked right past me and asked "where's the baby?", the first of many times that my children were put first. I remember my second C-section, you and Rob went back to work as soon as I was in recovery – what a difference the second time around!

You were the one who took me to sign my first child up for Kindergarten and you were there when your youngest grandson told you they wanted him to skip for Kindergarten screening and he told them skipping was for girls and proceeded to sit there. You were there for both of their high school graduations and I know how proud you were. I watched you cry the day our oldest left for Marine Basic Training and how proud you were when we drove to Parris Island South Carolina to see him graduate and again several weeks later when we went to Camp Lejeune North Carolina to see him graduate from The School of Infantry.

I remember the look of joy when our youngest went to College in Connecticut for welding and I know how you were looking forward to seeing him graduate. We know you were there with us that night and that you and Mom were both smiling. Dad, there have been so many times I needed to talk to you, and I can feel you with me.

I know you would have loved to meet your great granddaughter Kennly; she looks just like her daddy. I remember you bringing Bobby home from helping you in the shop and the only white area on him was the skin under his glasses. He was covered in oil, dirt, and grease and you couldn't see anything wrong with that. I can still see you operating the backhoe and the boys sitting on your lap, first Bobby and then later both boys.

They were always under your feet, never wanting to be anywhere else but Nanny and Grandpas. I still go to the cemetery and change the flowers, like you I am scared if I don't Nanny will come back and haunt me!! I remember our trips there together and now you are there too, it's not right!

I scream knowing that you should be here! Knowing I should have done more but not knowing what that would have or could have been! I still want to be that little girl who sat on your lap and hugged you, or the adult who still kissed and hugged good-bye before she left. How can I go back to our last Christmas, making it last even longer, making you stay longer? How do you turn back time to a place when all was right with world? Is it possible, will it happen if I wish hard enough?

I have prayed from the first night in the hospital to the day when they came out and said there was nothing else they could do. I prayed the doctor who was standing in front of me with tears running down his cheeks was mistaken and it was all a horrible dream as my knees gave out and I hit the floor. I would wake up anytime now! But the reality was, I was awake, and this horrible nightmare was truly happening.

I remember the calls I had to make. The first to your oldest grandson in California, who broke down and I could not hold him to comfort him, to your brothers and sisters, who were there for me during all of it. I remember the look on your youngest grandson's face as he arrived at the hospital after a 10-hour drive to hear the doctor say you were gone, I can still see him standing beside your bed, kissing your cheek, telling his grandpa good-bye one last time.

I remember everyone leaving the room and I just sat there on your bed holding on to your hand trying to will you back to life – I wasn't ready to let you go – I was angry that you would leave me, I was angry because there was nothing I could do but sit there and cry. I see the funeral, the Military honors, your oldest grandson in his dress blues, the friends who came and the stories they told, the tears that fell as the song "You can Let Go Now Daddy" played.

I remember every word to that song, it was so my life with you – from the little girl on the bicycle, the young lady you walked down the aisle, to the woman who had to let you go. Now, almost 5 years has passed, I wear your ring on my finger that you told me to keep for you till after the surgery, I keep your watch beside by bed because it means you are with me at some point in time.

The clothes you wore to the hospital are still in your bag, still in my closet. The heart shaped pillow they gave you after your surgery is next to my pillow because it was one of the last things in your arms. I still long for our nightly dinners, our daily phone calls, our laughs and our tears.

I want one more family reunion, one more day to talk to you. Mainly, I long to hear your laugh, your voice telling me you love me, seeing you sitting at your kitchen table drinking your coffee and easting your two cookies in the mornings, your arms hugging me and saying everything will be okay. I want one more of everything with my Dad. The moral if any of this story is to cherish your loved ones because at some point in time God will either want them back or you. We are not given a time table so live life like today is your last and make it count.

Memories and pictures are wonderful but nothing takes the place of being there in the flesh and blood. Live for today because we are not promised a tomorrow.

Learn more about Terry Sutton Hammond

Terry Sutton Hammond is an entrepreneur who is a first-time storywriter. She recently joined a journaling group where they have passed around ideas and subjects for their individual stories and visions. Ms. Hammond is also an Advanced Color Consultant with Mary Kay. Ms. Hammond lives on a farm outside of Shadyside, Ohio with her husband, dogs and cows. She has two grown sons and one Granddaughter.

Terry enjoys writing, crocheting, sporting events and spending time with friends and family. She enjoys baking and having Sunday dinners with her husband and two sons. Terry received a degree in Civil Engineering and worked in the construction industry most of her adult life. Terry now works for a Global Law Firm in the Finance Department. Terry and her family love to travel and have been to the Virgin Islands, The Keys, and The Grand Canyon on vacation.

Terry and her husband have also been to several Nascar Races at Richmond, VA., Charlotte NC., and Las Vegas NV. To contact Ms. Hammond please email her at terrylhammond@marykay.com.

Her Personal website is also www.marykay.com/terrylhammond

.

Conquering Cancer

Lyn Kyrc

Sparkle

As I write this, I am battling Chronic Lymphocytic Leukemia. It manifested itself in my bones, which places me in Stage 4 cancer. My course of treatment includes a strong oral Chemotherapy which is extremely costly--over $10,000.00 per month. It is hand delivered to me via a courier from Vanderbilt University Hospital in Nashville TN. This is all so overwhelming to me--a gal who moved to Nashville from a tiny two-lane, one taxicab town in West Virginia.

My most recent Bone Marrow Biopsy showed that the CLL was now entering my bloodstream which causes concern.. My Oncologist is hoping that by flushing the cancer from its compact state in my bone marrow and moving it to flowing freely in my bloodstream, it will be easier to eradicate. However, I am determined not to let the Leukemia win. I will maintain the same strong 'Sparkle' that my dear Mother always told me that I had. "Never let anything steal your Sparkle, Lyn," she would say.

Now, as daunting as this may sound, the takeaway from this is that when we are given adversity in our lives such as cancer, we have the option to crawl into a fetal position and call it a day, or dig deep inside ourselves and find hidden strength. My faith has always been very strong, but I never realized just how strong it was until I heard the word "Cancer".

When I was diagnosed with CLL, I was devastated! I was very scared.! Would I get sick? Would I lose my hair? Worst of all, I worried that I was going to die. I turned to my faith and my very dear friend Susie, who I refer to as my "Chemo Angel". She was by my side through each and every chemotherapy treatment and Bone Marrow Biopsies when I was originally diagnosed in 2008.

In time, I realized that I was trying to deal with my cancer by putting it in the back of my mind...pretending that it was not there. That clearly was not working. Finally I devised what I refer to as a "Wallow Window" when I am faced with cancer concerns or any adversity at all. This is going to make you smile, because it is rather humorous, but it works!. I found that if I give myself a two hour window of time to cry, sleep, scream, go shopping, punch a pillow or help myself to a big piece of cheesecake I could release some of the negativity that I was holding inside. At the end of my two hour "Wallow Window", I take a deep breath, brush the cheesecake crumbs from my shirt, and move on with my day. By acknowledging my adversity instead of putting it in the back of my mind and pretending that it doesn't exist actually lowers the stress level, and it is easier to carry on with my daily life.

I began reaching out to others to help them through their challenges in life. I began writing my story. I shared my story. I spoke with Women's Church and Civic groups and I focused on empowerment and overcoming adversities. I share my story of the "Sparkle" that my Mother told me about. We all have "Sparkle". I truly believe that out of something bad, some good always happens. We just need to believe in ourselves. It is through that faith in God and in ourselves that we find our "Sparkle".

I have had continued critical health issues since my first diagnoses of Chronic Lymphocytic Leukemia. My continued story will tell you about being diagnosed and hospitalized for weeks at a time with MRSA, a serious bacterial infection which entered my body during a major abdominal surgery. It returned later when I was diagnosed with Shingles which caused major nerve damage in my leg forcing me to use a walker and cane for 6 months. Through my faith and my inner "Sparkle" I worked with Physical Therapy until I could walk 2 miles a day without assistance! My Sparkle and I were unstoppable!

I began to keep a journal of my thoughts and prayers and I pulled from them when I was asked to share my story for The Soulful Pen in "100 Voices of Inspiration, Awakening and Empowerment". I call my story "Sparkle", and justifiably so. My story you will laugh. My story will make you cry. But most of all, I hope that my story will help find that beautiful inner peace from learning about your own "Sparkle".

Here is the beginning of "Sparkle":

"Again? I have cancer again? " Chronic Lymphocytic

Leukemia. It is in my bones, which puts me in automatic Stage 4 cancer right out of the chute, and there is no Stage 5. That is as bad as it gets, ladies and gentlemen.

No passing Go. No collecting $200. 00.. End of the road. I had been extremely tired the past few months, but I had just worked as Campaign Manager for one of the Nashville TN incumbent City Council members. The election was soon. I worked 18 hour days and I thought my fatigue was from my busy schedule. "But I am healthier now than I have ever been!" I told the Oncologist. Prior to the campaign, I had dieted and exercised my way to a 104 lb. weight loss and I'd been going through the application process to try to become a Houseguest contestant on the reality show 'Big Brother'!"

I was healthy and was free of the previous Chronic Lymphocytic Leukemia that I was diagnosed with 8 years prior. I did 6 rounds of chemotherapy and I was in full remission! During the original course of chemotherapy, I had lost all of my hair and was wearing what I referred to as 'my Hair Hat'. My hair just did not grow back in fully. I grew to love my "Hair Hat". It saved time getting ready for work. Five minutes and I am ready to go!

There are a few drawbacks in wearing a "Hair Hat", however. One Saturday I decided to wash my car, so I drove to the car wash. Once I had washed the car, I pulled over to the bay where I could vacuum the interior. There was a car parked next to me with two children in the back seat. I smiled and waved to the children as I grabbed the vacuum hose.. I took the end of the hose and turned to begin. Just then the hose slipped from my hand and hit the side of the door and the end of the hose landed square on top of my head and sucked the wig right off my head! I was mortified. All I could do was think of those poor children beside me looking at my horrid bald head, and my wig sticking out of the vacuum cleaner hose!! I felt like Lucille Ball in one of her comedy skits!

I looked at the children, and they were crying and I heard one of them say "The vacuum sucked her hair off"!! I pried the wig from the end of the hose and I quickly tried to reattach it to my barren head. I put it on. It was backwards. The children were crying and holding onto one another trying not to look at me, I took the backwards wig off and turned it around and out of the corner of my eye, I could see the poor Mother of those children and she was standing there with her mouth gaped open just staring at me in disbelief. All I could do was look at her and mouth the words "I. Am. So. Sorry"!

The children were still screaming so loudly, and for all I know, they may still be in therapy as a result of seeing the vacuum cleaner 'suck that lady's hair off'.

I got in the car as quickly as I could, and drove directly to the wig store and purchased some two-sided wig tape. I am happy to say that I have not had any further wig debacles, but I am mindful to vacuum the interior of my car in the parking lot in front of my apartment (although I am also very mindful to case the parking lot for random children just in case!) All in all, I had adapted well to wearing a wig. It was a small price to pay to have my health back. I love my wig! I have a sassy little chin length bob which was a style that I never could pull off before!... Boy am I Sparkling now!

All in all please hold tightly to your "Sparkle". Never allow it to slip from your grasp and always believe in yourself. God bless you and always continue to allow yourself to be illuminated by the Light of your Sparkle.!

Learn more about Lyn Kyrc

Lyn is a lady who is truly on this earth to be an inspiration to others. Although she has been faced with multiple adversities, she has been blessed to know so very many women and men who have shown her that with patience, perseverance and most of all with faith, you can do just about anything that you set your mind to. Lyn is originally from Moundsville, a small town in the Northern Panhandle in the beautiful hills of West Virginia and currently resides in Nashville Tennessee where she moved to be closer to her two grown sons...Dylan and Malachi. Lyn has always maintained her 'small town' attitude, and knows no strangers. She is self-taught through life experiences, and she wants to share those experiences with you. Lyn often mixes a bit of humor about those life experiences when she speaks with groups of women and men. She feels that a smile in the face of adversity is step one to overcome obstacles...

Lyn shares her story with various church and civic groups, with a small group of ladies sitting around the table having a cup of coffee, or privately on a telephone call or video chat. Lyn believes that life, itself is a classroom, and we learn something new every day that we can use to help someone else...

Always remember... Never let anyone ever steal your sparkle !

Website: http://www.LynKyrc.com

Krissie Aylward

The Greatest Gift

"Losing my mom and being diagnosed with cancer were the turning points in my life. The greatest gift was in the strength she left with me, as me."

My story starts here but it is far from all of my story. As my life has shifted over the last few years, many things have fallen into place and I am never looking back.

The Phone Call that Altered my Life

"Hello?" I answered, waiting for my mom to reply with her typical, "Hey, kiddo"

I had called her two days ago, to wish her a happy birthday and text her as well without any response. The caller id read MOM but it wasn't her voice that responded.

"Krissie, it's your dad……, I'm afraid your mother has died…."

The line went silent. I could hear the voices in the background, the hustle of feet on the wood floors. I'm sure I didn't hear him right. I couldn't have heard him right. I had just spoken to my mom a few days ago. I had just seen her a week prior. I had just been reassured by my aunts that she was ok, not feeling well, but she'd be ok. I was supposed to drive up to their house that Friday for her birthday and to celebrate Father's Day. What the hell was he saying??? Was this some sick joke??

"Are you fucking joking with me right now?" It was out of my mouth before I could stop it. The anger and pain in my tone could not be contained at that moment of shock and total disbelief. I didn't want to play this game. It wasn't supposed to happen like this. This is not what I had planned!!

"Why would I joke about something like this?" my dad responded, obviously distraught and confused.

And then came the slap of reality. The scream in the middle of the parking lot after little league practice. People standing around watching me as my heart was breaking. My boyfriend, my rock, trying to calm me. I felt like someone had punched me in the gut. I had no air coming in and I felt totally helpless. I was drowning and my mother would never be able to help me again. She was gone and I didn't get to say goodbye. I didn't get to tell her how much I loved her. Worst, of all, I didn't get the chance to help her.

My dad found her the evening following her birthday. He had gone up to her room the night before to wish her a Happy Birthday. She hadn't been feeling well and when he asked her how she was doing she told him she felt better. I smile today at those words because I can hear her telling him that. She never wanted anyone to take care of her but in reality, that was her biggest fear… who would take care of her if she got sick? Me, that's who.

There is not one single struggle that I have been thru in my 40 years that could have prepared me for that phone call. There is not one single heartache that hurt me to my core like the loss of my mom has.

The hours, days and weeks that followed are a blur to me. Almost like I was living in some surreal world. I felt numb but at the same time overwhelmed with emotion. You see it was the first time I had allowed myself to actually feel and be vulnerable in a very long time.

I told my boys that evening and the looks on their faces will be forever etched in my mind. The heartache and the sense of helplessness; the raw emotion broke my heart. Their grandma was everything to them and this was their first experience with death. I could see the anger, the fear, the confusion and ultimately the pain flood thru them. The hot tears burned their faces as they rolled endlessly down their cheeks. Their mouths would open but no words would come out. As we stood in the middle of their room crying and holding one another close I could feel the strength we have built and the bond we have formed as mother and sons take over.

We held one another up, taking turns sharing memories, asking questions, and figuring out how we would push thru this. We would push thru this together because that's what we do. We are a team and we stick together, good, bad and ugly.

I spent the month following my mom's passing making the weekly trek back home to check on my dad and take care of funeral arrangements. As I began to go through the things she left behind the feeling of abandonment became stronger and stronger. I found myself constantly asking "Why?" or "How could she leave me?" "How could she do this to me?" and the ultimate question, "What did I do to deserve this?"

Shame after Loss

Hadn't I been thru enough in my life? Divorced twice once at the hands of alcoholic/addict. The second at the hands of narcissistic sociopath who broke me into tiny pieces. A thyroid cancer survivor who found myself homeless with two kids in tow as I was released from the hospital after a full thyroidectomy. Spending a month recovering in a so-called friend's basement until I could find a place for myself and my boys to call home. Being harassed and ultimately threatened by my estranged husband while trying to remain strong and protect my boys. Unable to work for periods of time as I underwent RAI treatment to kill any remaining cancer and having to send my boys to stay with friends because the doctors said it was unsafe for them to be around me. Barely making ends meet and 'borrowing' quarters from my kids' piggy banks for gas and groceries. Slowly healing and trying to put together those tiny pieces during chaos.

And still more memories.

Exhausted, absolutely exhausted, but always making time for my boys and being at every sporting event to cheer them on. My mom was with me thru it all. Spending the day and night with me as I labored for hours with my first son. Being at the end of the bed to watch a miracle unfold before her eyes and seeing her first grandbaby born. Rushing me to the hospital as my water was breaking and my second son was on his way. Running into the delivery room just as her second grandbaby was coming into the world, six weeks too soon. Opening the door when I showed up with the clothes on my back, a diaper bag, and two babies, tears rolling down my face.

Willing to remodel her house when I was planning my great escape from my second husband and giving me hell when I decided to stay and not move back home. Calling me in a panic when she showed up to my house and my boys were being berated by their step-father and she was terrified for their safety. Holding my hand as the iv was placed in my other and laughing at the silly comments I made as they wheeled me in for surgery.

Listening to the ENT tell her that her daughter had papillary carcinoma and it spread to her lymph nodes. Hearing nothing but... "She will be ok. This is a curable cancer." Telling me that I couldn't quit my coaching business because it was what had changed my life. Celebrating holidays together and birthdays and ultimately watching a dream of hers come true as we sat in the presence of one of her favorite bands, Fleetwood Mac. A surprise 70th birthday gift I could give to her.

I made it through. Somehow.

As I began to clean out my mom's closet, I ran across somethings buried in the back. I knew she was very active in a service group and had gotten elected into many different prestigious positions during her service. What I didn't know about were all the awards and honors she had received. One being the Presidential Award for Service, one of the biggest honors one can be given. As I mulled thru the pictures and plaques, framed awards and articles, it became very evident to me who my mom was. She was a giver, a best friend, a story teller, and she served with a fire and passion like no other. It was in that moment I realized that my mom knew who I was as well. She believed so fiercely in me and saw the fire burning inside me just as it had burned inside her. In that moment all of my questions faded and I began to focus on her legacy. A legacy so great I had no idea how I was going to continue it.

On July 18th, 2015, I stood in front of my family and friends and what I had thought was a terrible joke was replaced with a cold hard slap into reality. I saw faces I hadn't seen in years and heard stories my mom had shared so passionately with her friends. Each one of them knew all about me and my boys, like they had lived it with us. Every person that spoke to me repeated over and over again, "Your mom loved you and your boys so much. She thought you all walked on water and could do no wrong. She was so very proud of you and her grandbabies and adored all of you." Those words said, stories told, tears shed and smiles shared are what got me thru that day. I delivered a eulogy to honor my mom and tell a story of my own. Standing strong and picking out faces that I needed to see in each moment of weakness, I could feel my mom with me. Hearing the laughs at certain points and then watching those tears roll down the faces of my boys as I shared with everyone how much my mom adored them.

A year has now passed since I received that dreaded phone call and we have grown so much. I have spent the past year really figuring out who I am and what I am meant to do. The belief that my mom had in me was so strong and her admiration and support so fierce yet so quiet it went unnoticed to me. I searched constantly for the words instead of opening my eyes and seeing.

It has become very clear to me what I am meant to do and that my mom knew that all along. However, she knew she had to let me figure it out on my own. Hence her quiet cheers from the sidelines and her unending expression of admiration to her closest friends. I have found my passion and it doesn't fall far that of my mom's. It is a passion for helping people, helping people find their way out of struggle and develop a belief system within themselves so strong that they become unstoppable. I have instilled this belief in my own boys and it is amazing to watch them grow. Although I am far from quiet when it comes to telling them how proud I am of their accomplishments and how much I admire their strength, much like my mom I do let them fail and figure things out themselves.

As I bring this chapter of my life to a close, I will leave you with this. In every struggle I have been thru I have also struggled to find the reason why. Why did this happen and what did I do to deserve it. I have come to this very answer; Everything happens for a reason. We must open our eyes and be ready to see that reason. It may take hours, days, months or years, but we mustn't shut our eyes. We must remain patient and open. I know that I went thru my own personal hell and suffered both mental and emotional abuse so that when I was faced with a life changing event I would be strong enough to push thru. I know I was strong enough to push thru my cancer because of that very deep inner strength.

I know that because of my cancer I was given a second lease on life and in a weird way that very cancer that could've taken my life saved my life and the lives of my boys. My mom's passing was a critical time in my life and although I thought I was unprepared at the time, I can look back now and say, I was fully equipped to rise above and push thru and it was my mom who made sure that I knew that.

Today I spend my time in the health and wellness industry and have found my passion and purpose. I AM a WARRIOR fighting each day to EMBRACE this BEAUTIFUL mess I am, INSPIRING other women to BELIEVE in and accept the BEAUTIFUL mess they are.

Learn More about Krissie Aylward

Krissie Aylward, a proud mom of two teenage boys whom she absolutely adores. A thyroid cancer survivor who is learning to embrace the beautiful mess she is while inspiring other women to do the same. Krissie is a fitness coach and entrepreneur. She has found her passion and purpose in creating success stories that change people's lives forever. Krissie can be found laughing and spending quality time with her soulmate, Chuck, motivating and inspiring a room full of fitness junkies, hollering and cheering for her boys at their sporting events or quietly working in her home office creating her very own success story.

Follow Krissie on

facebook www.facebook.com/krissieaylward1 or on

Instagram @krissie_aylward

Judi Moreo

Overcoming Cancer: A Journey of Faith

Surely, there had been a mistake. I was healthy. There was no pain. There were no lumps I could feel. All the tests had to be wrong. After all, they had redone the tests several times and the surgeon was the only one who said I had cancer. This was the most alone moment of my life.

Once I moved from disbelief to acceptance, my first concern was what would happen to my sister if I died? Who would take care of her? I couldn't die. I had to get well. There was no other choice.

The surgeon said I needed surgery immediately, so we scheduled it for 5 am the next morning, which just happened to be my birthday. When I awoke hours after the surgery, six nurses were singing "Happy Birthday."

At the follow-up appointment the next week, the surgeon explained I would need an additional surgery to remove a sentinel lymph node – then a round of radiation treatments and chemotherapy. I scheduled the surgery for the next month, but I started hearing a voice inside my head telling me not to do it. As the date grew near, I called the surgeon and asked how long I could wait. She said a couple of months, so I postponed the surgery. She sent me to see an oncologist who explained to me that lymph node removal is usually done at the time of the cancer surgery. He seemed surprised it had not been done.

I was fearful of radiation and chemo. Everyone I knew who had been through it had been too sick to work, had lingering side effects, and even though some of them are still alive, the quality of life they are living is substantially diminished. I didn't have the time required to go for treatment and absolutely didn't have the time or inclination to be sick. I couldn't make money if I was taking chemo and radiation and was too sick to work. I had to work. I needed to make money. I had to take care of my sister and myself. I was afraid of was living an unhealthy life – suffering side effects of cancer treatment.

I was very frustrated and confused. I felt I had no control over my own life. It seemed no one –not doctors, not family, not friends -- understood how important it was for me to make the right choice about treatment. I had more to consider than just myself. I had to find some way to get well or at least keep going at optimum efficiency if possible.

I started asking, "Why me? I have been a good person. I work hard. I try never to hurt others or do things that are immoral or illegal. I am a good citizen. I've really worked at becoming a quality person." Now, just when I arrived at a place in my life where I could start looking after myself and do some of what I wanted to do, I was diagnosed with cancer. I felt trapped as though I would never be able to live the life I wanted and it would soon be over. "Why me? It isn't fair. It isn't fair and now it's almost over." I've always known deep down that life isn't fair, but this certainly seemed to be definite proof.

When the doctors spoke with me, I felt like I was in enemy territory. When I tried to explain my circumstances, they told me I didn't have a choice. They insisted on treatments which would not accommodate the life responsibilities or the time restrictions I had. One doctor told me if I didn't do what she said I would be sorry. Another said that without having the chemo and radiation treatments, I would be dead within five years. Yet another said if I did have the chemo, I could extend my life for another five years. Isn't that the same five years? So, if I had the choice of living five years without chemo or living five years with it and its side effects, why would I chose to do it?

I began trying to figure out what I wanted to do with those five years. It didn't feel like panic, but it could have been. I knew for sure I wanted to be healthy until the day I die. I wanted to be able to do the things I wanted to do whatever they might be. Most of all, I wanted to be the one to make those decisions…not leave it up to some doctor who doesn't really know me or anything about me.

Because I was getting so many messages from the outside which conflicted with the messages I was getting from the inside, confusion and frustration began transitioning into anger. I wasn't mad about having the cancer. I wasn't mad at God. I was angry with everyone else telling me what to do with my life. I was also angry with doctors telling me that I only had a year and possibly a maximum of five years to live. I have never seen an expiration date stamped on anyone's forehead and I knew for certain there was none stamped on mine. Where were they getting these ideas?

At my next appointment with the surgeon, the explanations still didn't add up. She was now telling me it would be eight or ten lymph nodes she would remove. She showed me a pump that looked like a clear hand grenade attached to a long tube which she wanted to insert under my arm and down my side, so I could pump toxins out of my body. I couldn't think what to ask. I just knew I didn't want to do this. So, I said, "You are not going to make it as a motivational speaker. There is nothing you have said that would convince me to do that."

Surely, there was another way to find out if there was any more cancer in my body, so I pestered the oncologist who said, "Yes, we can do blood tests and a CT can." This made me realize one of the most important things cancer patients should do is get a second opinion before allowing anyone to cut us open or treat us in any way.

I started doing research, visiting clinics, and spas. I read books and watched movies about cancer, treatment, nutrition, and natural healing. I prayed for guidance, asking for a sign that I was doing the right thing. The voice inside of me kept saying, "No" to what everyone else was telling me to do. The more they insisted I have chemo and radiation, the louder the voice became.

A friend recommended a naturopath in Cedar City, Utah. The instant I walked into his clinic, I felt a sense of peace for the first time since this whole nightmare began. Dr. Holcomb greeted me with, "Let's see if we can get you well." That sounded like a really good idea to me. No other doctor had even mentioned getting well, they all wanted to talk about treatment.

After the initial examination, he put me on an intravenous drip of vitamins, minerals, and trace elements to boost my immune system. I sat for 2-1/2 hours with the tube feeding this mixture into my blood stream. Dr. Holcomb administered the drip, left the room, and came back with a book which he suggested I read.

It impressed me that he had "heard" what I had briefly shared and gave me a reference for dealing with my emotional pain. This was a doctor who did not see me as an illness. He saw me as a person. He would help me heal all my dis-ease, not just my body.

Before I left, Dr. Holcomb gave me a large packet of vitamins, herbal tinctures, and other naturopathic medicines as well as instructions on how to use everything. He then said, "On your way out of town, I want you to stop at the chiropractor down the street and get your neck fixed. I made an appointment and he's waiting for you."

He had noticed I had a stiff neck and was suffering extreme pain. I couldn't turn my head either way and hadn't been able to do so for the past year. This was his second observation and acknowledgement of something else which was affecting my health.

The chiropractor adjusted my neck and asked why I had gone to see Dr. Holcomb. When I told him about the breast cancer, he suggested I take Vitamin D3. He was the third person that week to bring Vitamin D3 to my attention. After a short discussion regarding the benefits of Vitamin D3, he said, "I will work with Dr. Holcomb to get you well." I asked to use the restroom before I started the three-hour drive home.

While in the restroom, I continued to pray about my decision to take the naturopathic route. Prayer was becoming a 24 hour per day activity. While praying, I looked up and saw a beautiful poster that read, "The Power that made the body heals the body. There is no other way." An incredible peace came over me. I had my sign. I must admit I had previously thought the sign from God would possibly come in the form of a white dove, a rainbow, or something equally transcendent. I hadn't expected it to be an actual sign on a wall. But, the voice was saying, "Yes."

Seven and a half months later, my oncologist gave me a clean bill of health. That was six years ago. I have made many lifestyle changes and today, I am enjoying a healthy, vibrant, and exciting life.

Judi Moreo, CSP, is a motivational speaker and author of *You Are More Than Enough: Every Woman's Guide to Purpose, Passion and Power.* She is the publisher of the *Life Choices* book series and *Choices* magazine. You can listen to Judi's motivational messages on her popular podcast, *"Choices with Judi Moreo."* Learn more about Judi at www.judimoreo.com or contact Judi at judi@judimoreo.com.

Spirituality & Enlightenment

Rev. Shelia Prance, PhD

Finding Myself

I am a southern lady who grew up in a small country church. I remember being awarded a "perfect attendance" pin for not missing Sunday school classes in an allotted period of time. We were required to quote the Books of the Bible, the Ten Commandments and various Bible verses. Our church was not large enough to employ a full-time minister.

The minister preached two Sundays per month and was also employed at another small country church the remaining Sundays. The preacher was an old man who did not graduate from high school. He had been "called to preach" at a young age. This man used the pulpit to quote Bible scripture and then provide his opinion regarding what he read.

Our church did offer Vacation Bible School and summer revivals. I received more training in arts and craft projects than Bible studies in Vacation Bible School. The summer revivals consisted of long sermons each night with miserable heat to deal with. I remember the church did not have indoor plumbing or air conditioning. There were two out-houses behind the church building. One for the men and the other for the women. There was always screaming from the ladies out-house as lizards were common residents. Paper fans with Jesus picture were provided to assist in making the services more comfortable. In my opinion, I grew up without a strong basis in Bible education.

When I was seventeen years old, I married my high school boyfriend. My parents married just out of high school and I believed it was the correct thing to do also. This is another story to be told later or perhaps never. I attended the church where my young husband grew up. This church was warm and invited me to join in. I gladly took my place as a Vacation Bible School teacher and worked with the children. The services were similar to what I was accustomed to from my home church. The preacher was a full-time employee and his messages were different than what I had experienced previously. The next fifteen years, I attended various churches searching for what I missed from organized religion in my youth. There is one Sunday message that broke the trust I had in the preacher at one certain church. The preacher chose to turn his message into a political rant. As a Southern lady, I sat through the message out of respect for the members of the church.

After the service, I spoke with friends on my way out the door, never to return with that congregation or minister. On my drive home from the service, my head was full of questions. Where do I go now? Do I find another church family? Do I want to deal with the church politics? What choices do I have? I knew I had plenty of chores to keep me busy on Sunday mornings with family responsibilities. I made my decision to stay home and forget about organized religion at that point in my life.

For several years, I spent my time attempting to "find myself". I worked a full-time job, married with one daughter and three step-sons. I attended college at night working towards a Bachelor degree. Obviously, I was one very busy lady. One night I was studying for an exam and thought about how nice it would be to take a class I was interested in and not a requirement for a degree. I actually set an intent which surfaced several years later. In 1991, I graduated from the University with a major in accounting after seven years invested in night school. The degree allowed me to apply for higher paying jobs and my career changed with duties and responsibilities.

In 2000, I met a gentleman in a spirituality discussion group. He spoke with a passion about his faith and beliefs. He talked about various current authors, books and workshops. I took notes and checked out different books from my local municipal library. This gentleman renewed my curiosity regarding what I had missed in my faith journey. He talked about "energy work" which included Reiki (pronounced ray-key). Reiki is a laying-on-hands method of healing that comes from the God-force. The energy does not come from within the healer, but through the healer. Reiki heals by flowing through the energy field and charging with positive energy. It is believed that Reiki is the same method that Jesus used to heal the sick. My research led me to a lady who was a Reiki Master providing classes with the attunements. Her location was in a city about one hour from my home. I became a Reiki practitioner in 2001.

My Reiki Master was also an ordained minister with classes for those who wanted to become a minister. I had not considered becoming an ordained minister when this class appeared in my path. I put preconditions around the ministerial classes. The classes were scheduled to meet weekly at night. I would be required to drive over two hours, after working all day, to attend the classes. The classes including homework assignments was one factor. My work schedule consisted of working for a Certified Public Accounting firm with 60 or more hours required weekly for the duration of income tax season.

I also had to consider the possibility of winter weather driving situations. Our household of six people would require adjustments along with additional financial resources required for my class. I kept asking myself "how can I do this?" My answer was very gentle. I knew without hesitation, I had to accept the opportunity. If I ignored this chance, the class would not present itself to me in the future.

I was ordained as a Metaphysical Minister in 2002 with a Christian faith. To this day, I do not know who is more surprised with my decision to become an ordained minister. My family and friends were taken back, but I was the one shaking my head regarding what I had gotten myself into. I consider the designation as a path to open doors for me. It has opened some doors with others being slammed in my face. I joined a local Hospice to offer my services. An older man was the head minister and he did not accept that women could hold the position. Unfortunately, I was never given an assignment with him in control.

Since the day of my ordination, I have continued to evolve to where I am today. I continue to work as an accountant for my main source of income. I am a Reiki Master and teacher working with individuals. In 2003, I found a book titled "The Theft of the Spirit" written by Carl A. Hammerschlag, M.D., a Jewish psychiatrist. He spent almost twenty years in the Southwest United States working with the Hopi Indians. The book provided a view at Native American traditions and culture I had never been exposed to. I was hooked and wanted to learn more. I earned my Master of Divinity (MDiv) and Doctorate of Philosophy (PhD) in Religious Studies with a focus in Native American Spirituality. The research for my graduate degrees was the most rewarding of my spiritual education. I discovered a common thread among the numerous tribes. I found a poem that connects direct to my heart.

Run your fingers through my soul,
for once, just once,
feel exactly what I feel,
believe what I believe,
perceive as I perceive,
look, experience, examine and for once,
just once, understand

-unknown author-

Part of my graduate research included attending a Pow-Wow held in my local area. A friend of mine is a member of a Lakota tribe. He introduced me to several of his Native American friends. They took the time to explain the significance of the dancing, the drums and other events taking place at the Pow-Wow. The sacred event is one I will always cherish as I was a witness to a portion of the Pow Wow and Native American culture. When I take time to meditate, I often think back to this event and hear the rhythm of the drums.

I have not worked behind a pulpit as a minister to this point. I realize this could change at any time as life happens in spite of other plans being made. I have counseled various individuals, performed marriage ceremonies, and held hands with patients. My path is changing as I work direct with individuals with terminal illness, their families and various civic groups. I have chosen to also work as an advocate for Domestic Violence Prevention, Women's Rights and Special Needs Individuals. I must provide a voice for those who cannot speak for themselves.

I found myself by taking inventory of what I had been taught, the books I read, my research and digging through my soul. I admit there were concepts evicted from my beliefs while I worked through the ministerial classes. This time in my life was emotionally draining with periods of uncontrollable crying. I reluctantly released the venom in my spiritual beliefs. The venom was the false and incomplete teachings from my childhood. It was the thoughts that stayed in my head whether they were true or not. It was the result of growing up in a patrilineal society.

The purging of inadequate concepts allowed room for my growth. My faith is a combination of numerous variables and unique only to me. I am a Christian without blinders. I have an open mind willing to listen and consider other concepts. I will read books recommended or attend workshops. I will make an emotional connection when the material speaks to me. I usually find additional information I was not aware of and adopt as applicable. When I am asked about my faith, I respond by telling people I am more spiritual than religious. In my opinion, spirituality is a personal relationship with a higher being. I find religion to be a set pattern for a group of people. I choose to use my ministry to educate others regarding cultural, social and civic issues.

I challenge you, the reader, what do you believe? Are you sure or just programmed to respond? Take inventory of your faith and belief system. I encourage you to remove the blinders and open yourself to new possibilities. Research has never been easier than what today's technology provides us.

Invest your time wisely in books and workshops to obtain other concepts and beliefs. Take a chance and attend a church service you had not considered before.

If you are not comfortable walking into a church, remember most services are recorded and available for podcasts by the next day. You could listen at your convenience. Are you ready to find yourself? I encourage you to be the best version of yourself. There is a quote I use after my signature on my email accounts. I hope you will adopt this quote in your life also. "Make your life a story worth telling" – by Adam Braun

Learn more about Shelia Prance

Shelia Prance is an author residing in Kentucky. She was born in Alabama and graduated from Jacksonville State University with a Bachelor of Science degree in accounting. Shelia is an ordained minister who works within her community. She has a *Master of Divinity* (MDiv) and a *Doctor of Philosophy* (PhD) in Religious Studies from Metropolitan University. Her graduate degrees were based in Native American Spirituality.

Shelia has spent her career as an accounting professional. She passed the Internal Revenue Service exams and is an "Enrolled Agent – Enrolled to Practice Before the IRS". Over twenty years of her career has been spent working in various Certified Public Accounting firms.

Shelia is a Certified Knitting Instructor through the Craft Yarn Council of America. She teaches classes for local junior colleges, adult education classes and churches.

Shelia is a Certified Reiki Master and provides this service through her ministry. As an accomplished home cook, she works with young parents teaching basic cooking techniques, menu planning and budgeting. She is involved in local civic organizations. She is a former Rotary member where she served as their treasurer. She is a member of the local chapter of Business and Professional Women. Her volunteer services also include being a board member of a local group working to fight racism in their community.

Shelia is a survivor of domestic violence from a previous marriage and works as an advocate for the prevention. She also works for Women's Rights and the Rights of Special Need Individuals. As a member of the local Democratic Woman's Club, she is currently working to register voters and educate them about the issues facing upcoming local, state and federal elections.

Shelia continues to work in the accounting field as the controller for an electrical contractor. Her plans include her accounting career, spiritual counseling, writing articles and books for publication and speaking engagements.

Website: www.pshelia.wixsite.com/mysite
Facebook: www.facebook.com/sheliaprance
Pinterest: www.pinterest.com/pshelia/

Ava De Guzman

God's Molding Process

Many of us have a sense to go in one direction or another based on life experiences, adversities, passion and giftedness. This is "God's molding process". Shattered dreams often lead to a world impacting destiny. I experienced this first hand as my upbringing seemed like a page from a Greek tragedy. At a young age, I had already experienced and endured some of life's greatest pain and sufferings. For over thirty years, I've harbored hurts and resentments over abandonment, neglect and abuse but did not have the courage to speak up. I was a prisoner of my own fear and shame.

At the age of four, I lived in a comfortable home with my parents and an older sibling. Though my father was not biological, he treated me like his own. I was loved and cared for. Unfortunately, I did not see the same love between my parents. They were constantly fighting and separated after a short marriage. My father, and stability, suddenly vanished and our life instantly changed. We moved into my grandmother's tiny home. As an elderly, she was also struggling to support herself. My mother started looking for a job to support us. Though she immediately found one, the income was not enough. She had to find better opportunities even if it meant working far away from us. When mother left the country for employment, my sibling and I were separated. I had never felt so alone and abandoned. I started losing interest in school and isolated myself from people. Since I didn't have many friends, I was constantly getting bullied at school. Thus, decreasing my already low self-esteem.

Years passed, and my mother didn't return. However, I never lost hope that one day she would return as promised. After many years of patiently waiting, she made good on her word and brought my brother and I to America. I was overjoyed and ecstatic for the long awaited reunion. I couldn't wait to share many precious moments together to make up for the lost years. Unfortunately, what I thought was going to be the best time of my life, turned out to be the opposite. What happened next was far from what I had anticipated. My brother and I were immediately dropped off at a relative's home straight from the airport. To make matters worse, my mother lived far from us. Weeks passed when I learned she was not going to be able to care for us. I realized that I had no choice but to practically raise myself. I was devastated. I didn't think it could get any worse but little did I know my miseries had just begun.

One horrible day, my worst nightmare had happened. I was molested and raped. I did not fight or speak up. I suffered in silence. I chose not to tell anyone fearing no one would believe me. I was scared and lived in shame. I didn't have anyone I could trust. I even blamed myself for my own tragedy. It brought back the same feeling when my mother had abandoned us twice. I felt alone, unwanted and neglected.

As I became an adult, I made many poor choices in life. I craved for love and attention in all the wrong ways. I had failed relationships including a divorce. When I became a single mother, I focused my attention and energy in raising my two daughters while juggling a new career as an entrepreneur. I spent many hours at work trying to grow my business. The workplace became my safe zone. My first start-up company became successful. Through the course of my career, I joined many business associations including women networking organizations where I met vibrant and passionate women whom I've established friendships to this day. They've become life-long trusted friends. I quickly gained new alliances and skills, thus, became more knowledgeable and influential in my industry. I was speaking in public forums and leading groups of professional women. My self-esteem and confidence blossomed.

Even with all the new found friends, success, and confidence, I felt unhappy and empty. I worked harder and spent money as fast as I could earn it. I showered my children with gifts to mask the guilt of spending long hours at the office. Over time, I acquired material wealth thinking it would fulfill me. I bought things I could not afford growing up, began traveling around the world, and started partying to experience things I had missed out on. I thought that as long as I was a good provider to my children and spent time with them during the week, I could party all weekend and still be a responsible mother. Through it all, I felt so alone. I knew I was only fooling myself and fell into deep depression. I refocused on making more money and opened my second start-up company which became another success. During my financial success, I remained lost and miserable.

As I explored my journey of finding happiness, I met a friend who shared his faith and life testimony. He gave me a book called "The Purpose Driven Life" written by renowned author and pastor, Rick Warren. I kept the book on my bedside table for an entire year without opening it. I was too occupied reading other self-heal books. During one of my low moments, I finally opened it after running out of other books to read. As I turned the first few pages, I was immediately confronted by the "Forty-day challenge", to read only one chapter a day for forty days straight. Out of curiosity, I took on the author's challenge. Within the first few chapters, I started finding inner peace and pure joy I could not explain. Half way through the forty-day journey, I found my real purpose for living, to empower women. On the fortieth day, while reading the last chapter of the book, I also accepted Jesus as the Lord of my life and surrendered my life to Him almost immediately. He turned my life around and I started giving back to the community. I became active in helping homeless people, found a Church to serve in, got involved in different caring ministries, attended bible study groups for fellowship, and eventually led a bible study group for single mothers and abused women.

Years later, I found myself back in my homeland for a short visit. What I thought was going to be a quick get-away trip to the Philippines, turned out to be a ministry of a lifetime. Shortly after returning home, I responded to God's call to start a non-profit organization helping underprivileged women and orphans in third world countries and the Philippines would be my starting point. Within six months of planning and praying for affirmation and confirmation, Bridge of Hope-World was born. Soon after, I started WINGS-Philippines (Women's International Network Giving Support), a program of Bridge of Hope-World to provide continuous support and skill trainings for homeless single mothers at different shelters in the Philippines. The focus is to help them get back on their feet and can provide for their children.

After decades of living in fear and silence, I finally found courage to speak up. I want to share my testimony to women living in despair in hopes of empowering them as they go through challenges and miseries. I want to encourage them to keep pressing on and never give up. If God can turn my own miseries and defeats into a purposeful life of victory, I firmly believe God can do the same for anyone willing to turn their life around and accept Jesus as their Savior. He has a GREAT plan for all our lives.

The Bible tells us in the book of Isaiah 30:18, "Therefore the Lord waits to be gracious to you, and He exalts himself to show mercy to you. For the Lord is God of justice; blessed are all those who wait for him.'. My ministry verse can be found in Psalm 82:3-4, "Defend the weak and fatherless; maintain the rights of the poor and oppressed. Rescue the weak and needy; deliver them from the hand of the wicked.' My life verse can be found in Proverbs 3:5-6, "Trust in the Lord with all your heart and lean not on your own understanding. In all your ways acknowledge Him and He will make your paths straight."

What Jesus did for me, He will do for you. Believe it for it's true. Sincerely ask Him for forgiveness and allow Him to take over your life. Only then will you truly overcome.

Learn more about Ava DaGuzman

Ava De Guzman founded two start-up companies in Northern California and co-founded a global company based in the Philippines. She is the President and CEO of ADG Referral Services Inc., a leading home health care agency in Northern California for over fifteen years. Ava is the President of Senior Services and Beyond Inc., a consulting firm for seniors and home-care providers. She is the President of Philus Technology Inc., an information technology consulting firm. She served as President of EBW (Empowering Business Women) and an active member of various local and international business women network organizations.

Ava De Guzman is the Founding Director of Bridge of Hope – World, a 501 (c) (3) non-profit organization helping single mothers, abused women, and orphans in poor communities worldwide. She is the Founder and International Coordinator of WINGS (Women's International Network Giving Support).

Her greatest achievement comes from being a single mother raising two wonderful daughters. She is prayerful that one day her own daughters will respond to God's calling, touch many lives, and make a difference in the world. Ava De Guzman is an active member of her home Church and serves in various caring ministries.

"I view faith and God's call as an integral part of my own life's journey as a single mother, business woman, and a follower of Christ." ` *Ava De Guzman*

Kaye Odom

"The Thought of Praying for God"

A few years ago, I shared with my small home group from church that I had prayed for God. I think it caught them off guard as it did with others I've shared this experience with. It's so interesting to see people expressions when I share that I pray for God. The leader of my small home group informed me that God does not need our prayers. I personally feel that's the beauty of praying for him because he doesn't need (anything at all). After ponder and trying to wrap their heads around why I would pray for God; I'm usually asked; Why would you pray for God? How do you pray for God? Do you think God can or will answer a prayer about Himself?

In September 1987, my 5-month old son was supposedly shaken to death by his babysitter. Two days before this incident my son and I attended Wednesday night Bible study at my church, and I rededicated my life back to God. I also dedicated my children to Gods care and protection.

I vowed on that night that nothing nor no one would ever turn me away from God again. My son's death was the worst experience of my life. I was later told that this incident made front page news and was the headline for most of the major news channels. My family loved, protected, and shielded me during this time, so I had no idea what was being said nor did I care.

My focus was trying to keep my heart and thoughts pure from anger because I knew that I could not ask and believe God to save my son with hatred for someone else in my heart. After my son was pronounced legally dead and taken from my arms I ran out of the hospital with such anger declaring that the enemy had not won.

Again, I vowed that I would be sold out for God that I would praise him, share his love, and testify to his goodness even more in Jesus name. My son's death gave birth to the prayer warrior within me, and she has grown even stronger in her faith and commitment to this day. My faith assures me God can and will answer a prayer about himself. God honors, loves, and protects our oneness with him. When I pray for God I'm praying for the world and all his creation, so yes, I believe with all that I am that God loves when I pray for him. The evidence is seen every day when he chooses to give us continued life and his unconditional love during so much devastation and destruction in our world.

Secondly, I'm usually asked how do you pray for God? One night in 1988 I was on the phone with my son's father who was in jail at the time and I couldn't stop crying, because I was telling him how much I love God. I was sharing with him that I wanted God to feel my love for him because it was so much greater than mere words could explain. My son's father tried to comfort me and assure me that God knew how much I loved him, but his words and prayers were not enough to quench the desire I had to allow God to feel the depth of my love for him.

My son's father begged me to stop crying before the phone cut off, but I couldn't. After the disconnect I continued crying, praising, and loving God. I know without a doubt I had touched God's heart because Jesus himself came down held me, and cried as he hugged me, held me, and rocked me until I fell asleep wrapped in the essence of his pure unconditional love for me.

I know Jesus was crying because I could feel his spiritual tears upon my face. His tears were warm, beautiful, and refreshing like tears of joy. At this point of my story, I'm always asked how did I know it was Jesus holding and rocking me? And, what does Jesus look like? I know it was Jesus because of the unexplainable comfort and peace of his presence. I'm certain most people are waiting for me to say he looked just like pictures the world has created of him. Jesus had no form nor image just presence.

The next morning, I prayed and asked God to allow my love for him to comfort him, bless him, and provide joy and peace to him as he continues to watch over, protect, and love our hurting world. I made my expressions of love to God with the full understanding that there is nothing and no one greater than God, and there is nothing and no one I can ask to bless and comfort Him but Him, however, I have no doubt I can touch His heart because of the oneness I share with him and my prayers of love for Him. God's heart and unconditional love is free and available to all, who diligently seek him with their mind, body, soul, and spirit.

In 1998 I was crying and whining out to God in what was supposed to be a prayer. I can't even remember what I was supposedly praying about (probably the usual stuff, job, marriage, kids). At that moment, I felt the overwhelming presence of the lord with me and I could clearly hear Him say in an audible voice "Stop all that whining and complaining. So, you think you got problems He asked"? How do you think I feel with the weight of the world to care for? For a split of a split second, God allowed me to feel the weight of the world. It was indeed unbearable and all I could do was cry, feel selfish and ashamed, and ask God for his complete forgiveness. I truly felt, received, and understood God's unconditional love for not only myself, but all His creation. Therefore, I pray for God.

Despite the difficult tragedies I have faced in my life and there have been many, I can honestly say that I have never been angry at nor blamed God. I have friends that are mighty prayer warriors, and women of great faith, however they have shown so much anger towards God at times, even so far as to tell God if he doesn't heal their child they will never serve him again. I don't understand all of God's ways, but I do trust that no matter what happens he has a plan and a purpose, and he will work it out for my good. "The Thought of Praying for God" was not the story I initially plan to write; however, it is the story I feel God wants me to share. I consulted pastors, my pastor wife, friends, and family for their input, because I did not want to offend anyone's belief. I was informed that praying for God is not Biblical. My sister reminded me that it is my life experience and my story to tell and no one can understand nor tell my story but me, because I lived through it and survived.

Last week my pastor told me that he did not know how, but he truly believed that God was going to use all my pain and trials as a testimony to help others heal. I received that word and declared that will be the beauty for my ashes. I am so grateful that God has allowed me to host and sponsor a support group for women of abuse, mental illness, and recovery. The group is called "Hot Chocolate with Ho Ho's". We eat, drink coffee (and hot chocolate), encourage and support one another, learn social skills, and create laughter (Ho Ho's).

Finally, researching praying for God did not pull up any results, so I researched Jesus prayer in the garden of Gethsemane to try and develop an understanding of Jesus the Son of God praying to God the father even though they are one. I found one study that stated Jesus prayed to God the Father and the Holy Spirit to allow them to feel and understand the human emotions of what Jesus was about to endure on the cross. I found that to be understandable, because I desire God to feel the depth of my love for him through my prayers of love for him to him.

Again, I would like to reiterate that I acknowledge and I am fully aware that God Is sovereign and supreme there is no one nor nothing greater than He. I personally choose to continue to pray prayers of love to God for God, because I love him with all that I am. He is my Father and I call him Daddy.

This is the relationship I choose to share with Him because he gives me the free will to do so, and because he has not told me to stop or that it is wrong to pray prayers of love for him. I have prayed for my future bloodline to enjoy, experience, prosper, be blessed and protected by God's unconditional love thru the mere thought of praying for Him. I now encourage them to pray for God to God in those times of darkness and confusion; when you don't know the answer or what to pray. Be assured God is the answer. Matthew 22:37 Jesus replied: "You must love the Lord your God with all your heart, all your soul, and all your mind". NLT

Catherine Kaye Odom is a Life Transition coach, Etiquette consultant, and creator of the iT2's (intelligent Thinkers x 2) children book series for and about students with special needs.

Learn More about Kaye Odom

I am a mother of 3 children 1 daughter Katherian (pronounced as K-Tree-Ann and nicknamed KoKo). 2 sons Ja'Terrian (Terry the "DJ") and Gabriel (Gifted Productions).I have 1 cool grandson Kevon, and two beautiful granddaughters Kyra, and Sabrina Starr who inspired one of the characters of the "iT2's". I love God with all that I am, and I'm on a journey to become the unconditional love that I share in my oneness with the One (God).

I love helping people discover their gifts and talents, volunteering in my community and city, hosting, encouraging, and helping the women of the women group I sponsor "Hot Chocolate with Ho Ho's".

Placida Acheru

The Power of a Good Laugh

"You take away all the other luxuries in life, and if you can make someone smile and laugh, you have given the most special gift: happiness". ~ Brad Garrett

I have been reflecting on the lessons life has taught me, lessons learned both as a child and through my life experiences. As I reflected on my journey, my memories took me to a day spent with my father. It was a very busy time for him as University Registrar. At various times of the year his deadlines seemed endless. He could not take time out of his schedule, so this occasion he decided to invite me to join him on his travels. I waited eagerly in anticipation of his car arriving to collect me. As it appeared, I rushed out of the house and jumped in. I loved days like this. I felt important. I felt like I was his support, helping him achieve his objectives for the day. We drove from meeting to meeting, with me riding "shot gun" armed will my favorite snacks!!

What made today particularly special to an impressionable sugar-fired 12 years old daughter was a chance meeting. We were skipping back to the car, when a young man approached. He had a huge warm smile on his face. He introduced himself as Stephen. "Good afternoon Sir", he said with joyously excitement. "Good afternoon Sir", he repeated. Stephen was in awe of my father. He shook my dad's hand with such enthusiasm I thought it might break off.

Stephen went on, sharing with my dad his joy of meeting him and thanking him for what he had done for him in the past.
My dad continued to smile and thanked Stephen for his words. I watched

closely how my dad laughed with Stephen. I wanted so much to be like my dad. I wanted to be someone that earned people's respect and love through their actions. It seemed like the whole world loved my dad. He always had a smile and a warm greeting for everyone.

Stephen left. My father turned to me and said "I do not know him. I must have done something good for him to make him that happy." I thought, so if he did not know him, why then did he behave in such a friendly way to Stephen. It was like they had been best buddies. I have a lot to learn I thought. Would I be that friendly to someone I did not know?

Seeing a perplexed look on my face, he whispered to me, "Be nice to the everyone you meet; because someday somewhere someone else will be nice to you and, it may not necessarily be the person you helped!"

I enjoyed the whole schooling experience and could not wait for the day I would be get my chance to go to University. Eventually the date arrived. I was a very independent young lady. I have always wanted to succeed on my own merit so I took a place in a University almost 10 hours travel from home.

The Nigerian postal service in the 1990s was very unreliable and it took my admission letter almost 2 months into my first academic year to make its journey to my home in Port Harcourt. I had a dilemma and needed my dad to help me. I had missed the deadline to secure accommodation. I was being told that all the hostels were now fully occupied. I could take my place at the University, but I would not be able to stay in the secure hostels. We were advised to take the option of private residence. If we failed, it was going to be a long return adventure. Driving in Nigeria is always an unpredictable adventure, especially at night time.

We arrived safely, amazingly without trauma. Was this going to be a good omen for finding somewhere to stay. It seemed not to be. We soon found that everything in my price range had gone and we were about to have to accept that I had missed my opportunity. As we drudged disappointed back to the car, my father was greeted by a man speaking in the native dialect of the town where the University is located. The man had mistaken my dad for someone else.

Finding two people that could not understand the local language created a curiosity in the stranger who was now interested in finding out something about us. We explained our pitiful situation in English. To our surprise this seemed to please our new-found friend. He joylessly smiled, "I might be the answer to your prayers. I have a room with a bed for your daughter. It is not on the list because the students living in the shared room refused to disclose that it had spare bed that was vacant. I have just come from viewing that room, so come with me". And in less than one hour I was settled in the most comfortable, spacious student room. Even the incumbent student liked me and we became great friends.

Before my dad left to return home he reminded me of what he told me almost nine years earlier. "You see", he said, "the good we have done in the past to others is now paying us with help today"

"So do unto others as you would like them to do unto you"

My father's wise words have never left me and played a significant part in forming who I am. "Do unto others as you would like them to do unto you" being my foundation, my golden rule in how I live my life. This rule has been and still is the bedrock of my daily living.

If I love and care. If I do good to all then life will be that I attract good back to me. No pain only gains. Right?

My years in University were the best. It did not want that part of my life to come to an end. Since graduation, I have stayed friends with some of the amazing people I met there even though I have moved thousands of miles from Nigeria.

As I walked out of that closeted University life and in began finding the life I had envisaged in my dreams, I found that "life" did not quite have the same plans in mind for me. There start to appear hurdles and obstacles manifesting themselves as people set on my making my journey, should I say, not so smooth. That with hindsight is probable an understatement. I should have said extremely bumpy.

My laughs began to disappear. I was finding it even difficult to raise a smile on some days. Where did all that love and hope go? What happened to that smiley girl with the golden rule that meant everyone smiled back with helpful intention?

My life began to slip into a series of failures and disasters caused by a very painful divorce, crushed self-esteem, self-doubt, the inability to express myself and fear of the what the future was holding for me. Despair was replacing the laughter in my heart. My fingers felt like they were slipping of the edge of my dreams and about to let me fall into a funnel of darkness. It was so dark, so deep, I could feel it pulling me. I cannot breathe. I needed a strong hand to pull me back up. I could not go back to my dad. I was too independent, strong willed, or should say too proud and stubborn to admit I was not the person I thought I was. I am a big girl and I should be able to fix me.

A ray of sunshine?

Turning on the television one day I found Joel Osteen – a Christian preacher. His message gave me a lift. I could not just see the light at the end of the tunnel, but he helped me feel its warmth. Oh, my God! I am still alive. I can feel love in my heart even with it so deeply hidden away.

I looked in the mirror and I decided. I will focus on only things that made me happy and so, the journey to rebranding Placida began.

One bible scripture came to mind and became my motto.

"Finally, brothers and sisters, whatever is true, whatever is noble, whatever is right, whatever is pure, whatever is lovely, whatever is admirable--if anything is excellent or praiseworthy--think about such things". ∼ Philippians 4:8 (NIV)

The more I focused on that scripture, the more love I began to feel inside.

I began to study me, yes! To find Placida, who is she and what does she want in life. My discovery found me creating a system that promises a shift and creates change when implemented. I began to play with my discovery asking friends and clients to try my process.

Not only did they begin to see change, they began to attract the things they have always wanted in life. My life changed before my very eyes. I found myself in a completely new career. Growth was inevitable.

My hearts desires were being handed to me by the heavens. Is this real?

I pinched myself a few times and yes! It's all real.

Another scripture stood out for me and it became my mantra. I soaked myself in every word. This scripture was unquestionably written for me.

Zephaniah 3: "Behold, at that time I will undo all that afflict thee: and I will save her that halteth, and gather her that was driven out; and I will get them praise and fame in every land where they have been put to shame. (vs 19)

At that time will I bring you again, even in the time that I gather you: for I will make you a name and a praise among all people of the earth, when I turn back your captivity before your eyes, saith the LORD (Vs 20)

Confidence returned and it was time to share with the world, my tips and tricks. So, I launched my Vision Activation Workshop. Testimonials began to pour in about the miracles the attendees where attracting into their lives. Word began to spread about this workshop and the wonders happening. Invitation to speak began to land in my inbox asking me to teach my tips and tricks.

Here are some of the lessons and steps I want to share.

They helped rebrand "Placida", ME to who she is today.

Forgive yourself and everyone else.

Hurt and pain eats you up, so the first thing is to forgive yourself for giving others the permission to hurt you so much. I had so much hurt inside; it was when I consciously began to forgive that I realized how much I was pulling myself down.

Stop comparing yourself with others.

You may think that the situations in your life has slowed you down from being all that you could have been. Focusing on what could have been only breeds more pain and hurt. Instead of moving forward, you are taking yourself 10 steps backwards. Having to start my life all over again at 37, felt like I had lost time. My clock was kicking and my energy levels not so good. To keep sane, I must focus on me and me alone.

Slow down and breathe.

We are in a fast world with lots of shining objects. There is the tendency to jump in at every opportunity that comes into your radar, alleging to be your solution to your next level. The trick is to slow down and breathe. Find you, your purpose and stick to the plan. When you find yourself being in too much of a hurry, remember to exhale.

Know your friends

It is said "no man is an island" and that your "network is your net worth". This just means that you need to have people around you who support your overall purpose and vision, whether in life or business. You can call them your network or your tribe. I found out that my inspiration is on the high when I am with my tribe. Learning new things became easy because I have the right people around me.

Look at the bright side of life.

Life will always throw stuff at you, it is not the stuff it throws that matters but your reaction to the throw. I have learned that if I look for the positive within the situation it immediately shifts everything.

And sometimes it is hard to see any positives, remember time and patience makes living this life easier.

Beautiful surprises when you trust God

It is difficult to trust in a God that you cannot see. The sure truth is, if you can trust in the knowing that he's got your back. You will begin to see him show up unexpectedly in your life. When I rested, and stopped trying to make things work, things began to fall in place. I began attracting beautiful surprises, as I call them. The question, might be, how do I trust? A good place to start, will be to just sit still and know that everything will be ok.

Latch to a Mentor

In other to enter the next stage of your life and to win you will need a Satnav. Your Mentor is like a good Satnav which will help you gain more clarity on your journey and to help you develop ideas that come to you as you go along. The journey is shorter because the mentor has paved the way for you.

My final words:

Life is for the living and it should be our commitment to ourselves to be happy and enjoy the journey. Be thankful for what you have and what you are about to receive, even if you do not know the how or when. Just trust that you will receive when the time is right. If you are in the process of rebranding you, here is a gift for you.

It's my "7 Proven steps to Rebrand YOU"

Get it here at http://placidaacheru.com/rebrandyou

Learn More about Placida Acheru

Placida Acheru, founder of Unleashed Women's Network and Coaching4Excellence, is a top UK Business Transformation Coach, International bestselling Author and Mentor. She is dedicated to guiding others toward taking charge of their lives; breaking through roadblocks to systematically transform their everyday into the power to create wealth. A straight-talking Business Coach, Placida helps clients to get laser focused on their goals. She has empowered thousands of business owners across the globe to become independent, gifting them the knowledge and passion to transform their lives. She specializes in helping clients to apply planning, mapping and financial strategies to build a successful business.

Placida uses her own powerful story of how she has overcome significant personal obstacles to encourage and motivate others. Her social media reach is over 100,000, and the recent launch of her online magazine - Her Inspiration, reaching 680,000 in its first week. Placida has been featured in digital prints (People.co.uk), NHS Conferences, TV shows (Sky 182 Ben TV, OH TV, The Sporah Show) She's also on the list of Top 100 Most Influential Black People on digital/social media drawn by eelanmedia.com She also hosts Keep Your Dream Alive Radio, featured on iTunes.

Too often the vision we hold for ourselves and our lives remains stuck. Deciding what we want in life is the hardest part of acting. Do you know what you want?

Placida inspires her audience through her signature events

http://womanunleashyourpotential.com
http://visionactivationworkshop.com
http://freedomlifestyleincubator.com

Connect with Placida

Website: http://placidaacheru.com
Facebook Business: http://placidaacheru.com/Facebook
Twitter: https://twitter.com/Placida_Acheru
Instagram: https://www.instagram.com/placida_acheru/

Nakeisha Geddes

Inner Strength with God's Assistance

"There are only two way to live life. One is as though nothing is a miracle. The other is as though everything is a miracle"

-Albert Einstein

If you are one of those people who have had the pleasure of knowing me, you would agree that I live life as though everything is a miracle. I try to focus on the positive within the negative, and seek God's assistance to help me move forward whenever I'm having difficulties.

Life in Canada has been a rough road, and believing in God and having faith in him has helped me throughout the way. Whenever I'm having difficulties I would cry "Yes! Crying is healthy", and ask God to see me through. "He hasn't failed me yet". I am a very spontaneous, risk taking individual, who sometimes doesn't think about the outcome. I believe that the more I think about the task at hand, the less likely I will do it, due to self-doubt taking over.

I use my obstacles as an opportunity to challenge my weaknesses which fuel my motivation. I think if people are more willing to fail and accept their challenges, they would be able to move forward, and not carry such heavy mental loads, filled with anxiety and fear of what's not to happen. Life is full of positivity, and people seem focus too much on the negative and its energy. There are so much more positive situations to be grateful for, if people could only open their mind to receive it through good faith.

Ten years ago I prayed to God for a career change, and I knew at the time I had to have faith in him, and that he'd deliver as he always does. I'm the type of person that likes to make plans, but also goes with the flow because I know that life take its own path.

Without any knowledge or experience within the disability or mental illness field, the Lord guided me in a direction to help me grow in areas that at the time I didn't know I needed growth.

My first day working with adults who has developmental disability was very scary. I wasn't sure what to do or how I would be able to impact their lives, since I thought they had limited abilities. In my mind I wasn't equipped enough to make a difference or empower these people with exceptional needs.

As days, weeks and even months went on, I realized that I had a lot to offer and the adults I was supporting weren't any different than I was. They were very willing and open minded with accepting me with my lack of experience, and I came to realize that they had more faith in my abilities, than I had in myself.

As Saint Augustine once said "Faith is to believe what you do not see, the reward of this faith is to see what you believe"

This goes to show how God has a way to place you in an environment that best suit your abilities or allows you to seek out potential you've looked over. Individuals with disabilities must live their lives in faith every day, and sometimes their entire world depends on others and their ability to put their needs first.

As times went by I became more energetic and started implementing skills I thought I didn't have; I found it amazing how God could find purpose within us to do his work. I became so attached to my job, I began to advocate while going beyond my duties to ensure their needs were met. Everything happens so fast that I didn't see the growth within myself; I was changing in a positive way and had no idea.

Ten years later, my perception has changed; I stress less about life stressors and accept life for what it is. Whenever things don't go the way I have planned them, I would remind myself "I'm not in control and things happens for a reason", I would seek out alternative methods of getting past my obstacle and move forward.

Over the years my parental skills have changed a lot; I am less traditional with my ways of discipline, and I am learning to listen more to my children's needs. I understand that no two children are alike and I am able to focus on my children's strengths and not their weakness. With three sons and a daughter, by working in the field it has helped me to understand that every child learns at a different paste and through different methods.

We parents need to have patience, and with time our children will reach their full potential. We also must understand that sometimes we pressure our children with our hopes and dreams, not realizing that our children need to live their own life and not the ones we failed to accomplish. Often I would talk to other parents and they sometimes express how their children have disappointed them because they are not living up to their expectation. However, in life we need to realize that when we place expectation on others they will always disappoint us; because no one person has the same idea of success.

I have become a very strong individual in ways I didn't think was possible. I have developed strong advocating skills, and determination to accomplish any issues that surrounds me. I have learned how to stand up for what I believe in, and not to be afraid of the outcome. Working with individuals with developmental disabilities has empowered me in many ways I cannot explain, and due to this I can empower those around me.

Accepting people for who they are is one of the biggest lessons I have learned. We all have something about us that others might not like, but the pros outweigh the cons. When we focus on the positive in people they tend to shine more in your eyes, and their negative behaviors don't seem to matter as much. I began to realize that a person's behavior doesn't define who they are, and when we change our perception about the person, you will realize their qualities.

Finally, I've learnt that we are all equal with different abilities, and that we all have a disability. It's easier to see other people's fault before our own, and I could identify that I have ADHD (Attention Deficit Hyperactivity Disorder). I am always on the move, always looking for something new to do and never afraid to start over. I love taking chances because it brings new excitement, and gives me that rush in the brain that I have created a dependency for.

Sometime we enter people's life with an agenda and an idea of the changes we can implement in their lives. We plan our lives and do not realize that life has its own plan for us. We often have tunnel vision and are close minded about the outcome. These pass ten years I have come to realized that the individuals I'm currently supporting, have had a tremendous impact on my life. I know that I am walking away with so much more than I have given; this has been a remarkable journey for me, and is a life time accomplishment.

Ten years ago, I remember praying to God to point me in the right direction that he's guided me, and I was so stressed out at my current employment to the point that I didn't want to return in an unhealthy setting. Growing up, the adults around me always said "what God has planned for you, no man can take way". I strongly believe that God answer prayers, and all you have to do is have faith in him. God answered my prayer and placed me in a challenging position because he had more faith in me than I had had in myself.

God knew that I needed to change my ways and my perception of what living was all about; he also knew that I had skills that I wasn't aware of. I strongly believe now that my purpose in life is to impact those around me in a positive way, and to help them seek and accept their inner self. I am able to have a positive outlook in life situations and tend to advise those around me to look at the brighter side of life.

Little did I know that individuals with disabilities have so much to offer, and to me they are our everyday heroes, because they live the kind of life that most of us wouldn't be able to survive, and yet they are one of the happiest people I know. I get to walk into a working environment daily and receive the warmest welcome and no matter what happening in my life that day, I'm able to leave knowing that I was wanted and appreciated by the people that I support. I can't imagine any other environment that could have such a positive impact on one's life.

Yes! There is a difference between the person I was before I started working with Adults with Developmental Disabilities and the person I am now, I appreciate life more. I started to focus more on my happiness and not allowing life stressors to keep me down. I have a lot to be thankful for, and working in this field helped me realize this. As I mention above, I also realize that I am not in control of my life, God is. God has given me so much over the past ten years, and I have seen tremendous growth in my life. I give thanks every day that God has answered my prayers and placed me in a healthier environment, where I was able to discover my strength, courage and wisdom.

"I may not have gone where I intended to go, but I think I have ended up where I needed to be" -Douglas Adams

Learn more about Nakeisha Geddes

Nakeisha Geddes is a Co-Author of 100 Voice of Inspiration, Awakening & Empowerment. She is a writer by day and a reader by night.

At the tender age of sixteen (16), Nakeisha was living on her own with little or no support. She has faced many challenges and obstacles throughout her life; however due to great determination to succeed, she is currently living a life that she is proud of. Nakeisha is full of life and has a way about her that makes everyone feels zestful. She is a wife and a proud mother of four (4) children; her first born was diagnosed with ADHD (Attention Deficit Hyperactivity Disorder) at the age of four (4).

Nakeisha has been working with individuals with Developmental Disabilities for ten (10) years and she is very passionate about her work and the people she supports daily. A strong advocate for fairness and equality she oftentimes finds herself advocating for people who are not able to adequately represent themselves. Nakeisha's motto is "Never regret your past: because it's your past that makes you who you are". Nakeisha hopes to empower her readers with her writing, by motivating them to love themselves as they are.

Email: nakeisha_geddes@hotmail.ca

Lisa Frances Judd

THE GIFT OF A 'NEGATIVE LIFE THEME'

It's time to heal

What is a 'negative life theme'?

Many of us experience repeated situations throughout our lives that trigger deep emotions revealing a 'negative life theme' that requires healing. Do you find yourself in *similar situations* repeatedly in life? Do you feel an intense wave of negative emotion each time these situations happen to you? It may be a different day with different people, but you are left feeling familiar negative feelings and you ask yourself why? Your negative life theme is hidden from your conscious mind and when your negative life theme remains hidden, it controls you unconsciously.

Your negative life theme is like a magnet, it pulls to you every opportunity to show you the belief or pattern in your life that you need to transform. Everyone has a 'negative life theme'.

Just as we develop a 'positive life theme' reinforced by feelings of love and connectedness to ourselves and others, we have a 'negative life theme' reinforced by feelings of disconnectedness from ourselves and others.

We are often taught in society and family life to 'avoid' negative feelings at any cost. What I want to share with you is that negative feelings are not your enemy; they are your friend. They are trying to help you heal and grow emotionally, mentally and spiritually, if you will let them.

Below I share some of my own major life events to illustrate what I am talking about. I've purposely written this section in the third person. As you read it you may see yourself in some of it.

- ✓ A child is born into a family that does not want it.

- ✓ The child is rejected by her Mother and Father from birth.

- ✓ The child is given to family members (maternal Grandparents) to take care of.

- ✓ The child is an identical twin. The other twin is not rejected; but the twin tragically dies from cot death at 3.5 months.

Both Mother and Father leave the child permanently with maternal Grandparents, divorce and move on into new lives.

- ✓ The Grandparents don't cope well and the child is passed around to various family friends in its first year of life. Eventually coming back to the Grandparents who raise the child to adulthood.
- ✓ The child never sees her Father or paternal family and they don't have any contact with the child.
- ✓ The child only occasionally sees her Mother who marries again and has other children (whom she does not leave).
- ✓ The Grandmother raises the child but often tells her that she was not wanted by her Mother.

Have you worked it out yet?

My personal 'negative life theme' is SEPARATION.

I was rejected, abandoned by my parents; I lost my twin and then passed around to three different families in my first year of life. This set me up to be unable to form healthy close bonds and to distrust people because they "always leave me". Of course, as child I did not understand the wounding of my 'negative life theme'. I just felt that I was 'unwanted' and a burden to my Grandparents. As the years rolled on, this pattern continued to play out in my adult life.

Maybe you will see some parallels with your own life experiences here:

- ✓ The girl turns into a young woman and seeks attention and love by becoming intimate with young men way before she is emotionally and mentally ready to do so.

- ✓ The young woman tries constantly to get her Mother's approval by being good at things, only to be rejected repeatedly in favor of her siblings.

- ✓ The young woman eventually contacts her Father who is indifferent and rejects her again.

- ✓ The young woman throws herself into a career to try to 'be good enough' to please her family and be acknowledged.

- ✓ The young woman loses her maternal Grandparents who raised her (the only stable relationships in her life).

- ✓ The young woman marries a young man who is not emotionally available to her because of his own 'negative life theme', therefore reinforcing her feelings of separation.

- ✓ The young woman tries to be the perfect wife and mother to her own children, seeking the love and approval of her family. Of course, nothing she does is 'good enough' for her Husband, her family and now her in-laws as well.

After many years trying to make her marriage work she ends up divorced. She re-marries happily but has a distant relationship with her step children. Years later, her only Son develops a terminal illness and she wrestles with this tremendous anticipated loss.

So, my 'Separation' _negative life theme_ continued into my adult life but now I am very conscious of it and do my best to stay conscious of it as I continue to work on my own healing on a deep level. Do we all find our 'negative life themes' and heal them? The short answer is NO. It takes courage to face your negative life theme and be willing to feel its deep pain while transforming it into something healing and healthy.

Many people avoid their 'negative life themes' altogether. Here are some ways we all do this:

- ✓ By self-medicating – alcohol, drugs, sex addiction are some examples.

- ✓ By blaming everyone else in their lives for their own misery.

- ✓ By working all the time hence always super busy and having no time to allow the pain in and work with it to heal.

- ✓ By playing the 'victim'.

- ✓ By becoming hermit like and just avoiding people where-ever possible.

- ✓ By using aggression and bullying to cover up feelings of inadequacy and pain.

How Can You Find Your 'Negative Life Theme'?

Here is a list of activities that *you can do right now* to identify your life theme.

- ✓ Do what I did. Starting in childhood write a point form list of major life events that have happened to you that caused you to feel negative emotion.

- ✓ Sit quietly, take your time and ask yourself: How did I *FEEL* at the time these events happened? Be brave and allow yourself to temporarily put yourself back in that situation to evoke the emotions.

- ✓ Write down all the feeling words that come to you to describe your emotions next to each life event.

- ✓ Look at the feeling words you have written. Do you see common themes? Are words repeated or do they have very similar meanings?

Which ONE WORD sums up best the deep painful emotions at the time of these life events? That word represents your 'negative life theme'. How can you transform your 'negative life theme' into something positive and healing? Knowing your negative life theme is a big step forward towards self-healing. You now know what you need to heal and you know what type of situations and events will trigger your 'emotional hot buttons'.

The good news is that your emotional negative response to trigger events will diminish over time; as you start to heal the wound created by your negative life theme.

Things you can do NOW to start healing your 'negative life theme'.

- ✓ When you find yourself in a repeated situation and that old negative life theme rises inside you ~ *choose to respond rather than to react.*

- ✓ Reacting is impulsive and unconscious while responding is staying conscious of the negative life theme. Remind yourself that you can respond differently this time. Take a few deep breaths, think and respond in a calm and non-attached way.

- ✓ If people disrespect you in a trigger situation, instead of arguing or trying to prove you're right gently remind others that they are stepping over your personal boundaries. Part of healing the negative life theme is to refuse to allow people to continue to hurt you.

People will treat you the way you have allowed them to treat you. If you have let others manipulate you emotionally, mentally or physically you must set *new boundaries* in line with your new found understanding of negative life themes.

It's possible that some people in your life are attached to your negative life theme. If you have asked them to respect your personal boundaries and they refuse and continue to try to get you all upset; it's time to let them go. If they are family members, then at least limit your time with them.

Find a supportive group of positive people who are working on their own self-healing and self-growth. Like attracts like! Lastly and importantly, if you find your personal negative life theme becomes emotionally overwhelming, *seek professional help* quickly. During some of my darkest times on my healing journey I have chosen to work with wonderful professionals in both alternative and traditional psychology. These professionals helped me immensely and if you have a very deeply rooted negative life theme, they will help you too. Prioritize Yourself.

LEARN MORE ABOUT LISA FRANCES JUDD

Lisa Frances Judd is a Published Co-Author in the no. 1 International Best Selling Book *Women on A Mission (Teresa Hawley-Howard)* Lisa is also a professional Australian Artist and Creative Business Owner at: QuirkyHappy.com a business that spreads joy via art printed gift and home décor products. Learn about your 'Negative Life Theme', what it is, how to reveal it and most importantly how to start healing it. Lisa shows the way using her powerful personal experience facing her own negative life theme.

Website: http://www.QuirkyHappy.com
Joyful Art printed Inspirational Gift & Home Décor products that uplift and inspire.

http://www.LisaFrancesJudd.com
You can contact Lisa about her contribution to this book and her creative business via email: lisafrancesjudd@gmail.com Lisa is also available for Speaking Events.

Contact: 61+ 247545369 or Mobile 61+ 438074714

Nikesha Tilton

<u>Activating Your Power Zone</u>

"How I Found Power Through HOPE"

People have always told me, "Kesha, you should be an attorney!" They have asked me, "How did you get to be so strong?" These are phrases that I tend to hear from those who know me well. People often turn to me for advice or to assist them with navigating through situations that leave them feeling helpless or wronged. I guess you can say, I've developed a "unique" (some may call it unconventional) way of affecting change. These are traits that would not normally be associated with an extreme introvert such as myself. Introverts usually tend to be emotionally drained because of interacting with large groups of people. Introverts find great joy in solitude. I love my "me time", but I also love helping others. I find strength in empowering others and helping them use their voice.

I haven't always been this way. There were times when I wouldn't speak up. There were times when I lived under the impression that "someone else would fix this" or thought the "system" would fix itself. I didn't possess the amount of self-esteem or confidence that was needed to use my voice. So how did I get from that space to where I am now? The short answer...I chose HOPE!

I have come to the realization that I am who I am today, not because I have always had things work out in my favor, nor because I possessed the confidence or boldness to use my voice or chase my dreams. But, I'm here because I got sick of feeling defeated. I got sick of seeing others being defeated. It is an eye-opening experience when you witness someone reach their breaking point and you realize that you have the power to be a conduit for change. Our society has always capitalized on our fears. When people feel powerless they are less likely to fight. When hope is gone, people are willing to accept what is and are unable to see what can be. I want to share a situation that occurred with my SUN (son) that had me feeling hopeless. However, I chose not to remain in that space and doing so unleashed a power that was inside of me, that can no longer be contained.

The Story of my SUN (My Son)

My SUN is 12 years old. I noticed that his grades weren't where I thought they should be. My first instinct was "he just needs to try harder". I even called him lazy and unmotivated. Soon, I realized that there may be another reason for the difficulties I was noticing. He is a smart young man, but certain things just weren't sticking. I began to think that maybe he had a learning disorder like dyslexia.

I researched this disorder and quickly noticed many similarities between the listed symptoms and the traits that I witnessed at home. I began to research dyslexia in depth, and learned that this disorder has many layers and can manifest itself in a variety of ways. I knew the first step to getting him the help he needed, was to get him assessed. I contacted his school about my concerns and they quickly setup a meeting with me, the school counselor and a few of his teachers. During this meeting, the teachers didn't share the same concern.

They informed me that they would access my SUN and schedule a follow-up conference to discuss the results. After a few weeks, I was told that there were no indicators of him having dyslexia and no other concerns existed. I immediately became confused; he displayed serious traits at home. I saw it in his reading, his writing, his spelling, his comprehension. Why was there a disconnect? Where do we go from here? These were questions that immediately began to circulate in my mind. It was in that moment that I felt hopeless!

Being a parent unlocks a reservoir of unconditional love and strength that you may not know you possess. Most parents would have accepted the school's assessment as a fact and did nothing.

Well, I couldn't allow this to be the end. I continued to research the disorder and could find some strategies that I can implement at home. I also contacted my primary care provider and sought a second opinion. Eventually, it was determined that he did in fact have dyslexia. I became disheartened that the school failed to properly diagnose him. I then wondered how many other children have been misdiagnosed. I joined some advocacy groups and became more involved with the school, with the goal of affecting change at the policy level. I am happy to say that my SUN is now a business owner and a soon to be author of his first book. You see, we didn't allow life to happen to us. We chose HOPE.

Merriam-Webster's dictionary defines hope as a "desire with expectation of obtainment" or "to want something to happen or be true and think that it could happen or be true "I possessed a spirit of expectations. I expected my children to be successful, I knew with hard work we could change the direction we were headed. Hope is an action word. It is not enough to profess you have hope, you must put your hope into action through work.

I am an introvert who activated my Power Zone through speaking up for issues that I am passionate about. I found my voice through advocacy and being an agent for change. I currently empower individuals and businesses by equipping them with the necessary skills and strategies to develop SMART goals and implement effective plans of action to reach their desired level of success.

Are you operating in your Power Zone? Are you currently experiencing a situation that has let you feeling hopeless? A quick way to gain power is to declare your desires. What are your expectations for yourself, your family, your spiritual life, your career, your finances, or your health? What are some immediate steps you can take that will catapult you into your desired direction? The journey of life will cause you to take several detours. I urge you to remain focused and strong. Never let difficulties distract or deter you from your destination!

Danielle P. Coulter

Irish Whiskey, Green Grass & The Elders

"Cerebral Palsy does not stop (Turbo) as I have named Danielle Coulter. She goes after life with both hands and feet" – Carla

In October 2016, I went to Ireland on my uncle's band, The Elders, tour for my 3rd time in my life. Every year The Elders who are an Irish rock band take their fans on a tour of Ireland. It's a lot of fun. We are in Ireland for ten days and every other day we move to a different town. It is hard to move every other day when you have CP, but it is worth it to get to see everything and hear my uncle play in the band.

Every time I have been to Ireland, it's always a new adventure for me. I have been in castles, pubs, and old houses. I even have been where they make Irish whiskey and Guinness. In 2014, we went to see how the Irish whiskey was made. After the tour, we did a testing. You'd think that I was going to pass on it because of my CP. Well, it was my holiday and I joined in with everybody else. I did my testing with my straw. I can't drink anything without a straw. After we were finished, I told my mom that I was a little dizzy. She had to help me back on the bus. When you are as little as me, a little alcohol can mess you up big time.

In the three years that I was in Ireland, my favorite place that I have visited is the Aran Island. We took a 45 minute ferry ride to get there. When we got on the Island, we took a little tour of it. It was a beautiful little island with cute little houses and horse carriages. After about 30 minutes we stopped somewhere. I had no idea what we were about to do. We walked to a little courtyard and our tour guide handed us tickets. I took my Mom's arm and started walking up a pathway up a hill. We were walking on gravel and my right foot was turning in a lot. A man who was on the tour with us asked if we needed help. I told him yes and my Mom asked me why? I told her about my right foot.

As we were walking we could see the green grass and a lot of beautiful plants. We also saw old rocks that were for a fort for sometime in the past. The Wild Atlantic Ocean was in our view the whole way up the hill. The sound of the waves hitting the cliffs was powerful and beautiful to hear. One of my friends past us and told me, "I thought that I wouldn't see you here, but here you are." I told her yep and I thought this was going to be a long way up before we get to wherever we were going.

After a while, the gravel path turned into a rocky hill that lead up to a fort. As we started up the rocky hill, we wound our way up and picked out the easiest way up. People were calling me a mountain goat when they saw me going up. We finally arrived at an archway that led into the fort, the view gave me a breath of fresh air. The view was amazing. The grass was an Irish green and some rock form the fort was in the ground. You can see the waves coming up on the cliffs, because one of the walls of the ring fort had fallen off at some point in time. My mom and I heard my aunt yelling at us that we made it and to come up to the second level of the fort. So, we went on up.

When we got up to the second level, we looked over the wall and at some point I sat right by the edge and looked out at the view. It was amazing and I took in everything that I saw. It felt like I was in a dream, but it was real. It was worth all my energy to climb that huge hill to see an amazing view from the ring fort. When I got back down to the little courtyard, I had to put my arms out like airplane wings to keep my balance to get over to the picnic table to set down. I was tired and my legs were like noodles. I was so tired but it was worth it. It was a story to tell and I am happy that I just told it to you.

It is a lot of fun when your uncle is in an Irish rock band and you can go on tour with him in Ireland. It's always fun to see old friends, family, and make new friends. Also, you can jig the whole night away when the band is playing in a pub. Every time I go to Ireland it is always a party and a new adventure.

Email: Danielle.P.Coulter@gmail.com

Website: http://www.dancanshred.com

5 Time Bestselling Author "If Dan Can Shred"

Rosa G. Corsini

"To thine own self be true"

(William Shakespeare's "Hamlet Act 1" scene 3, 78-82.)

"Lessons learned became the Divine key to the best relationship I could have ever asked for"

"To thine own self be true," "to thine own self be true," "to thine own self be true? Is there really a manual that I could have read that would have helped navigate me through life? If I had read the Bible, would all the answers to what I was experiencing going to be given to me? Possibly, but that would have required me to be patient enough to read the "word" and understand it and then smart enough to apply it. I wasn't evolved enough nor experienced enough to know how to navigate through a world filled with evilness, competitiveness, lies, deceit, jealousy and envy.

I was perplexed. How could I, a strong, intelligent, educated, self-made woman be lured into that type of world? Desperation? Lack of Self-love? Seriously, how and why?

Excuse my naivety but I wasn't trained on the school of darkness. I wasn't trained on not wanting the best for another human being let alone selflessly giving of myself to help another. But what happened? How could it be that one's goodness would be the very thing that others wanted to destroy.

Is it that others are that deeply disturbed and thoroughly miserable that they need to ease their internal strife and boost their esteem by bringing others down? Really? What type of dysfunctional personality was I dealing with? Please read on.

It was November 2004 and I reluctantly accepted an invite to meet a man that had interest in me. I had no knowledge of "Jack" but trusted the friend that organized the introduction. He appeared confident, generous, self-made...qualities to consider in a potential long term partner, right?

I was on the top of my game. I had completed my MBA the year prior. I held a significant real estate portfolio. I launched a nutraceutical company that was now in its 4th year. I was financially sound and aside from being an Entrepreneur, I was still gainfully employed in my career. I mean, WOW, I had "the goods!" And all this was achieved by the age of 34!

Jack flattered me and was quite charming. He was excited at the potential of being my partner. He would tell those around us that he was so lucky to have found me and that he knew he couldn't do better. He wanted to marry me. I was impressed! This all within a short period of time...could it be real?

I didn't question much and went along. I was excited at the thought of what life could be with a man that was so excited about me and about us. I felt that finally, I had met someone that I could start a family with and just do life together.

Not long in to the relationship, in tears, Jack shared that he was having financial difficulties and was on the brink of bankruptcy. He told me that it was due to having to pay out his now ex-wife, to whom had been married to for only a year, for having an affair that led to a pregnancy and now had a 3-year-old son that was estranged from him.

He was so emotional and so convincing that he wanted normalcy back in his life and that he was truly sorry for all the hurt he had caused his ex-wife, families and this little boy that I truly believed him. I felt his pain and had compassion. I felt that we were perfect for one another and could get through anything together.

Now recall, that I said, I was on the top of my game when I allowed Jack into my life and that I had "the goods." Anything I needed, he was there and so helpful. In return, I took the time to listen to his woes, understood his concerns and had extreme compassion for his struggles. I felt needed and he felt understood. I didn't question if what he was sharing with me was true, I believed him and why not, he was good to me.

I worked with Jack to help rebuild his life, while mine was put on hold. I did the bare minimum to keep my life afloat while I tended to his needs. He was demanding on my time and very aggressive with his needs.

The more we spent time together the more I noticed personality traits that did not resonate with the core and essence of me. Where was the Jack that I fell for and allowed into my world?

Jack began to portray behavior traits that were erratic. He had extreme highs and extreme lows. He was violent and did not think twice about damaging property to get his point across. On social nights out with friends, he drank excessively to the point of embarrassment.

The more I began to pull away, the more aggressive he got in ensuring I was not going anywhere. He made sure that everyone knew I was with him.

It's funny how we fall into repeated patterns in our life and how, despite our deep intuition, we still settle. You will see a bit later just what I speak of.

I felt the need to share what I was experiencing and opened up to a close girlfriend, "Jezabel." I didn't understand what was happening. Jezebel, concerned for my wellbeing, asked if I wanted her to speak to Jack, as she felt she understood him better. I agreed. At this point, I did not know what to do and was fixated on wanting to get married and starting a family.

Matters did not improve and the stress and anxiety of being with him was unbearable. I finally found the strength to end the relationship and refused to accept his calls or see him. The more strength I showed, the more he reacted negatively. He was acting psychotic!

About 3 months later, a close family member contacted me and said that Jack had reached out to her. She felt that I should reconsider meeting with him and felt that he had changed. Doubting this, but hopeful, I reluctantly agreed to meet and we met.

Once again, the Jack that I fell in love with was back! Everything was perfect and we were making plans! I thought, maybe, maybe he did learn from my absence. He convinced me that he wanted me to be fully integrated in his life and business and that there would be no need for me to have separate businesses that did not involve him. And more importantly, he wanted to get married and start a family with me. I agreed and began liquidating in preparation for my new life. After all, why would I need to have anything separate from him? We married in September 2007.

That was the beginning of the end of the relationship. The "Jack" that led to the breakup, was now back and worse, we were now married!

Jack's financial troubles continued. He disclosed that he bartered services for my engagement ring and needed to pay the Jeweler a $10,000 difference. He promised to pay me back within a couple of weeks. I agreed. A couple of weeks went by and no talk or sign of the repayment. I was so hurt. After a month, he asked if he could borrow $25,000 to buy some equipment and this time he wrote me an "IOU" and joked about paying all the funds back within 30 days. We laughed and I agreed. Against my internal strife, I trusted Jack and thought no sane person would go through all this...for what and why? His behavior spoke louder than his words yet, I was determined to make this marriage work. I was still hanging on to the "Jack" that was good to me and so excited about us.

Thirty days came and went and I overheard Jack making plans for an extensive trip with a few of his male friends. A feeling of anger overtook me. I demanded that he pay me back. Jack did not like to get challenged and got violent and accused me of being selfish and unappreciative?? Really??? Today, I can say typical behavior of a sociopath but then, I took it to heart and was so hurt and confused. I did not have the tools to deal with such a personality.

I questioned everything about myself. Was I selfish and unappreciative? Was I not a supportive spouse? Everyone around me seemed to be enjoying their lives and here I was, depressed and feeling so alone. This was not what I thought marriage was going to be like. I did not dare tell my family that I felt I had made an error in marrying Jack, so I continued to find comfort in sharing with Jezebel, after all, she understood Jack the best. She once again offered to speak with him and I agreed.

A few weeks passed and after a long day at work, I came home and there was Jack and Jezebel laughing and drinking wine together in our home. I was shocked and asked, what was going on? Jezebel looked at me and said, "we are like a brother and sister, nothing is going on." A feeling of anger overtook me but I calmed myself down and questioned myself and wondered if there was something wrong with me. They were laughing and having fun, and so was everyone around us, but me, I was feeling miserable, crazy, depressed and anxious!

One day, a voice inside encouraged me to pay close attention to Jack's behavior. I began counting pain meds and checking his phone. It was clear, Jack was taking drugs and pursuing a relationship with Jezebel. The pieces of the puzzle were coming together.

I confronted Jack and he denied it all. I demanded he end his relationship with Jezebel. He refused and got violent. With conviction he assured me that if he had wanted Jezebel, he would have married her. This time, I did not believe him. I cried and screamed "YOU LIAR, YOU CHEATER!!!" I stormed out to my car. Jack tried to reconcile. For a few months we teetered back and forth but I did not give in. It was not long after that I found Jack and Jezebel together. My last words to Jezebel were, "you want my life, you can have it, because this is not worth fighting for!" The charade was now over.

I left for good. Not only was this a failed marriage for both of us but he repeated the very thing he had so much remorse for. I had no use for continuing a life with liars, cheaters, drug abusers, alcoholics, sociopaths and emotional bullies. I had peace about moving on. No longer was I going to be played a fool. I had my family and that was all I needed. Unfortunately, it was not going to be that easy. Both Jack and Jezebel were going to ensure my demise.

A continuous stream of negative events went on, for what seemed like forever, that just about broke me emotionally, spiritually and financially. The more I tried to make sense of everything the more I got confused and encountered more of the same. I thought...WHAT IS WRONG WITH ME??? I cried. I screamed to God asking for answers. Why was the world being so cruel to me? What did I do to deserve such punishment? The two people that I trusted betrayed me and now felt empowered to orchestrate my demise.

I persevered and kept moving forward, despite it all. At one point, Jezebel, dyed and cut her hair to look like me. This was now getting diabolical! Jack and Jezebel appeared to be succeeding in their bullying quest to bring me down. Me, the woman that had it all and always did things right, couldn't seem to get anything right any more. My desire to have a family created such desperation that allowed such a pathetic existence into my life. What was I thinking to have a drug user, excessive alcohol abuser and sociopath into my life? Obviously, I wasn't thinking. And what about Jezebel? A woman that I confided in and considered a dear friend, betrayed me. For what? So she could have the prize...Good riddance!

Seven years have now passed and Jack and Jezebel are no longer together and worse, Jack continued with his cheating, drinking, drug abusing ways. As for Jezebel, she is still alone and no further ahead in her life. Her jealous, envious, conniving ways caught up with her. Emotional bullies only get so far.

As for myself, I am now celebrating my first-year wedding anniversary with Michael, a precious and beautiful soul. Our meeting was nothing less than divine. God introduced him when I cleared the space for him to arrive and I was standing strong. Although, I have lost valuable years to start a family of my own, my faith in love, and life, are being restored with Michael each day.

As difficult as it was to relive this past that no longer exists, I wanted to share what I consider a gift today to have gone through this experience. It is my gift to give back to you. And despite all the pain that I endured during those years with Jack and the years that followed to heal from it, I am no longer the same person today. I do not want to be.

I now have the gift to know what true love is and how it feels. I now have the gift to know that a true friend will only want and wish the best for you. I now have the gift of knowing the power of family. I now have the gift to know that if something does not seem right, it most likely is not. As "Helen Keller," wrote, "The best and the most beautiful things in the world cannot be seen or even touched, they must be felt with the heart." Blessings to you all.

Learn more about Rosa G Corsini, MBA BA CHRL CHC SRC

An accomplished professional and entrepreneur, Rosa spent 25+ years directly involved in the mental health of others through her profession as a senior in human resources management and as a health coach, promoting health and well being. Throughout the years, her generous, compassionate, and empathetic ways, attracted a string of dysfunctional personalities that almost led to her demise. Her faith in God and having a strong love for herself, gave her the strength to remove herself from the dysfunction and move on. After 8 years, she chose to share her story in hopes of inspiring others to do the same. This journey, now being shared with you, is her gift to give back. Professionally, Rosa holds an MBA, is a Certified Human Resource Leader (CHRL), a Certified Health Coach (CHC), a Sub-Conscious Restructuring Coach (SRC), is President of iRTH Foods, and President of YourHRDirector.ca. She is happily married to her husband, loves her family and enjoys creating precious moments.

Julia A. Royston

What Do You Tell Yourself?

It was 1963 and the doctor said, "It is a girl!" My parents were thrilled but concerned when they saw that my toes were pointed east and west rather than north and south. For the first nine years of life, there was much time and money spent on doctor visits. "Julia has a terrible speech impediment." "Julia's vision is 200/200 rather than 20/20." "Mr. and Mrs. Foree, Julia has failed the hearing test." A nurse said in a crowded gym for all to hear, "Julia Foree's weight is 100 lbs. and she's six years old." There have been countless unhappy moments surrounding my weight but, overall, I've had a happy life. I have wonderful, loving parents, two sisters who were opposite from me but somewhere behind those grimaced faces they really do love me.

In everyone's life there are good and bad times, achievement, excitement, disappointment and failure. I have had my share. Over the course of my life, I have learned to maximize the positive and minimize the negative. I don't avoid or run from negativity in my life but I realize that I can't control others or dwell on their opinion of me.

Being the fat girl, wearing glasses with a speech impediment wasn't pretty and wasn't fun. As I got older, I had the nerve to shade the lenses color on my glasses. Sometimes it was rose, other times it was brown and once it was even blue. Yuck, what was I thinking but I was trying to make the most of my poor vision by trying to make it as stylish as possible. Surprisingly, I always had friend. I was fun, cute for a fat girl, people often said, outgoing, talkative and gifted. My gift is what saved my life. At nine, I sang my first solo in church and my life changed forever.

I had a gift like no other nine-year-old or some teenagers for that matter. Throughout my teenage years, I didn't have many dates with boys but I had a lot of dates to sing in churches around the city, state and nation. From the eight track player to the record player to the cassette tapes to boom boxes and CD players. I had it all. My parents gave me all of the tools to support my gift. The one thing they couldn't give me was a positive self-image. I had confidence on the stage, academically above average in the classroom and played a musical instrument through college but when I looked in the mirror, I didn't see much. I would laugh at myself more than anyone laughed at me. My family often tells me that I wasn't as fat as I made myself out to be.

But, it's what you tell yourself that counts. Self-talk can demean you more than anyone else can. I had great friends who would defend me against anyone. I went to dances. I went to prom. My family went on vacations every year and in my circle, I was popular. I didn't live in a dysfunctional family or was abused by anyone. I did every conceivable diet known to man but lost and gained weight repeatedly. It was frustrating but it took a toll on my self-esteem. Remember it's what you say to yourself, how you see yourself and the boundaries, limits and tolerance level that you place on yourself that matters. Maximizing the positive should have been easy because there were so many positive things going on in my life, but instead, I allowed the one negative aspect of my life to magnify and intensify my poor self-image.

In my senior year in college, there was a young man stationed in the military who came to my church. He was handsome, manner able and suddenly took an interest in me. It was a shock to me. I had so little experience that I was hesitant, skeptical and turned him down repeatedly but he didn't take no for an answer. There were several other young women and their mothers who were certainly interested in him, but he chose me. Finally, I had a good announcement, I had a boyfriend, then a fiancé and then a husband. It was a miracle. It lasted for four years as a couple and eight years on paper.

It is now 1993 and the announcement from my ex-husband that ended the marriage was, "My mama says you have to go." This was clearly the lowest moment in my life. I was more than 1100 miles from home, little money, in my night gown, rollers in my hair, my clothes being tossed into a suitcase by a man who said he loved me but his mama said I had to go so I had to go. This was the last straw of a situation that had too many details to name here but this was finally it. I had had enough of a bad situation. At that moment, it didn't matter about my weight, it mattered about my life. I stayed that night but the next day, I acted. I quit my job, emptied my bank account, called my father to decide to have someone come and drive me home. I had a safe place to be until they arrived and it was all set.

I got home, worked temp services and then enrolled in a graduate program which I completed in one year while working two jobs. I was headed in a new direction with new people to meet, places to go and things to experience.

What did I learn?

Love Yourself – Sure, I should take care of myself, eat better, exercise more and maybe lose weight but what good is a perfect body with a tormented soul? I first had to fall in love with me. This is not an arrogant, self-centered, self-absorbed, can't stand to be around her type of love, this is a love of myself so that I can be the best self that I was destined to be. You don't love yourself when you allow yourself to stay in toxic mental, emotional and financial relationships. Loving yourself is determining the good and abundant life that you want to live and what that looks like for you. Denying yourself that abundant life is not loving yourself at all. Over time, I had to learn how to put limits, set boundaries, be the final approval or disapproval of who and what was going to be in my life. Love yourself enough to take care of yourself, mentally, spiritually, emotionally, financially and physically without fear or regret. Love yourself enough to walk away and don't look back.

Limitless Life – My father always said that I could do anything any human being could do. I not only remembered it but I started doing it. I had no responsibilities to anyone but myself. I was finally going to be true, good and honest to me. I took the limits off of my life and over time, the control out of the hands of others including my family. When I recognized who I really was and realized the life that I could lead, there was no stopping me. I have never been a natural risk taker, but I have taken more risk since 1993 than I ever thought possible. Through tears and pain, I decided as long as I can, breath, think and believe that I can, I can and will. Take the limits off of your life!

Live Out My Purpose – I found my purpose as I walked out my journey. It wasn't a perfect path because I am not a perfect person. I have made mistakes, bad decisions and trusted some wrong people but I acknowledged the mistake, held myself accountable, got back up, got on the right road and got moving even faster than before. I discover more about myself each day, month and year that I live. Each time I say yes to something new, discard the unnecessary, remove all distractions, love without hesitation, I am greeted with a new gift, talent, ability and opportunity to live.

Look with New Eyes – When I look in the mirror, I wink, blow kisses and tell myself that I am smart, cute and talented. Sure, I see the defects but call them possibilities. My husband tells me that I'm beautiful, intelligent and that he loves me every day. I am grateful but if he never said it, I have to look myself in the mirror and see someone smart enough, good enough, worthy enough to be a success in every area of my life. It's how you see yourself and what you tell yourself that matters.

Learn More about Julia A. Royston

Julia Royston is an author, publisher, speaker, teacher and songwriter residing in Southern Indiana with her husband, Brian K. Royston. Julia and her husband spend their time overseeing the operations of BK Royston Publishing, LLC, Royal Media Publishing and Julia Royston Enterprises to provide quality, informative, inspirational and entertaining materials as well as writing and business consulting. Julia's first love is music. She travels the country singing, giving music workshops and music consultant. By profession, Julia is a certified, technology teacher with the local public school system. In Julia's spare time, she loves to people watch, support other small businesses and watch the Hallmark Channel.

Website1 : www.bkroystonpublishing.com,
Website 2: www.royalmediaandpublishing.com,
Website 3: www.juliaroystonenterprises.com
Website 4: www.juliaroyston.net

Angela Aphayvong

Discovering My Self Love Through Sensual Energy Therapy

Hi my name is Angela Aphayvong, I live in St Thomas Ontario, I'm a mother of three amazing boys who I refer to as my Gents, married to my high school sweetheart and been together for 15 years. I am a Sensual Energy Healer and the creator of Sensual Energy Therapy.

I grew up in a few places in Ontario. Belleville, Aylmer, Dorset, Niagara Falls and St Thomas. My parents separated while I was young. I don't recall much memory of them together, other than a time with the two of them screaming at each other in the kitchen. My mother provided for 3 children, myself, my sister and brother, after she left my father. We moved around a lot, as needed.

My father has remained in Dorset almost his entire life. I recall as a child my mother would always seem to settle for men who didn't value her and at times it felt like she abandoned her children. I realized the effect my parent's relationship and separation had on me. Growing up I had so much stored anger, wondering why my father couldn't be loyal to my mother, why he couldn't love her unconditionally, why my mother allowed such disrespect and why she couldn't put her kids before the men who treated her like she was of no value.

As children, we are what is reflected around us. What we see, hear, feel becomes embedded into our little minds and bodies. We become a model of our parents, families, friends...the people we share our life with. I believe it is up to us to open our eyes and do the work that is needed, constantly growing and to become a better version of ourselves and not let our past define us.

With the knowledge I have gained over the past 9 years, I've realized I was angry with my parents for not setting an example of unconditional love within our family and each other. I always wondered why they didn't value each other or their marriage. My father's disloyalty had a huge effect on my mother's self-worth and my own as a young girl becoming a woman. Her first love...this explained why she wasn't fully able to put her children, nor herself before men who treated her badly.

I've found it so helpful to become more aware of why people do what they do...looking deeper into the situation or the person and recognizing what they may have gone through as a child. This doesn't mean we can't change these behavioral patterns. It will take hard work and dedication but it's possible. I don't hate my parents in any way. I love them unconditionally and appreciate them for all they have done for me. I understand they did the best they could with the knowledge they had. Nobody is perfect after all, we all have things we need to work on and areas we wish we could change. But life is about being in the moment and finding that something every day to be grateful for.

As a child whose self-love/worth was very low, I found myself looking for it elsewhere, not realizing it at the time of course. When you feel so lost and just want to be excepted for who you are, trouble can be just around the corner, even if our intentions are good. A life changing experience that had kicked me in the ass was a simple Toronto shopping trip with my best friend at the time. I was living with my dad and step mom, I was about 14, 15 years old.

My girlfriend was spending the night at her Uncles house in Toronto and asked me to come along. I had been to her Uncles before so I felt comfortable going. The time we spent shopping was wonderful. Considering where we lived at the time, was beautiful, but had very limited shopping options. It was a Saturday evening and we had finished up all our shopping and was about to settle in for the night.

Our sleeping arrangement was me on the couch and my friend on the floor in front of me. I started to doze off and the last thing I recalled was her Uncle sitting on the floor beside the both of us while on his laptop. I thought it was odd he was sitting there instead of upstairs with his beautiful wife and three precious girls, but I brushed it off and went to sleep. I was sleeping on my stomach and was awaken to the feeling of someone rubbing up against my ass (overtop of my pajama pants).

I was frozen and right away realized it was my friends Uncle. I could believe this was happening to me!! The thoughts that rushed though my head...Is this happening to me!? Was I dreaming?? What do I do!!?? I was in horrifying shock and felt like I had nowhere to go. Why I didn't yell and scream, I ask myself this to this day! I'll never understand why, but I wanted him to think I was sleeping so I squeezing everything as tightly as I could, tucked my arms under my stomach and prayed for him to leave. He didn't leave and tried to still have his way by pulling my pants down slightly and forcing himself from behind.

After attempting several times, he finally gave up and got off me. I remember feeling like he was still in the room, so I stayed still in that position for what felt like forever. I finally opened my eyes and turned my head, only to have his face directly in front of mine. He asked me "Was that ok?" my response was "Is what ok?" I for some reason wanted him to think I had no idea what just happened. Maybe because I knew I had to spend practically a full day at his house still before going home with my friend and her parents.

He rolled his eyes, got up off the floor and went upstairs. He never came back down and I didn't go back to sleep. At the first sight of light outside I crawled beside my friend and woke her up to tell her what happened. I was in complete shock to hear her response..."That doesn't surprise me" is what she said. I couldn't believe it!! Then she removed her blanket and looked at me shocked because her pants were off... I was extremely confused and felt this was something he maybe was doing to her and she wasn't saying anything.

 I desperately needed a shower and didn't want to be alone so I asked my friend to come with me. I remember feeling so dirty and disgusting, and felt even more sick to my stomach when we passed his middle daughters bedroom, finding him in bed with her! I'm not saying he did anything to his daughter, but your guess is as good as mine. After the shower and painful wait before leaving that day, I had never been happier to be safely home.

It took me some time to tell my step mom, but when I did she immediately helped me by reporting to the police and finding me a wonderful counselor. I went through moments of blaming myself for what had happened, and of course this triggered more of my low self-love/worth issues. The counselor reassured me this was normal emotions to be feeling being in that situation. The police investigated my case and found his fluids on my clothing through a process they call a Rape kit.

Considering he was denying this happened, it really helped my case. Two years later it went to court. The day of the hearing it was to my surprise that my friends Uncle was able to represent himself as his own lawyer and question me. I knew he didn't stand a chance in helping his case, but I was shocked and hurt that the system would allow this! When all was said and done, he was sentenced to two years in prison.

So how was I going to do my own personal growth work and use this as a tool to help me grow spiritually, physically and mentally, and not become a victim by it?

I decided to face it directly. I created Sensual Energy Therapy, an Art Form of Healing Dance Therapy for woman. Through this class I would be held accountable for the negative thoughts and feelings towards myself. I would gently recognize this and dismiss those negative thought, replacing them with positive ones. This at times was definitely a challenge, but once I recognized it and blocked out my ego from interruption, it began to pave the way for me. I went from not wanting to look at myself in a mirror, to embracing who I am and loving what I see in the mirror.

I couldn't help but be drawn to the beauty I was feeling through the art form of dance and the energy flowing through me and around me.

I found through Sensual Energy Therapy I could help repair much of the damage of my childhood, and truly believe it can help others who may have had the same or similar issues as I did as a child. Sensual Energy Therapy has helped me to face my issues, brake down my insecure walls and rebuild my self-love/worth from the inside out.

I see it in so many young girls these days, searching for something that will make them feel ENOUGH. Even as we become mature women, many of us are constantly searching for something that's missing and I'm convinced that this connection with the core of your feminine being through Sensual Movement/Dance, is one of the keys to raw happiness and vitality. Through intense self-love, a myriad of transformation can occur in life and can be infectious!! And I am on a lifelong mission to share this beautiful gift with other women.

Thank you so much for taking the time to read my story, as this has been another wonderful way of deep healing for me.

Email: ooohlalalcb@gmail.com

Website: www.ooohlalalcb.wix.com/sensual-movement

Facebook: http://www.Facebook.com/OoohLaLaMovement

Queen Iawia

Finding my Voice

"My fear of public speaking has eased since I learned to love myself in total completion." – Iawia

I always admired the Ladies who stood up in Church and read the announcements. They always stood very stoic and articulated themselves well. I wanted to be that woman one day but I was shy and beat down. Lacking self-confidence for many years I struggled. I had no idea what it took to be that women or speak like that.

As you will read, my childhood experiences caused me to create physical reactions in my body from self-hatred of my voice. Since that time, I have found so many new and fun outlets, including getting into nature and using oils for aroma therapy to help ease my anxiety. You can too.

Do you know that Public Speaking it is the number one fear in the World? How many of you are afraid to speak in public? The average person ranks the fear of public speaking greater than death. I have recently put myself out of the box and won a speaking contest!

People would rather be dead than stand up in public and speak. I was so afraid to stand up and speak publicly and I made this my number one goal in my life, to overcome, because I allowed it to control my life for so long and I was depressed and anxious because of it. Speaking in public causes a tremendous amount of anxiety in my life as well as the life of thousands of others. You are not alone if you are afraid to speak in public or if you become anxious, before speaking.

This is my Story

Growing up as a child, I stuttered and kids would make fun of me. Walking home from school some of my classmates would ask me to say something like house. When I attempted to pronounce the word house, it sounded very different. It sounded like hhh-hh-aaaase. And all the kids would laugh at me, and I would be very embarrassed. This ritual occurred daily for a brief period in my life, every afternoon walking home from school.

I was also told such things as "shut up", "be quiet", "only speak when spoken to", or "children should be seen and not heard". Having these harsh statements told to me so much, created an imprint in my subconscious and became part of me growing up. So much of our childhood is never healed and so many parents make the dire mistake of saying these things to kids, even today.

As a young child, I was frequently choked and always feared I wouldn't be able to breathe afterwards. Everything I basically did was bad. Rarely was I praised for anything. It was always something I did or forgot to do.

My childhood formed the basis of why I am so passionate today about showing parents how to raise empowered children.

I wasn't a bad child but I was very mischievous when my Mom was at work. The rigid ideas of our household were unbearable at times. I learned to be anxious and depressed at an early age and was afraid of everything and everybody. I had very low self-esteem and the only fun I had was laughing and playing with my brothers. I was always frightened and tense, rigid. I didn't understand it at the time, I thought it was normal.

I was the oldest girl and one of my brothers and I were very close. We always caught *whippings* together so we could share our feelings openly and honestly with each other. After our beatings and our parents were out of sight, we often laughed until we cried and the laughter was our release. We always laughed out of our parent's earshot, otherwise my Mom would think we were laughing at her and beat us again. It wasn't unusual for us to receive several beatings in a day.

All this tension, drama, and fear affected my voice. Being timid and having deep fear came out through my voice. When I went to live with my aunt briefly while I was learning the prayers for my first communion, I became even more fearful and timid. I was afraid to speak in front of my aunt and often forgot the Creed when I attempted to recite it. If I made a mistake I was instantly pounced upon and beat by my Aunt.

This behavior to this day has caused me great anxiety before I speak. I was learning disabled as a child and no one was aware of it. During those years there was in the (special class) and it was for severely learning disabled students. I often had to recite things over and over until I remembered. I learned everything from memory and only remembered it long enough to pass a quiz. My mom was uneducated and unable to help me. I was on my own and since I had a burning desire to be smart, I was on the *B Honor Roll*. I could read well but never retained the formation.

I was never called upon to speak in front of the class except in the 3rd grade. Each student was given the opportunity to teach the class. I did so well teaching the class that my teacher Mrs. Lillie Mae Jones *told me I was going to be a great teacher one day.* Those words always stuck with me until this day. I wasn't the smartest kid in the class but I could teach.

Many years later I was a senior in High School and was called upon to give a report. I was so anxious and my voice trembled the whole time I read my report. I refused to quit but stood there with dignity and pride, refusing to give up, till the end, and sat down. I was very embarrassed and was never asked again to give a report orally in that class. I was also the only black girl in the senior class, because it was the first year that the school was integrated and it was 1966.

I began to hate the sound of my voice and the more I projected hateful energy toward my voice the worse it began to sound. I never spoke up for myself or said anything if I was in a room full of people. The only conversations I ever had were with my close friends and some family members. I would never ever sign for anything that required me to speak in public and especially out loud. I had no problem holding a conversation with my friends, brothers and sisters. I was afraid to speak up in meetings and always had something to say but it he words never came out.

My voice began to change and respond to the hatred and abuse. I began to develop signs and symptoms of Spasmodic Dystonia. I had smoked for over 25 years and drank frequently. These things contributed to my vocal issues. I was on a roller coaster ride to destruction and didn't know how to ask for help or get off. I suffered in silence and the fear and anxiety manifested itself more to the point of paralysis. Not a physical paralysis but a mental paralysis. I had delved deep into the pits of hell and was locked in my own private prison. Smiling on the outside, hurting on the inside, hating the sound of my voice and afraid to open my mouth. When someone comments on my voice I cringed and sank deeper into self-pity.

I had much to say but the words just never came out. I also hated it when people made a comment about my voice. Year after year I suffered in silence and prayed for me to be free of the fear to speak in public. Year after year it felt as though I failed. No one knew the pain and agony I felt and I discussed it with no one. I smiled on the outside and suffered on the inside. Someday the pain was unbearable and I would have thoughts of suicide. The pain and agony were unbearable at times. Oh how I longed to be able to stand up and speak well.

I decided to seek help and in my pursuit spent thousands of dollars on some therapy and programs that did nothing for me. Everyone I spoke with promised they had a solution but nothing worked for me. I was finally diagnosed "Spasmodic Dystonia". It's a condition when the vocal cords spasm at will. Again I continued to hate the sound of my voice.

The biggest disappointment and heartbreak was not being chose to participate because of the sound of my voice. I was ostracized and discriminated against even in Church.

I suffered in silence because of three things: The depression, anxiety, and the sound of my voice. I decided to become a lecturer in Church and prayed to God for my healing.

I believed whole heartedly I would be healed. I didn't realize the extinct of the fear until I stood up to lecture in the Catholic Church. It all came back, the fear of standing up in front of my Aunt resurfaced and I experienced it all over again. Healing of my old story was necessary to this day, to be a speaker and an author. It was in that old story where my voice would continue to be muted until I learned how to heal it. I continued to pray reverently. A Church member came up to me and told me after one Sunday Mass that II at that I was the worst lecturer she had ever seen.

I was devastated and quit the program for approximately 6 months. I continued to pray and nothing happened. The anxiety and panic attacks continued and my depression soared. I remember one Sunday many years ago I was scheduled to lecture and was sitting in Church and panicked so bad I became paralyzed and couldn't get up. Luckily, the person sitting next to me was a lecturer and I asked her to do the reading for me. At that moment, I hated myself. I continued to suffer in silence and wondered how long was God not going to answer my prayers. I had courage if I didn't have anything else and I continued to get up and speak for many years.

I was and still am very determined to win and overcome all my insecurities. I was anxious all the time and never really knew what it felt like on the inside to be at peace. I was constantly warring with myself. I associated most of the anxiety to my childhood because of our household and living with my abusive aunt.

One minute we were sleeping and the next minute we were awaken by our mom telling us to pack our things we were leaving and moving back to Louisiana. There was always some type of drama in our home and my Mother also was depressed and easily agitated. It didn't take much to set her off. It's amazing how things of our childhood can still affect us today as Adults.

I remember writing affirmations over and over about the sound of my voice such as: I am speaking boldly clearly and confidently. My voice is powerful and strong.

Tablet after tablet of paper and pen markings, and nothing changed with the sound of my voice. I got Reiki treatments and tapping treatments and nothing changed. I had energy work done and my voice remained the same I was desperate and willing to do whatever it took to overcome my speaking issues. It seemed as this it all failed. I felt abandoned by God and that my prayers were in vain. I was applying action with my prayers and nothing. Was I doomed? Was this an issue I was destined to live with the rest of my life? I know some of you reading this are wondering the same thing. When will it change? Rest assured it will change for you in time.

I made a firm decision to face my fear.

I joined Toastmasters because I wanted to be a better speaker. After a year with Toastmasters I later joined The Speakers Academy and continued to be a part of Toastmasters.

I remember the very first time I joined Toastmasters I was sitting in the meeting and silently praying they wouldn't ask me my name. I arrived late and the meeting had started. After the meeting the President asked me what was my name and I stated it very timidly. I almost didn't go back because of that one encounter but I remembered the reason for my initial visit and decided to join.

One Sunday I was to speak, and my voice was shaking, my anxiety was out of control and with the two together I panicked. I was so angry with myself I wanted to run and hide, I sounded like a shrill piercing scared, broken record all in one. Dressed immaculately, I was very embarrassed and question God at that moment as I walked away from the lecture, about my healing. I hated myself for not doing a good job and losing it.

I always practiced my readings many times before I was scheduled to speak. At home practicing in the mirror I was calm as I practiced readings and felt comfortable reading. On Sunday I panicked. When I asked myself why, the answer was the anxiety I always felt before practicing the Apostle Creed in front of my Aunt. After all those years it still affected me.

The very first Speech I gave and it was called the Ice Breaker. I was very anxious but felt safe and secure because I knew the members. I wasn't really comfortable however and was very happy when I sat down. I received a good evaluation and I secretly hated the sound of my voice but was doing nothing to change it.

One day a friend stopped by my home and told me about an app that I could get that helped the vocals to become stronger. I purchased the app and began to practice daily. I also joined a Meet Up group; *Overcomer's 101*. It was a group for people with social anxiety. We would meet every Sunday at a designated place.

With the help of our group leader I was encouraged to do something to face my anxiety and grow. I chose to give a speech and be the Guest Speaker. I was working with a coach and it was a waste of money and time. On the day of the event I was anxious but with courage did a fair job. I received a good evaluation from friends and family.

I continued to do everything in my power to improve and speak boldly, clearly and confidently. I prayed fervently and always failed. I dusted myself off failed again and got back up and dusted myself off. This went on for many years but I was determined to win so I continued. With the encouragement from Toastmaster members, my Coach and a few friends that constantly encouraged me, I would have quit. I wanted to quit many times but there was something inside that wouldn't allow it.

The anxiety and depression caused me to isolate myself from people and every time I said anything I was aware of my voice. It was as if I were watching and listening to the sound of my voice Ready to criticize it, waiting for it to make a mistake, no wonder it responded negatively to me.

The more I became aware of my thoughts and how I sounded it made sense. If there is a part of your body that you absolutely hate that part of your body will respond and become ill and sick. I began to tell my voice "I love you" and do mirror work. I began to tell myself I'm grateful that I have a voice and can speak. I reminded myself of all the people who wish they could make a sound or speak, but couldn't. I made up my mind to never pay another person any money to help me because I had to be honest and open with myself. With honesty I could rebuild and start over. I loved the sound of my unique voice.

I continued to practice my vocal exercises daily, read out loud and say tongue twisters to keep my voice strong. I continue to struggle with the anxiety and depression as well. Am I there yet? No but every day I work on my vocals by doing the vocal exercises and reading out loud. I use Essential oils, Herbs, Prayer and CBD to help with the anxiety. I also chose to have balance and enjoy my life to the fullest.

If you struggle with hating any part of your body know you are doing more harm than good. Stop and go deep within to figure out why you hate that part or allowed a certain thing to happen. Be honest and quit fooling yourself.

Am I there yet with my voice? No, not yet I continue to strive to overcome and slowly my voice is changing. Do I still struggle with anxiety? It's a daily struggle but some days are better than others. I still have days where I battle depression and it's a real challenge daily often but it has gotten so much better. Writing has helped me tremendously as well as being truthful and honest to myself.

If you suffer from silent anxiety and depression and especially if your voice was paralyzed as a child, here are some tips for you to use to get out of the low spot and feel better.

A. Believe in yourself. Your past is the past. Believe so hard until it happens
B. Be honest with yourself. What really happened? Why are you anxious and insecure?

C. Write about how you honestly feel
D. Get out and find support groups or Meet Up Groups
E. Pray for yourself and have unwavering faith. Pray and believe you will get it
F. Get out and laugh and spend quiet time in nature
G. Get rid of people who aren't supportive or deadbeat friends
F. Travel and meet new people
G. Be Grateful and always give thanks
H. Get out of your comfort zone and be Courageous

I have found that using Therapeutic Grade Essential Oils and Hemp Vape supports my anxiety. And again, become aware of your thoughts always. Never be afraid to seek professional help if you need it. There are lots of good Therapist out there. My main takeaway point is for you to never give up. We are all in this together.

Learn more about Queen Iawia Amen

IAWIA: I am What I am!

My name is Queen Iawia Amen. I am a Nurse and worked years in Long Term Care and as a Psych Nurse. As a child, I was abused mentally and physically. Most of my life I've struggled with anxiety and depression that began when I was very young. My passion is helping people overcome their Depression and Anxiety. I also suffered Domestic Violence and issues with Drugs. I overcame Drug Addiction and finally left my abuser, and I'm available to speak on:

Anxiety and Depression
Domestic Violence
Substance Abuse

Website: http://www.byiawia.com

My picture book will be releasing soon! Keep up with me on Facebook @PatSam

Jamie Timmons (Jai)

Why Me? What Child Abuse Taught My Inner Me

Growing up in a home filled with violence taught me several life lessons; unfortunately, when I became of age (in my late 30's), I had to un-train and un-teach everything I thought to be true! Let's travel down the road of lessons, shall we?

I remember the wedding day quite clearly. It was my mother's second marriage and she was marrying a man who was a stranger to me. When she met him, he was a truck driver. She was gone a lot with him on the road. Then there was the day of the wedding. It was in a small room, that I can remember. All my sisters were there, my grandmother, grandfather, and other close family members. My mother seemed so happy. This man was still a stranger. I didn't like him, probably because I did not know him and he made no attempt to know me or my other three sisters.

I never called him "daddy" or even "stepdaddy". When he would walk in the room, he would give me and my sisters this look of disgust. Maybe he didn't feel that way, but that's how I felt whenever he looked at me. I felt violated, as if his stares undressed me. I can't explain it; all I knew is that I did not like him.

When my mother got pregnant and had my baby sister, his daughter, that's when things changed…. or shall I say, became more apparent. His evil stares would turn into verbal vomit. He would say things like, "you're so stupid", "go to hell", "you're nobody", "your own daddy doesn't even give a damn about you", etc. Oddly enough, I remember more of his actions than his nasty words.

Though there were many, many instances of fighting this man, and yes, I mean physically fighting a grown man, there is one that rings loud and clear to me. I was about 16 years old. He had come home drunk, as usual, and there was no bathroom tissue in the house. He went on his violent rant of verbally vomiting all over me and my sisters, in other words, verbal abuse. Calling us all kinds of profane words. Words I cannot use in this book. "Lazy" is the cleanest version appropriate for this platform. So, I, being the only one who talked back to him when he went on his rants, stood up and spit back at him. I said something to the effect of, "well you don't buy anything in this house anyway so why are you mad?!"

That pissed him off even more and he reached to grab me. We tussled for a while until he slammed me on the floor, put his foot on my throat, cutting off my air supply, and bent over to continue yelling (and spitting) in my face.

As I struggled to breathe, he stood over me with that look of superiority refusing to give me air. Then he said the words I will never forget, "Where are you going? No damn where until I say so!" He clearly knew he had complete control over me and I was at his mercy. He was determined to break me of my strong-will attitude.

To make this long story short, the cops were called, perhaps by the neighbors. The police called me a wayward teen who need to learn some respect for her elders, then walked away as if I wasted their time. They walked away with my respect and trust in the law and police. They walked away with my hope, leaving me feeling alone and desolate with no one to come to my rescue. Leaving me to take matters into my own hands. It was up to me to protect my family.

Those words spoken to me by an angry drunk were burned into my soul as a teenager and at that very moment I declared I would never be controlled by a man ever again. I would kill him first. So I began to search for ways to get rid of the man who made my life and my sisters' lives a living nightmare! I plotted to kill my then-stepfather. I had so much anger and hatred in my soul for this man. And for every man since then, except for my grandfather who was heaven sent. And when my grandfather died, so did my idea of a good man.

A couple of days before I was about to commit the murderous crime, my mother came to me with a U.S. Navy brochure and persuaded me to join the *military*. Unbeknownst to her and my sisters, I was about to commit the ultimate crime. Hatred filled every fiber of my being as a young 17-year-old high school graduate. My family did not know the extent and depth of the hatred inside of me. I kept it quiet. I kept it inside. But it was boiling! All I wanted was that man dead. My mother saved my life, and his, by signing me up to join the military.

The road to healing was a long one. I had no idea how broken I was when I left home at 17 years old. I had no idea how those life lessons distorted my perception of marriage, love, men, parenting and self-worth. My self-esteem was nonexistent. But my will to never be at the mercy of a man was stronger than ever. I plotted against every man I ever met, including my husband. I trusted no one. Though I would convince myself that I loved them, I did not. I was incapable of loving a man when I honestly felt that they were all evil and out to hurt me. Oh boy, was I broken!

For years, I carried an aggression in my heart towards men. Every relationship was doomed from the start. Everything was a fight. I would be angry about something petty and blow it all out of proportion. I would snap back with my sharp tongue. I searched for his weakness and used it in arguments to belittle him and his pride. I would make them fall in love with me, then cheat on them with their best friend or brother; then tell them what I had done. I was ruthless and cold-hearted. I was on a private mission to destroy every man in my path, but I told myself that it was self-defense. It became a senseless game to hurt them before they hurt me.

My husband was the first man to say to me one day at our kitchen table, only days in of a fresh new marriage, "I'm not your uncles." A light came on in my soul at that moment and I began therapy. That is when I realized that I had been living a path of vengeance all my life. That is when I realized I didn't have to fight every man; and that every man is not out to hurt me. That is when I realized that there are some good men out in this world.

But again, the road to recovery and healing was a long one. A lot of men fell into my snare. I hurt a lot of men, convincing myself that it was for my own protection. I had a vicious vengeance plan against all of them. The road to recovery was a long one. Fast forward to the present. I am weeks away from turning 40 years old. Over the past 10 years, I've worked on my core (my heart), un-doing what had been done to me as a kid. Un-learning and re-training my heart, mind, and body to value humankind, starting with self-love and appreciation. Transforming and renewing my mind to God's mercy and love, and thus sharing it with the world through my words of inspiration, empowerment and enlightenment.

You may ask, "How can someone so broken and damaged turn over a new leaf just like that?" First, I say it wasn't just like that. It took years of therapy and hard work on self. Secondly, it was, and remains to be, my faith in God. At my lowest point in life, when I hit my rock bottom, my soul cried out to God to be rescued, renewed and healed.

They say you are a product of your environment, and I wholeheartedly believe that. So, I am extremely cautious of what environment I am a part of. Though I could not control the environment in which I was raised or groomed, when I became of age of accountability and aware of my state of mind, I knew I had the authority to make decisions to better myself. To be committed to this journey of healing. And to pass along the hard lessons of life and redemption. I changed my story, and you can too! "My past does not define me, it refines me." – Jai

Learn more About Jamie "Jai" Timmons

Jamie Timmons, also known as Jai (pronounced Jay), is a best-selling author, blogger, radio show host and visionary. She self-published her first memoir, It Is Forbidden: The Untold Story of Child Rape Survival, and has spent a good amount of time and resources empowering others to tell their story and be free from the pain of it. She founded Matters of My Heart, an emotional support program for victims of abuse, where she aides in the transition from a place of hurt to emotional healing. Her message is, "***My past does not define me, it refines me.***"

Holding a dual graduate degree in International Management and MBA, Jai has travelled to Kenya, Tanzania, Uganda, Indonesia and Cambodia to conduct research with government officials and children affected by the worst forms of child labor, including child trafficking. This travel has broadened her senses to different cultures and lifestyles; and has created a deep respect to all mankind, with all ethnicity and backgrounds.

The pain of Jai's past has developed into a passion to help others like her, realizing there are people hurting all over the world. Her purpose in life is to be the voice of the child (boy or girl) who is being abused by someone they know, yet they do not have the wherewithal to verbalize the abuse. Jai declares, "I will continue the fight to bring awareness to what is done in the dark, expose the ugly truths, and create an environment of healing for the hurt."

Her focus now is to partner with organizations with the same mission. Jai strongly believes in partnership. "***Together, we can eliminate domestic violence and sexual assault in this world!***" As such, Jai is an active speaker/volunteer for the Rape, Abuse & Incest National Network (RAINN), the nation's largest anti-sexual assault organization.

The bottom line: Love Doesn't Hurt.
Website: www.mattersofmyheart.com
and http://jaitheauthor.com
Visit Jai's Amazon author page at amazon.com/author/jai

Sundi Sturgeon "Sponsor"

Using Your Voice to Help Others

"I learned many life lessons on forgives after domestic abuse and now help others find their joy" - Sundi

Domestic Violence effects everyone. It is not just the problem of the abuser or of the victim. One in Four women will experience abuse in her lifetime. This is a horrendous fact. But it is a fact, one we can no longer ignore. Every nine seconds in America a woman is beaten by her partner. Children are growing up during this abuse. They are witnessing and sometimes experiencing it. That's why it is important to speak up. To speak out and make a difference. I am sharing my story with you. To help you understand and to hopefully save another life.

I am using my voice to help another woman or man who is a victim. I know I can make a difference by no longer remaining silent. By choosing to tell my story. By choosing to make a ripple in the sea of life. I will use the pain I overcame and survived; to empower and inspire the next generation.

My story will change the world and make a difference. Will you? So, let me give you a glimpse of my story, just a moment in time of the life that led me here. Just a small part of my story. Of how I became a victim and then a survivor.

I found myself in the parking lot of a convenience store at 2:00 a.m., in a panic and on high alert. I exited my 'Chevy Luv' pick-up truck to call my parents from a payphone. Thank God we still had payphones in 1993! I let my parents know I was ok and that I had escaped. I stood there on the phone with no idea if he would find me as he always seemed to be able to track me down. I am speaking of my abuser, Dave; he was my partner at a tumultuous time in my life!

Today more than ever I understand that Dave had patterns that he brought forth in his DNA and we all have them. But the Angels will only allow us to stay in alignment with those people who resonate with us on a deep level. As I was speaking with my parents in the dead of night, he came tearing into the parking lot with one of his friends.

"Oh God! He found me again, "I thought as my mind and heart raced.

He jumped out and literally levitated across the parking lot toward me! I dropped the phone and ran inside the store as he was cursing and threatening to kill me like he had on numerous occasions. The shame I felt for staying was nearly as intense as the fear I felt each time this happened.

See, I brought my own set of patterns to the relationship and because of the DNA in my family, I seemed to attract a shadow side of me of which I didn't know I could change. And the words continued to spew…

He began throwing my belongings from the truck, then jumped in, revved the motor as he backed up, screaming: "if I can't have you, nobody will"! He threatened to drive through the front of the convenience store windows. I stood behind the counter with the clerk screaming and crying, as the clerk called the police, yelling at him, "you better leave now", as my parents hung on the other end of the phone outside, hearing the screaming and tire screeching they prayed fervently for my safety.

My heart broke each time this happened but I always felt in my soul there were protectors around me. Sometimes it felt like I had many personalities because of my emotional shifts before, during and after the abuse - but I now feel certain it was the protection of Angels.

I was stranded there with no vehicle, freighted and alone, but felt my abuser had been carried away by Angels. Did the Angels come rescue me in my time of need? As if my abuser had been called away or pushed away by angels, he left in a fierce manner out of the parking lot with his friend following. I was left standing there, stranded with no vehicle frightened and alone.

The clerk at the convenience store said: "You need to get away from that man, he is dangerous" and I responded, "I am trying to, he tracks me down wherever I go, he is crazy"!

This is a glimpse of one of the last days with my abuser. It was my normal at the time. I lived in fear. I was a domestic violence victim. I felt alone and scared. Like many other women do. Like thousands of other victims do daily. He was completely in control. And my fear was as strong as my shame. But I chose to leave and change my destiny.

This was my life and sadly it is the life of thousands of women today. There are women who are now reading this looking for a way out. I know when they read my story and know I survived and made it to the other side, they will be empowered to begin to plan to leave. The more we share our stories and use our voices to change the world, the better place it will become.

Angels are all around us, they are here to help us, guide us and protect us. Had it not been for my Guardian Angels I would not be here today. I know they were watching over me. They were guiding me to my new life. The life where I will use my gifts and voice to inspire, empower and guide others. I will no longer live in fear. I will no longer be abused. I will no longer live in silence. I will raise my voice and speak out. Will you join me? Will you be a world changer? Will make a difference for the next generations? Will you use your voice?

Learn more about Sundi Sturgeon

Sundi Sturgeon is a Certified Reiki Master, Intuitive Empath/Healer, CHT, NHC, a certified Doreen Virtue Angel Practitioner, and is currently enrolled in a doctorate program in integrative medicine with a focus in holistic/quantum medicine which will be completed in 2016.Sundi is also a wife, mother, and grandmother who is devoted to caring for Earth's living beings. She is a resident of Kihei, Maui, where she lives with her husband, Joseph as Quantum Energy Healing practitioners.

They co-founded the Holistic Light Rejuvenation Center, an educational and charitable organization promoting holistic and cellular rejuvenation services. Sandi's story has been included in Pink Think, Grow Richer, Activating the DNA of Wealth, In the Presence of Angels, and Women on a Mission,

Trials, Tribulations and Triumphs.

You can contact Sundi

Website: http://www.Soulpurposemission.com
Website: http://www.Holisticrejuvenate.com
Holistic light rejuvenation center 808-463-9898
Sundi offers Skype and phone appointments so connect with her today!

Claudia Ibarra

<u>The Awakening</u>

In my early twenties, my friend and I liked meeting new people online. It was very hard to meet guys with a population of under twenty thousand people in a small town in Virginia. I lived in Shenandoah Valley, the Blue Ridge Mountains. At the time, I was working full time and going to college.

When this event happened, I was taking a break from college and my friend decided to meet this guy she met at the dating site online. However, she didn't want to go alone. I decided to take her on a little road trip and meet her online friend. In addition, he was at his friend's house and wanted us to meet him there. I had no idea he was blind and we had to take him home. We were driving for a long while. It was getting dark we were lost. Luckily, I had my laptop with wifi service. Smartphones didn't exist at the time yet. We only had regular cellphones in the mid-2000's. I ask him for his address, but something told me to give my laptop to my friend for her to enter his address. It was around August and it was the hottest time of the year.

I decided to roll down my window because I was getting claustrophobic. While I was looking for my wallet. I found a piece of hematite on the car floor. It must have fallen out of my purse. Hematite is a protection stone, like a magnet.

So, I decided to pick up the stone and put it on my dashboard. While, I did that this man put a gun under my breast. He told me to give him my wallet. The man quickly turned into a monster and put a gun under my breasts. He was not actually blind, but had just lied about being blind to try to lure us away.

It was this event that implanted in me the desire to study the Angels and healing in such a way that I learned how to deeply love myself. – Claudia

Topic: Women in the Military

Laurasha Sadler-Lovett

The Ultimate sacrifice of Moms on Duty

Have you ever wished someone would have told you the uncut raw truth to motherhood? I know I have a lot, but nothing made me wish this more than the time I had to fly my son from Okinawa, Japan to Greenville, SC before I was about to make the ultimate sacrifice of a mother serving her country.

Hello my name is Laurasha and I want to share with you not only the moment my nightmare became a reality, but the blessing that came out of it.

I remember the day like it was yesterday. It was in the summer of 2007 and I was told that my name was on the list for a deployment. At this point I had been in the Marine Corps for 5 years and I was stationed in Okinawa, Japan during my second enlistment contract. I knew my time would come but deep down inside I did not want it to come.

My boss, Gunnery Sergeant(GySgt) Foster pulled me in the office and said "Sergeant Sadler this is going to be hard for me to say this but your name is on the list for the 6 months' deployment coming up in 4 months. I tried to get them to change it but they wouldn't do it."

I said with a nervous chuckling laugh "It is okay GySgt and I appreciate it but remember this is what I signed up for". But, deep down inside, my heart had sunk to my tailbone. I knew at that moment I had to keep my cool. He then proceeded to tell me the rest of the plans and what we needed to do to get prepared.

I was listening but I wasn't listening because in my mind I had to figure out how I was going to tell my precious three-year-old that mommy had to go away for six months. As the day went on I started to fill numb because all could do was replay that conversation in my head. When we got off work I went to the PX which is our store on military bases to pick up a teddy bear for my baby boy.

I wanted him to have it because I needed him to have something that would remind him of me. Then I went and picked him up at daycare. When I got there, I had to pull my emotions together because I did not want him to see me crying. I walked in and he ran to me and gave me a big hug like never before.

Tears started rolling down my face because it was like he knew something was wrong but he was telling me that it was going to be okay. When we arrived home, I told him today was Mommy and Son fun day. We are going to eat junk food and watch power rangers all night and sleep in late the next day since it was the weekend. I texted my friend and told her that we were not going to be at the brunch. Of course she asked and I told her. She completely understood why I was cancelling.

Just as much as it was hard looking at him and knowing what was about to be happening it was a going to be even harder for me to tell my mother. She was going to flip a wig. As we were watching Power Rangers I kept watching the clock because I knew the phone was going to ring soon. As I sat watching the clock it seemed like time was zooming by so quickly. Then before a blink of an eye, it happened. The phone rang. At first I just looked at the phone and let it ring and ring until it stopped.

Then she called back again and this time AJ answered the phone and said "Hello mee-mee". I could hear her ask for me but I was trying to avoid the inevitable. As he handed the phone something took over me. I said "I was in the bathroom, my bad". I do not know why I said that but I did. That was all I could say because I could not bring myself to tell her the news. I felt bad about lying but in my mind I felt I was protecting her. So I thought anyway.

A month had passed and it seemed like the time was zooming by. During this time, I stared preparing paperwork such as my will, updating my life insurance, and the most important paperwork of them all my Power of Attorney. A Power of Attorney is a legal document that you can give to someone you trust to handle things in your name such as car note, bills concerning your home, or your kids well-being while you are deployed.

My Gunnery Sergeant let me do these things on my own instead of with the group. He could see how this was weighing me down. One day he took me in his office and said "Look Sadler, I know this is hard for you. But you got this. You will be back with your son before you know it. I have deployed many times and the time flies when you are over there." I look at him and said "Gunny, you don't understand. Your wife takes care of the kids while you are gone so they are not 100 percent pulled from their element.

Your house is still running on the daily momentum for the most part, mine is not. I should take my son to my mother's house and give her permission to handle my son as well as other things. You do not have to do that. I am the only one my son knows on a day to day basis. I am all he knows right now."

He looked at and said "You are not the first military mom to do this and you won't be the last. So, deal with it okay." My eyes got real big and I had a shocked look on my face. He saw my body language shift and started to say something until I asked to be dismissed. Once I left the room all I could think about was "How could he say that? He doesn't understand and he never will! I can't believe he said that? He really hurt my feelings but guess what he was right."

Later that day I went out in town to a local traveling agency and did the first step. I purchased a round trip ticket and a one way for my baby boy back to South Carolina. That day I had to remove my mommy hat and feelings and put my Marine hat on and do what I signed up do. That was to serve, fight, and protect my country. But no one ever told me that it would be hard to do this when you become mother.

A whole week went by and I was clearly trying to avoid my Gunny because of our last encounter. On Friday after the debriefing for the weekend Gunnery Sergeant told everyone they were dismissed but for me to meet him in his office. Of course, I was nervous, confused and wondered what else he could possibly say to me about my personal life. I went in his office and stood at parade rest and stared at the wall waiting for him to come in. Once he came in his office he told me to have a seat. I did what he said and sat down in the chair. He started off by saying how he knew I was avoiding him all week. But then he went into a shocking moment. It went like this.

"I talked to my wife a few days ago about our conversation and she really jumped on my head. She told me I was being really insensitive about the situation. She told me how it feels from a mother's point of view. I honestly never thought about it. I just know I have seen so many women do it and they seemed fine. So I felt you should have been the same way. Then I called a really good female friend of mine

and asked her for her opinion on it as well since she is a Marine and my wife was not.

When she told me how she felt inside but didn't show it because she didn't want to seem weak, it broke my heart. I never knew how hard it could be on you all. I just felt like you should suck it up and do what you have to do. I want to apologize for what I said to you earlier this week and know that I am here for you whenever you need to talk about this."

By this time tears were rolling down my face because I now know another Marine mom felt how I am feeling now. But my question is why are we not sharing this with other moms? Then I said "Thank you Gunny I appreciate it. I want you to know that I bought a round trip flight and AJ a one-way home. I need to take a week of leave to get him settled at my mom's house is that okay?" He was shocked! He asked "When did you do that?" I told him at lunch time. I let him know how the last time we talked he said something that struck my core. He told me he was glad that it helped and to go home and love on my baby. Plus, my leave would be approved.

The day had come for me to travel back to the stateside. We had our bags packed. I made sure I packed his favorite toys and movies along with the bear I bought him a few months ago. The drive to the airport seemed long and quiet. As we were boarding the plane my eyes got watery. I had to snap on to my emotions quick before AJ saw me. I didn't want him to feel like something was wrong. Once we were on the plane he sat in the window seat, just amazed at the view.

He was a typical three-year-old boy. He wants to see everything, touch everything, and ask a million and one questions. Out of the 13-hour flight he slept about 9 hours. During the time he was sleeping I would hold him and silently cry and think about all the "what if's" moments. When we landed in South Carolina I felt a happiness over me. It was something about the crisp fresh air and the awesome feeling of being back home. I was super excited to be surrounded by family during this crazy time. My mom picked us up from the airport. I do not know if she was more excited to see me or AJ. I am sure it was AJ. It had been about a year and a half since she seen us in person. She just hugged us so tight I thought she was going to crush my lungs. But I was happy to feel her arms around me. I felt a sense of relief, and it was almost like everything was going to be okay. The ride to my mom's was great. I told her that I just wanted to relax and get AJ settled.

I did not want family coming over or even know I was in town but my close family members. She told me that she respected my thoughts and understand.

That week went by like a big blur. Next thing I know my mother was driving me to the airport. The moment I was dreading was finally here and I was hating every minute of it. As we were walking into the airport my chest started to tighten up and my body was getting heavy.

I checked my bag in and we started walking towards the terminal for boarding passengers. Before I went through that section I moved to the side so I could say my final "see you laters." I grabbed my son and kissed him all over his face while squeezing the life out of him. I want to get enough hugs and kisses to last me the whole time I will be gone.

Then I hugged and kissed my mom and granddaddy. Then I went back to my AJ to get more hugs. In my mind I was thinking "Damn this going to be harder than I thought. How could I let him go? I can't do this but I have to be strong for him". I let him go and looked him in his eyes and said "Baby I love you and will always be with you in your heart." I handed him to my mom and walked through the boarding passengers only areas. I told myself not to look back but I could help it I did and it break my heart. He was waving at me until he realizes he was not coming with me. He started crying and trying to jump out my mom arms. I quickly turned around and tears started rolling down my face.

I boarded my plane and sat in my seat and cried my eyes out. The lady beside me asked me if I was OK. I told her no, I wasn't. At that point she called for a flight attendant. When she came over the lady asked me what was wrong. I wiped my face and looked at her and said "Ma'am, I just flew my son from Japan to here to drop him off at my mother's house while I go back to Japan to deploy for 6 months or more. He is my life and I cannot handle my emotions right now".

She hugged me and said come with me. She put me in First class and let me straight out to rest and be comfortable. Why was she rewarding me? This was the worst feeling I had ever felt in my life. I had now named myself the worst mother ever. How can a mother put anything before her child?

What I later learned was that I was showing my child what it meant to commit to something bigger than yourself. I showed him something I could never verbally teach him. To this day my son remembers that moment but he always says it was because America needed me and he was okay with sharing me because I was the best mommy ever.

Angel Davison

Living with Lupus

I served in the United States Marine Corps from 2003 to 2011. This experience was one of my many proud accomplishments in my life. Just like any job you will experience many different highs and lows. In a world where the ratio of men is higher than women, as a female Marines there are several odds already stacked against us once we graduate boot camp. We are supposed to be strong mentally and physically, disciplined and well groomed, we are expected to perform our military duties equal to our peers, we are expected to be 100% dedicated with ambition to always put our career first. So, the moment we become mothers, wives, or fall ill you can expect for judgement to be passed. When you experience this, you will either need to have thick skin as tough as nails or it will physiologically break you there's really no in between. For me I had an emotional breakdown because I had never been subjected to such cruelty in my life. Here's my story.

For the past six years, I know what it feels like to wake up in the morning and be in unbearable pain and have to come muster up the strength to make it through it the day. I know what it feels like to go to the doctor's office in tears and they can't figure out what's wrong with you. I know how it feels to go to bed scared at night because you don't know what's going on with your body and if you'll be blessed to see another day. I know how it feels to be prescribed different medicine to only treat the symptom and not the cause. I know how it feels to push through the pain, unexplainable fevers, fear and exhaustion every day.

By the year of 2009 I had served overseas, was married with two children, and had obtained the rank of Sergeant. At this point in my life I was truly happy I felt like I had everything I ever wanted, a family, good friends, I was financially stable with a successful career. But what seemed like at the blink of an eye it all changed when I started to experience some life changing events with my health. These changes limited my daily living capabilities and duties as a Marine. As a Food Service Specialist going to medical was considered as you being a weak Marine, because our job really isn't strenuous. You know your body and when sometimes is wrong, sometimes pain is not weakness leaving the body, so I felt like I had no other choice than to seek medical attention.

I had a constant headache and always felt weak, one day I black out at work from dehydration which lead to me having a seizure. From this seizure, I experienced temporary memory loss. I would fall out of company pt (physical training) runs due to unbearable pain the pain I was experiencing was unexplainable. If the working condition were too hot my skin would break out in unknown rashes and my fellow Marines didn't want to be around me from not knowing if it was contagious or not, and lastly, I experienced an allergic reaction to the annual immunizations that we are required to receive.

During this year I lost up to 40 pounds drastically with no logical explanation. I went from a healthy lean 145 pounds with 10% body fat to 105 also loosing muscle mass. My hair began to thin and fall out, and I'm not talking about the normal shedding, which made it difficult to keep my hair in regulations. After 60 days which felt like pure torture like time was standing still, I was finally placed on a limited duty board.

This medical documentation was altered to my needs to help make my duties as a Marine more manageable while protecting myself. Everyone from my Company Commanders and Staff Non-commissioned officers (SNCO's) who are my superiors, my fellow Non-commissioned officers (NCO's) and even junior Marines had something negative to say about my health conditions.

At this time, there wasn't an actual diagnosis to explain what was going on with me and mainly because it wasn't happening to them for them to understand or care what I was experiencing. They would say things like "Oh we can't depend on her because she's sick." Or "How do you expect to be a leader of Marines when you can't lead them in physical fitness because of your so-called condition?" These types of statements were hurtful because it's not like I could control what was going on with me, and even on my worse days I still went to work and gave it my all. I felt like I was being treated as like an outcast by the same organization I signed my life away to serve and protect and it was one of the worst feelings in the world. I considered being a Marine more than just a job, and I cared about the people I worked with like they were family. After being placed on limited duty it was no secret that I was terminally ill, there were a few coworkers who understood but still didn't come to my defense which was also discouraging. It made me feel like why do I continue to give 110% of my efforts when this is the outcome?

What's frustrating about the health and insurance department is when something is wrong with you they are trained more to give you a temporary cure (which I like to call a band aid) instead of taking the time to figure out the cause and the cure. So after a whole year of feeling like I was a medical experiment or should I say test dummy, with undergoing several different tests, studies, treatments and medications taking all these different medications to treat the symptoms but not cure the cause of it.

During this year my possible diagnosis went from Chromes disease, rheumatoid arthritis, HIV/AIDS, leukemia and other cancers, sickle cell anemia, and epilepsy. All my test results come back normal or negative but my blood work panels were still abnormal. After each doctor's appointment I was relieved that my illness wasn't what the doctor thought it was but also nervous because there was something wrong but the Naval doctors just couldn't figure out exactly what. I was finally referred to a specialist at the internal medicine department that seemed to actually care about their patients, after reviewing my medical record, lab and test results she put me on the right track for medical treatment and provided me with a diagnosis that made since. At the age of 25 I was diagnosed with Lupus. Lupus is also known as systemic lupus erythematosus (SLE).

In February 2010 life as I knew it had changed forever and at that time I didn't see any positivity in sight. I felt like everything spiraled out of control, my career was coming to a fast halt when I had different plans in mind, my marriage was falling apart which left me as a single parent of two toddlers with one of my children being a special need, and I began to question my faith in religion.

Often I felt like I no longer had a purpose in life and that being diagnosed with this incurable disease was a punishment. I wouldn't wish this type of pain and suffering on my worst enemy. Fast forwarding to 2016, five years later after my diagnosis I am finally comfortable in sharing my story and raising awareness on living with Lupus.

What is lupus? Lupus is a chronic autoimmune disease that can damage any part of the body from your skin, to your tissues, joints and organs. There are several underlying issues and symptoms that come with having this disease that tend to last longer than six weeks and cause a significant lifelong disability, and then there are some patients that only suffer minor inconveniences. Lupus symptoms vary depending on the patient but can include fatigue, anemia, joint pain, skin rashes and ulcers, fevers and pain. Also common symptoms of having lupus are anxiety, depression, blood in urine, headaches, joint stiffness, sensitivity to light and heat, and unexplainable weight loss. Most of the symptoms lupus patients experience are also confused with arthritis. The types of doctor that will treat this illness are the pain management department, Rheumatologist, and an internal disease specialist.

Just like any illness I have my good days and my bad days, in the beginning of my journey my bad days outweighed the good. Sometimes it's physiological like it's a mind over matter fake it until you make it kind of thing. What helps me through my bad days are three things, number one my faith in believe in a higher power, two having a good supportive system of friends and family that are there for me through the good, the bad and the ugly. These people take the time to understand how Lupus affects me and aren't judgmental.

And lastly having motivation to keep pushing, not only do I have to live for myself I have to live for my children. I push through my illness everyday basis to be strong for my boys, who are now the ages of ten and eight years old. When they are grown I want them to know that I tried my best to provide them with a better life and childhood then I had and to be just as proud of me as I am of myself. Maybe one day I'll be someone else's inspiration. I surprise myself sometimes because as the saying goes "You never know how strong you are until being strong is your only option."

Shantell Gutrick

A Tribute to Military Soldier Moms

Joining the military after graduating high school wasn't my Plan A, attending a four year university was my plan, but that plan was interrupted after I had my second child as a teenager. I knew that it was my responsibility to take care of my children, and I had to figure out what I needed to do to ensure my children were taken care of financially.

Honestly, I never thought I was made out to be a soldier, I didn't think I was that tough or that I would be able to pass basic training. However, I had to suppress all of my excuses and fears and join the military for my children. I was scared shitless -- for real, but I knew my children's lives dependent on my success in the military.

Being a mother is already a tough but, but being a soldier on top of being a mother is challenging. As a soldier, we were required to put our country first and our family second. On a daily basis, we were required to report to our units very early in the am morning to participate in physical training.

Following physical training, we had enough time to shower, and then we had to report to work, where we were required to work at least 7.5hrs -- if not more. As a mother, you have very limited time to spend time with your children or family during the week. It was also possible that on the weekends, the time I had with my children would also be limited. Basically, this was a very tough time of doing what I needed to do to care for them.

Each soldier is required to pull overnight guard duty, and at times that duty is done on the weekends. As a solider, we know and understand we are parents, but we also know and understand that if we fail to adhere to the militaries rules and regulations, it can result in the soldier facing legal issues. I was blessed enough to be married during my time of service. My husband picked up the slack where I left off. I must admit there was time I was jealous of his relationship with the children because he was closer to them than I was. I truly felt, at times, we were experiencing role reversals.

I wanted to be home with my children, or spend more time with my children, and he be the soldier. I can admit there was a bit of jealousy and bitterness, but I knew that I had to stick it out. I had to realize that what I was doing in the military is helping my children or family. I think there should be more services offered to single soldiers who are mothers.

They truly struggled with maintaining their military career and being a parent. It is already difficult to be a single parent, but can you imagine being in the military as a single parent. Although I wasn't single, and I had help, I still felt at times that majority of the responsibility was on me and if I failed, my family failed -- my children failed. There was so much weight on my shoulders, and I must be honest to say that is weight that I didn't care to carry.

Even more challenging than being a mother was being a military mother. There are soldiers who miss out on their children's birthdays, school activities, important milestones, etc. It breaks a mother's heart to miss those precious moments, but they know they must do what is required of them to care for their children.

While I was in the service, I was fortunate enough to never be deployed, but I did reside overseas in Germany, and there was a time my oldest daughter wasn't with me. It was very hard not knowing when I would see her, and when she would move to Germany to be with the rest of her family. I missed my daughter and I loved my daughter, and being separated from her broke my heart. I had a similar experience when I decided to enter the military, and I had to be away from both of my children for 5 months. That's a very long time.

Letters and telephone calls didn't help at all. In fact, it made missing my children and family worse. I can only imagine the mothers, whom are soldiers, who are deployed for a year at time. The separation anxiety is unreal and it's something that all mothers who love their children, and who are called upon by the military to deploy, train, etc. endure to make a better life for their children.

Joining the military was strategic, and I knew this was the best opportunity for me to take care of my children. Honestly, it will assist with housing, utilities, health and life benefits, and stable employment. I sacrificed myself so that my children could have better. So that they can live a better life. I recall every obstacle, every run, every range I participated in, I repeated my children's names.

Repeating their names allowed me to remember why I joined the military and its importance. It reminded me that I had two children depending on me, and who needed their mother to pass basic training. Their lives depended on me, and I wasn't going to let them down. Basic training was tough, but I survived it. The military woke up the leader within me, and ever since then, I never stop being a leader. I never stopped accomplishing goals, no matter how difficult or challenging they were. Although I am not on active duty, and I'm a veteran, I am a soldier.

Although the military wasn't my initial desire, today I'm grateful that I made that decision to join. Being a veteran has afforded me many opportunities, and I've grown tremendously due to my service to my country. It's a decision that I will never regret, and that I'm grateful for. If you can speak to a military female soldier who is a mother, please do so. Listen to her share her reasons for joining, and the sacrifices she has made to provide for her family. Pray for her and encourage her, she most surely will appreciate it and she needs it.

To all my sisters, female veterans, I am proud and grateful for all the sacrifices that you've made to serve your country. Your sacrifices are not going unnoticed and know that I've walked the same walk as you. Continue to stand proud, and your family/children will forever be grateful for everything you have done for them. You may get discouraged from the early morning PT, the military politics, guard duty, being deployed, but remain encouraged. Hang in there! You got this Soldier!! You got this Marine!! You got this Airmen!! You got this Sailors!! It's Your Time to Shine™! HOORAY!!!

From The Soulful Pen – Thank you for your Service.

Renee Sallee Doughty

<u>Beautiful Warrior: Push past the pain</u>

Encouragement for my sisters

Hey Beautiful Warrior! Yes You! Wait, you don't know you're beautiful and you're a warrior? I can prove it. Have you ever or are you experiencing any traumas like divorce, depression, Post Traumatic Stress Disorder (PTSD), financial set back, low self-esteem (the list goes on) in your life? If yes, then you're a warrior.

Per Merriam-Webster's Dictionary, the definition of a warrior is: A person who is or has been in warfare; A person engage in some struggle or conflict; or A person who fights in battles and is known for having courage and skill. The definition of beauty is: The quality of being physically attractive; the qualities in a person or a thing that give pleasure to the senses or mind; A beautiful woman.

Therefore, per these two definitions you are a beautiful warrior!

My desire for you is to embrace the beautiful warrior that resonates inside of you. She is there, just waiting on you to PUSH PAST your circumstances and move toward what God has for you. I'm here to tell you that you can experience peace, joy, love and wholeness in your life. You can go from Pain to Beauty!

Right now, you're probably saying "ok that sounds good but I don't have the strength to push through anything, I just want to throw in the towel". Well, before you quit let me give you a few examples of pushing past the pain. One example I can give you of pushing past pain is that of a mother giving birth. Despite the labor pains, despite the opening of her cervix, she pushes through the pain and on the other side of that pain she delivers a beautiful baby. Another example is that of an Athlete, yes I know you've heard that one before but, it's too good to pass up so here it goes. Athletes' go through physical pain to train their bodies. Pushing past any discomfort to get the results they need to achieve the desired goal. Depriving their bodies of certain foods (now that can hurt bad), long practices, getting their bodies to do the impossible. They push themselves to receive the goal; that championship ring, the gold medal, and the covenant title of champion. I so love those examples just thinking about them keeps me motivated and not wanting to quit.

Having been exposed to war and diagnosed with Post Traumatic Stress Disorder (PTSD) and Major Depressive Disorder (MDD), I know there were plenty of times in my life I didn't feel like pushing so I stopped pushing. Tried to drown out the depression and the nightmares with alcohol and it got worse. I didn't want to function. I didn't want to live.

I still experience those times of wanting to stop, but now I push anyway, no matter how I feel, or no matter what negative thought comes to my mind. It doesn't matter if depression tries to invade my space that day, I push! Now, I try to incorporate self-care days where I take time out for myself. I also incorporate my faith in God in my healing process. Believe me, my journey hasn't been easy but with the help of family, friends, and other individuals I push! Through prayer and supplication, I've learned to lean on God. I've learned to trust Him through the pain.

While deployed during the Gulf war, what I experienced left a lasting impact on my life. I could paint a picture of how a Scud missile exploded in our camp with fire and chaos everywhere. I could tell you how it felt to lose dear friends and comrades who died in the desert while evacuating Iraqi soldiers when their Blackhawk helicopter crashed. I could even tell you how I had to push through two divorces, homelessness, losing custody of my children, and thoughts of suicide. But those stories are for another time. Right now, I want to tell you not to focus so much on the circumstance that's causing you the pain but to focus on some things you can do that will help you through the pain, I call it "Your Pushing".

You can mediate, write in a journal, get involved with helping local organizations, find a support group, and therapy. For me, my "Pushing" came from all the above, plus prayer and studying the bible. And I'm always finding new methods of pushing. Some help some don't, it's a process. When you begin to push, you'll find out you are not alone. You are not the only one going through these struggles. You'll also realize the feeling of hopelessness will begin to subside. Your sense of purpose will be restored and you can move forward.

Before, I let you go I want to share with you how diamonds go through a rigorous process. Yes, even diamonds had to push! It's amazing to me how diamonds are formed. Underneath the Earth's crust it is very hot and extreme pressure. The combination of these high temperatures and pressure is what's necessary to form diamond crystals but it doesn't end there. The diamonds must go through a violent volcanic eruption to get to the surface. When you look at a clear-cut diamond in all its majesty you don't see the process or the pain the diamond had to go through. You see the beauty. Like the diamond, you must first go through high temperatures and high pressures; you may have to go through someone leaving you, foreclosure, or even depression, for God to get to the deep parts and form you so that you can come out and shine. Show us your beauty, you Beautiful Warrior!

I encourage you to Push Past your pain, trust God through your process, and embrace His peace. God will give you beauty for ashes, the oil of joy for mourning and the garment of praise for the spirit of heaviness. You can go from Pain to Beauty. Keep Pushing!

"You will keep him in perfect peace, whose mind is stayed on You, because he trust in You" (Isaiah 26:3 *NKJV*).

"To console those who mourn in Zion, To give them beauty for ashes, The oil of joy for mourning, The garment of praise for the spirit of heaviness; That they may be called trees of righteousness, The planting of the Lord, that He may be glorified"(Isaiah 61:3 NKJV).

A Wife's Prayer

Hello Lovely Lady!

I pray you are enjoying the beauty that surrounds you as well as the beauty that is within you. Today, I wanted to share with you this prayer I wrote for a client awhile back. As a wife, I understand how sometimes marriage can be challenging. If you are having some issues in your marriage such as, but not limited to, lack of communication, adultery, financial setbacks, addictions, and/or abuse; I do encourage you to seek the help of a good Spirit-led Christian Counselor and to also pray for yourself, your husband, and your marriage.**

Today, marriage is often taken lightly as is evident with the divorce rate at an all-time high and co-habitation the norm; there is no real commitment. And believe me; I know a thing or two about divorce. I have been divorced twice. I have come to learn that we as wives must fight for our marriage. We have a responsibility to the marriage process as well. In my previous marriages, I had no idea that I had to fight. At that time in my life, the effects of the Gulf war had started to appear. I was depressed, angry, and confused (and that's not even half of it). I didn't pray about my mental and emotional state. I didn't pray for my husband or my marriage. I didn't take authority over my situation. I just let life run me over and cried to God when it hit the fan.

After many lessons learned, I've come to appreciate my current situation. My husband and I have made an uncommon commitment to fight for our marriage. A commitment to seek help from godly counsel when needed, to pray for one another, to hold each other accountable, to love one another even when the other is not so loveable, to pray together and to always put God first. My dear lady, the prayer below is for you. To fight for and to take authority over your marriage, remember you are your husband's helpmate. Help him be what God has called him to be and pray for him. And as you pray for him, your marriage, and yourself, watch God move on your behalf.

Father God, I worship You, I give You all honor and praise, and I magnify Your Holy Name. Father, I lift my husband to You and I ask that Your Will (not his will) be done in his life. Line him up with Your Word; help him to see who he is in Christ and give him a clear understanding and certainty that he was created for a high purpose. Enable him to walk worthy of his calling and remind him of whom You've called him to be. Protect him from the temptations of this world. Protect his heart and his mind. I pray that he would begin to hunger after You and seek Your face.

Now Father, I ask that You help me become the wife You have called me to be. Strip away any pride that I might have toward my husband and our relationship. Show me clearly what it is that You would have me to do concerning my marriage. Holy Spirit, come, give me guidance on when to speak and how to speak to my husband. Knock down the walls that I have put up, soften my heart toward my husband and give me that peace that surpasses all understanding concerning my marriage.

Father, I come against anything that would hinder my marriage from going forth and prospering according to Your Word. For no weapon formed against us shall prosper. Father, I thank You for Your covering, I thank You for Your love and I thank You for hearing and answering my prayers. In Jesus mighty name Amen

I encourage you to pray daily with boldness and with the confidence for God's perfect will to manifest in your marriage.

Meditate on the following scriptures

Genesis 2-18; 20-24, NKJV

18 And the Lord God said, "It is not good that man should be alone; I will make him a helper comparable to him." **20** So Adam gave names to all cattle, to the birds of the air, and to every beast of the field. But for Adam there was not found a helper comparable to him. **21** And the Lord God caused a deep sleep to fall on Adam, and he slept; and He took one of his ribs, and closed up the flesh in its place. **22** Then the rib which the Lord God had taken from man He made into a woman, and He brought her to the man.

23 And Adam said: "This is now bone *of my bones, And flesh of my flesh; She shall be called Woman, Because she was taken out of Man."*

24 *Therefore a man shall leave his father and mother and be joined to his wife, and they shall become one flesh.*

(If you are experiencing physical or emotional abuse get out of harm's way and PLEASE SEEK HELP NOW!)

Love & Blessings,

Renee Sallee Doughty

Learn more about Renee Sallee Doughty

Renee Sallee Doughty is a disabled Army veteran whose wartime experience led her to a place of darkness and depression. The transition from military to civilian life was not easy and Renee found herself struggling for stability. In and out of jobs, becoming homeless, losing custody of her kids, and receiving a DUI, are just a few of the outcomes that came from some of the choices she made while suffering with untreated Post Traumatic Stress Disorder (PTSD) and Major Depressive Disorder (MDD). Out of her painful experiences, Renee wanted to help women veterans not make the same choices she made and live a life of peace and balance.

This desire led her to the founding of Combat Boots to Makeup Brushes, Inc., (www.cb2mb.org), a nonprofit organization whose mission is to create a path of healing and wholeness for women veterans, who suffer with Post Traumatic Stress Disorder (PTSD) and other disabilities both seen and unseen. The organization is educating, equipping, and empowering women veterans to embrace their inner peace and outer beauty through Health & Wellness Seminars, Spiritual Retreats, Coaching, Peer Support, workshops and practical assistance with everyday needs. Renee and her staff believe this holistic approach in addition to clinical support can radically reduce the number of suicides in the veteran community. Renee has become an inspiration to many women veterans who have experienced trauma. Her words of encouragement and real life example of pushing through despite the odds has given them hope and purpose. She believes by showing the veteran they are not alone and equipping them with the tools they need to overcome emotional and mental scares, they can become whole again and live a purposeful life. Renee is a Certified Spirit-led Christian HIS coach™, Ordained Evangelist, Author, former Makeup Artist, part-time event Host and Comedian. She is married to Brannon Doughty. They have a wonderful blended family of 7 beautiful children, (4 boys and 3 girls)

Combat Boots to Makeup Brushes, Inc

Po Box 265 Wake Forest, NC 27588
(919) 727-6937

www.cb2mb.org
admin@cb2mb.org

Poetry

Poem: Elizabeth Blade

<u>Write to Inspire: Your Desire</u>

Each of us has a body, a mind and a heart to make what we do within the time we have, it's important to spread wisdom, inspiration and to create an impact in other people's lives.

In a world filled with negativity, each of us can create positiveness and goodness. We can empower one another and lift our voices.
Our voices need to be heard, if we have a story within us, we must share it with the world. Within our universe, we can push beyond our limits.

To desire, to take ourselves higher.
A lot of people I know, including myself, write through the pain, the anguish. We watch the words dance along the page. The words written time and time again we rearrange.
Trying to find the splendour the voice, the words to be heard. Voices that put you down are all absurd. We are the voices of the chosen words we speak.
We are our own forever. We write our own endeavours and we are in charge of our inner destinies.

Whenever someone says to you that your goals and dreams do not matter, I say to you is this. Do not listen, do not give it a second thought, feelings are sold and bought what we preach is what we are taught.

We must train our inner minds that THIS IS OUR TIME, we are the bells that chime.
We are the wind that blows. With every whisper of our names is where we will be. Every single thought, expression, is the way we feel.
Feelings we have ARE real. We have the appeal to spread a message and a good one.
The world around us is dying and so many of us are crying but we ourselves can uplift our voices to the ones that need to hear it.
Everyday someone is through something bad in the world, messages that are forever told or the ones that remain silent. So much never ending violence. Lay down your guns, stop breaking the laws.
Our knees have fallen to the floors; our tears are forever making waves. Who is going to save your day? Who is going to save mine? A bell is rung; a bell has chimed. The church bells are playing them today.
We have lost so many innocent people. The devil has its way and we stand idly by. Watching the innocence of it all. Our hearts cry, our souls cry too. If it can happen to me, it can happen to you.
Feelings feel so unglued.
Heavens above and hell is below, we watch the ones we love disappear and go, the ground gets sour, the planet is being devoured by war and greed. Everybody wants and everybody needs, again we are brought to our knees. You have planted the seed in my mind, that no one or nothing is good enough in this world.
But if we seek we shall find, everything that matters and everything that rhymes. We are the chimers; we are the doves that fly. We can make the difference in this world. YES, YOU! AND I!
So, spread the words of positivity that we all long to hear, bring the love back into society lets hold it near and dear.
We can do anything if we truly try. We are the 100 voices or more. We can raise our voices. We can raise them as one. We will find our setting sun.

Learn More about Elizabeth (Liz) Blade

Born in Melbourne Australia and raised in Adelaide, South Australia Elizabeth Blade has been one thing all her life and that has been a dreamer. Elizabeth is in the middle of writing a variety of novels and books for all ages. Through the years Elizabeth has written poetry, she believes that it has helped her overcome some troubling times in her life. Her first release that was debut in April of 2015 was a ebook called In Motion With Devotion Volume One more are to follow as each volume will be something new and a change of pace in various topics. Elizabeth will have a re-release of her book A Rising Moon on Domestic Violence set the be released in later 2016. Domestic Violence is in every corner of the globe. Through experiences witnessed or feelings that have delved inside due to media attention and news stories, Elizabeth decided to write a book about this. As a strong advocate that wants to see an end to this mindless violence she is determined to have her voice heard.

Through a poetic manner, she whisks you into the world of poetry that she likes to call unique and 'a world of its own'
Website: http://www.elizabethblade.com
Email: moondance_81@me.com
Twitter: @Moondance_81
Facebook: https://www.facebook.com/ElizabethBladeWriter

Poem: Erin Stevens

<u>Confusion</u>

Do I lead?
Do I follow?
Lead who?
To what?
Do we go quickly? Not too quickly. If I go too slowly will we make it in time?
In time for what?
To Meet who?
To get what?
Is there anyone there?
Will anyone know when I get there?
Will I know?
Will I know when to stop leading and to follow?
Follow who?
To what?
To where?
Are we there yet?
Will we know when we get there?
Do I follow quickly? Not too quickly. If we go to slowly will we make it in time?
Will I get lost?
Will my leader turn back to find me?
Will they know I am lost?
Will they look for me?
Will they miss me?
Have I gone too slowly?
Did I go so quickly that I did not pay attention and I got lost anyway?
The path is covered in snow.
There are no tracks to follow, and no one to lead.
No leaders and no followers.
Just me............ Alone and Confused.

Erin Stevens

Deanna Caroline Bosworth

TAKE LIFE BY THE HAND

In life there's just one moment,
A chance to make a stand,
Make today that instant,
Take life by the hand.

We have this day we're living
And not one moment more,
To make this life we're given
Something worth living for.

Don't wait for tomorrow!
There is no time to wait
For every plan we borrow,
We can not know our fate.

When the morning lingers nigh
Shadowed by the rain
Take each breath with deepest sigh
For it'll never come again.

Grasp each gift of nature
Wind, moon, stars, the seed
The grandest gifts from our Creator
Fulfill our every need.

When the day is ended
Father hear my prayer,
First to thank you for today
And one more day to share.

A day is but a heartbeat
In your grand universe
And like a fleeting moment;
A lyric unrehearsed

So let me sing with all my heart
To praise your Precious name
As you commence your skies to part
And pour your healing rain.

My life is just this moment,
Lord please take my hand.
While today is mine, this instant
It's my chance to make a stand.

In life there's just one moment,
A chance to make a stand,
Make today that instant,
Take life by the hand....

In life there's just one moment,
Take life by the hand.

Intense Health & Wellness

Jill Birth

The Journey Worth Taking, Is The One Within

I know what it's like to struggle. Believe me, I know every excuse that people can give for not being able to lose weight and change their lives because I've probably used every one of those excuses myself. It's still a struggle for me some days not to revert to the old me and give in to my food addiction. There were some days that I literally made it through my weight loss and personal transformation on my knees, in prayer. Day by day, though, it became easier, as I felt myself changing inside and out.

I am Jill Birth - a recovering food addict. I started my first diet in the 3rd grade when my school nurse told me I was "One Fat Little Girl". I went home from school that day, cried to my mom, she put me on "a diet" the next day and that was the beginning of my "dieting career".

Since that day, my whole life revolved around my weight. If I got up and weighed myself in the morning, I was on top of the world if my weight was down a little yet felt like a beast if I was up a few pounds. Despite my seemingly idyllic family life, supportive parents, and activities through grade school, Jr. high and high school, the real me was trapped somewhere deep inside myself. It wasn't a happy place to be. I even let my weight control my marriage. My poor husband didn't know what he was going to come home to - Jekyll or Hyde.

I was the mom that was sitting on the bench at the park too embarrassed to play with my kids. My son was told that he had a "fat mom" - so he didn't want me to come to the Jr. high school for anything; not even to pick him up if he was sick. He'd rather stay at school sick than be embarrassed again.

Reaching 263 pounds and feeling self-defeated knowing that I had over 100 pounds to lose, I knew that I could not do this alone. I had tried everything out there over the years to release the weight, even trying out for the Biggest Loser Show on TV. In fact I have 24 "before" pictures, taking a picture each time I started a diet, just hoping that this was the diet that was going to work for me! I finally reached the lowest point of my life in May 2010. I realized that there was only one way to make a complete SHIFT and that was through the Lord and finding a program that was simple, one that would become a lifestyle, not a diet!!

I had learned from my previous mistakes. I couldn't let my past failures continue to haunt me. I was determined to succeed this time. I was ready to transform myself—and my life. I had accepted the fact that I was addicted to food. I started attending 12-step addiction meetings almost immediately. In my heart, I knew this would be the key not only to my own success, I would soon be able to help many others achieve theirs as well. All I wanted, was to be an inspiration to others like the Biggest Loser Contestants were for me.

God dropped a nutrition system into my life that I knew I could follow and I started feeling amazing! My energy was increasing as I was releasing pounds and inches safely and quickly. I was feeling like an entirely different person as I worked through the 12 steps and started working through my "own steps".

As I started working through these steps, I found out about a "body transformation challenge". This contest, we found, wasn't just about weight loss - it was about a total transformation in every area of your life. I got excited, I was ready to compete. I was going to win that title and make my lifelong dream of inspiring other people. I knew winning the Challenge was going to require dedication and commitment. I now had the clarity and certainly to do it. I was confident that I would be successful.

I went right home and got to work. Now that I had this huge goal, I mapped out my strategy. I knew how much weight I wanted to release—my goal was to release half of my original body weight of 263 pounds, which was where I had started with the first challenge 24 weeks before. That meant releasing another 31 pounds. Not only that, it meant that I needed to get fit. Fit. I needed to plan my exercise strategy as well as my food intake. I could do this. I would do this.

I decided that one of the first things I'd do would be to put my dream out there on my vision board. I tacked up all kinds of inspirational sayings and pictures. And then, looking at that picture of the lean girl running, I decided to sign up for a half marathon. I printed off a program called "Couch Potato to 5K" that I found on the Internet and began following it. This seemed like the easiest and most affordable way to release body fat and build up the lean muscle I needed to truly transform my body.

Gradually, I started running instead of walking, pushing myself at first to go from one mailbox to the next, then picking out more distant landmarks as I started running a little more every day. At the same time, I stuck faithfully to my nutritional cleansing program. In addition, I decided to keep a journal. Doing that was, without a doubt, one of the single most important steps I took toward becoming more aware of my eating habits and how those habits were linked to my emotions.

By May 15, I'd done it. I had cut my body weight in half—from 263 pounds to 132 pounds. I had decreased my clothing size from a size 22 to a size 4! I was fit and ready for that half marathon. I was never prouder of myself than I was on the day I crossed that finish line. I had achieved so many things that I never could have imagined accomplishing when I was a child. I had learned to manage my demons and get truly healthy. Shoot, I had even become a half-marathoner!

I took my kids to St. George, UT and my oldest son pointed to the top of a mountain and said "Mom, let's climb that mountain tomorrow". I had never climbed a mountain and started doubting myself. Then something came over me and I said "Let's do it!". The next morning, we climbed the mountain and sat side-by-side at the top. He turned and looked at me with tears in his eyes and said, "Mom, thank you for getting healthy for us". It was at that moment that I knew I wasn't going to sit on the side-lines any more - I was going to LIVE MY LIFE!

A mere five days later, I had my "after" pictures taken, or what I like to call my "photo shoot." This was fun and exciting—a far cry from the days when I used to hide if anyone took out a camera because I was so embarrassed by my size.

I received a phone call that I was one of the finalists for the challenge and that they would announce the Grand Prize Winner in San Diego that August. At 39 years-old my mom bought me my first prom dress, since I never went to a boys choice dance in high school.

When I arrived in San Diego for the celebration, I was excited. My anticipation had built to a nearly unbearable degree, yet it was heightened even more by multiple photo shoots, one right after the other. Everything felt surreal as people attending the event kept approaching me, excited to meet me and shake my hand or hug me. I loved every minute of it. I had no idea that so many people had been following my progress on Facebook or had watched my YouTube video—the one I'd made for my Challenge portfolio and decided to post myself, which apparently had gone viral.

i was excited by the attention. It was so heartwarming to hear people say, "You've inspired me so much, Jill. I love you," "You lifted me up," or, "You made me feel like I can do this, too!" I was finally living my dream of inspiring others!!!

Finally, the big moment arrived. When my name was announced as the winner of the Transformation Challenge, I felt like I'd won the Miss America Pageant. Me! The person who was once too afraid in high school to deliver a verbal report, and the same girl who quit her public speaking class in college because she was so self-conscious about her weight! It was exciting and surreal at the same time.

It was the biggest win of my life—so far. Reaching my personal goal wasn't about winning money or releasing weight in the end. It was about knowing that I had worked hard to accomplish a goal I had been dreaming about for so long. No more humiliation, no more shame. I had addressed my food addiction. I could hold my head high, and my kids saw it all. I had finally crossed the finish line. By releasing half of my body, I had won my life back at last. Now I could begin to live my dream of helping others. I could not wait! Now, my passion is in helping others make that shift and achieve their dreams and goals. I believe that everyone deserves a chance to walk through life with a healthy body, walk in confidence and live the life of their dreams emotionally, mentally, physically, financially, spiritually and in their relationships. I LOVE MY LIFE! You can find out more information about me and my story and the steps I used to create my dream at www.jillbirth.com and if you are looking to make "The Shift" you can find me at

Website: www.focusedfaithevents.com http://www.jillbirth.com

Follow me on Facebook: www.facebook.com/jillbirth

Dr. Patricia Kennedy

How would you feel?

You are in your early 30's, seemingly healthy, active and living the 80's dream of work, family and fun. To the outside world your life seemed perfect. Suddenly you become aware of the fact that you are not functioning as you had always known, and perceived to be normal. Your body starts to rear ugly symptoms and your mind becomes foggy with the usual day to day tasks of life. Embarrassed, feeling defeated and scared, your world as you know it is falling apart... body, mind and spirit!

That was my reality and at the time I was in panic mode; no inkling that it was a wakeup call or a blessing in disguise until much later.

As a fulltime Registered Nurse and my mother as a retired RN, I sought some answers for myself and pulled out my nursing manual to discuss my symptoms with my mom. To my shock and the obvious concern of my mom, I had all of the symptoms of Multiple Sclerosis. As a woman from the 50's, I downplayed the symptoms, I kept the secret that everything was normal, as it always was and kept pushing to keep the flow of my family's daily activities. That is what we knew to do as women of that era. Be stoic, invincible and always someone that everyone could count on regardless of your personal struggles.

At the time this was playing out in my life, it was the 80's. The mindset and sometimes downright craziness of what was happening back then and close around me perpetuated my silence and fear to share the imperfections of my life with anyone.

It was an era of opulence and hedonistic values for many. We were socially driven, hardworking and reaping the reward from a society that aimed to please and feed our dreams! Nothing was unachievable or unworthy of taking the risk to experience it!

Women were overachieving and continually working on being super mothers, super wives, friends, and colleagues. We strived to be time-management queens, multi-tasking machines and what I called, "domestic air traffic controllers"!

The visit to my family doctor was very difficult. In fact, I put it on the back burner for months to muster up the courage to attend. In his office I felt the heat of my face as if my father had scolded me in front of my friends. I felt weak to have to admit that I was not all right and everything was not great. I laid the cards on the table and shared my concerns. He looked worried and I became weepy, so unlike the character I was portraying.

He tested me for everything possible including Tuberculosis which at the time was having comeback. I was investigated for six months and offered six pharmaceuticals for life, including antibiotics- go figure! I made visits to a specialist and had tests for six months. I listened intently to the expert opinions. At one point I was hospitalized for serious symptoms of dizziness, spinning and vomiting for ten hours. After two ambulance rides, numerous tests and an experimental drug given to me in emerge, I realized this is not how I wanted my life to play out.

I felt defeated. It was time for some soul searching, prioritizing and 'getting real'!

How would I get my power back?

My first "aha moment" was retrospectively looking at my youth. I realized with my mom's advice, that I had to revisit my natural roots; my German and Austrian grandparents' way of life. I needed to be picking the vegetables out of the garden, wash off the dirt and manure and make a full-spectrum, healthy meal full of love and conversation. Let food be thy medicine.

Taking final responsibility for what I had become, I read every book I could get my hands on, went to every seminar and searched out every natural medical modality. This was the era before the internet when you had to work hard to search, learn and sample. I did this because I started to understand that another world in medicine existed, not just a pill for every ill!

A world of natural prevention, around for thousands of years existed in my community with passionate, brilliant leaders, teachers and practitioners. They knew what I did not know, and I became a holistic sponge with a timeline. I wanted to experience everything!

I also realized as a mainstream RN, trained in the seventies, that the system was becoming more robotic, systemized and clearly driven by the pharmaceutical industry. Natural medical physicians and practitioners stayed low key and I felt timid and trapped at times in my own skin. The old world of nursing including backrubs, hugs, patient and family conversations, caps and uniforms, body, mind and spirit had faded into a business approach. My mom was trained in the 40's where like the veterans at the time, the nurses were proud, conscientious and sacrificing. The original nursing persona was created with those core values. You always cared, were there for others and had an ethical responsibility to assist whenever you could.

The idea that I had a voice began to surface in my psyche. It was my body, my mind and my spirit and I oversaw where I went from there. I started to get my power back and take control of my health and wellness!

The natural medical door opened to the world of training and sharing. I studied practices of Reflexology, cleansing, detoxification, colon hydrotherapy, bio energetics and energy practices to name a few.

After living with my devastating symptoms of MS, six months of investigations and no concrete cause found, I spent three years turning a corner and finally becoming healthy. I started to be in control, got educated and empowered myself with my new found voice.

It was my responsibility to share this knowledge, subsequently change my family dynamics and make sure all of my children were exposed to the health and wellness approach. It was a powerful learning which would change ultimately the future for my children and their children.

I had become a powerful, healthy woman. I had faced and changed the direction of my life in a moment of falling apart, being ignorant of the actual control I had over my body and the basic foundational healing brilliance of the human body, mind and spirit!

Little did I know that this was only the beginning of my life's purpose!

The True Purpose Revealed!

As I move forward on this journey of life with four amazing children, five grandchildren, a respectful and supportive partner and many cherished friends and colleagues, I realize that just when you think you get it, you really have no idea what lies in store for you. The universe will interject and your path will turn yet again.

My frustration with our mainstream medical system on many levels, transitioned me into a world of home care and becoming an assessor for veteran's affairs (True to my heart as my father proudly served). My Natural medical preventative hat was still on working and loving my part time business. Taking the leap to full time prevention was an unknown.

Then it happened! I sat in a room with a palliative woman my age and her three beautiful daughters caring for her on her hospital bed in the living room that they had shared so many intimate moments in. I observed and grieved for them for hours. I became aware of some powerful thoughts in my head that this is not right, is not necessary and is truly devastating. I felt a force overcome me and a voice inside my head say, "what are you doing? This is not where you belong!".

I left that shift, went home and decided to jump in with full force to the natural preventative arena. I knew that this was my calling. I felt an overwhelming sense that this was where I wanted to be and where I could help most. I knew from a natural and preventative perspective that you are not just dealt a bad hand and have no control over your destiny. Life is about choices and you have the freedom to choose and the freedom to change. As a woman growing up in a restrictive world of the 50's and 60's I felt my options were always so limited.

I now know and want to share with future generations that "The sky is the limit!". Never underestimate your talents and power to make a difference. Believe in yourself and the message you want to give to others.

I have learned and observed that any adversity, devastating physical ailment, or tragedy can become a blessing in disguise. *As a grandmother warrior, I want every woman to know that you have the right to be informed regarding anything you do to your body, mind and spirit.* You will be limited in thinking and options if you do not realize that you control the environment of your cells and again are not just dealt a bad hand.

Also, to understand as I have learned over the years with my journey shared, there are two forms of medicine to be respected. The brilliance of acute care in mainstream medicine and the empowering, natural and preventative focus in the world of holistic, complimentary or natural medicine.

The integrative approach is and should be the new approach with you in the driver's seat, educated, empowered and making informed decisions regarding your health and wellbeing.

Dr. Suzanne Denk

The Alchemy of Change

"Alchemy: a seemingly magical process of transformation, creation, or combination."

There was a time in my life where I dreaded change. The mere thought of it paralyzed me in my tracks. Leave well enough alone. Don't rock the boat. Status quo is a good thing. Throughout my life I have learned to understand that change is more of a noun than a verb. This new inner realization has given me hope and taught me that change is always for the better, even if it hurts now. The pain of change is only from the fear of change, so I have learned to embrace it along the way.

Gradually, as I grew older, I realized that not only is change inevitable but it is a magnificent catalyst for a journey we would maybe have never taken if not for that change, if not for those unforeseen circumstances that propels us forward in life.

Being afraid of change can keep you stuck, quite literally. We wake up one day and find that we are stuck in am unfulfilling relationship. We find ourselves in a job that sucks the life out of us with its relentless demands. We become accustomed to, used to, what we believe it is that society expects of us. Don't change it. Stay with it, year after year after year until finally, one day...

You wake up and you find that changes, although very scary, can make you feel more alive than you've ever felt before. This happened to me after I ended a long-term stagnant marriage. I stuck around in this marriage, overstayed it because I was afraid of what my future would be.

You see, I was nearing traditional "retirement age" and I had concerns about financial future. Turn on the television, and you see a senior wringing their hands with worry about their future. Would it have been better – or shall we say easier – to have stayed there?

Maybe there were financial gains to be had, but the costs associated with staying were too high for my liking. I was becoming someone I didn't know, someone I didn't particularly like. I got tired of being sad, of being angry. I felt smothered, like I couldn't take a deep breath and really be who I had become. I needed to grow.

Slowly, I did just that. Day by day, I grew stronger inside, hearing the song in my heart, the song and love of Spirit, like I had never felt it before. I realized that it was a magnificent thing to embrace this newly – evolved woman, to release her to the world. My Spiritual journey began long before I realized it had begun. I seemingly woke up one day and knew who I was as a woman, knew that I was much more than my husband ever thought I was or could be, and that, quite frankly, I did not want to share this new self with anyone other than myself.

I stayed. And stayed. And stayed. Until, one day, in the middle of yet another argument, something in me was ready to spring forth. I remember walking around a corner and thinking, "this is what it feels to have your heart broken". I have come to believe that most woman can tell you the exact time and place when they realized that they had had enough, that they were done with the destructive ways of an unbalanced relationship.

From that day on, I slowly made plans to break free from my unhappy marriage. I remember telling him that I did not love him as a wife should love her husband, but it didn't faze him. I remember telling him that I would no longer tolerate abusive language, but that didn't faze him. I slowly put little bits of money away in a safe place with a friend.

Finally, the day came when I left. Unable to take his overbearing ways any longer, I loaded my car with my clothes and went to a friend's house. I have the most amazing, generous friends who have opened their hearts and homes to me while I was going through that time in my life.

Although I lived separately from him, I still did not fully embrace change. I was still afraid and reluctant to pull the plug, if you will, and file for divorce. During the 3 years where we lived separately, I had frequent contact with him. I didn't want to hurt him, but in doing that, I was only hurting myself. He wanted to remain "friends" but when I thought about HIS definition of what it is to be a friend, and then I thought about MY definition of what it means to be a friend, I realized that there was a great divide between the two of us.

All the while, I was making changes in my life. I was meeting new people, trying to do new things. I co-authored a book with 11 other amazing women, and traveled by myself to Nantucket. I had never traveled alone before, and I found that it is an amazing experience. Each time I tried something new, I felt myself grow stronger and more fulfilled. I re-connected with many old friends of mine, taking each of these relationships to a deeper level of friendship, one that is so very heart-centered and amazing, full of love and respect for one another.

The journey to being a single woman has been long and arduous. It was a very messy divorce, with him thinking that I was abandoning him, and that he deserved so much more than the laws in my state allowed. You see, I realized during that time that what I left behind, a house, furnishings, and all the trappings of life, is all STUFF. I got what I wanted: that which has a heart and a soul. I wanted my 5-pound dog.

The changes seem to be coming faster these days, but I welcome them with open arms as I realize that with change, comes amazing growth and opportunities. Opportunities to do things we may never have thought of doing. Change encourages us to look in different places to grow. I no longer fear change, as it has been good.

I reflect back, and see where these changes have led me. We make plans for the future and POW! Life throws you a curveball. That's OK because along the journey that I call life, I've learned to get out of the proverbial batter's box and take a swing at whatever comes my way. I have hit many home runs and grand slams taking a swing at the chances that have come my way.

Don't be afraid to get out of your self-imposed, limiting box of beliefs. The limitations were never there. We have a tendency to put obstacles in the way when we're afraid to take action. But, have you ever asked yourself, "what if I succeeded?" How would your life look then? You'll never know until you try it. Don't look at life through the lens of regret, or through the rear view mirror of your past and what has already happened.

How can you go through life, move forward through life, if you don't look forward, through the windshield? Move on past the limiting beliefs and have some "Limitless, Boundless, Unstoppable" beliefs. I have found that by embracing all the changes that have come my way, I can fully experience life.

Even though life doesn't always turn out how we think it should, you can always find some good in each moment. Dare to take chances. If someone had told me 10 years ago that I would have experienced so many amazing things, or that I would have met so many magnificent people, or learned so many important life lessons, I would never have believed them. I was living a life full of limiting beliefs, even though I never knew I was doing just that. Because I dared to take chances, dared to believe that I deserve all the goodness that the Universe has to offer, and dared to open my arms and heart to receive all that goodness, I live a very fulfilled life.

Are there times where I wonder what is next or what will my future bring? Absolutely. I make plans and something changes. I have learned though that the changes always bring even more to my life than I had before. Sometimes I don't see the benefit right away, but I always carry the intention and belief that it is good, and that I am exactly where I am supposed to be at the time I am there, experiencing exactly what I am supposed to be experiencing, meeting those and reconnecting with those as it is supposed to be.

I don't know what my future holds, where I will live, who I will meet, or what I will be doing. That's OK, because change is an amazing catharsis that I now embrace like I've never embraced it before. I know it is all good, and that I, too, am changing each day. Life as I once knew it bears no resemblance to the life I live today. I can't wait to see how each day unfolds, the wonderful people I meet, and the amazing experiences that will come my way.

For as they come into my life, I welcome and embrace them.

Learn more about Dr. Sue Denk

Suzanne Denk, Psy.D. (Dr. Sue) is a Spirit-Guided Transformational Psychologist who helps people realize, embrace, and step into their true power. As a catalyst for change, she is passionate about empowering others to reach deep within to accomplish what they never thought they could accomplish. An expert author, her feature articles have been published at ezinearticles.com, as well as her blog at drsuewisdoms.wordpress.com. In addition, she is a contributing author in "Inner Circle Chronicles, Book 1 (Anne Deidre, editor).

Contact information: drsue1030@att.net

Facebook: Wisdoms from The Heart Publications

Darlene Ondi

Back to ME

"Daddy!!! Daddy!!! Don't Daddy!!! Please DDDaaaaddddyyyy!!!" I screamed these words as the tears were pouring down my face. I was no more than 3 years old and my father had caught me with a pack of matches. I don't recall much of the memory, other than ending up held between his knees.

My dad was a large and a very strong man. What I remember of the incident is that he took each one of my tiny tender little fingers and burnt them until the ends of them blistered. I remember jumping and screaming and he held on so tight. I remember looking at him and wondering why he was hurting me so, as he went from finger to finger, then I don't remember much at all.

This incident began a very ingrained fear of my father. My father seemed to get some form of sick joy taunting me and making my life difficult for most of my life. He once tried to kill me. My memories of my childhood are staggered. What I do remember are usually traumatic incidents and in the back of my mind I'm asking, "Where is my mother?" I was a child that was invisible to my parents and dismissed by my siblings. What I came to understand many years later is that I was different and they didn't know how to deal with me so they just didn't.

I wouldn't conform to their unwavering and strict standards, and I would be punished for it. I was given much responsibility and was pretty much looking after myself by the time I was 8. I was already buying my clothes by the time I was in grade 6 so my parents didn't go out of their way to buy things for me. At sporting events that I exceled at, I went alone. I was never given money to care for myself or heaven forbid, have fun. I just learned to deal with the lack of support, and being without.

I am grateful to now be a conscious being and very mindful of others. I consider kindness and compassion my greatest virtues. Being an empath I feel the suffering and pain of others. I have the capacity to pull their darkness and their Light from within. It is a gift that I am learning to embrace and embody.

At age 50 I had the revelation that my greatest gift to myself was me. In the past I owned opinions of others that I would take on as the truth, such as you're stupid, you're not worth anything. I despised the term, (Because I said So). It is a painful term when you are an intelligent and curious child. I could never understand why any human becoming or as I know now...unconscious being would want to harm, hurt, degrade or control.

Control. Let's speak to that a moment. I have come to realize that all of us do it. There are those that loudly portray it and to most of us, it's familiar. What about those subtle, passive-aggressive ways like not returning calls, or saying you are showing up to something where someone counts on you and not have the courtesy to return a call? What about dismissing someone? It's all control!!!

One of my biggest lessons after returning from what I will term, "a dark night of the soul" experience was that at 48 years of age I realized I had absolutely no idea who I was. I returned to Canada to start over after I had been fraudulently terminated, ostracized, by a global women's empowerment organization. I had sold everything to follow a dream that ultimately became my biggest nightmare. No one came to look for me.

They had been told that by the founder, a woman from Tehran, that I was healing at an ashram. I found myself homeless, starving, suicidal with what I now know was "Post Traumatic Stress Disorder". I came back to Canada to start over. I had nothing and I promised myself that I would never again live in fear or give my power to someone else. I worked at a golf course raking bunkers at 4am in the morning for minimum wage while I searched for every healing modality to try to fix me. I thought I was broken. I wanted the pain to go away. I hid from the world for three years. I couldn't speak without crying so I shut off my voice. The experience in the USA was so traumatic that I started to stutter, and my two ring finger nailbeds rotted in my hands. I learned later that this is where you hold your emotional energy. I was so full of fear I couldn't even stand myself. No outside modality worked

Ilyana Vanzant made a very powerful statement that holds much truth. She shared we stay in the familiar, no matter how painful, to avoid the unknown where the pain could possibly be greater. Sleeping with the enemy. I was hanging on to pain and suffering. It is all I knew....my little girl....so familiar. It was important now to break the cycle!!!

You sometimes think that it can't get any worse....well it can!!! I was bringing experiences to me that were how I was feeling inside. It was obvious that I hated myself!!! All I had to do was look around at my surroundings. I had to take a long hard look at myself and start the work that was necessary for me to own my journey of taking back my power, owning my power and learning to love myself fully. The fact that I had to be completely disempowered by a global women's organization to learn to become empowered. I learned to never hold anyone in such high esteem that you put them on a pedestal because they are human and will disappoint you and...if you truly want to discover someone's character, give them power and then give them money. Everything will be revealed!

In 2012 I found myself in the chrysalis of life. It took becoming a mush of nothingness, crawling and flailing to come through many challenging lessons to the discovery of myself; the journey back to me. I cannot count the rivers of tears I have shed realizing that I had given the gift of myself away and all I needed to do was to own the fact that I was utterly Magnificent!!! My discovery-I was unique and I was here to shine! There was and never will there be another me! My very short time on this planet was for me to claim my right to be here and make the difference that I chose to make.

I jokingly share with people that I did not work on the reserves of northern Manitoba as a social worker for the money. I sincerely love people and have always wanted the best for others. If I knew then what I know now I may not have chosen that profession but I know in my heart that if I assisted the life of one native child than I did make the difference that I was here to do. Now that I have more life experience under my wings I know that I choose to do this now on a much grander scale with like-minded beings. And who would have ever known that the business model of people to people marketing would be a vehicle that would allow me to do the mentoring and inspiring of my heart's calling. More interestingly is that it is in an industry that I would never have imagined...health, beauty and skin. I chuckle even thinking about it now as I always considered myself more of a tomgirl and never really paid attention to all of that "pretty stuff", and then.....BAM!!!

Hit me over the head with the 2x4 to get my attention...No wait, that was the entire wall of China that had to fall on me before I became aware to where I was being guided. Remember that control I mentioned earlier? Well I thought that I was in control. Guess what!!! I was never in control, and so began the process of surrender and letting go.

I have a deep understanding now that we are divinely guided to bring out our gift and that is the gift of us, being our highest and most incredible selves. We are here to be in joy and when we are in joy we bring joy to the world. It's as simple as that. Another lesson... what is simple to do is also simple not to do.

I trust that many will not take the five decades that I did to get it. Now that I own my power and take responsibility to claim my ability to create the world in which I live....I say, watch out world!!!

I've got this!!! This is my time!!! Time to live and enjoy every moment!!!

Learn More about Darlene Ondi

Darlene is a published author, speaker, and best known for her gift as being an Intuitive Connector. She has created revenue of $1Million+ through creating events and visceral experiences across North America with women from all over the world. Known as the "Go-To" woman for two global CEO's, Darlene is taking her talent as an Entrepreneuress to build community and gatherings. With 25 years of entrepreneurial experience, Darlene delivers impactful and insightful knowledge to those who are ready for their true transformation.

After coming through a two-year journey of a "dark night of the soul" experience, Darlene delivers a real and raw message with teachings that will accelerate your life path and shift your very way of being. Darlene is about empowering women and inspiring them to flourish into their authentic selves now! She also has a category-creating technology that creates your beauty from the inside out.

Darlene is all about living from a space of Pure Love, Joy and Empowerment no matter what your stage of your life. You become what you DECLARE yourself to BE!

Here's to Creating Beautiful Lives!

Caron Kavanagh

Stop Pleasing: Start Serving Beginning with You

Confession time: My name is Caron and I'm a recovering pleaser. Yes, I know that sounds silly, however, this trait has wreaked havoc in my life. So, what's so bad about pleasing others? Over the years I've learned that there's a big difference between pleasing and serving.

My first experience in pleasing started with my parents. I wanted to be a "good girl" and not disappoint them, behaving in public, getting good grades, being happy - as my mom called me "the consummate cheerleader", all in the space of a turbulent home environment. The story that I created was maybe if I did everything right, Dad wouldn't yell at Mom.

Over the years I found myself committing to do things with and for friends, family, bosses, colleagues and my community when I really didn't want to do them. I didn't want to look bad or disappoint anyone. I found that my self-worth was wrapped up in not disappointing and looking good in the eyes of others.

I spent 24 years trying to please my husband, trying to keep peace because I didn't want to argue, saying what I thought he wanted to hear even though I didn't feel that way, being who I thought he wanted me to be, etc. I morphed myself into who I thought he wanted me to be, although he never asked me to do this. I became someone I didn't know or even like. This way of living was completely inauthentic and it was a lot of work and truly exhausting! On the outside I appeared to "have it all" and on the inside I was miserable and suffering in silence.

This pleasing others and not wanting to look bad also worked in my favor, for awhile. I became the top performing sales person for 4 different companies in 3 different industries making a comfy 6-figure income. We owned a beautiful California home, went on expensive vacations; enjoyed fine dining. However, there was a price. I drove myself into the ground and my health suffered. I spent my life living from the neck up and was not at all connected to my body or my spirit. I was burned out, stressed out, I couldn't sleep, I was exhausted during the day and needed caffeine to stay awake. I became moody, developed digestive issues, and started putting on weight.

I got sick and tired of feeling sick and tired and took the first step to get on track by seeing a holistic doctor. The first thing she did is put me on a wellness program that shifted my health within the first few weeks. By feeding my body vibrant superfoods, cleansing out harmful toxins and impurities and taking in nutrients that help combat stress, I began to heal my body. I gave up caffeine yet my energy became vibrant and abundant! I started sleeping a full 8 hours and began feeling happy again. My digestive issues went away and I released 20 lbs. and 27 inches! Hippocrates said "Let thy food be thy medicine, and thy medicine be thy food", and I totally took this on. By healing my body, I also realized I could help others do the same. This was my introduction into serving others. Since this day, I have helped hundreds of people optimize their health and vitality, which feels amazing! This is a completely different feeling than pleasing. Pleasing eroded my self-worth and self-confidence. Serving gives me a sense of purpose, brings me joy and increases my belief in myself.

As a Wellness Coach, I pursued a delicate balance between pleasing and serving. I really wanted to help others and make a difference in the world. But, I also wanted my clients to like me. I didn't want to upset them because they might quit. I took on clients that were not ready to make a change; I wanted their well-being for them more than they wanted it for themselves. I found myself dragging people through the program, feeling like a mother hen, trying to convince my clients into taking care of their health for not only themselves but for the sake of their loved ones. I felt like I was "carrying the weight of the world" on my back. Although this is a metaphor, I became so stressed out again that I threw my back out and was literally on the floor for 10 days because I was unable to sit in a chair or lay in a bed. Ugh, guilty again of pleasing versus serving and this time it got me flat on my back! My intentions were really true to serving, however, my actions were still in the realm of pleasing. I didn't set any boundaries. I didn't release clients go who were less committed than me.

O.K. Caron, how many signs do you need before you start loving yourself enough to put yourself first, create boundaries and start speaking your truth? I learned that pleasing is giving to get something, while serving is giving to give from the heart. Pleasing is coming from a place of fear and selfishness; such as wanting to create safety, be liked, look good, not disappoint, not rock the boat, keeping peace or getting attention, praise, love or accolades. This all feels yucky. Serving and giving to give coming from love and it feels amazing! Yes, we get something from giving to others; feelings of joy, peace, love, connectedness. These are far more satisfying and make me feel so much better! So then, why not serve ourselves? Was I neglecting to serve myself as well?

It was time for me to practice some rigorous self-care! Many times I heard flight attendants say, "put the mask on yourself before helping others". I use this analogy a lot with my clients because I believe this needs to be our mindset. When I started making myself a priority, my life shifted. It started with my health by getting my nutrition on track. I scheduled my workouts and yoga on my calendar and they became non-negotiable appointments, like I would treat a client appointment. I created these "self appointments" and blocked out time for me. I started working on my spiritual practice. I started getting up earlier every morning to meditate for 20 minutes and doing daily affirmations. I began keeping a gratitude journal and scheduling the things that bring me joy like spending time with girlfriends. I started saying "no" when I didn't want to do something versus saying "yes" because I didn't want to disappoint someone. What I found is that by putting me first, and doing things for myself, I had more energy and more capacity to give more of myself to others. My self-confidence improved. I became a better daughter, friend, wife, coach, neighbor, leader, etc.

What I learned is when I began to serve myself, because my soul is full, I can be of greater service to others. <u>We cannot give from an empty well</u>. I also learned being authentic and true to myself not only feels good to me, but it also shifts how others relate to me. As I care more for myself, I become happier and more joyful which changes my energetic vibration and shifts what I'm attracting into my life – positive people, more money, miracles show up, etc. Caring for and loving ourselves first has a massive ripple effect to our loved ones. We are taking responsibility for our own happiness and not putting that chore on others. As Marianne Williamson so beautifully states, "As we let our own light shine, we unconsciously give other people permission to do the same. As we are liberated from our own fear, our presence automatically liberates others."

Self-care and self-love are strategies to grow love in the world. Do you now see how caring for ourselves can impact our loved ones? Now my friend, it is your turn to serve yourself first. Commit to speaking your truth and saying yes when you mean yes, and no when you mean no. Open up your calendar, schedule time to feed your mind, body and spirit. Schedule time with friends, time to paint, take a bubble bath, read, get a massage or a facial, garden, take a martial arts class, do yoga, whatever brings you joy! Trade with a friend or neighbor to watch the kids so you can have more "me time" and she too can create her own me time. The possibilities are endless! Ready, set, GO!

Learn More about Caron Kavanagh

Caron Kavanagh is a "Lifestyle Mentor", speaker and trainer who focuses on helping women optimize balance, vitality and confidence in their lives. Caron has been an entrepreneur and business owner for 7 years and has successfully mentored over 250 clients. She has been a top income earner in sales and new business development in three different industries and worked for small and large companies such as Starbucks Coffee Company. Caron has received industry awards for outstanding service and contribution to her associates.

She is a Certified Yoga Instructor and a graduate of Landmark Worldwide. She is also a practitioner of Krav Maga. Caron has also shared the stage with world-renowned author Dr. John Gray. She is an expert in helping people achieve optimal health and vitality so they can live to their highest purpose.

Caron is the ideal blend of head and heart. She is passionate about helping her clients to achieve their goals and dreams so they can have a life they love, and live it powerfully! Through her own trial and error of creating a balanced life, she provides proven systems that when integrated, produce transformational results in physical and financial health. These outcomes include vibrant energy, mental focus, less stress, weight loss and residual income.

To work with Caron and/or schedule a complimentary Breakthrough Strategy Session, visit her website: www.caronkavanagh.com.

Terryn Barill

Greece, Bikinis and Self-Love

"In moments of gratitude, I revel in her strength, her resilience, how much I've put her through and she still carries me every single day."

The breeze is cool, cooler than I thought it would be, but it's a counterpoint to the heat of the sun, so I'm enjoying the feel of it. My skin heats up, still salty from the water. Then the breeze kicks and, drying me, caressing me, relaxing me.

For the moment, there are no screaming children, no loud groups of tourists, nothing but the sun, the sand, and the sea.

It has taken me days to get this relaxed. I'm here in Santorini, Greece, on a travel package that was cheaper than going to Boonieville Florida. It's off-season, and I'm on the less-touristy east side of the island. There are no gleaming white cities here, but there also aren't a lot of stairs, so my often-surgically-repaired back and knees are thinking me.

The whole thing would have been cheap and glamorous, if not for the overpriced retreat that I got suckered into. I haven't had a real vacation in 3 years. I used to love doing retreats and spiritual getaways, back before I was married to a much more practical man. Now single again, I was excited for a new adventure. I was going to do deep work here, guided by a master healer, who also happened to be a friend of mine. Bonded by the instant intimacy that the work requires, our small group would become friends, forever connected through this shared experience.

That was what was promised - a retreat to restore you in body, mind and soul in the beautiful location of Santorini.

I've spent the entire retreat alone and ostracized, my former friend has shown herself to be a petty and unprofessional woman, and I didn't have enough time with the group to bond to anyone.

Thank G-d.

The day I arrived was fine. My friend met me and another participant at the airport, and we all chatted during the short drive to the hotel. We dumped the luggage in rooms, and walked to a seaside restaurant for lunch with the members of our group that had already arrived. The lunch conversation was light and fun.

After lunch, we walked back to the hotel, with the intention to change and head to the beach. My friend and I ended up talking for about a half hour. She laughed at how engaged I was during lunch, she said I led the conversation, and she loved it. Maybe I should have paid more attention to that comment.

She's been traveling in Europe for almost three months. There have been many times when the travelling wasn't fun, when we had calls and texts and message conversations, trying to get her on an even keel.

Originally, I wasn't going to come to this retreat. She was so excited about putting on her first retreat, in her home country of Greece, and I was excited for her, but I wasn't feeling it for me. Then a few months ago, I started getting this feeling. A feeling that maybe I needed to do this. So internally I made a deal. If there was still a single room available, because I don't share rooms anymore, I would do it. There was one single room available. I took it as a sign, and I booked it. I've been saving, so I paid in full. It turned out that because I paid in full, she could make the deposits on the hotel.

Sitting on the beach that first day, I chatted with the others, feeling frumpy and fat. Thanks to a health issue, I'd put on a lot of weight very quickly, and I had been disgusted by my own body and ashamed for feeling that way ever since. I've had a complex relationship with my body. In moments of gratitude, I revel in her strength, her resilience, how much I've put her through and she still carries me every single day.

I was a bodybuilder in my 20s, kept up through my 30s, and pretty much coasted on that through my 40s. Now well past 50, not only was I not healthy, but I had put on this weight in a way I had never gained weight before. I had cellulite for the first time in my life. I had rolls around the midsection that I could feel every time I sat down, and it fueled my disgust. The clothing I wore was for hiding the fat, and if I could have claimed that muu-muus were coming back in style, I would have jumped on that bandwagon so hard it would have broken the shocks and flattened the tires.

I looked to my right and saw a huge deeply tanned woman in a tiny bikini. "She looks how I feel" I thought, focusing on her size, my **Inner Comparison Queen** in full power. And yet, I knew I wasn't that big. Later in the water, I saw other women, bodies as soft and white as mine, none wearing an old lady flowered one-piece with tummy control. Everyone could wear bikinis here. I shook my head at the thought. It's not me. I haven't worn a bikini since I was 7, largely because I play in the water, and I got tired of the bottoms coming down. It was a strictly functional choice.

The next day was a sightseeing day, before the retreat officially started.

I woke up at 5:30a, wondering why I was awake in the darkness. Did some meditation, went to journal, and realized what day it was. 9/11. The day my world changed. Somehow in the whirlwind of getting ready to go to Greece, getting to Greece and being in Greece, I'd forgotten. Or maybe just tried to forget.

A very heavy full day of sightseeing had been planned, with an assumption that everyone would be physically capable of doing it. I did the volcano hike, tough even for those fitter than me. High heat, uneven unstable terrain, and a steep incline are never a good combination for someone who has the back and joint issues that I do. She opted out.

By the end, I was in severe pain and overheated, shaking from low blood sugar and lack of calories in my system. I opted out of the strenuous swim, knowing what it would do to me. During our "lunch and beach" stop, there was no beach, and another woman in our group was also shaking and feeling ill. Everyone rallied around and took care of her. I didn't want anyone focused on me. It was taking all my energy just to hold it together.

I had said repeatedly throughout the day that I didn't want to do the activity at our last stop, climbing over 300 stairs, at a steep incline. I told them I would just wait at the bottom. She heard me every single time, and didn't say anything. When we arrived, I realized there was no possible way around doing these fucking stairs, because our ride home is from the top. She had known, and didn't say anything. Very quickly it became apparent that I wasn't doing well.

I did what I always do when in severe pain...I power through. They had donkeys, but for anyone who has back issues, riding a donkey up a flight of stairs isn't helpful. So I am doing the best I can, stopping when I have to, pushing through because I can't stop too long, and doing a damn fine job dodging the donkey poop all over the stairs, if I do say so myself.

When I'm almost at the top, she comes by and tells me "listen to your body". I say "We're a ways past that." She gets upset and peels off to tell the others. I can see her gesturing at me, and can hear the tone of her voice on the wind. I don't care. I AM taking care of my body. I am doing what I am required to do to get through this, this thing I did not choose to do.

I ended the day hobbling and alone, using all my energy to hold it together. If I'd been depleted and in need of restoration when I arrived, now I was well past reserves. I've been carrying the burden of 9-11 all day. Climbing those stairs, climbing the side of the volcano, it reminds me of The Pile. Details come back. The details will break your heart every time.

The next morning, I woke up crying. All the sorrow I should have released the day before is coming up today. My beach shoes disintegrated the first day, so after breakfast, I wander off to find replacements. Thanks to missing a turn, I walked further than I had planned, and my feet were now rubbed raw. Fabulous. But I found a cheap pair of flip flops...and a bikini. It was cheap and my size, and I figure this is the place, right?

As I arrive back at the hotel, I see a message "I need to talk to you NOW. I'll be waiting on the patio for you." Okay. Not liking the sound of this, but I go. It was every bit as bad as you imagine, and probably a bit worse. I'm barely holding it together and she's telling me I'm too aggressive and ruining the retreat for everyone...and it hasn't even started yet.

I was told that my pain is "inappropriate", " that I am "too angry / aggressive / combative /assertive", and that I am "making it harder" on her. All I did is what was asked of me. All I did was give more of me than what I had to give. I gave when I was well past empty, and received anger and humiliation in return. I am told to not talk to any of the other participants, and to "not bring my energy to the retreat".

That first "healing session" was uncomfortable. I just sat there. Can't share, comment or participate, that would be "bringing my energy to the retreat", not to mention that it would require talking. I didn't understand why she was doing this. I run workshops all the time, and when someone comes to me in pain, I don't respond with anger and self-centeredness. It is my responsibility to ensure that everyone gets what they need, it would never occur to me to ostracize someone.

I head to the beach for some real healing after the healing session. The bikini remains hidden in the closet. I can't even look at it. I am resolved to not cry in front of anyone. They see me, and walk right past. I can see them from where I'm sitting, talking and continuing the conversations. I will hold to her requests of me, because if what she said was even remotely true, I certainly wouldn't want anyone else's retreat ruined the way mine has been.

I sit in the silence, listening to the wind and the waves and the sounds of life all around me, feeling very disconnected. I can hear my thoughts of anger, of judgment, that victim voice that cries out "Why me?". I spend the next 18 hours in silence, releasing everything around the retreat and the loss of a friendship. I cry. I rage. I journal. I cry some more. I use the tools I have in the toolbox and I see the situation for what it is -- that without me, this retreat never would have happened. That I needed a silent retreat, but I never would have done it for myself. That I always do what others ask of me, and I give more than I have, especially to those I care about. That my friend is petty and unprofessional, and only likes me when I am doing / being / acting the way she wants me to. It is an old pattern, and one I need to remove from my life.

As the sun comes up, I am empty. Cried out, no longer angry. I will go to the "healing sessions", but I am not willing to spend the energy to contain myself and have a rotten time. I'd rather be alone and happy. I'm happy that today is an "integration day", which means I am on my own and can spend my whole day under a beach umbrella reading novels. As I open the closet, I see the orange bag. I haven't even tried it on. I pull it out and put it on the bed. "It's so small!" My mind runs through rationalizations, "I should at least just try it. I don't have to wear it." I try it on.

And burst into tears. I am standing alone in my hotel room, tile cold on my feet, barely capable of looking at myself in the mirror, doing one of those ugly-cries of terror and fear and "what will they think" and "what am I doing". My breath is ragged. I consciously begin to relax my shoulders. I take a look at it. Tentatively, tenderly, I notice that I'm not as bad as I thought. In an evil judgmental moment, I notice that I certainly don't have the muffin rolls that she does. Okay, enough of that. Positive focus. Deep breath. I can do this. There is no physical reason why I can't do this. And if I don't have friendly support, well, at least I am surrounded by strangers who don't care at all.

I put on my cover-up. I gather all my stuff in my bag. I flip-flop down to the beach, which has become my happy place. She is already there, but I find I don't care. I grab a lounger on the opposite end, make myself comfortable, and...I sit there in my cover up. I can't do it. Okay, maybe I can. It takes me an hour that feels like three to get up the nerve to unwrap and dash down to the water. I dive in, feeling the arms of Mother Ocean caressing me, holding me. I can feel the salt on my cheeks, a combination of tears and sea and success. I laugh out loud. I run my hands down my sides, feel my little tummy, which doesn't need spandex control after all. I am fully IN my body, and it is a glorious body. I feel sexy for the first time in years. I feel strong and powerful. I know that this week isn't what I had planned, but it is exactly what I need, and I need more ocean in my life.

Later, on my third trip to the water, I stand at the edge, no longer dashing in. I can no longer be less of who I am to make others more comfortable. I can no longer put myself last, or punish myself for mistakes made. I am unapologetically me. Three days later, I figure out that my bikini looks even better when I don't wear the top upside down.

Learn more about Terryn Barril

If you want to sit in a circle and sing Kumbaya, Terryn is **not** your girl. She also disapproves of reliving your trauma repeatedly, or wallowing in what is wrong. She is a PTSD and trauma recovery expert because she's <u>lived</u> it, not because she read about it in a book, and that keeps her focused-on things that make an immediate impact on your life and then help you to keep moving forward.

After 15+ years of DoD deployments, Terryn found herself with combat-related PTSD. It took her 10 years to come all the way home. After leaving service, she spent time as an EMT & emergency planner. It was as a 9-11 first responder in NYC that the last piece of the puzzle fell into place.

Terryn began running PTSD programs for veterans and emergency responders in 2001, but it wasn't long before she was asked to work with a wider audience. She has worked with genocide survivors, cancer survivors, people in deep grief, forced retirees, professional athletes who had career-ending injuries. Terryn knows what it's like to be blindsided by life, to look around and think "It wasn't supposed to be like this." She gives people practical tools to re-build a life worth living, even if it's not the life they had planned on.

Karen Davis-Foulks

The Greatest Hoax Ever Played on a Human Soul! Shift Out of Chronic Disease Care Stress

"Life Begins Where Fear Ends" OSHO

There was no fear in me when the doctors did a medical procedure on my mother Shirley R. Hardy without my mom's permission or mine. I was not afraid to tell them to reverse the procedure and stop managing my mom's sickness to keep her alive by any medical means necessary. My mother had told her medical doctor, the Gastroenterologist of 15 plus years that she would not do dialysis that when that time came to let her go, she was tired. She had tried everything that was requested of her and still she did not get better. She told me that when she could not speak for herself anymore do not let them keep her here when she cannot do for herself no matter what they said, little baby.

Little baby is the name that my mother would give me as a child when she wanted me to hear what she was saying to me and understand that she meant what she was saying. My grandmother Ruth Bond would do the same thing that my mother did. She would say Karen don't let them keep me here on her way to the hospital in 1988. My mother is there with me, and she would say that to me, I was 31 years and nowhere in my consciousness did I understand why she said that to me and not my mother.

Later in life, I would come to know the inner truth of what my grandmother was sharing with me all those years of her working with the elders and assisting with their transitioning. I would visit with my grandmother often in the home where she worked and lived. I would assist her when I was there. This period would come to shape my life in the future. It's like the new health care information that is showing us that it is the environment that is controlling our cell life not so much your genes. This information from the field of epigenetic which states you are more than just your genes.

Genes don't just turn themselves on or off they are express. Bruce Lipton shares this information in his book The Biology of Belief. This book should be required reading for all people. I would emerge in the future of time as a living example of the information shared in Bruce's book from the seeds planet in my subconscious mind. I would live a disease free-thinking lifestyle without even knowing why I lived the life I have. Growing up I never would accept what the doctors said about my health. Why western medicine and pharmaceuticals never seem helpful to me. People still were sick not getting well.

That day in 2011, I can hear the doctors in the emergency room asking my mother all kinds of questions about her directives for her health care. Knowing all the health challenges and surgeries that she had had before and after her choice of not going on dialysis in 2005 I stood there listening to my mother with that tone in her voice. She said my doctor; her gastroenterologist he knows what I want. My paperwork is in my medical records, and my daughter (pointing to me) knows what to do. Right then they would have my mother sign new paperwork. We would be there for hours as I see my mother getting weaker by the hour and no treatments are being administered to her as I sit there quietly. Finally, they gave her life water and began to ask me health question about my mother at the same time informing me that they are going to admit her.

Without telling me what they found out and why the doctors chose to ask my mother all those questions have her sign new paperwork admit her to the hospital now you are going to ask me what is wrong with my mother. Can I give you her medical history? In my mind, you got to be kidding me you are asking me what is wrong with my mother and what is her medical history. No, I cannot answer you did my mother just give you that information. No, I cannot answer your questions, I DO NOT SPEAK FOR MY MOTHER when she can talk for herself any answers you need contact her doctor and read her medical records. Oh! The doctor is not happy with my reply, who am I, not to answer him and the other two doctors that ask me the same question.

I am very conscious of the standard medical practices between doctor, patient and the responsible person or child of the patient so no I will not speak for my mother you tell me why you are admitting her. The doctors stop talking to me and says to my mom transportation has been called and walks away. It is past midnight, and it was a long day in that ER. I am in thought my heart is racing, and my body feels weak as I am driving home. What just happen why the doctors didn't tell me anything, my mother may not make it through the night.

I go to my mom's house given to her by my sister Saundra after her death in 2001 much too early before her 48th birthday. My mother would witness the death of her first child and that of her third child in 1969 before Kevin was two years. Shirley would also come to lose her fourth child Franklin before his 30th birthday in 2002. A mother's greatest heartbreak is to outlive her children.

I would be her last living child Karen Davis-Foulks the special child, the child that always saw things different and responded to life different. I am anchored in my career, my passion no longer just a nutritionist, lymphologist, stress and relaxation specialist. I am also a pioneering quantum health and healing wellness specialist and conscious self-healthcare educator. An energetic cellular reader and human body water purifier transformer and cell shifter. Yes, that is me 16 years ahead of time sharing the future in health care.

I sat there in the living room with tears in my eyes all alone crying and crying I know what I am feeling and I know what energy is saying to me get prepared Karen. My mother, my mom I could see it in her eyes I felt it in her spirit my mother was leaving why the doctors would not just say that. Sleep just will not come; thoughts will not stop the feeling of wanting to share with someone no siblings no husband, no friend to call. Don't want to panic my nieces I will call everyone tomorrow after I get to the hospital and learn what is going on.

Now readers hold on to your hat this happen with my mother in 2011, the next day when I got to the hospital. The doctors had stop my mother from dying saved her life did a medical procedure and put a life saving device in her body. My mother had just told them to do nothing to extend her life and they did. The doctors did not follow my mother wishes and kept her alive by any means necessary. So, Yes I honored my mother wishes and told the doctor speaking to me to reverse the procedure and tell my mother that you want to do that to her and place her in a nursing home. Shocked he was and Yes, I meant what I said reverse the procedure.

It is 2014 and to my surprise my mother has thrived for the past two years. She was not as dire as the doctor had told me when they want to move her to a nursing home in 2011 with that device in Shirley. Shirley would show signs of cognitive dysfunction and brain fog when she returned home from the hospital after they removed the device from my mother so I must pay attention to my mother's health choices. I am not take control of her health choices but monitor what she was choosing and what the doctors was saying and doing to her. She would tell the cardiovascular doctor that she would not have vein surgery on her legs, like she said in 2007 no more surgeries and do nothing to keep her alive.

Now my mother is seeing a cardiologist and I know her from her work in the community. She tells my mother to change her diet, take supplements; to juice and to stop smoking or that she would be having surgery. I told my mother that I knew her doctor and if she did what she said she would keep improving. And that she DID she was released by her cardiologist in 2013 told to return within a year.

I never had a conversation with my mother once she was released from the hospital in 2011 and she never had a conversation with me about those events and no one in my family or the medical establishment or any doctor of hers ever did.

Remember reader doctors don't talk to each other nor do they all work from the same model but they all see the body as separate and there part has nothing to do with the success or failures of other doctor's parts. It is a reductionist mindset of treatment and healthcare YOU DON'T MATTER just their science. The holistic approach from her cardiologist was a match with what my mother had heard me say, teach and live for years.

Mother is no longer seeing the cardiologist, she is now in the control of her beloved doctor the Gastroenterologist, and she calls him her boyfriend. How stupid of me. How in creditably stupid of me to think that everything was the same with my mother and her doctors and the medical establishment with me and them with my mother. We never had a conversation with her doctor the gastroenterologist I will share with you later why that never happens.

I cannot believe how stupid I was to think that there was no repercussion from my actions in 2011. I should have remembered what the medical doctors did to my marriage when they told my husband that I tried to kill him also because I follow my husband instructions and told them no they could not do a procedure on him that they wanted to do. Oh! This is major to this part of my story because it doesn't end here in this story this is only the beginning of the middle of the life and legacy of Shirley R. Hardy beloved mother, grandmother, godmother and devoted daughter of the Elks for 60 years of her life and what was done to her daughter the pioneering quantum health and healing wellness specialist.

What do you do when everyone walks away from you doing the time your mom is dying, and you are accused of denying her medical care and of killing her? When it is time for her funeral you are denied the right to speak at your mother's funeral and the pastor Michael Bell don't mention your name in his eulogy and tells everyone that Shirley told him a secret in 2010.

How am I living after my family members, husband, partner, pastors, and friends, members of the community, colleagues, doctors, lawyers, and strangers worked to make me look insane and crazy? What was done to my mother by family members agreeing with them and to me because you were told to honor my mom and let her transition with dignity and off medication in 2011 and 2014? My mother made her transition in August 2014 and what they did to her and me is unbelievable but I will share this whole story that was played on my life and how the medical establishment treated my mother over the 12 days in the hospital where she died after being put in a fake coma because I would not let them move her to hospice care.

That is what they made everyone believe that I had done to cover up what they had done. What did they all do to us my family relationships, my work, my lively hood and my living space? Listen to my real-life radio show as I continue to share this story as I rebuild my life from nothing.

It is 2016 and my life is still turned upside down and inside out, did I imagine this all is my mother still alive and it was all a hoax an illusion. I go see Rev. Willie Wilson I know I can trust him, he will help me, I am tired. He doesn't even ask me why am I there he just say repeatedly for 20 minutes to my question can you help me find out what is happening in my life no one is talking to me and you won't believe what has happen. Rev. Wilson look me in the face and say repeatedly GO TALK TO YOUR FAMILY Rev Wilson you know I am my family who am I to go and talk with my nieces my two cousins. I came to you because I wanted help in finding out way all these things were happening to me my career, my living hood.

Thank you very much Rev. Wilson I will not be asking my family anything in 2016. You and everyone else that planed this Hoax and deception on my life will read it in my book and Still I Rise. Welcome to the new world of Health Care we are moving from disease care 2 Conscious Self-Healthcare so awake up Americans disease care is DEAD!

Topic: VIP Entries from our Kids and Volunteers!

Thank you so much to the writers who submitted their stories within minutes of my announcement that we needed a few more articles. Over the course of 4 months, we have worked tirelessly as a team to build each other up, but, some authors had issues that prevented them from fully committing to writing. When the call went out, you were there. Thank you from the bottom of my heart. CWH.

Jacqueline M. Broadenax, Age 8

My mommy is like a Red Rose.
She is passionate and bold!

My daddy is like a Purple Lavender.
His fragrance is strong and powerful!

My sissy is like a Pink Lily.
She is neat and sweet!

My nana is like an Orange Zinnia.
She is persistent and resilient!

I am like a Blue Violet.
I am a naturalist and a foodie!

My family is like a flower garden.
We are all different but beautiful, together!

Family Flowers

Jacqueline M. Broadenax
8 years old

Jacqueline M. Broadenax is your typical kid with a huge personality. She comes from a family that believes in serving and Jacqueline is no different. She plans on being a police officer, a Solider in the Army, or the President of the United States of America. Currently, Jacqueline is writing her first children's book addressing the subject of sexual abuse on America's school buses. Jacqueline is the daughter of Zara R. Broadenax and older sister of Sabrina E. Broadenax, both are fellow authors in 100 Voices of Inspiration, Awakening & Empowerment.

Sabrina E. Broadenax, age 5

The Pink Butterfly

Sabrina E. Broadenax

5 years old

The pink butterfly flies......
Across your head.

The pink butterfly flies......
To the beehive.

The pink butterfly flies......
By the people.

The pink butterfly flies......
Over to the flower.

The pink butterfly names......
The flower Princess Rosie.

The pink butterfly gives......
Princess Rosie a kiss.

The pink butterfly gets......
Nectar from kissing the flower.

The pink butterfly flies......
Back to the beehive.

The pink butterfly helps......
The bees with the nectar.

The pink butterfly turns......
Into a bee.

Then she goes home,
For a goodnight sleep!

Sabrina E. Broadenax is the sweet, shy type until she gets to know you, then her bubbly personality shines. She plans on being an artist when she grows up because she loves to paint. Currently, Sabrina just loves being a girly-girl by doing dance, tea parties, and coloring. Sabrina is the daughter of Zara R. Broadenax and younger sister of Jacqueline M. Broadenax, both are fellow authors in 100 Voices of Inspiration, Awakening & Empowerment.

Additional Stories & Bonuses

Jennifer Diaby

Creative Ideas to Build Your Brand Or Name On Social Media

Hello my name is Jennifer Diaby, and I am the CEO/Founder of Growth Women's Prayer Ministry. My online ministry is to encourage and uplift women who need to heal. Women who have been abused emotionally or any other type of circumstances such as: marital problems, divorce, infertility, low self-esteem, weight issues, or the loss of loved ones, etc. Growth Women's Prayer Ministry is well-known on Facebook for posting inspirational prayers, scriptures, and messages daily. The followers of my page visit to read God's word to heal from emotional hurt and pain. To start a brand or name on social media and begin to be followed by an audience always know your platform. These are some of the questions that should come to mind before making a public page on Facebook, Twitter, Instagram, and LinkedIn. What is your purpose of using social media for your brand? What is the mission of your social media pages? Who do you want to follow you? How do you plan to advertise and grow your audience? I will elaborate by answering each question.

What is your purpose of using social media? The purpose of Growth Women's Prayer Ministry public page is to reach women across the world to encourage and uplift them to heal from situations that have caused them emotional pain or hurt.

What is the mission of your social media page? Growth Women's Prayer Ministry mission is to help to bring healing to women through prayers, scriptures, encouragement and inspirational quotes to build a closer relationship with God. My page is about showing love to save souls for Christ.

Who do you want to follow you? Everyone who needs encouragement: the brokenhearted, the lost, persons who feel rejected, those who are suffering with anxiety, depression, worries, and fear. Individuals who are sick and praying to God for healing and restoration. Anyone struggling with financial problems. Women dealing with infertility and need prayers for the fruit of the womb.

Married women have experienced or presently experiencing marital problems. Also, men who are on my prayer ministry page can be part of the prayers.

How do you plan to advertise and grow your audience? It is several ways to advertise through Facebook. Select how long you want to run your sponsored ads along with the amount you want to spend. Make your social media pages as interesting as possible to attract people to visit and then follow you. On the rise and increasing in numbers of followers on daily basis I actively stay involved working on new creative ideas to capture my audience attention. For example, I create my own memes with an inspirational message for women. I normally find a beautiful background that will compliment my topic. It is important to interact with my followers and reply to messages. I observe and research what would interest my audience from diverse groups of backgrounds and countries. I have followers not only in the United States but also internationally. My page is there for women from different walks of life and age groups. Even though, it is a women's prayer ministry I also have men visit and follow my page as well.

Another thing important about being on social media is creativity. You have to think of creative ideas to keep your audience wanting to stay following your page. I post quotes that are intriguing that will be shared from my page and bring new followers. Social Media can be easy and fun but it requires putting in time and effort. Sometimes it may require creating advertisements to reach a larger number of people on the different social media sites. Choose to post things that compliment your page and grab the attention of visitors and those who follow you.

Jennifer Williams

When One Door Closed Virtual Media Opened My Window

Hey Ya'll, I'm Jennifer Williams, a lady with a personality between Dolly Parton and Pamela Anderson minus the boobs. I come from a very small town in Alabama called Glencoe with a population of about 8,000. I was raised in a very filtered environment, pg-13 movies were scandalous and the internet was of the devil. I did not discover the world of internet until I was working on my degree in college and my professor could not believe I had not yet done a term paper with internet research. Let me just say the wealth of knowledge that I gained on Woodstock from the internet became addictive. I made a 98 on a term paper for the first time ever! I loved this "new" computer program.

In a small town, the ideal dream is you graduate high school get married and have babies. So, to follow tradition my high school sweet heart and I got married a year after high school and remained in our small town, we had our first child a year after we were married. The ideal small town couple struggling with jobs that paid little more than minimum wage. I found a job working over the internet. I lived in hell for 11 years, I was physically and emotionally abused. Although I was my family's only source of income I was nothing, if you ask my husband. I would hear 24 hours a day how I was never going to be good at anything and how I wasn't attractive to him or anyone else. In his words," I should be grateful he put up with me."

In a small town, this is not something you want anyone to know about because we lived in a white picket fence neighborhood, meaning everything had to look and act a certain way. We had a lot of friends and attended most socially elite functions. I was offered a better job working outside of our home for a plastic injection molding company based out of Florida.

I would use the internet to get jobs for the firm I worked for and to stay in contact with our customers and owners. I was convinced by several of my Florida coworkers that a move to Florida would benefit my marriage and my family. Worst case if it lead to divorce I wouldn't be stuck in a small town with a reputation of a failure due to my failed marriage. I did accept a new job and moved to Florida after meeting these people over the internet and gaining a support system that made me feel like a beneficial person. I became operations manager for a firm that built picture frames for Carnival cruise lines and made a substantial income. At this time, I had no clue what Facebook or my space was.

My small-town divorce became a nightmare even with-out social media because the gossip fields were nuts. I had to return to Glencoe for a custody trial for my sons. I get off an airplane to hear that I am doing drugs and left my husband for a rich old man in Florida. I felt I couldn't even hold my head up to go to the grocery store because a small-town judge had taken my children without any proof or a hearing to hear about my job or the years of torture. My reputation was scandalous and I lost all my friends.

As the trial has went on more and more rumors get exaggerated but I began to talk to people outside of our community and learn how these small town people, women mostly, have small town mentalities and I needed to shrug it off and say to hell with it. I met a lady with a group called Rose haven. Rose Haven helps women coming out of abusive relationships.

The Rose Haven lady and my attorney will never know how much they changed my life. I lost my job in Florida due to the time I had to spend in Alabama fighting for my boys. It's hard to find a job in a small town when everyone bases hiring off of word of mouth and reputation. Once again, I returned to the internet taking side jobs here and there. I went back to college to acquire a degree in paralegal so I could help other women in my situation.

I took a job as a bail bondsman so I could study and make money. I had by this time moved back in with my parents- I didn't have my sons so I didn't have to have a home or a regular income because I had in my mind nothing. As I began to gain knowledge of law and help the people I ran into at the bail bonds office I was introduced to my space and met my second husband. We dated over the internet and telephone. I began to fly to Miami and see him and eventually got married and had our son. He began to isolate me after we got married from family and friends. I began to use the internet to talk to my friends and family because I was online doing my school work most of the time. I had gotten in touch with several classmates and I would forward them pictures of the beatings I was receiving. They helped me find the strength to get out. When I left my son was 6 months old and all we had was what I could fit in my car. I used Facebook to sell things and to get back on my feet. People read my story and would donate furniture and clothing to my new son and myself and I began a new life with my 6-month-old son and myself.

I continued to pray and fight for the best for my oldest two boys. The visitation once they moved to Mobile, Al was tiresome because my oldest felt mistreated and didn't want to return to his dads. He began to hyperventilate and sob at the drop offs. My ex-husband wouldn't allow me to talk with the boys on the telephone or visit on their school trips.

My oldest, Daniel, began losing weight and failing in school. I prayed clung to hope and continued to fight for my boys to come home. Once given a court date through God the judge asks to speak to my sons and "let them decide who they wanted to live with" I had not been allowed to see the boys or talk to them in 3 weeks! I remember sitting in that court room my ex telling the judge I wasn't important enough to see my kids. The judge gave me 30 mins after court to see my boys and get hugs. Poor Daniel said," mom I'm leaving with you, today right?" I was speechless. I explained we had to wait on a court order. He laid his head on the desk and sobbed Benjamin seemed ok he was bouncing around just happy to get mommy hugs. My ex interrupted our visit because he and his wife had plans and needed to leave - it would be another month before I was scheduled to see the boys.

I prayed daily and many of my friends did as well. I will never forget 6 pm on a Friday night in November I received a call saying," Jennifer this is Tom King (aka my attorney)" In my mind I just knew one of my kids had died. That's how the devil works he wants us to think the worst. I sat quietly couldn't respond for holding my breath then he continued,"

I wanted to tell you personally and just got in from court I have some papers for you." Again, I was speechless thinking great now I don't get to see them at all. He then said very excitedly," can you go pick up your son tonight? You now have Daniel-they split the boys but go bring him home." I was at a book signing and couldn't help but cry because God worked in my favor. I had given up all hope. Benjamin didn't have as hard a time being returned to his dad it did and does hurt they separated them but at least one of my babies wouldn't be hurting. I arrived in Mobile within 5 hours my parents and I didn't even pack we just jumped in the car, my job gave me the night off and I arrived to another battle. See, Satan is relentless when God is working he wants to act like a boa constrictor and tighten his hold. My ex brought a sobbing Daniel with a pair of girl capris and a shirt that was too small and shoes too large that a neighbor gave him and drops him off at city hall saying, "take him I'm done."

Daniel was sobbing. He said," mom I have no clothes. You're broke because you have the babies. But I have you right I'm home?" I have never cried so hard in my life I held him - tight and didn't want to let go. I said," baby boy you're going to have more than you dreamed." Daniel was 15 when I got him back and within the past 2 years I have been blessed with over time and my now 17-year-old has his own car and name brands like all the others kids. He plays football in high school and is up for scholarships. I don't have his brother back because he says," I can't make dad cry like Daniel did he'll die. Mom you're strong I love you but I can't leave dad." I still fight when there are times he's making bad grades. I don't get to talk to him on the phone or attend his sporting events. They still fight and make my 17-year-old sleep on the floor when he visits but God has given us a peace that is unexplainable.

Moral of my story when we give up all hope it seems that's when God shows up and fixes our problems. I'm not saying I don't struggle because I promise you I do and I'm no angel but I keep my faith strong and my knees weak. I kid folks and say I'm a hippie pray warrior. I pray twice a day and if my sons are happy and healthy I don't care where they live because I just want to see them smile. I live by the verse Philippians 4:13 I can do all things through Christ which strengthens me. No matter what you are going through put God first and he will show up and show out.

Dianne Kottle

The Great Awakening

Currently the planet is going through an epic energetic shift in global consciousness and frequency upgrades, unlike anything we have seen before, and it is happening rapidly. *People are quickly awakening and gaining access to their own light, their own power, their own information, their own truth.*

With this level of change, comes great challenges (opportunities for learning and growth) and disruptions that may rock you to your core, as you release the old and make room for the new emerging energies to come into form.

The old structures must fall; the limitations must be released; the castles of corruption must crumble to the ground. Essentially, we must empty out the garbage first, removing the layers of trash from our lives that are clogging the pipes and stopping the flow, before we can be filled with and hold, the high frequency light that is available to all of us, now more than ever before.

We are entering a new era, a time where many of us are cracking open out of our old hardened shells, shedding limiting belief systems and toxic thought patterns, dismantling the false structures of control, unhooking from the planetary programming grids and busting through the illusions of fear and separation, that are designed to intentionally keep us small and stuck and complacent, dependent and enslaved; and we are instead gaining new levels of awareness and embracing the true essence of who we are at the core soul level of our being.

We must stop dimming our light and hiding in the shadows of fear.

Now is the time to fully step up into our creative manifestation power as a collective consciousness — as a unified sea of our unique individual voices, whose authentic expression, whose particular specific sparkle, when united in our bright shining light and connected empowerment, creates a tidal wave of healing alchemy, a shimmering ocean of infinite possibilities, weaving together a tapestry of high frequency crystalline light packets of information and sacred geometries, creating the golden grid of the new paradigm.

Why do we dim our light?

Simple. We are programmed and conditioned to from birth. It is bred into us from day one, woven into the very fabric of our society. We see this out-pictured as agreed upon social norms, via our corrupt political system, through standardized government funded public schooling (which among other things, inserts its own agenda of controlling what, and how, we learn) and in belief system constructs that are constantly hammered into us, designed to limit, constrict and abolish free expansive thought and expression; all under the guise of freedom of course. We are taught to stay in the box and follow the rules, color in the lines, dot your i's and cross your t's like a "good little boy or girl", to be rewarded, to graduate up to the next level, which simply means moving up to the next little box with a new tight little lid, that is promptly set and sealed firmly in place.

We are controlled and manipulated through our food and water supply, not being told what we are really consuming, yet being told it is good for us when it is brimming with chemicals and hidden toxins that our bodies can't possibly process, which results in dis-ease and a litany of illnesses on all levels (mental, emotional, physical, spiritual, energetic). We are forced to vaccinate our children who become sick from the poisons and toxic substances they contain. We are told lies of fear through the news and media, as if they are truth; we are really only shown what fits the specific agenda of those with the power, the puppeteers who are installing, and then pulling our strings.

We are groomed to be Muppets (aka: mindless puppets) and become hypnotized sheep, who follow blindly, sleepwalking our way through the world, after being led through enticing magical fields filled with beautiful scarlet poppies whose intoxicating aroma of manipulation and unconsciousness makes us check-out, and serves to lull us into eternal sleep. My god, we are even taught to count sheep as children to help us fall asleep at night.

We are constantly being fed fear and propaganda as truth, which conditions us to doubt our natural instincts; so we choose to stay in our separated boxes of imagined safety because we are so afraid of what we are told is "out there", beyond the iron clad walls that are built around our hearts, to "keep out" and protect us from the boogeymen, and other things that go bump in the night.

Is it any wonder we are too petrified to even turn on the light switch to see if there is really a scary monster in our bedroom lurking in the shadows or hiding under our bed?

We are so traumatized we hide under the covers, paralyzed and trembling with fear, anchoring our feelings of powerlessness even deeper into our incredibly impressionable psyches.

We are pumped full of fear based, hyped-up, trumped-up scenarios (diversions and red herrings), designed specifically to distract us and keep us focused away from the real solutions, and even the real issues, whose discovery of does not serve the status quo, nor the hidden agenda, of keeping us numbed-out, dumbed-down and completely disconnected from the actual real conspiracies (not theories) that are going on, often being hidden right under our noses, in plain sight.

We are told to only believe what we can see, what is "proven" by mainstream Newtonian Physics, which does not address or even acknowledge the effect of consciousness on outcomes (The Observer Effect is a basic premise of Quantum Physics, which simply put says: the mere act of observing something, influences it, and changes it on a quantum level) which affects and changes everything, in a major way.

So we are taught to buy into an old outmoded system of Science that does not accurately reflect the forward movement, the upgraded consciousness (or even the role consciousness plays on matter for that matter) and ignores the new model of the world we are actually living in and experiencing today. It reflects instead a closed system that is now exploding from the pressure of the heightened creative consciousness bursts of the planet expressing itself as higher light frequency, in an entirely new expansive way.

We are taught this because mainstream acknowledgment and acceptance of the Quantum world, is a threat to the current dysfunctional systems run by the select few governing elite, in positions of high power, who financially benefit from the old models staying intact; they profit by keeping us sick and afraid. New thought and change frightens and threatens the old regimes, the corrupt elite groups, the old outmoded structures, that are now beginning to crack and crumble from the pressure, as we enter these new energetic times, where the rules and the rulers are changing.

When we live in a matrix of fear, we are anchored into the lower denser frequencies. The vibration at this level is thick and dense and heavy and dark. This is designed specifically to keep you hooked into the program of control, tethered to the hamster wheel at the bottom of the dark ocean, running endlessly through mazes of circular loops, going nowhere, while eternally drowning and gasping for air.

You really think anyone is thinking about enlightenment or spiritual evolution in that scenario?

Imagine Maslow's hierarchy of needs. At the bottom of the pyramid, you have safety and survival. At the top, you find self-actualization and transcendence. To access these enlightened states of being in frequency, you must move up in vibration. And as long as you are strapped to the lower energies and denser frequencies scrambling to get your most basic needs met (and not die), you are trapped, hooked into the control matrix of fear, pain, unconsciousness, unworthiness.

In essence, you are suppressed, hypnotized by the very convincing illusion that says "you are unable (not powerful enough) to ever set yourself free".

The programming and fear is so thick at this level, it is insidious, infused in everything and found everywhere; so we believe that it is normal and that it is "just the way things are". We become a valley of complacent cows and submissive sheep waiting to be slaughtered by the very hand that fed us the lies to begin with that keep us enslaved and unaware, all the while oblivious that we are even enchained.

Yet we are the chained elephants conditioned to believe we are stuck and rendered powerless, by the tiny little stake in the ground tied to only one of our enormously powerful feet.

The distortions and corruption is layered and hidden (running very deep indeed). It is woven into the very fabric of what we are taught to trust. It is sprinkled into our "health" food, added to our "clean" water supply and laced into the "natural" supplements we are told will keep us healthy. All this is done with a big fake smile dripping with enticing false promises, that find and push on our pain points, inflicting scarcity and fear and lack consciousness, to convince us of an illusion designed specifically to keep us in struggle; to keep us separate; to keep us subdued; to keep us from questioning; to keep us from remembering how powerful we truly are.

Well this is not normal and it is not the only available option. Not by a long shot.

It's time now for you all, especially the Light Workers and Way Showers, the Earth Angels on this planet, the Empaths and Energy Healers, and everyone else who has a deep soul calling to help others awaken to their own light, to start shining your own light more brightly than you ever have before — on these illusions, on these distortions, on the garbage that the masses keep consuming as if it is caviar, guzzling down like it's the finest bottle of Dom Pérignon, remaining drunk, wandering around in a constant dazed collective stupor, from the countless hypnotic bubbles of toxic corruption that are consistently coursing through their bodies on an automatic drip system.

It is time for a massive wake-up call to all of humanity — to remember and ignite your own inner light; to come together in the frequency of love, truth, and collective empowerment; to know that we are so much more powerful than we were ever taught to believe. How do we share this message with those who are hypnotized and asleep?

We do this by being the light; by speaking our authentic truth; by releasing our own dark shadows that want to drag us into debate and separation and superiority, triggering our need to be right or better than others (or however this 'right' vs. 'wrong', 'good' vs. 'bad', 'us' vs. 'them' separation power struggle out-pictures specifically in your life); we lead by example, sharing our messages of empowerment, worthiness, connection and love with the world, through our own unique authentic voices of truth.

By doing this we will reach a critical mass, a tipping point of awakening, where a new morphic field is created and becomes its own powerful force of light, whose unique signature stands tall, like a glowing lighthouse in the thick dark fog, shining brightly, guiding the way home to those vessels who are lost at sea, being tossed about in the crashing storm of monstrous waves. This is how we create the new paradigm; this is how the new way, the new energies on the planet, come into form; this is how a new world is born.

This is a call to all of you who came here to help awaken the planet.

Please get your own house (your own internal world) in order pronto, so that you can do and be what you came here for. Because the world is waiting for you: to stand tall; to shine brightly; to stop apologizing for who you are and be your true authentic self; and to play your specific role in the awakening of the planet and human consciousness to the absolute fullest now. It is time for what I call, The Alchemy of Awakening. And so it is. Aho. Amen.

Shontina Gladney

Stop Pressing The Pause Button On Your Dreams!

As we move forward we must continue to look ahead instead of over our shoulders while carrying large bags of guilt or pain with little to no hope for tomorrow. As we desire to have better days than those we have created for ourselves. We must move forward with the Wisdom and knowledge our past has bestowed upon us. There is no wrong or right way to move forward towards the plans God has for us. But what is wrong is the failure or lack of effort we choose to put forth. Yes stepping forth into the unknown can be a very daunting thought, but if we put our mustard seed of faith into action we can run forward and not faint.

 If we continue to move forward God will assure that every step, we take HE is right there through every step. Let's choose to not go back, it's worth us moving ahead. How will we choose to use our second chances is the question we must ask ourselves? Our past is over, did, done, complete, God has renewed our mind and thinking to look towards everything HE has in store for us. Now it's up to us to pick up the pen and write our stories, one page at a time. Releasing us from all bondage as we run into our wealthy place of peace, joy, and abundance.

Shontina Gladney

Hasina Brinson

A Hard Decision

Embarrassment is an emotional state worse than fear when it comes to domestic violence. I am a survivor of an abusive relationship. It took two years for me to be able to admit that. This was after eight years of being abused by my ex and trying to hide it. However, it is a fact. Even now as I write, I am still struggling to come to terms with the level of success I have been able to achieve on a small scale because of getting out such a dangerous situation. I am also, for the first time, admitting that it took a great amount of strength and determination to move forward.

There is no amount of advice that can prepare a woman for the difficulties of making a decision when she has had enough. There is no amount of persuasion that will convince her to take back a relationship that she doesn't want any more. The thing is that for a domestic violence victim, it can take a long time to come to that point, if she gets there before she is permanently or irreversibly hurt.

As I was going through counseling, and as I attempted to get help from the State Attorney, the police, my family, and others, there was an underlying theme. Everyone talked about fear, and Stockholm syndrome, and low self-esteem. I am not trying to discount these valid points, but one thing that I have not heard emphasized is the amount of embarrassment involved for a victim of domestic abuse.

You see, no victim ever wants to talk about the abuse that she suffers at the hands of someone who is supposed to love her. This is the most hurtful, shameful, and *embarrassing* part of being a victim. Luckily, when in polite company, it is not something that will be talked about in one's face. The downside of this is that there is a false sense of security in the illusion of "keeping the secret", because it is not a secret. Not ever. It will not be a surprise to those who know you best that you are being abused, just as it will not be a secret when you finally walk away from the relationship. This is not to say that you will do so unscathed. There will be scars. There will be tumultuous feelings of loneliness; there will be internal questions and guilt. The barrage of emotions will be overwhelming at times. However, I am here to say that you can do this. Nothing worth doing is every easy, and as they say, "Rome was not built in a Day..."

If you are a victim of abuse, people know. Your neighbors know. They hear your screams at night. Your coworkers know, because they see how disheveled or stressed you appear to be after an episode. Your kids know, because they are often the ones who throw themselves in front of the blows to keep you safe. This is an entire network of people who are aware that abuse is happening. However, no one can get you out of an abusive situation and keep you out of it, but you. I want to share a little bit of my story and my triumph with hopes that it will inspire someone who is experiencing something like take steps to save her life...

The night of the super bowl was pivotal in my decision to get away from my abusive relationship. In my case, my neighbors heard my screams each night when my ex came home drunk and high. They could also hear my body hitting the walls and the floor when he pushed me. These same people would smile at me and speak, and not mention that my screams had kept them up the night before. This night, I was at home with a new baby, and he, let's call him Matt, was over at a super bowl party with one of our neighbors. The men had traditionally taken this opportunity to bond over BBQ, beers, and, I later found out, hard drugs.

The phone rang while I was sitting on the couch playing a video game. Yes, I love to play video games. Tomb raider is one of my favorites. My daughter was young at the time, and I didn't want to take her with me amongst the smoking and the cussing. I stayed at home to play my game. The young lady on the other end of the line clearly did not expect a female to answer.

"Hello?" she said timidly, "Is Matt around?"

"No dear," I replied, "whose calling?" A pregnant pause followed this question.

"Well," she said, "This is Nikki, and I, um, call Matt sometimes to help me to get clients." She said softly.

"Clients?" I said, oh okay, you work at the car wash too? Okay, I'll tell him," I began,

"No," she interrupted, "I am a, well, I, do, well, I have clients, male ones, and he helps me with that," she finished.

I said, "oh, okay. Well he's not here, but I'll tell him to call you," I said without missing a beat. My mind started racing. So, did this girl just tell me that Matt was her pimp? What? Christ almighty! I thought. This man was watching our daughter while I was at work and entertaining whores? What the... I packed the baby up and walked down to the party. Matt had taken the car down there, and I wanted my keys back.

I began to wonder what I didn't know about this man, the father of my children, who demanded that I trust him, and who had been getting progressively meaner to me. When I got to the party, I told him to give me my keys. He looked at me with red rimmed eyes, and slowly reached into his pocket. The room had gone silent, but I hadn't noticed. I was so distraught. "Oh," I said, "Nikki called."

"Who?" he asked loudly moving close to me.

"The hooker you've been helping get clients," I replied. Even the game was muted at that point. All eyes were on me. Every man in that room, whether he lived on the same complex as we did or not knew what Matthew was doing. They also knew that he had a girlfriend whose ass he beat regularly. At that point I did not care that I was the topic of conversation for most of my neighbors and friends. I did not care that he might try to kill me for embarrassing him. I also did not care that he was looking at me with a frown that said, "Bitch I will beat your ass!" All I cared about was getting my keys, and getting as far away from him as possible. He stood still in surprise and handed my keys to me. I took them, and turned on my heel to leave. I went home with the intent to pack some things for my little one and I and get gone. I did not know that he had followed me home. I wasn't clear to me just how much danger I was in until he came into the house and slammed the door so hard that the building shook.

"How could you embarrass me like that?" He roared from the living room. I was in the bedroom. I hurriedly placed my suitcase back into the closet and sat down next to my baby girl, who was looking around with a confused look on her face, trying to figure out what all the noise was about. Now my little one was about four months old. When Matt came into the room, he was so angry, and screaming so loudly that spittle was flying from his lips. I cannot remember much of what he said, but I recall him screaming about being embarrassed repeatedly.

I sat stock still on the bed and watched him. I did not move to grab my daughter; I did not even breathe. At some point, he rushed over to the bed and grabbed my foot, pulling me down to the floor. I kicked him with my other foot, and this only made him angrier. He pinned me to the floor and punched me in my face, and neck until I couldn't breathe. Then he picked me up from the floor by the front of my shirt and slammed me. I felt my ribs crack on impact. I couldn't even ball myself up to protect my face from his blows, I just lie there on the ground, trying to breathe as Matt paced back and forth over me, yelling.

After a while he left the room, and I could hear him pacing around the house, still mumbling. After some time, I rolled over on to my side, and tried to see if my daughter was okay. She was on the bed, making little noises, and trying to look around. She had not moved or rolled during the entire episode. I didn't immediately go to her, because I was terrified that he might come back, and that he might try something else, or harm her as well. He really seemed to forget she was in the room. This same was true years later when he strangled me as she stood in the doorway watching him. He told his attorney later that he did not realize what he was doing until he saw her watching him.

Matt did come back into the room, as I knew he would. He paced in and out for a while mumbling, and looking around the room wild-eyed. I had dragged myself into the corner as far away from the bed as possible. I did not believe that he even saw our daughter, but I did not want to put her in danger by placing her in his sights. Also, at the time, I would have been unable to protect her if he decided to snatch her away from me, and leave the room. My chest hurt, my face hurt, as did my legs, and I was so ashamed that the neighbors has heard me screaming. I was so embarrassed about the fact that they would know that I knew what they knew about the hell I was living in. This is what I mean when I say your situation is not ever a secret. Even after this ordeal, I stayed around for five more years. Even after I understood that my secret shame was no secret to anyone, I stayed in the relationship.

When I walked away for good, it was just as much of a secret as I thought the abuse was. The night I called the police and finally made my report, I didn't share the event with anyone. It was not until I had gone to court twice for my restraining order that my mother found out what I was doing. I made up my mind to walk away and to take my family out of the stressful situation. Now, I have attained a Master's Degree, and I am working and taking care of business. It is not easy, but I am now able to turn away those who question my motives, my single status, or where my children's father is. I learned that my life is the one that means the most to me next to those of my children. There are needs that we have, that I can get fulfilled on my own, and I do not need to submit to an abuser. I hope that whomever reads this will gather strength from this except of my sordid tale. I hope that if you know someone who needs help that you will be able to let them know that abuse is not a secret to anyone, and embarrassment is only a temporary emotion. Don't let emotions make your decisions. Realize that you are special, and important, and that *no one* deserves to be abused. There is help there, if you're willing to take advantage of it.

Debra Whittam

An Excerpt from: Everything That's Been Waiting

Back in 1975, when I was senior in high school, Phil and I were best friends. He had moved to our small village of Delanson sometime at the end of third grade. It was time of learning cursive, reading longer chapter books and boys and girls running together on the playground. At that age, it didn't matter that much. It wouldn't be long, though, before there would be the awkward separation of the sexes and even being seen speaking to the opposite sex meant something close to marriage.

In fourth grade Phil was in my class. I remember him being an intense young man already at that age. He was already very handsome and tall with Irish heritage pouring forth in his blond hair, blue eyes and striking angular face. I don't remember thinking those things in quite that way back then, but now, looking back, he was a change from the regular country boys I'd known since Kindergarten. Phil had the manner of an old soul in his lean, lanky presence.

Mr. Valentine, a music teacher, came to our school during our fourth grade year. He loved putting on plays for these young grades and would make these productions as elaborate as our small village school budget would allow.

During choir practice, after the holidays were over and the New Year had begun, he asked who would be interested in being a part of a play where big and small parts would be available. As I remember, most of us auditioned for parts and those not interested in doing that were put to work building sets, painting and working the curtain and lights. This was quite a daunting undertaking for one person and twenty or so fifth graders. We were to put on H.M.S. Pinafore. Phil and I were the first to raise our hands to audition. It would be that way until we graduated.

Back then we glanced at each other with wide eyes and big smiles. We wanted the same thing. We loved singing and performing even though neither of us had much experience in either. We had no idea how much our paths would cross, intertwine and become one during the course of time.

The following year was the Mikado. We learned a great deal about one another with each month's experience of long, after school rehearsals, in a way much different than a knowing of each other from sitting in the classroom, groups at a lunch table or the chaos of the playground.

On stage, in each rehearsal, the actors learned the depths of each other's fears, sense of humor and the vulnerability of going through hours of repeated scenes bringing with it exhaustion, at times bitter despair at others brilliant excitement. Phil and I grew closer through the years that followed as each new musical director, especially in high school, cast us as a couple. There was Hello Dolly in tenth grade where we played Barnaby and Minnie Fay. Being together was natural and easy on stage, at his house to go over lines and on our long walks through the trail in the woods from my house to his.

Phil was attentive, patient, caring and a very gentle partner. He was, to me, like a basket of safety where I could land whenever my troubled soul overwhelmed in fear and despair. For me, I was a selfish, self-centered seeker of attention. His was a given so I ventured out from his protective friendship to see who else was there to provide me with what I needed. Inevitably I returned each time to Phil, his friendship and belief in me.

Being with Phil was a safe haven from my own anxious mind. I felt he was a friend I could always rely on especially as the years flew and we found ourselves in our fun and expectant senior year.

As a senior year generally goes, friendships were ended, begun anew or reaffirmed for a commitment to last a lifetime. That high school year Phil and I spent many nights together or on the phone. That one phone we had in my house in 1975, hanging on the kitchen wall for all to hear and ask about who was on the phone and why. It was our only connection to the outside world at that time. I had to ask permission to call anyone and allowed just a certain amount of time to talk. When the phone rang it alerted all of us in the house that someone was being called and all hoped it was for them. The only exception was my mother. She perched in her prominent spot of the sofa demanding to know who it was on the phone and what they wanted.

When I shouted to her, "It's Phil." She simply said, "Okay then." She and my dad really loved Phil. He was just the person they could imagine for me. Someone able to handle my mood swings, excitability and force of ideas and excitement of the next thing to do and place to go. I didn't think of him that way at all. He was my Phil, my confidant, my constant, and my protector even or especially when either of us had loves of our own.

Many nights after school I'd go to Phil's house where his family was far less disruptive. They didn't worry that when dad came home fights might break out and his parents were easy to be with and speak with. We'd go up to his bedroom and laugh, teach each other the instruments we played. He tried to help me blow into his trumpet. I couldn't imagine working that hard to get a note out! I guided him through the learning of the clarinet. Phil's smile was worth any and all silliness on my part. I knew we would be okay as long as we were together.

As our class prepared for the all-important Senior Prom in the spring of '75, most of us decided to go as a group of friends paired up only for pictures and seating at the prom. With a class of 63 students, most of us were friends with only a few couples that seemed to be in another group and mindset entirely.

The evening of the prom Phil and I were excited to be together and with our group of seniors many of who had been together since Kindergarten. It turned out to be a great prom. We all had a good time in the auditorium, basketball court, gym space turned into a wonderland of crepe paper and twinkly lights. I don't remember much in the way of alcohol. I'm sure the punch was spiked, hard to imagine getting anything past the eagle eyes of the teachers present to keep order if chaos ensued.

After the dance was over we all piled into Brian Pavlic's van. He was going to drive us all to our houses; we would run in, change quickly and come back out to hang out after for the long night ahead.

He had this 1972 Chevy van, which had no seatbelts and could fit as many of us as could shove in. Phil, I and about six others jammed into the long back seat while the rest of the van filled with anyone headed in the direction of the after party. Brian's parents owned a restaurant so he was the kid with the most money and had all the things that could bring. Later than night Brian would roll that van and most were seriously hurt. Brian would pass away not many years later from drugs and alcohol. He spent years in and out of hospitals and rehabs. But that night he was our ride and we were all grateful.

Once on our way in the van Phil, who was pushed up against me and me against the inside part of the van and in that very dark, close place said, "I'm in love with you Deb. Could we have sex tonight?"

Sue Urda

Get The Funk Out!: Release Your Funk

I know very intimately what it feels like to be in a funk. Perhaps you do too. Or maybe you were in one and didn't call it that. You might recognize a funk by these symptoms: lack of enthusiasm about pretty much anything, unexplained tears, lethargy, anxious moments for no apparent reason, feeling depressed, lingering sadness, angry outbursts or anger bubbling beneath the surface, feeling unloved or unworthy, not caring about things you used to care about, moodiness or an overall dark mood, or seeming inability to take 'normal' everyday actions. Often a funk feels like a near complete disengagement or wanting to be disengaged from life. At the lowest level being in a funk feels hopeless and completely apathetic.

Basically, being in a funk feels pretty #&%>$@ lousy.

So how can you release your funk? It's simpler than you might think but not necessarily easy or fast. It all depends on your motivation.

The first step is recognizing you're in a funk and caring enough to want to get out of it. You have to desire a change in order to remove yourself from the grip of your funk. You have to decide that feeling lousy and just going through the motions is no longer acceptable to you. Or at the very least you have to want to feel differently than you've been feeling and be willing to take even a little bit of action out of the state you've been in. Depending on how long you've been in a funk and how deeply you're feeling it, this first step may be the hardest - and I will tell you from experience that it is worth doing.

Once you've made the decision to get out of your funk you're one to step two: You must name it what it is. You must admit that you're not feeling like yourself and that something needs to change for you to feel better - and always that something is you. You can choose to change your mind, habits, or surroundings. It might be as simple as getting your butt off the chair or couch and moving around. Go outside, take a walk or even sit on the grass, and breathe in some fresh air. Or if you want to really go for it, exercise. Exercise stimulates your entire body and delivers more oxygen to your cells and your brain. It gets the heart and blood pumping faster and this physical stimulation will also stimulate your emotional state. Energy creates emotion, and that's exactly what you want to engage when you're in a funk - you want to *feel your feelings* and create movement of them instead of staying stuck in the muck.

You might choose to change the habits you've gotten into like drinking every night, going to work late, yelling at your kids, numbing out with TV, surfing the web or online games, just sliding under the radar at work, or avoiding people. Start with baby steps.

Any step no matter how small is a step forward.

The third step is the conscious decision to release it. Now that you've recognized your feelings, decided to make a change, and created movement from your stagnant funk, you must commit to letting go.

**You must consciously choose and declare
that you no longer wish to be mired down.**

First, look at the aspects of your life that have been negatively affected by your funk. Think about what you've missed out on. Think about the relationships that have suffered. Think about the crappy way you've talked to people and yourself. Think about the effects on your physical and emotional health. These things may be tough to look at, but what they help you to do is create leverage - leverage to want to let go of your funk. You can even write them down and burn them as a ceremony and means of release.

And now that you have leverage, you can move into the positive aspects of letting go. Think about the reasons you'd like to feel better. Imagine the respect and love you will experience from your loved ones and coworkers. Visualize moving easily through your day, actually smiling and communicating freely, even helping others to feel good too.

Now that you have leverage on two fronts - the positive and the negative - you can more easily make the decision to release your funk.

Leverage brings more ease to your transition and transformation.

The fourth step is to do something different or opposite. If your funk kept you from engaging with friends or people in general, make a date to hang out with someone. If your funk kept you from going outside of your room or your home, go to the park, the mountains, or the beach and enjoy the magnificence of nature. If your funk kept you from being productive at home or at work, jump into a project and commit to seeing it through. If your funk had you eating unhealthy foods excessively, choose a healthy substitute and notice the deliciousness of natural foods and the lightness of your body.

Affirmations are also a great tool and very helpful in releasing your funk. Most likely you were practicing some pretty negative self-talk in your funk, and now you must turn it around. Affirmations are a way of programming your subconscious and shifting your attitude and actions.

Sometimes when you start affirmations they feel like lies. That's okay.

Eventually you start to believe yourself and live into the beauty and promise of your own words. Start with phrases like: I am one with all of life; I am happy and vibrant and strong; I handle all situations with grace and ease; I know how to manage stress; I am a loved and loving child of God. You can also create affirmations that are specific to your personal desires.

In saying these phrases out loud to yourself you will shift your mood and begin to care more about what's happening around you and the people in your life. And perhaps most importantly, you'll care more about yourself and the quality of your own life.

Shifting out of a funk is not for sissies.

It is real work, and it is worthwhile work. And it is deserving of an immediate start.

Pulling yourself out of a funk can feel like a rite of passage.

And in many ways it is. It is you telling yourself that you are worthy of feeling good. It is you caring enough for yourself to re-enter life. It is you loving and valuing yourself enough that you bring your whole self back into the fold of human engagement. It is you deciding that life is here FOR you and not against you like you have felt in the past.

You are powerful beyond measure and it all starts with the story you tell yourself about yourself. You are stronger than you know and more capable than you imagine. You are worthy and deserving of great good. Simply by virtue of you being alive right now you are justified to actually enjoy life. You are a vibrant example the Divine and you are a glowing light being imbued with pure love.

My wish for you is that you feel all of this and allow good back into your life. Do not block the flow of abundance, grace, and joy. Know that you are magnificent and miraculous. You are awesome!

Maggie Holbik

A New Social Way of Doing Things

I grew up in a very small town in Northwestern Ontario, Canada. I went to a one room school and when I graduated in the eighth grade, there were only 7 children left in the entire school. The school closed permanently not long after. Some tell stories of walking for miles to get to school, well I rowed a boat to school. When I was 10 years old I upgraded from oars to a six horse Evinrude motor. I was quite proud of this. High School was 70 miles away and I had to board with people while attending this new school with multiple classrooms. I would catch the Grey Goose bus on Friday evenings to return home for the weekend and back to town on Sunday nights. It was quite an experience that taught me more independence early on.

Growing up in the 'bush' taught me many things and I am forever grateful for my upbringing. I have learned to be resourceful, resilient, independent and respectful of mother earth. My mother was a great influence in my life. She believed in taking chances, that you could do anything you set your mind too, and that you could do anything that you wanted in life. One of her favorite sayings that I remember her saying often was "Oh, you can to!" My mother passed away in 1993 and the older I get, the more I cherish her teachings.

My parents were originally from Wisconsin but came to Canada on their honeymoon and ended up eventually moving to Canada to operate a small tourist resort, which is where I was raised. Life wasn't easy for them as they made a business, a new life, and a family in the remote wilderness in Northern Ontario. As with everything though, blessings and gifts come from these situations. My parents through example, taught me all of those great things mentioned above about being resourceful and resilient etc. Times were not easy and more so for my older siblings. I am the baby of six siblings, and by the time I came along at least we had electricity J

I have always been a person who has had many interests and a genuine love for life. Over the years, I have dabbled in many things. When I discovered Numerology, and learned that I was a Life Path number 3, my life truly changed and everything made sense to me. I was better able to understand that it was not so much about 'what I was doing' in life, but it was more about 'who I was being' while I was doing. What I mean by that is that, I truly feel that my job here on earth is to uplift, inspire and motivate others in whatever form that takes.

Whether I am coaching someone one on one, having lunch with someone, or speaking to hundreds or even thousands of people, it is all about who I am being. I truly believe our life purpose is not about a task or occupation, but more about how we are serving the world while we perform this role.

Things really became clear for me when I was in my early 40's. I remember being at a funeral and I was asked to read a poem for someone because they were not comfortable getting up there and reading it. I could not wait to get up there and share his message. It was in that moment, that I later reflected on, when I truly knew speaking and communicating was my greatest passion and that it was the perfect platform to uplift, inspire and motivate others. The funeral analogy was what really did it for me because two of people's greatest fears are public speaking and speaking in particular at funerals. So I knew when I was ripped to get up there, that my calling was becoming very clear to me.

I have always had a passion for personal discovery and understanding the soul's purpose. I have had an interest in palmistry, numerology, Chinese medicine, Quantum Physics, Reconnective Healing ,health & wellness, and more. I am currently completing a diploma in Applied Nutrition with the Alive Academy out of British Columbia, Canada. At some point on my bucket list is Iridology. Iridology is based on the scientific study of the iris -- the colored part of the eye. Like markings on a map, the iris reveals physiological conditions, psychological health risks, challenges and/or strengths of various organs and personality traits. I am fascinated with anything that will help individuals with clues to 'who they are'.

When I became a Certified Life Coach in 2005, everything came together for me as far as my practice goes. I was certified with the Life Purpose Institute and they are known for helping 'Rainbow' people like myself. Rainbow people are people who have a lot of interests and need a way to channel them for productivity and enjoyment. Life Coaching did all of this for me. I was then able to tie in all my passions under one umbrella, coaching and speaking! It was a magic formula.

I currently coach people in both life and business coaching and offer workshops and lectures on various topics such as Finding Joy in your Life & Work, Natural Health Seminars, How to Work from Home Effectively, and many more.

The icing on the cake for me was when I jumped into Social Media! I say jumped in because I did. I loved it and jumped in with both feet. To me, social media is like a giant canvas. I see myself as a 'Communication Artist' and social media is my canvas. Here I can create beautiful expressions and share them with the world and in turn I might inspire, uplift and motivate others. At least that is my hope. I consider this form of communicating as serving the world and to me it is an art form. Some people like to paint, cook, or to do crafts. For me my creative art is using social media and expressing myself. It gives me tremendous joy. When people make fun and say "Oh you should get a life.. too much time on the internet" or something to that effect, I smile, because that is about them. For me, it is en-Joy-ment and I always honor things that are important to me, just as I respect others choices for themselves.

Two of my greatest joys and what I consider to be gifts in my life are my spouse Don and my daughter, Sivanna Rose. Don is not only my spouse but my partner in life and my greatest supporter. We truly believe that all relationships whether love, friendship, or any type of relationship, should never be from a place of 'need' but more so from a place of "I want what you want for you". We believe when we live this way we are free to be who we truly are and we also know we are free to leave if we so choose.

The interesting thing is that when you know you are truly "free" to choose what you want, and there are no conditions or ultimatums, you truly want to stay. We see a relationship as more of a support system to uplift, uphold and encourage each other to follow our dreams, rather than a tradeoff situation. Ex. You do this and I do that, you can do this if.... At least this works for us and I am eternally grateful for him in my life. He is loving, compassionate, kind, wise, tenacious, an extremely hard worker, and is a main go to person for everyone in his life. We now have a blended family and one of the things I love most about Don, and always have, is that it was important for him to take care of and be there for his family. I could not imagine myself with a spouse who thought different. Our family is now a true example of "Love is all there is" and challenging circumstances only make us stronger. I also have gratitude for all of my step children and grandchildren and even a new great grandbaby!

My Sivanna Rose, who is now 10, has been one of my greatest experiences when it comes to Joy and opening my heart to a love I never knew existed. I was one of those people who did not have children but knew everything about raising kids. You know the type I am talking about lol J

Sivanna was a surprise pregnancy. I found out I was pregnant at age 39, on my late mother's birthday. I was in complete shock! Well it turned out to be a life changing miracle for me. On the same day, I had found out I was pregnant I had coincidently donated all of the baby clothes I had held onto for 13 years donated to me from my sister. I gave them away because there was no need for them. Ha ha, the joke was on me. It's amazing how life works isn't it?

Sivanna was premature at 32 weeks and that was a very scary time; however, there is a cute story that goes along with this. On April 1, I pulled an April fools prank on my best friend and birthing coach, telling her I was in labor. I will never forget what she said. "Okay, which hospital?" and I said "We only have one duh" lol. Well speed ahead exactly one week. I go into premature labor and call her and she doesn't believe me! I had to get Don on the phone to get her to know that it was really happening.

I remember being very calm when arriving at the hospital. I had this sense of knowing and trust because a few days before I found out I was pregnant and when I was completely in denial of everything, a voice that I now believe was my daughters came to me and said "Don't worry everything is going to be okay". So, I just trusted. I even had Don leave and check in on his work. I ended up having an emergency C- Section that day and she was born at 2:09 in the afternoon. The scariness came after.

The first major issue was that her lungs were not developed enough. I was terrified. I remember kind hearted friends and family telling me not to worry and that she would be fine. I was in a cloud. I just wanted someone to say "this must be scary" because I did not really feel inside that we for sure knew it would be okay. That taught me a great lesson in life and I now use it in my coaching practice and in my life. Sometimes people just need to have their feelings acknowledged especially when there is no clear cut answer. It is a way we can hold space for people.

Sivanna spent 36 days in NICU and I made over 100 trips to the hospital to feed her and to be with her. That was a tough time. I continually had a fear that a nurse would drop her or that she would stop breathing, or some other fearful thought. I think the combination of a new mother's heart opening along with tubes and machines, would do just about any new mother in J

When Savanna did come home she was colicky and that was a long stretch as well. However, now she is my beautiful 10-year-old who shines her light in our lives every day. She is charming, witty, pretty, and wise, but most of all she is healthy and has a passion for life. She really lives in the moment and her joy is contagious. I am honored to be called "Mom" or "Momsy" as we sometimes say. Everything about the whole experience for me feels divinely guided and I am continually amazed by the gift of life itself.

I recently celebrated my 50th birthday and asked people who attended my celebration to write a note about a memory we shared, a connection that we had, or if in some way I have inspired them in life. I wanted to know now and not at my funeral listening from the other side. The notes were very moving for me and I cherish them dearly. I was really glad I asked for this. It was a wonderful gift to get.

When it comes to appreciating the people in our lives, we should do so more often. We often wait until it's too late. A few kind words can really make a huge difference in people's lives.

I am looking forward to the next phase of my life. What's in store? I am hoping to continue to do things that bring me joy. One of which is spending time at my cottage at the lake where I work and play from anywhere, thanks to technology. My place at the lake has been something I have worked toward my entire life and it's a dream come true.

I am both fortunate and grateful that I also have a best friend who comes to my cottage, or camp, as we say in Northern Ontario. Together we inspire and support each other while also embracing the element of nature while we both work and play. I love spending time in nature as it feeds my soul and inspires me.

I believe that it's important to have close friendships in life. When we experience closeness with another person it can be a form of unconditional love and I feel grateful to have found that. Erika is not only my close friend but she understands and inspires me to bring my essence into my work. It's hard to explain to anyone but it's a magic formula. I feel very fortunate to have the best of both worlds (friendship & business) when we are together. I will continue to pursue my various income streams which are rental property management, speaking, coaching, my wellness center, Digital Marketing & Web design Business and my online business, CashBackRocks.com.

I have enjoyed being an entrepreneur my entire life and it has thrilled me to help many others find success and leveraged income. I feel it is very important to follow our passions and to create resources so that we can live the best life possible. Abundance is there for all of us. So often I see people confused about money. To me money is just a tool and like a tool it can be used to build or to destroy. For example, a hammer can build a house or destroy and damage a house... it is all how it is used. Money is also a tool and when we have the tools (resources) things flow easier and we are not consumed by making every decision based on affordability. Life is much easier when the issue of 'not enough' is removed.

I will continue to do the things I love and to use my 'Joy Meter'. My Joy Meter is the gauge I use for everything and I teach it to all my clients. Whatever you do, eat, hear, see, or are about to experience, simply ask the question. "Does this bring me joy?" Does my heart lift or drop? Once you start using this it works every time. For example if a friend asks you to go for lunch with them, what is you initial feeling? Yay or Nay? It's simple really and the more you use your joy meter the easy it gets. In fact, it becomes automatic.

For those of you reading this, I encourage you to be true to your heart , to follow your bliss and to be your authentic self. I wish you much health, happiness, and joy.

Maggie Holbik is a Life and Business coach who resides in Canada. She coaches both individuals and businesses. Her greatest passion is to uplift Inspire and motivate others to success. She is also a public speaker an owner of a Wellness Center in Canada.

Conclusion

Soulful Pen Publishing wants to thank you for bravely reading 100 Voices of Inspiration, Awakening and Empowerment. Our mission is to provide affordable publishing services to anyone who has a desire to be published as an author. Our programs are designed to create authors, then publish stories. The SoulSpiration series features many authors as you see in this book. We also offer book coaching and 1:1 mentoring services.

Carla Wynn Hall has helped 1000's of women write out their stories. Her relentless effort in holding the space for women to heal painful stories, is noted in her extensive social media outreach. Carla is a 10-Time bestselling author and her newest book "The Soul Code for Women" can be purchased here:

http://www.bit.ly/thesoulcode

www.TheSoulfulPen.com

http://www.facebook.com/thesoulfulpen

http://www.twitter.com/soulfulpen

http://www.linkedin.com/in/thesoulfulpen

THANK YOU AGAIN!

Manufactured by Amazon.com
Columbia, SC
02 April 2017